CHINA

Texts in Regional Geography
A Guilford Series
Edited by James L. Newman, Syracuse University

www.guilford.com/GTRG

Regions can be defined in many different ways; in this series, the focus is human geography. Volumes in the series cover large areas, such as Europe and sub-Saharan Africa, as well as smaller ones, such as Cuba. Each author is a recognized expert on the region in question, ensuring that students and other readers will be guided by the best that human geography has to offer.

Cuban Landscapes: Heritage, Memory, and Place
Joseph L. Scarpaci and Armando H. Portela

A Geography of Russia and Its Neighbors
Mikhail S. Blinnikov

The Europeans, Second Edition:
A Geography of People, Culture, and Environment
Robert C. Ostergren and Mathias Le Bossé

Africa South of the Sahara, Third Edition:
A Geographical Interpretation
Robert Stock

Latin America, Second Edition:
Regions and People
Robert B. Kent

China: A Geographical Perspective
*David W. S. Wong, Kenneth K. K. Wong,
Him Chung, and James J. Wang*

CHINA
A GEOGRAPHICAL PERSPECTIVE

David W. S. Wong
Kenneth K. K. Wong
Him Chung
James J. Wang

THE GUILFORD PRESS
New York   London

Library of Congress Cataloging-in-Publication Data

Names: Wong, David W. S. (David Wing-Shun), author.
Title: China : a geographical perspective / David W. S. Wong, Kenneth K. K.
    Wong, Him Chung, James J. Wang.
Description: New York : The Guilford Press, 2018. | Series: Texts in regional
    geography | Includes bibliographical references and index.
Identifiers: LCCN 2017027337| ISBN 9781462533732 (pbk.) | ISBN 9781462533749
    (hardcover)
Subjects: LCSH: China—Geography. | Human geography—China.
Classification: LCC DS706.7 .W66 2018 | DDC 915.1—dc23
LC record available at *https://lccn.loc.gov/2017027337*

Many maps throughout this book were created with ArcGIS® software by ESRI.
ArcWorld™ and ArcMap™ are the intellectual property of ESRI and are used
herein under license.

Preface

WHY HAVE WE WRITTEN
CHINA: A GEOGRAPHICAL PERSPECTIVE?

China, the world's largest country in population and fourth largest in area, became the country with the largest total gross domestic product in 2016.[1] It has become a superpower, exerting significant influence globally. Because Europe is in flux partly owing to the United Kingdom's exit from the European Union, the coming era is likely to be dominated by the United States and China, with Russia as occasional player. For a full comprehension and appreciation of global society and its dynamics, both present and future, acquiring a better understanding of China is essential. Books about the Chinese economy and politics are numerous, but books providing relatively comprehensive and up-to-date coverage of China from a geographical perspective are few. The current book is intended to fill this void.

China is probably changing faster than nearly any other country in the world. Because of this pace of change, together with China's unique characteristics of development and styles of handling issues, trying to predict its future is enormously challenging. However, this book should provide readers with a solid background on, and understanding of, China from a perspective incorporating two main approaches to geographical study: the "systematic" approach, covering specific topics and themes across a geographical area, and the "regional" approach, covering particular regions within a larger area in greater depth. Many people in Western nations do not understand why China experiences certain problems or why its government acts in a certain way. Knowledge about China gained from this book's dual approaches will help readers better appreciate and comprehend China's existing issues and the decisions that it may make in the future.

ORGANIZATION OF THE BOOK

The book is divided into three parts—Part I, "Background"; Part II, "Thematic Topics"; and Part III, "Selected Regions"—plus a concluding chapter. Part I includes an introduction to China (Chapter 1), its physical geography (Chapter 2), and its population (Chapter 3). These chapters thus offer overviews of fundamental aspects of the country. The topics covered in Part II include agriculture (Chapter 4), economy (Chapter 5), urban systems (Chapter 6), rural China (Chapter 7), transportation (Chapter 8), and environment (Chapter 9). The chapters in Part III cover three major regions: coastal China (Chapter 10); the peripheral regions in the north–northeast, west, and south–southwest (Chapter 11); and the Chinese territories outside the mainland—Hong Kong, Macau, and Taiwan—which, together with the mainland, constitute "Greater China" (Chapter 12). The final chapter (Chapter 13), "China at the Crossroads," considers future directions for China.

Together, the chapters offer a relatively comprehensive assessment of China. While they are connected to a certain degree, they are independent of each other; thus readers do not need to read chapters in a specific order, and most of them can be read independently without losing the context. Nevertheless, reading the three background chapters first will be beneficial.

Since cultural and political geography affect many aspects of life in China, these topics are interwoven throughout the book rather than covered in separate chapters. For instance, the introductory chapter (Chapter 1) explains some major aspects of Chinese culture, including its languages and religions. Cultural geography is also highlighted in Chapter 3 on population and in Chapter 11 on the peripheral regions, particularly in respect to minority populations. The formation of Chinese rural culture, its characteristics, and its recent erosion due to economic growth are discussed in Chapter 7. Political geography is mostly discussed in Chapter 1, but it is also touched upon in the chapters on the peripheral regions and "Greater China" (Chapters 11 and 12) and in the concluding chapter (Chapter 13). Chapter 13 also discusses tourism, which is an emerging economic force in China and is regarded as a potential tool for furthering and sustaining the country's economic growth.

PEDAGOGICAL FEATURES

Because this book is intended for use as a textbook, it includes several pedagogical features. The beginning of each chapter includes a list of learning objectives to highlight important themes or interesting topics in that chapter, as well as a list of key concepts and terms. Throughout the book, notes are used extensively to point students to online resources, including data sources, news sites, and reports. Many of these sources go beyond those usually used in traditional academic research, providing different perspectives on China and up-to-date information. The book's Appendix is a list of websites where information about China may be found. Although this list is not intended to be exhaustive, it includes websites for government agencies, major nongovernmental organizations, and the more reputable news media. In a companion website to this book (see the end of the Contents for further information), we also provide lecture slides for instructors. These slides include summaries of the major topics and points covered in all chapters, as well as all maps, tables, and figures.

Still another pedagogical feature of this book is the use of boxes in every chapter, discussing special topics or issues for China in general or for specific local regions. While these topics may not attract a great deal of academic research, they reflect the unique experiences of the people, and therefore deserve attention and explanation.

AUDIENCE

The book is intended primarily as a textbook for an undergraduate course or an introductory graduate course on the geography of China. Instructors may also assign selected chapters or the entire book for an advanced undergraduate course or a graduate seminar; these readings will facilitate discussions or further research in these advanced courses. Moreover, the book can be used for courses in areas other than geography. Teachers of courses in Asian studies, global studies, and international development, at both the undergraduate and graduate levels, who wish to provide a geographical overview of China and in-depth discussions on different aspects of China from a geographical perspective should find this book valuable.

ACKNOWLEDGMENTS

The conception of this book is partly attributable to Dr. Max Lu at Kansas State University; his edited volume with the late Professor Chiao-Min Hsieh provided the inspiration for the current book. A large portion of the book was completed by David W. S. Wong while he was teaching at the University of Hong Kong (HKU); he and the other authors are grateful for the support provided by the Department of Geography at HKU. We owe a particular debt to Tina Tsang, who magically turned our ideas and rough sketches into professional-level graphics and figures. At The Guilford Press, we are grateful to Senior Editor Barbara Watkins, Senior Production Editor Laura Specht Patchkofsky, and Copyeditor Marie Sprayberry, whose editorial skills transformed our manuscript into a readable text. We are also thankful to Editor in Chief Seymour Weingarten and Senior Editor C. Deborah Laughton for their patience and trust, despite the long delay and many setbacks on this project.

Finally, we must acknowledge several institutions and organizations for providing many of the geographical data used in this book. The data on China's political boundaries and topography are from Version 4 (January 2007) of the China Historical Geographic Information System (CHGIS) dataset, maintained by the

Harvard–Yenching Institute and Fudan University Center for Historical Geographical Studies. Some hydrological data are from the National Fundamental Geographic Information System (NFGIS). The copyright on the NFGIS data is owned by the National Administration of Surveying, Mapping, and Geoinformation of China. Political boundaries for countries outside of China, as well as some river network data, are from the ArcWorld data provided by Esri Data & Maps.

NOTE ●●

1. https://www.cia.gov/library/publications/the-world-factbook/ rankorder/2001rank.html#ch (retrieved February 24, 2017).

Contents

PART II. THEMATIC TOPICS

PART III. SELECTED REGIONS

CONCLUSION

The companion website *www.guilford.com/wong-materials*
provides lecture slides, maps and figures from the book,
and additional photographs.

CHINA

PART I
BACKGROUND

CHAPTER 1

Exploring China
The Aspiring Dragon

LEARNING OBJECTIVES

* Comprehend the current international status of China and its overall geographical setting.

* Become familiar with China's political and administrative geographies.

* Be aware of the brief history of China with respect to its territorial expanse.

* Survey Chinese languages/dialects and religions.

* Understand the organization of the book.

KEY CONCEPTS AND TERMS

closed-door policy; economic reform; superpower; globalized China; China proper; autonomous regions; municipalities; special administrative regions (SARs); administrative hierarchy; Great Leap Forward; Cultural Revolution; Four Modernizations; Chinese culture; Romanization *(pinyin)*

What do you associate with the word "dragon" (龙 or 龍)? Smaug in *The Hobbit*? Harry Potter movies? A dictation software package? Bruce Lee? The dragon is often associated with China and the Chinese. It is an important element in Chinese mythology and the only imaginary creature in the Chinese zodiac. Chinese dragons are usually wingless, and in Chinese culture the dragon symbolizes power and success. In fact, dragons often symbolize nobility and supremacy, and in ancient time, their use was reserved for Chinese emperors. The robes worn by the emperors were called "dragon robes" because they were always embroidered with dragons. The Chinese regard themselves as "heirs of the dragon" (龍的傳人) (Hou, 1980).[1] Many Chinese companies have "dragon" as part of their names, so that the legendary power of the creature will be associated with the businesses. (Put the Chinese character for "dragon" into an Internet search engine, and you will find many Chinese companies' names.)

However, through much of the 19th and early 20th centuries, China was far from powerful. The last emperors to rule China, the Qing dynasty, were politically incapable of dealing with foreign powers. Following the fall of the Qing dynasty, a series of destructive events occurred; these included the civil war between the Communist and Kuomintang parties, World War II, and several missteps in the early era of Communist rule. These cost China dearly, and the road to recovery was long. From the founding of the Communist People's Republic of China in 1949 until the early 1980s, China adopted a "closed-door policy," with no foreign investment and no private ownership of farms and businesses. The country's economy was largely isolated from the outside world. China was regarded as a sleeping dragon—but one day, it was believed, the dragon would awaken to flex its strength and muscle. This began to happen in the 1980s, as economic reforms opened Chinese cities to foreign investment, and China started to experience unprecedented economic growth. As the world has become more globalized, China's economic power has increased, penetrating into many corners of the world. Products labeled "Made in China" have flooded the marketplace. Indeed, for many types of products, it became difficult to find ones that did *not* carry a "Made in China" tag.

From global and regional perspectives, where does China stand today? In the globalized economy of the 21st century, all countries are connected to a certain degree. Global forces affect local situations. Therefore, knowledge about China is valuable not only for grasping what is happening on the other side of the world, but for understanding other parts of the world, including the Americas and Europe. For example, economic prosperity in China affects many prices in the United States, including those of housing and energy. Being able to think globally helps people act best locally. The following section summarizes some aspects of China's current status in the world. The remaining parts of this chapter offer brief background discussions of China's geography, history, culture, and basic geopolitical administration.

WHERE DOES CHINA STAND GLOBALLY?

Today China is at the top of many lists. It has the largest population in the world, currently approaching 1.4 billion. How long China can hold this title is not clear. India's population is not far behind, and population growth in China has come almost to a halt in recent decades. (Chapter 3 covers many population issues in China.) China also ranks first in the world in the following areas: exports, reserves of foreign exchange and gold, production and consumption of electricity, numbers of landline and mobile phones, and length of waterways (Central Intelligence Agency [CIA], 2016). China and Japan are the two largest foreign holders of U.S. Treasury securities—that is, U.S. national debt (U.S. Department of the Treasury, 2016). This fact has been used in jokes, but it has also become an important political issue.[2] China is now the world's largest greenhouse gas producer, and a key player in combating global climate change. (Chapter 9 discusses the role of China in global environmental change.)

BOX 1.1. China: World "Superpower"?

For most Westerners, it is debatable whether China can be labeled as an international "superpower," joining the elite ranks of the United States, Russia, and a few European Union countries. However, several Chinese achievements suggest that the designation may not remain debatable for long.

China has an ambitious space program that began as early as the 1970s. In the 1980s, China launched communication and earth observation satellites. In 2003, China launched its first manned space flight, orbiting the earth 14 times. In 2008, a Chinese astronaut completed a spacewalk. In 2011, China launched a space lab, similar to the International Space Station jointly built and operated by the United States and Russia. Three Chinese astronauts arrived at the space lab in 2012. The 2013 landing of a robotic rover on the moon indicated that China was getting close to its goal of putting a Chinese astronaut on the moon (Strickland, 2014).

China is also building its military might, particularly its naval power. In 2012, China commissioned its first aircraft carrier, the *Liaoning* (named after the province), which was retrofitted from a Russian–Ukrainian ship. While the *Liaoning* is designated as a training ship, its commission laid the foundation for the future development of China's naval fleet. China has launched the construction of its first domestic aircraft carrier (Panda, 2016). It will likely join the service in late 2018 or early 2019.[a] Among other nations' commissioned aircraft carriers, the largest are the U.S. Navy's *Nimitz*-class carriers, which weigh over 100,000 metric tons (mt) and are over 330 meters (m) in length. The United States has 10 of these, including the *USS Dwight D. Eisenhower* and the *USS Carl Vinson*. The *Liaoning* is the second largest *Kuznetsov*-class carrier in the world, weighing over 59,000 mt and over 300 m long; it is similar in size to the Russian carrier *Admiral Kuznetsov,* after which the *Kuznetsov* class was named. Clearly, the United States and Russia dominate in naval power, although the United Kingdom is trying to catch up with the newly built *Queen Elizabeth* class, weighing over 70,000 mt. Reports have indicated that China is planning to construct four aircraft carriers at the size of 50,000 mt.[b] Unless other countries such as Russia or France suddenly get started building aircraft carriers, China may have the second largest fleet of aircraft carriers after the U.S. fleet in the near future, and it will be surprising if China does not try to dominate the seas, at least in eastern Asia.

Only a handful of countries have nuclear-powered submarines. Obviously, the United States has the largest number. Other Western nations with nuclear submarines are France, Russia, and the United Kingdom. Among Asian countries, only China and India have nuclear submarines. According to some speculation, China has at least six nuclear submarines in operation, and another five to 10 are planned. Given all these developments in space exploration and military expansion, China definitely considers itself to be a superpower nation. Do you consider China to be among the superpowers now?

---

[a]www.scmp.com/news/china/policies-politics/article/2090723/china-launches-first-home-built-aircraft-carrier-latest.

[b]http://mil.news.sina.com.cn/2014-02-13/0908764011.html.

In 2010, China overtook Japan as the second largest economy in the world in terms of total gross domestic product (GDP). Economic experts predicted that China would soon take first place from the United States in GDP (Barboza, 2010),[3] and this occurred in 2016, as noted at the start of the Preface. This huge expansion of the Chinese economy is partly due to the increasing wealth of the Chinese. Initial public offerings (IPOs) of company stock often create millionaires overnight, especially for high-value companies such as Facebook. The largest IPOs in the United States have been those of U.S. companies (e.g., Visa, General Motors). However, the IPO of Alibaba, a Chinese e-commerce company that claims to do more business than Amazon, was the largest in U.S. history. China commissioned its first aircraft carrier in 2012, joining just a few countries in the world with such military technology. The Chinese landing of a robotic rover on the moon in 2013 put China into the same league as the United States and the former Soviet Union in space exploration. All these developments signal China's arrival as a major global player both economically and politically.

Chinese culture has spread to almost all continents through a centuries-old stream of Chinese migrants. Chinatowns are found in many major European cities (e.g., London, Paris, and Amsterdam), most major North American cities, the two largest cities in Australia (Melbourne and Sydney), and many Southeast Asian cities.[4] Chinese immigrants are also found in Latin American, African, and Middle Eastern nations. While many older Chinese immigrants have little direct connection to today's China, they are nonetheless manifestations of the far-reaching impact of this country and its civilization. More recently, China has begun having an impact on the global society through its tourists. These can be found not only at major tourist attractions, but also in less frequented but exotic places, such as the former Soviet bloc countries of Romania and Slovakia.

At the same time, many foreigners have visited, worked in, and even migrated to China. It is not unusual to see Western tourists visiting major Chinese cities and prime tourist sites such as the Great Wall, the Forbidden City, and Xi'an. Tourism, both international and domestic, is a major economic engine in many Chinese cities and a secondary effect of Chinese economic reform. The primary effect of this reform has been the overall expansion of economic activities, particularly through attracting foreign investment. International firms have established factories and other business operations in many Chinese cities, and these new business establishments have attracted many foreign workers, some of whom become Chinese citizens. According to the 2000 Chinese census, 941 foreigners became naturalized Chinese citizens. The number increased to 1,448 in the 2010 Chinese census (National Bureau of Statistics of China, n.d.).[5] Given all these facts, China's imposing international status is undeniable in today's global society.

GEOGRAPHICAL SETTING

Although China's economic engine has elevated its worldwide political and military status, its geopolitical location in East Asia has made it a regional leader, while also creating some issues (both old and new) with neighboring countries.

Figure 1.1 shows China with its neighboring countries. It is the largest in area among its neighbors except for Russia. With over 9.5 million square kilometers (km²), China ranks fourth in the world in area (but, nevertheless, it has only one time zone!). It is over 1 million km² larger than the fifth-ranked Brazil. Although Canada is second largest in area and the United States is third, they are only about 390,000 and 230,000 km² larger than China, respectively. These countries are all dwarfed by Russia, with over 17 million km². China is separated from North America to the east, and from Australasia (Australia and New Zealand) to the southeast, by the vast Pacific Ocean.

With its large land mass, China's borders with its many neighbors are over 22,000 km long, but its coastline is only about 14,500 km long (CIA, 2016). The neighbors to the northeast and north are North Korea, Russia, and Mongolia. To the northwest are the Central Asian countries of Kazakhstan, Kyrgyzstan, and Tajikistan. To the west are Afghanistan, Pakistan, India, Nepal, and Bhutan, and to the southwest are Myanmar, Laos, and Vietnam. China has strong political ties and satisfactory diplomatic relationships with many of these neighbors, some of which have had or still have adverse relationships with Western countries (e.g., North Korea, Myanmar). China's longest-lasting diplomatic concern with its neighbors has been the territorial conflict with India, but there are also boundary disputes with Bhutan and Myanmar.

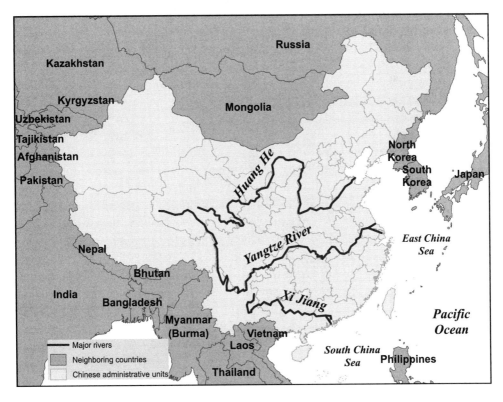

FIGURE 1.1 Locations of China and its neighboring countries in Asia.

China is currently in a high-profile dispute with Japan over the ownership of the islands of Senkaku (the Japanese name) or Diaoyudao/Diaoyutai (the Chinese/Taiwanese names) in the East China Sea. Other disputes include those over the Spratly Islands (Nansha Islands or 南沙群岛 in Chinese) with the Philippines, and the Paracel Islands (Xisha Islands or 西沙群岛 in Chinese) with Vietnam; both these island groups are in the South China Sea. The conflict with Vietnam over the Paracel Islands has been heightened by the discovery of undersea oil, and China has started to set up drilling platforms in the South China Sea. The conflict has escalated from verbal clashes to physical collisions between ships of the two countries. China's recent construction of an airstrip in the Spratly Islands through large-scale land reclamation has drawn international condemnation. As China's economy has grown, political tensions have intensified along these territorial fronts.

INTERNAL TERRITORIAL DIVISIONS

China is divided into 23 provinces (including Taiwan), five autonomous regions, four independent municipalities, and two special administrative regions (SARs), as listed in Table 1.1. The autonomous regions and municipalities have the same status as the provinces, regardless of their territorial and population sizes. Their names, to some extent, reflect aspects of their territorial, political, historical, and administrative characteristics.

The municipalities were originally cities (市). Partly because of their population size, and partly because of their special political and economic status, they are under the direct control (直辖) of the central government, rather than their respective provincial governments. The municipalities are substantial in both area and population. For instance, Chongqing used to be the largest city in Sichuan province, with a population of just a few million. After it became a municipality in 1997, its boundaries were expanded significantly through annexation; in 2010 it had more than 10 million people, compared to 26 million in the entire Sichuan province (National Bureau of Statistics of China, n.d.). These municipalities have populations larger than several of the smaller provinces.

The five autonomous regions are all in peripheral areas and border China's neighbors (see Figure 1.2). While China's dominant ethnic group is the Han Chinese, there are 55 other racial/ethnic groups in the country (see Chapter 3 for a detailed discussion). The populations of the autonomous regions are dominated by some of these ethnic groups, and the full name of each region indicates its predominant ethnicity. For instance, the Zhuang is the largest ethnic group in Guangxi Zhuang; in Xinjiang Uyghur, the Uyghur is the largest group; and the Mongolians are the largest group in Neimenggu or Nei Mongol (Inner Mongolia).

The two SARs of Hong Kong and Macau were created as historical legacies of the colonial era; Hong Kong was a colony of the United Kingdom, and Macau a colony of Portugal, until the 1990s. Their histories and situations are discussed in detail in Chapter 12.

TABLE 1.1. English and Chinese Names of the Different Administrative Units in China

Type of unit	English name	Chinese name (in simplified version)
Province (省)		
1	Anhui	安徽
2	Fujian	福建
3	Gansu	甘肃
4	Guangdong	广东
5	Guizhou	贵州
6	Hainan	海南
7	Hebei	河北
8	Heilongjiang	黑龙江
9	Henan	河南
10	Hubei	湖北
11	Hunan	湖南
12	Jiangsu	江苏
13	Jiangxi	江西
14	Jilin	吉林
15	Liaoning	辽宁
16	Qinghai	青海
17	Shaanxi	陕西
18	Shandong	山东
19	Shanxi	山西
20	Sichuan	四川
21	Taiwan[a]	台湾
22	Yunnan	云南
23	Zhejiang	浙江
Autonomous region (自治区)		
1	Guangxi Zhuang	广西 – 壮族
2	Neimenggu or Nei Mongol (Inner Mongolia)	内蒙古
3	Ningxia Hui	宁夏 – 回族
4	Xinjiang Uyghur	新疆 – 维吾尔
5	Xizang (Tibet)	西藏

(continued)

Type of unit	English name	Chinese name (in simplified version)
TABLE 1.1. *(continued)*		
Municipality (直辖市 or 市)		
1	Beijing	北京
2	Chongqing	重庆
3	Shanghai	上海
4	Tianjin	天津
Special administrative region (SAR)		
1	Hong Kong	香港
2	Macau	澳门

[a]The People's Republic of China officially includes Taiwan as one of its provinces.

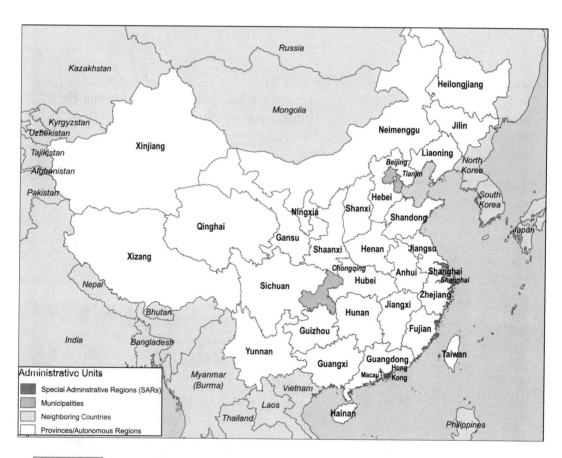

FIGURE 1.2 China's highest-level administrative units: provinces, autonomous regions, municipalities, and special administrative regions (SARs).

Provinces, autonomous regions, and municipalities constitute the highest level of the local government hierarchy, reporting to the central government directly. Officially, the next levels down the administrative hierarchy are the county (县) and township (乡). However, unofficially, the prefecture (地) level is between the provincial and county levels, and beneath the townships are villages (村). The structure of these several administrative levels is further complicated by another type of administrative unit, the *shi* (市). This Chinese geographical entity is often loosely labeled as "city," but it encompasses cities or city regions at various levels of the administrative hierarchy (the provincial, prefectural, or county level). The functional and economic relationships among entities at different levels within the hierarchy are discussed in Chapters 4–6.

Whereas the names of U.S. states are rarely associated with their geographical features (a few exceptions are West Virginia in respect to Virginia, the two Carolinas and the two Dakotas in relation to each other, and Mississippi and Missouri in relation to their bordering rivers), the names of many Chinese provinces are related to specific geographical features or provide geographical references. For example, in Chinese, the four directions are 东 (*dong*) for "east," 南 (*nan*) for "south," 西 (*xi*) for "west," and 北 (*bei*) for "north." (The italicized words in parentheses are Roman alphabet versions of the Chinese characters, based on their sounds; such words are called *pinyin*.) Thus, for instance, Guang<u>dong</u> province is in the east, and the Guang<u>xi</u> autonomous region is in the west. He<u>bei</u> and He<u>nan</u> provinces are on the north and south banks of <u>He</u> (河), a river—or more specifically, the Hwang He or Yellow River. Similarly, Hu<u>bei</u> and Hu<u>nan</u> provinces are north and south of <u>Hu</u> (湖), a lake—that is, Dongting Lake (洞庭湖), one of the largest lakes in China.[6] The province name Sichuan is quite geographical, as the word *chuan* (川) means "rivers" in Chinese, and the provincial territory is drained by several rivers. In Chinese, another word for river is *jiang* (江). (Note that the *jiang* in the Xin<u>jiang</u> autonomous region is not "river" in Chinese, but a "frontier" or "territory" [疆]; "river" and "frontier" have the same sound in Chinese.) Several provinces' names include the word *jiang*, implying that rivers are located in or near them. For instance, the *jiang* in <u>Jiang</u>xi refers to the Gan River (赣江), a river flowing from south to north across the province into the Yangtze River. Similarly, the provincial name of Zhejiang is derived from the Zhe River, and the provincial name of Heilongjiang is derived from the Amur River (Heilongjiang, which literally means "Black Dragon River," is the Amur's Chinese name), the river separating China from Russia/Siberia. The autonomous region <u>Xi</u>zang (also called Tibet) means "the western [*xi*, or 西] Tibetan [*zang*, or 藏] people." Another autonomous region, <u>Nei</u>menggu or <u>Nei</u> Mongol, is also called Inner Mongolia, as *nei* means "inner" in Chinese; the name signifies the Mongolia closer to China, as opposed to the independent country of Mongolia (which used to be called Outer Mongolia). Thus many Chinese place names refer to their geography, and their names are quite geographically meaningful to the Chinese.

THE ORIGINS OF CHINESE CIVILIZATION

Today the world is largely dominated by Western civilization. In most parts of the world, you can usually find someone who knows English, and very few non-English-speaking countries can escape the influence of American merchandise and brand names (e.g., McDonald's). However, Western civilization is relatively young compared to the Chinese. China is one of the four ancient civilizations, the others being Babylonia, Egypt, and India. All these ancient civilizations originated along river valleys: the Tigris and Euphrates for the Babylonian, the Nile for the Egyptian, and the Indus for the Indian (note that River Indus is within the current boundaries of Pakistan). For the Chinese, the Yellow River (Huang He in Figure 1.1; we use these names alternatively) is regarded as the cradle of Chinese civilization. It is the sixth longest river in the world. Although only the second longest in China (the longest being the Yangtze River), it has been closely tied to Chinese civilization, history, and societal well-being for centuries. It is also called the "mother river."

It is believed that Chinese civilization began in the general area of the North China Plain and the Loess Plateau, shown in Figure 1.3. The ruins of primitive communities dating to 4000 B.C.E. have been found in Banpo village near Xi'an in Shaanxi province. Note that the Huang He generally flows from west (highlands) to east, but it turns north and then back south before continuing eastward, partially circumventing the Loess Plateau. This plateau is made up of lightweight yellow silt accumulated over centuries; the soil is quite thick. The river also carries much silt,

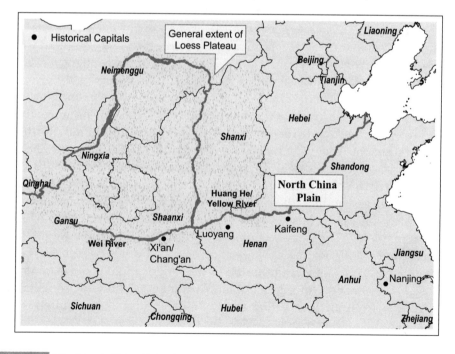

FIGURE 1.3 The North China Plain, the Loess Plateau, and the lower Huang He (Yellow River), the cradle of Chinese civilization.

which gives the water a yellowish color. This is how the Yellow River got its name. The yellow earth is relatively fertile and easy to work with for agriculture. The soil of the plain and the river have been supporting the ever-growing population of China since ancient times. Feeding into the Yellow River is the Wei River. The confluence area experiences frequent flooding (Figure 1.3). The characteristics of the landscape along the Yellow River are discussed further in Chapter 2.

Information about Chinese history is accessible from various sources,[7] and therefore this chapter and this book provide only a brief overview. Like that of all ancient civilizations, the earliest history of China is uncertain, but starting with the Western Zhou dynasty (ca. 1050–256 B.C.E.), the historical record is supported by many documents and artifacts. Various dynasties ruled China over the past 3,000 years or so, but the influence of the ancient dynasties was geographically restricted to an area including the Huang He valley and extending just south of the Yangtze River. Many dynasties were short-lived and experienced turmoil from invasions by the "barbarians" in the peripheral regions. To survive, these dynasties had to relocate their capitals from time to time. The locations of these historical capitals, shown in Figure 1.3, reflect the geographical sphere of influence of ancient Chinese civilization.[8]

Xi'an or Chang'an and Luoyang, on the southern banks of the Yellow and Wei Rivers, were the capitals for many ancient dynasties. Later, Kaifeng, a city east of Luoyang, was also a capital. But these cities within the same region were often flooded or even destroyed. Therefore, later dynasties chose cities farther away from the river, including Beijing (today's capital) and Nanjing. To some degree, the geographical area defined by these capitals reflects the core region of China.

TERRITORIAL EXPANSION: ASSIMILATION OR INVASION?

Due to relatively favorable environmental conditions—good soil in the Loess Plateau, and a reliable water supply from the Yellow River—early Chinese society was an agricultural society consisting of the Han Chinese ethnic group. Agricultural skills and technology in ancient times enabled this society to support an increasing population. As population grew, its territory expanded outward from the Yellow River. Regarding themselves as civilized and culturally superior, the Han Chinese believed that they were the descendants of gods, and that the surrounding races with different cultures should be submissive to the Chinese emperors. This worldview is well reflected from the country's name: "China" in Chinese (中國) means "the central kingdom." At the same time, these tribal populations intermittently attempted to invade the Chinese territory. Most of the races in the north and west were nomads. Eventually, under the rule of Qin Shi Huang, the founding emperor of the Qin (秦) dynasty, the Great Wall was "built" around 210 B.C.E. to protect the kingdom from "foreign" invasions (see Box 1.2).

Through wars, the Han Chinese conquered peripheral territories originally occupied by various tribal nations over time. When those tribal populations in the periphery became submissive, most of them adopted the Chinese culture and

BOX 1.2. Is the Great Wall of China Still "Great"?

The Great Wall of China (see Figure 1.4) is a wonder of the world and a United Nations Educational, Scientific, and Cultural Organization (UNESCO) World Heritage Site.[a] Although credit for building the wall is given to Emperor Qin Shi Huang, it was not entirely constructed during his reign. He just took different wall segments built earlier by nations he had conquered to be joined together into a continuous military structure across north central China. The eastern end of the Great Wall is at Shanhaiguan in Hebei province, and its western end is at Jiayuguan in Gansu province, crossing several provinces in the North China Plain. The original segments extended over 8,000 km (over 4,900 miles), but the wall was further expanded in dynasties as late as the Ming, with a total length of about 20,000 km (about 12,400 miles) today. Despite the length of the structure, the claim that the wall is recognized from space is questionable.

The building of this gigantic structure reflected long-term conflicts between Chinese agricultural societies and the mostly nomadic populations in the north and west of China's core region in ancient times. The populations residing to the north and west were regarded as barbarians who lived in physically adverse conditions (dry, cold, and rugged terrain) and wanted Chinese land with its more favorable conditions. Different segments of the wall were originally built by different nations to fence off these invaders. Different materials were used to build the different segments of the Wall; the workers utilized what was available locally. Materials included dirt and wood in lowland areas, while stones and bricks were used in more mountainous areas.

To defend their nations against the foreign populations, soldiers were stationed on the segments of the wall. Fortresses and watchtowers were built along the segments, so that soldiers could congregate and keep watch. To facilitate movement of soldiers from one part of the wall to another, horse tracks were built along certain parts of the wall. Underneath some parts of the wall were shelters and stables to house horses and sometimes animals to feed the soldiers.

Managing and maintaining this gigantic structure today are not easy tasks. The cost of keeping the wall from normal deterioration is exorbitant, and protecting it from human destruction (including vandalism) is almost impossible. As a result, the Great Wall today is in great disrepair. Although segments of the wall with many visitors, such as the segments north of Beijing, are kept in reasonable shape, those in more remote parts of the country with fewer visitors are in terrible condition. Portions of the Wall have collapsed, and some of the auxiliary structures have been destroyed. Thus, at least part of the Great Wall is no longer that great.

[a]http://whc.unesco.org/en/list/438.

civilization, and gradually they were assimilated into the larger Chinese society. Over time, the Han Chinese civilization was quite successful in expanding toward the south, southeast, and northeast.

However, the assimilation process was not equally successful across all peripheral regions. The nomadic races in the north and west were quite stubborn in their responses to the ancient Chinese policies. Eventually, the Mongols, under the leadership of Genghis Khan, invaded China and launched the Yuan (元) dynasty (in approximately 1279 C.E.). This was the first time in Chinese history that the entire country was completely controlled by a "foreign" emperor. After several temporary and partial occupations by foreign races, the second time that the entire country

FIGURE 1.4 Part of the Great Wall with fortresses. (Photo: David W. S. Wong)

was taken over by a "foreign" race happened in 1644, when the Manchus from the northeast established the Qing (清) dynasty, the last dynasty in Chinese history.

During these foreign occupations of China, foreign cultural practices were introduced and eventually absorbed into Chinese culture. The conquerors also gradually adopted Chinese culture. To a large extent, the expansion of the Mongol kingdom across Asia and toward Europe helped spread Chinese civilization to other parts of the world. The efforts of the Manchu Qing emperors to consolidate their territorial control unintentionally anchored Chinese civilization firmly in southern China, while other peripheral regions experienced different levels of Chinese cultural influence.

Although the Qing dynasty (1644–1912 C.E.) was able to control most of what is currently Chinese territory, there were military challenges from foreign powers, including Western nations. However, the real challenge came from the ideological realm, when Chinese educators were exposed to Western democratic societies and political systems. In 1911, a revolution led by Dr. Sun Yat-sen[9] started in the city now known as Wuhan (the so-called Wuchang Uprising). Eventually the movement toppled the last Chinese emperor and established the Republic of China. Sun Yat-sen is regarded as the father of modern China because of his democratic ideology. Unfortunately, the following four decades were consumed by civil war between the Communists, led by Mao Zedong, and the Kuomintang (the nationalists), led by Chiang Kai-shek, as well as invasions by the Japanese starting in the 1930s.[10] The nationalist government left the mainland in 1949 for Taiwan, which they designated as the

Republic of China (ROC), while the mainland Communists formed the People's Republic of China (PRC), significantly influenced by Russia's Communist ideology.

The Communists failed to bring prosperity and peace to the mainland in the early era. Besides involvement in the Korean War (1950–1953), the social and economic campaign called the Great Leap Forward (starting around 1958) was a major economic setback and was partly responsible for widespread famine. The Cultural Revolution (1966–1976), which was a political and ideological campaign, shook the social and cultural foundations of China with its push to replace the traditional Chinese value system with Communist ideology. Chinese traditional culture had heavily relied on the teachings of Confucius, but Confucian values were subjected to attacks. The collateral damage included not just short-term economic turmoil, but long-term destruction of human capital, as universities were dysfunctional for years and intellectuals were labeled as "class enemies." The Four Modernizations (in agriculture, industry, military, and science/technology) and economic reform in the late 1970s set a new course for economic development. Contemporary societal culture since then has been dominated by what often are superficial materialistic relationships and money-making goals.

The downfall of the Qing dynasty and the succession of the Communist party were major turning points in contemporary Chinese history. Between these two events, China lost peripheral territories to neighboring countries. Thus the Communist party has made major efforts to regain and maintain firm control over these peripheral regions, which constitute an "outer China" dominated by cultures other than the Han Chinese, whereas the core area dominated by Han Chinese culture is known as "China proper."[11] The question thus arises: What exactly constitutes contemporary "Chinese culture"?

ONE "CHINESE CULTURE": FAR FROM THE TRUTH

When Westerners think about Chinese culture, the first thing they may think of is Chinese food. Consider the many scenes on TV with coworkers or friends eating Chinese takeout meals in offices or at home. You can find Chinese restaurants and takeout places even in small U.S. or European towns. But Chinese food is only one of many manifestations of Chinese culture, although it is among the four main dimensions of daily necessity: clothing (衣), food (吃), accommodation (住), and transportation (行).[12] These facets of life are heavily influenced by local environments, such as the types of food that can grow in specific regions, and the types of clothing people need because of local climatic characteristics. Beyond these four main dimensions, however, the essence of Chinese culture and its variations can be seen in two elements: languages/dialects and religion. We discuss these next.

Languages and Dialects

Before the Qin dynasty (221–206 B.C.E.), written Chinese characters varied across different kingdoms. After Emperor Qin Shi Huang conquered these kingdoms and began to unify the country, he launched several sensible standardization measures to facilitate the unification.[13] One of these was to standardize the currency: Round coins with square holes at their centers became the official currency. A standard currency made commercial transactions in daily life more convenient. Another measure with a long-lasting impact on China was the standardization of written characters.

Chinese is written in characters. Each character represents one syllable in speech; it can be a word on its own or can be combined with other characters to form another word. Characters may have a single part or multiple parts. Many characters are derived from physical objects and thus are called "pictographic." For instance, the character 山 means "mountains" and is like a simplified drawing of mountains. Characters can also convey abstract ideas and thus are referred to as "ideographic." A simple example is 中, which means "center," with a stroke down the middle to divide the rectangle. Moreover, multiple characters or parts of characters can be combined to create new words ("logical aggregates"). For example, the character 田 represents "fields" or "cropland." Adding some "plants" to the top of the "fields" character creates another character, 苗, which means "seedling." Some characters combine meaning and sound ("phonetic complexes"). Thus combining different characters representing objects, abstract ideas, or sounds can produce characters with new meanings.

This flexibility in combining basic characters and using multiple characters to form words makes Chinese a very rich language, capable of describing complicated and abstract concepts. On the other hand, learning this language is more challenging than learning the 26 letters of the English alphabet. There are about 1,000–3,000 commonly used Chinese characters. Some studies claim that there are about 80,000 Chinese characters; clearly, many of these are small variations on the others. Still, learning more than several thousand characters is beyond the capabilities of most laypersons, although there are some systematic ways to learn and remember them.

The forms of Chinese characters have changed over time, and the current forms are different from those adopted during the Qin dynasty. Characters representing objects in ancient times were more like drawings of the objects, but today's versions are much simplified. In fact, the simplification of characters has been the historical trend. Currently, two versions of Chinese characters are commonly used. In mainland China, the official version is the simplified version, while in Hong Kong, Macau, and Taiwan, the traditional version is still used daily. The following are examples of the traditional and the simplified versions of characters, respectively: those for "horses" (馬, 马) and "fish" (魚, 鱼). Two other interesting features of the written Chinese language are that characters do not have singular and plural forms, and verbs do not have different tenses.

Whereas the Roman alphabets of most Indo-European languages help convey the pronunciation of words, sounds and characters in Chinese are not one-to-one matches. The Communist government expanded the Romanization of the language by using the Roman alphabet to represent the sounds; as noted earlier, these representations are called *pinyin*. However, in Chinese a sound may carry four distinct tones corresponding to different words (characters) with dramatically different meanings. For instance, *zhu* in *pinyin* may mean "pig" (*zhū*, 豬), "lord" (*zhǔ*, 主), or "to live" (*zhù*, 住), just to name a few possibilities, depending on both the tone and the context. *Pinyin* captures tones with diacritical marks (shown over the *u* in the examples just given) to help differentiate different words. *Pinyin* is the system through which most foreigners learn to speak Chinese these days. Learning the characters is still very much a matter of memory and practice.

Although written Chinese was standardized by Emperor Qin Shi Huang, spoken Chinese is far from standardized. Not only are there numerous local dialects, but the "official" spoken language varied from dynasty to dynasty throughout Chinese history. At the end of the 18th century, the Qing dynasty adopted the Beijing dialect, Mandarin, called Guoyu (国语 in simplified characters and 國語 in traditional), as the national language. The PRC kept Mandarin as the official spoken language of the mainland, but renamed it Putonghua. The ROC in Taiwan continued using the name Guoyu for the official language. Over time, the two official languages diverged slightly, incorporating new local terms and modifying pronunciations according to the local dialects. Generally, however, people from the two sides of the Taiwan Strait (which separates the mainland from Taiwan) can communicate without much difficulty. Indeed, in recent decades, people in different areas of China (the mainland, Taiwan, Hong Kong, and Macau) and Chinese people living overseas have been interacting more frequently than before, partly due to economic needs; thus they have started learning the written characters (traditional and simplified) used in other places, as well as the rudiments of different dialects.

Although Putonghua (Mandarin) is the official language, and is used and understood by the majority of the people in China, many people still use their local languages or dialects for daily communication. In the peripheral provinces and autonomous regions where ethnic minority groups reside (see Table 1.1 and Figure 1.2), ethnic languages are likely to be the dominant means of communication. Ethnic languages, as opposed to dialects, have both written and spoken forms (see Figure 1.5). For instance, the Zhuang, heavily concentrated in the Guangxi autonomous region, has an official written language based on Latin script, although the old Zhuang script, Sawndip, was based partly on Chinese characters and was similar to Vietnamese. The Tibetan language shares some similarities with the Burmese language and has its own distinctive writing system. Similarly, the Uyghur language is based on the Turkic language system, but is distinctive enough to be a separate language. These are some of the languages recognized by the Chinese central government as additional official languages in these autonomous regions.

On the other hand, many people speak local dialects. Although some dialects have similar pronunciations for some words, other words are unintelligible to nonspeakers of these dialects. The geographical distribution of local dialects is complicated. People in neighboring towns may speak significantly different dialects. However, several dialects are spoken by relatively large numbers of people. In southern China, Cantonese is spoken by many residents in Guangdong province (its capital, Guangzhou, used to be known as Canton), by people in some neighboring areas such as Guangxi, and by the majority of people in Hong Kong and Macau.

FIGURE 1.5 The pictures on the wall are Dongba characters (東巴文). Dongba is a written language of the Naxi minority in southwest China. This wall is found in the historical city of Lijiang, which is a UNESCO World Heritage Site. The inscription on the wall literally means "Guess Word (Character) Wall"; it invites tourists to guess the meaning of each character written on the wall. (Photo: Kenneth K. K. Wong)

Cantonese is a dialect because it does not have its own writing system. Like many terms in many Chinese dialects, some terms in Cantonese do not have official written forms and cannot be written in Chinese characters.

Another dialect spoken quite widely, particularly in southern China and Taiwan, is Hakka or Kejia. This dialect originated in northern China, but many people speaking it migrated to the south, including Taiwan, and to Southeast Asian countries because of wars. In some large cities in southern Taiwan, such as Kaohsiung, public announcements are made in two languages and two dialects: Guoyu (Mandarin), Minnanese or Taiwanese (i.e., the dialect spoken by the "natives" of Taiwan), Hakka, and English. Minnanese is a dialect widely spoken in Taiwan. It is akin to Fujianese, which is commonly spoken in the mainland province of Fujian across the Taiwan Strait. However, in Fujian, many other highly localized dialects are found. Where a large number of ethnic groups congregate, highly diverse local dialects can be found, such as in some parts of the provinces of Yunnan and Guizhou in southwestern China.

To summarize, China has a highly diverse language system, with many dialects and languages. This diversity reflects the fact that Chinese culture is not simple or homogeneous; nor are the Chinese people.

Religion

Similar to the highly diverse language system, religion in China is also diverse and complicated. Regardless of how capitalistic the Chinese economy may look today, the political ideology of the Chinese government is still Communism, which means that the government does not recognize any God or gods. Atheism was a major mobilizing force during the Cultural Revolution, when capitalist ideas, religions, and traditional cultural elements (including Confucianism) were suppressed and attacked. The teachings of Confucius, strictly speaking, do not constitute a religion, but they served as the moral and ethical foundation of Chinese society and culture for centuries. The Cultural Revolution dismantled this foundation, reducing personal (including familial) relationships to highly materialistic ones, and thus changing the ways people dealt with each other.

Officially, the Chinese constitution protects religious freedom. Article 36 of the constitution declares, "Citizens . . . enjoy freedom of religious belief," and "The state protects normal religious activities."[14] Article 36 also states, "Religious bodies and religious affairs are not subject to any foreign domination." This article sets up the government's management guidelines of religious activity in China. Through the State Administration of Religious Affairs (SARA), only five religious groups are recognized, and only activities organized by these five groups are considered "normal religious activities." These officially recognized religions are Buddhism, Taoism, Islam, Roman Catholicism, and Protestant Christianity; for the purposes of Article 36, the long-standing debates about whether Buddhism and Taoism are religions are put aside. However, the phrase "not subject to any foreign domination" in Article 36 stipulates that these religious groups have to be "independent," not under the influence or support of organizations outside China. Thus the Roman Catholic churches in China are not under the control or patronage of the Vatican, as other Roman Catholic churches throughout the world are. Religious organizations also have to register with SARA in order to "enjoy" religious freedom in China.

But governments do not have beliefs; only people have beliefs. So what beliefs do people in China have? Many studies and surveys have been done to try to estimate the numbers of believers of different religions, but this research has been difficult for a variety of reasons. One of the main difficulties is the definition of "religion" among the Chinese people. Chinese religious mentality is family-oriented and highly localized. Traditional folk religion, including the practice of ancestor worship, is pervasive and influences different aspects of Chinese life. Folk practices have also been mixed with the practice of the official religions, such as Taoism and Buddhism. As a result, when people are asked what they believe, their religious affiliations may be mislabeled as Buddhism or Taoism when they essentially practice ancestor worship or another folk religion. According to one study, the total religious population in China was about 300 million in 2008, just before the Beijing Summer Olympics.[15] Among this population, about 100 million were estimated to be Buddhists, over 20 million were said to be Muslims, about 16 million were reported to be Protestants, about 13 million were said to be Taoists, and about 4–5 million were noted to be Catholics. Unfortunately, these numbers cannot be verified, but they give us a general idea about the sizes of different religious groups.

Buddhism is a foreign religion imported from India. Although Buddhists probably constitute the largest religious group in China, not all Buddhists are alike. In China there are three main Buddhist sects: Han, Tibetan, and southern Buddhism. Han Buddhism is the largest group, with adherents widely spread across the country. Its religious practices have penetrated into various aspects of Chinese daily life, and have mixed with some traditional folk religious practices. Tibetan Buddhism entered into Tibet through Nepal and India, and evolved to become a major sect of Buddhism. It is also called "Lamaism" because the word "lama" refers to a spiritual leader. Some lamas, including the famous Dalai Lama, are regarded as reincarnations of previous leaders. Southern Buddhism entered southwest China, particularly Yunnan, from Burma and Thailand. Monks in southern Buddhism can marry and eat meat, and their vows do not have to be lifelong.

Another imported religion is Islam. Unlike China's other religions, Islam is a "family-based" religion; that is, children born into a Muslim family are "automatically" Muslim, and converting to another religion is strongly prohibited, if not completely forbidden. Moreover, the adoption of Islam is closely related to the racial/ethnic characteristics of the population. Several racial/ethnic groups in China have strong Islamic affiliations, including the Hui and Uyghur. High concentrations of Muslims are found in the Xinjiang Uyghur and Ningxia Hui autonomous regions and in several western provinces, although the Muslim population is quite widely spread over the entire Chinese territory. The dominant type of Islam in China is Sunni. The Muslim population, particularly the Uyghur in Xinjiang, is of concern to the Chinese government because of occasional unrest. They have significant religious and language differences from the majority of the people in China, and are racially and ethnically close to Central Asian populations west of Xinjiang. Because a significant proportion of the population in these western provinces and autonomous regions are Muslim, the number of Muslims in China is sizable.

The primary domestic religion in China is Taoism. The word *tao* means "road" or "way," which in this context means the general principle guiding the universe. A Taoist concept is *yin–yang* ("dark–bright," or 阴-阳), which refers to the idea that two seemingly contradictory forces can achieve a balanced state, complementing each other. The concept has been used to describe relationships between men and women, and has been applied to marital arts and numerous other aspects of daily life. Taoist practices have also intermingled with traditional Chinese folk religion, and to some extent with Buddhism.

Western-style educational establishments were introduced to China during the late Qing dynasty, mainly through the efforts of Christian (both Protestant and Catholic) organizations from Europe and North America. This was a major cultural infusion in contrast to the traditional Chinese educational system, which served only the elite classes. Christian missionaries, particularly those sent by the Catholic Church, were present in China before the Qing dynasty (see Figure 1.6).[16] Over time, more missionaries arrived, and their operations expanded. Although the Cultural Revolution destroyed churches, and the Communist party closed churches that were receiving Western support, more recently the Chinese government has allowed the reopening of Protestant and Catholic churches as long as they are registered with SARA. As noted earlier, these churches receive no financial and administrative support from Western countries, in order to satisfy the stipulation in the Chinese constitution that religious establishments should be independent of foreign powers. Many perceive these churches to be controlled by the Chinese government, and thus many Christians have formed "house churches," establishing a sizable "underground" community of Christians. These churches have been occasionally harassed by local officials; however, the Chinese government's tolerance of Christianity seems to be increasing slowly over time.

To summarize, not only do different religions exist in China today, but certain groups have flourished significantly, although reliable statistics are difficult to obtain. There is some tension between religions and politics, with the Muslim population in the west currently receiving the most negative government attention. Religious practices in local areas are highly diverse, especially among the smaller minority population groups in the southwest. Given the diversity in both languages and religions, therefore, Chinese culture is hardly a unified system shared by all Chinese.

FIGURE 1.6 St. Joseph's Church is one of the four historic Catholic churches in the Roman Catholic Archdiocese of Beijing. The construction of the original church was finished in 1655 by Jesuit missionaries. Due to renovations and reconstruction, the current structure dates back to 1904. The church, commonly known as Wangfujing Church (王府井天主堂) or Dongtang (東堂, the East Cathedral), is located in the Dongcheng district of the city in Wangfujing Street. (Photo: Kenneth K. K. Wong)

A LOOK AT WHAT'S AHEAD

This is a textbook about the geography of China. In general, the study of geography can be approached in two ways: "regional" and "systematic." The regional approach divides a geographical area into smaller regions, and each region is studied in detail across different topics, such as the physical environment (e.g., climate, landform) and human activity patterns (e.g., population, economics). The systematic approach organizes the study by themes or types of phenomena. This book is special in that it combines these two organizational approaches. The first nine chapters are organized by themes or topics; the next three chapters are dedicated to examining selected regions in detail. The book ends with a brief chapter considering future possibilities for China.

The next chapter, Chapter 2, provides an overview of the physical environment of China—the basic physical geography of the region. Such knowledge is essential to understanding other aspects of the country. Chapter 3 describes the characteristics of the population of China, including its demographic structure, geographical distribution, and racial/ethnic groups. Chapter 4 focuses on food production and consumption in China. Given the large population of China, a major concern is how to feed its people, and thus its agricultural system has to be efficient. Today's China cannot be separated from its economic power; therefore, Chapter 5 addresses the economy of China from a geographical perspective. Related to the booming economy is the growth of cities. Chapter 6 provides an overview of China's urban system and the process by which the nation is becoming more urban. Currently about half of the population in China is found in cities or urban areas, and most discussions have been focusing on these more developed and richer places. However, what happens outside the cities affects the cities themselves, and thus Chapter 7 discusses China beyond its cities. To support the growth of the economy, the expansion of ities, and the interactions between cities and rural areas, an efficient transportation system is needed to move people and commodities. Accordingly, the structure and development of China's transportation system are reviewed in Chapter 8. The economic prosperity and development of China have not come cheaply; the environment has paid a high price. Chapter 9 addresses environmental issues from a Chinese perspective.

The next three chapters are dedicated to some of the more interesting regions. China's most economically developed areas are scattered along its coast; Chapter 10 provides a more detailed discussion of this coastal region. The periphery of China is where the political and cultural influences of Chinese and foreign cultures interface. These boundary regions with great physical and cultural diversity are much less developed, but are of great concern to the government. These areas are addressed in Chapter 11. Chapter 12 focuses on Hong Kong and Macau, the two SARs, plus Taiwan; these three geographical entities were created under unique historical circumstances. The book concludes with a brief discussion of future directions for China in Chapter 13, "China at the Crossroads."

Much of the literature on China, particularly on its economic and social development, seems to take the general position of "convergence theory." That is, this literature assumes that China will become more like the rest of the world, particularly Western countries, as it continues to develop. We do not dispute the possibility that China will become more "Westernized." It is undeniable that many aspects of Western culture are already well received in China (e.g., fast-food chains such as McDonald's and KFC are everywhere). The standard and style of living in Chinese cities have also grown more like those in Western cities. However, we believe that underneath these superficial similarities, China is unique and quite different from the West. In geography, each location is unique, and so China's geography is unique. Nevertheless, certain processes are universal, and those processes are functioning in China. Therefore, while geographical concepts, theories, and models are used to frame discussions of the Chinese situation throughout this book, the uniqueness of China in all these aspects is also highlighted. Not just the physical environment of China is unique; its population composition, demographic history, rural–urban migration mechanisms, trajectory of economic development, expansion of transportation systems, causes and magnitudes of environmental degradation, and so forth, are all "Chinese style." Another special feature of this book is the use of boxes to highlight interesting phenomena and other unique aspects of China that are likely to interest most readers. It is our hope that the book will provide readers with an overview of the ever-changing China and a foundation on which they can build more knowledge about this country.

NOTES

1. See also www.youtube.com/watch?v=50dyyevLH6I.

2. www.youtube.com/watch?v=TYKAbRK_wKA.

3. http://data.worldbank.org/data-catalog/GDP-ranking-table (retrieved August 28, 2016).

4. www.chinatownology.com.

5. A high-profile naturalized Chinese citizen is Allan Zeman, who was a major developer of Lan Kwai Fong, a small neighborhood in Hong Kong that is a popular site for expatriates to drink, dine, and socialize. Zeman, a Canadian by birth, became a naturalized Chinese citizen in 2008.

6. http://global.britannica.com/EBchecked/topic/609044/Dongting-Lake.

7. One of the many sources is the List of Rulers of China (October 2004) in the Heilbrunn Timeline of Art History, www.metmuseum.org/toah/hd/chem/hd_chem.htm.

8. http://afe.easia.columbia.edu/timelines/china_timeline.htm.

9. www.historylearningsite.co.uk/sun_yat.htm.

10. www.history.co.uk/study-topics/history-of-ww2/sino-japanese-war.

11. There are no generally agreed-upon definitions or boundaries of "China proper." However, a map and some explanations are available at https://depts.washington.edu/chinaciv/geo/land.htm (retrieved August 30, 2016).

12. Many people claim that China is a nation that likes to eat. Chapter 4 discusses the agricultural system, as well as related local cuisines.

13. Qin Shi Huang is one the most frequently mentioned Chinese emperors because of his contributions, his "iron fist" in controlling the country, and his lavish lifestyle, including the creation of the famous terra-cotta warriors and horses for his mausoleum in present-day Xi'an (http://whc.unesco.org/en/list/441).

14. http://en.people.cn/constitution/constitution.html.

15. www.pewforum.org/2008/05/01/religion-in-china-on-the-eve-of-the-2008-beijing-olympics.

16. Although Christians had arrived in China during the Yuan and earlier dynasties, the most famous early missionary was probably the Italian Jesuit Matteo Ricci, who started his work in Macau and later moved to Beijing around 1600.

REFERENCES •••

Barboza, D. (2010, August 15). China passes Japan as second-largest economy. *New York Times.* Retrieved August 28, 2016, from www.nytimes.com/2010/08/16/business/global/16yuan.html?pagewanted=all.

Central Intelligence Agency (CIA). (2016, July 11). China. In *The world factbook.* Retrieved from https://www.cia.gov/library/publications/the-world-factbook/geos/ch.html.

Hou, D. (1980). *Heirs of the dragon* [Album]. Hong Kong: Rock Records.

National Bureau of Statistics of China. (n.d.). Tabulation on the 2010 Population Census of the People's Republic of China. Retrieved from www.stats.gov.cn/tjsj/pcsj/rkpc/6rp/indexch.htm.

Panda, A. (2016, August 29). China's first homemade carrier could take to the seas later this year. *The Diplomat.* Retrieved August 29, 2016, from http://thediplomat.com/2016/08/chinas-first-homemade-carrier-could-take-to-the-seas-later-this-year.

Strickland, E. (2014, January 3). Timeline: China's space program, past and future. Retrieved from http://spectrum.ieee.org/static/timeline-chinas-space-program-past-and-future.

U.S. Department of the Treasury. (2016, July 18). Major foreign holders of treasury securities. Retrieved from www.treasury.gov/resource-center/data-chart-center/tic/Documents/mfh.txt.

FURTHER READING •••••••••••••••••••••••••••••••••••••••

Hsieh, C.-H., & Lu, M. (Eds.). (2004). *Changing China: A geographical appraisal.* Boulder, CO: Westview Press.

Naughton, B. (1995). *Growing out of the plan: Chinese economic reform 1978–1993.* Cambridge, UK: Cambridge University Press.

Naughton, B. (2007). *The Chinese economy: transitions and growth.* Cambridge, MA: MIT Press.

Zhao, S. (1994). *Geography of China: Environment, resources, population, and development.* New York: Wiley.

CHAPTER 2

Physical Environment and Resources

Diverse and Abundant

LEARNING OBJECTIVES	KEY CONCEPTS AND TERMS
★ Comprehend the geographical and physical settings of Chinese territory. ★ Recognize the diverse physical and environmental conditions. ★ Understand the relationships among plate movements, landscape features, the hydrological system, and topography. ★ Understand the relationships among the climatic, biotic, and soil systems. ★ Recognize the connections among energy, metallic ore resources, and China's development.	topography; tectonic plates; Pacific Rim or "Ring of Fire"; hydrological system; monsoon climate; typhoon; climatic region; vegetation zones; chernozems; loess; fossil fuels; rare earth elements (REEs)

DIVERSITY OF LANDSCAPE: A BLESSING OR A CURSE?

As noted in Chapter 1, China is the fourth largest country in terms of area (after Russia, Canada, and the United States). It extends from about the center of the Eurasian continent to the coasts of the North and South China Seas. This huge territory includes a variety of landscapes, with highly diverse topographic conditions, climatic characteristics, and vegetative covers. However, it also includes a disproportionately large amount of land with poor resources or unfavorable conditions. China possesses a fair share of lowlands in the east, areas with decent climatic conditions, and abundant deposits of important natural resources. But a significant portion of its territory, mainly in the west, has a relatively harsh environment, including the world's highest plateau and one of the deepest basins on earth. It also has one of the world's major deserts, and the extensive dry land around the desert is extremely vulnerable to becoming desert as well (a process known as "desertification"). Although China has often claimed to be the "land of abundance" (地大物博), it is under many constraints from nature, and some of these constraints are quite serious.

This chapter focuses on the physical and environmental characteristics of China, including its natural resources. All of these physical conditions and environmental characteristics influence, if not determine, the locations of human activities to a large degree. Physical characteristics can act as restrictive factors on human activities. For instance, the frigid climate at the northeastern edge of China creates a hostile environment for human settlement, although there are sparse settlements in the region. Similarly, the extreme landscape features of western China, such as the Tibetan Plateau and the desert-like basins, are unfavorable to settlement. On the other hand, physical characteristics can act as enabling factors, facilitating the presence of certain activities. For instance, the southeast coast of China has a relatively mild climate with access to ocean resources, and is thus highly populated. Hainan, the island province off the southern coast, has a tropical climate during most of the year and is a major tourist attraction. Certain locations in western China are rich in natural resources and have significant settlements, despite their aridity. In general, areas with more desirable physical conditions attract human settlement, and thus these areas' resources are exploited and utilized more heavily. Areas with less desirable conditions are less likely to attract settlement. Thus the physical landscape is better preserved in those areas, and the natural resources are less likely to be exploited. To some extent, therefore, the harsh environment may offer protection. Developing comprehensive knowledge about different aspects of the physical environment allows us to better understand and explain the geographical distributions of various human activities.

The physical environment of a country is largely determined by its general location and its geographical setting. In this chapter, we first discuss China's geographical setting and general location, comparing these to the setting and location of the United States. Then we describe the topographic layout of China (including the variations in elevation) and the major landscape and hydrological features, such as rivers and lakes. The well-being of a large proportion of the population of China relies heavily on these rivers and lakes. We next discuss climate, a subsystem of the physical environment; we focus on the monsoon, which is the dominant climatic system in southern and eastern China. Major types of vegetation, soils, and biomes found in China and their general locations are then discussed. Topography and climate are major factors affecting the development of soils, and soils strongly influence the types of vegetation and the potential for agricultural practice. Finally, natural resources are part of the natural environment. Although there are many types of natural resources, our discussion focuses mainly on energy sources (fossil fuels, hydroelectricity) and metallic ores, as these are closely tied to the development of the modern Chinese economy.

GENERAL LOCATION AND PHYSICAL LAYOUT

China's location at the eastern end of the Eurasian continent provides strategic access to the oceans. China's overall position falls into the middle latitudes of the Northern Hemisphere: The majority of its territory falls between 23 and 43 degrees North. This is north of the tropical region, but far south of the polar region.[1] (See the map in Table 2.1.) The midlatitude location is characterized by a relatively mild climate, but it is also influenced by monsoon climatic conditions, which include tropical maritime influences in summer and polar continental influences in winter.

The vast geographical extent of China from north to south and from the coast to the continental interior provides a variety of climatic types. This great variety of climatic conditions across the country creates highly varied land cover characteristics and surface geological structure. Other significant factors affecting the surface landscape include the underlying geological structure and topographic conditions.

TABLE 2.1. A Comparison of Physical-Environmental Characteristics between China and the United States

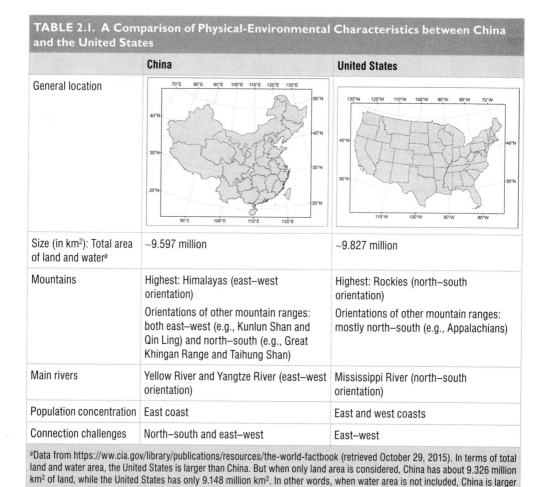

	China	United States
General location		
Size (in km²): Total area of land and water[a]	~9.597 million	~9.827 million
Mountains	Highest: Himalayas (east–west orientation) Orientations of other mountain ranges: both east–west (e.g., Kunlun Shan and Qin Ling) and north–south (e.g., Great Khingan Range and Taihung Shan)	Highest: Rockies (north–south orientation) Orientations of other mountain ranges: mostly north–south (e.g., Appalachians)
Main rivers	Yellow River and Yangtze River (east–west orientation)	Mississippi River (north–south orientation)
Population concentration	East coast	East and west coasts
Connection challenges	North–south and east–west	East–west

[a]Data from https://ww.cia.gov/library/publications/resources/the-world-factbook (retrieved October 29, 2015). In terms of total land and water area, the United States is larger than China. But when only land area is considered, China has about 9.326 million km² of land, while the United States has only 9.148 million km². In other words, when water area is not included, China is larger than the United States. Also note that other sources report different figures for the two countries' areas.

One way to develop a portrait of China's physical environment is to compare its characteristics with those of the United States, which is similar in size. Table 2.1 compares several physical and environmental characteristics of these two countries. In terms of topography, China has the highest plateau, with some areas over 8,000 m (26,246 ft). The adjacent Himalayas, the tallest mountain range in the world, have some mountains over 7,000 m (22,965 ft) in elevation; Mount Everest, partly in the Tibet autonomous region and partly in Nepal, is the highest mountain (over 8,800 m/28,870 ft). The highest mountains in the U.S. Rockies are slightly over 4,000 m (14,000 ft). Mountain ranges in China have different orientations, some running north and south, but many running east and west. In the United States, mountain ranges mostly follow a north–south orientation. Due to landscape characteristics and climatic conditions, the population in China is heavily concentrated in the eastern part of the country. However, one of China's challenges is to connect people in different parts of the country, from north to south and from east to west. Population distribution patterns are part of the problem, as are physical barriers inhibiting human mobility.

In the United States, population is concentrated along the east and west coasts, although some large cities (such as Chicago, Illinois, and Dallas–Fort Worth, Texas) are found in the interior. Many of those interior cities are found near bodies of water (e.g., Chicago is located on Lake Michigan), while other interior cities have historically strategic locations (e.g., the Dallas–Fort Worth metropolitan area was important to the cattle trade and was developed as a railroad center). Historically, the residents of the United States faced challenges in connecting and communicating along its east–west axis, given its mountain ranges. The north–south connections were less of a problem (geographically, if not politically!). The following sections discuss different aspects of the physical environment of China in detail.

PHYSIOGRAPHIC SYSTEMS

A physiographic system may include many elements: topography, or elevation; different landform features, such as mountains, valleys, and basins; and hydrological features, such as rivers and lakes. Plate 1 shows the detailed topography of China. (For this and all other plates in this book, see the color insert.) The general impression is that China's land surface is rugged and uneven. Traveling westward from Shanghai on the coast, one goes steadily higher in elevation across a series of hills and ridges, plateaus, and elevated basins. The landscape is highly heterogeneous across the country, but in many areas, the landscape varies tremendously even at the local geographical scale.

The overall topography of China can be described as a series of steps ascending from east to west, with elevation increasing from the southeast coastal area toward the west. Although this picture is generally correct, it misses prominent features in specific regions. For instance, southwest China has the features with the highest elevations (the Tibetan Plateau and Mount Everest at 8,850 m/29,035 ft, according to one of several measurements on the highest elevation), but northwest China has the lowest elevation point in the country (the Turfan or Turpan Depression at 154 m/505 ft below sea level).[2] Thus, the most extreme landscapes are found in western China. On the other hand, eastern China is not uniformly low in elevation. Major mountain ranges are present in the east, and coastal areas are not all flat. China's eastern coast abuts extensive neighboring seas, and their depth on China's continental shelf is generally less than 200 m (656 ft). There are more than 5,000 islands on the continental shelf. In sum, the topographic structure of China is very complex, and the landscape features are very diverse. To better comprehend the distribution of landform features and topography, we need to understand the major underlying forces affecting the formation of China's land surface characteristics.

Plate Tectonics and China's Landscape

Why is the highest mountain, Mount Everest, on China's doorstep? Why is the world's highest plateau in southwest China? The reason is the plate tectonic system. It is the major underlying force that has built the Himalayas and the Tibetan Plateau, and that causes all seismic activities.

According to plate tectonic theory, the earth's crust (lithosphere) consists of several plates "floating" on the top of molten magma (hot fluid underneath the earth's crust). These plates move away from or collide with each other, causing different types of volcanic activities and producing different types of landform features.[3] China is located in the eastern part of the Eurasian Plate, which is a relatively large plate in the system (see Figure 2.1). This plate extends east beneath the Pacific Ocean, under Japan to the east, and under most parts of the Philippines to the south. Another large plate to the east of the Eurasian Plate is the Pacific Plate, which sits under most of the Pacific Ocean. However, between these two large plates is the relatively small Philippines Plate. To the south of the Eurasian and Philippine Plates is the Australian Plate.[4]

These plates are subject to movement over time. Figure 2.1 indicates the general directions of the plates' movements. The Eurasian Plate and Pacific Plate move toward each other, squeezing the Philippines Plate. Therefore, the Philippines and Japan, which are located close to or along the edges of these plates, experience frequent volcanic activities and earthquakes as results of plate collision. On the other side of the Pacific Plate is the North American Plate, and these two plates also move against each other. Figure 2.1 indicates areas with high risk of earthquake. Many of these vulnerable areas lie along the edge of the Pacific Plate, including the Philippines and Japan on the western side, and the western coast of North America (including Alaska and Mexico) on the eastern side. All these areas together are known as the Pacific Rim or the "Ring of Fire," reflecting the volatility of the earth's crust along the edge of the plates. The edge of the Pacific Plate is quite far from Chinese territory, and its movements are not of much concern to the mainland.

On another front, the Australian Plate moves northwestward, pushing toward the Eurasian Plate. These two plates collide along the boundaries of China, India,

Bhutan, and Nepal, where the Himalayas are located. Theoretically, when two plates collide, one possible release of tension is through the uplifting of the earth's crust, creating a mountain range. This accounts for the formation of the Himalayas and to some extent, the high Tibetan Plateau. Partly because of the "squeezing" between these plates, southwest China, including Yunnan, has relatively rugged terrain.

Figure 2.1 clearly shows that an area at the junction between the two plates in southwest China is at high risk for earthquakes. From Bhutan, Nepal, and northeast India, to areas within Chinese territory in Xizang (Tibet), Yunnan, and Sichuan, earthquakes are quite common. Most of the world's strongest earthquakes have occurred in the Pacific Ring of Fire and at the interface between the Australian Plate and Eurasian Plate, including Indonesia. The 10th strongest earthquake to date occurred in Xizang (Tibet) in 1950.[5] Figure 2.1 may give the impression that China is not subject to this kind of natural disaster. However, China has more than its share of deadly earthquakes.

According to the China Earthquake Administration (CEA), China has at least 495 areas where earthquakes are a constant threat.[6] The CEA plans to identify all other major active quake zones in China by 2020. This information will allow the CEA to conduct better monitoring and analysis, prevent damage, and create emergency rescue plans when earthquakes occur.

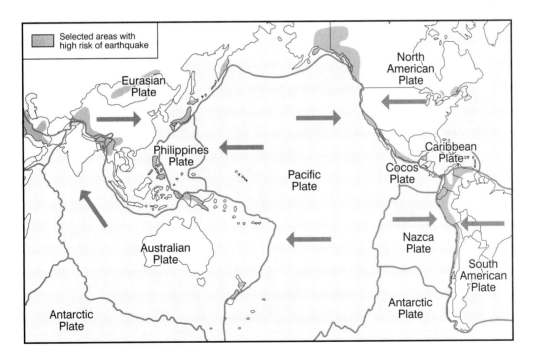

FIGURE 2.1 Major tectonic plates, their directions of movement (arrows), and areas with high risk of earthquake (dark shading).

BOX 2.1. China Is Shaking

Most of China's earthquakes are associated with the geological fault structures called "seismic belts" (see Figure 2.2). The most devastating earthquake ever recorded occurred in Shaanxi province in January 1556 (during the Ming dynasty). As shown in Table 2.2, four of the deadliest earthquakes to have occurred in China are the Shaanxi earthquake (1556), the Haiyuan earthquake (1920), the Tangshan earthquake (1976), and the great Sichuan earthquake (2008) (see Figure 2.3 for photos from the Sichuan earthquake). These quakes are ranked in Table 2.2 according to the number of deaths they caused. Much of the death and damage resulted not from the quakes themselves, but from the lack of earthquake-proofing measures. For example, the enormous human casualties of the 1556 earthquake

were mainly caused by the collapse of cave houses within loess and by the starvation that followed.

Even with today's state-of-the-art technology, earthquakes are still difficult to predict and to monitor precisely in the short and medium terms. However, they may be predicted in the long term, and thus heavy damage might be avoided. For example, the city of Tangshan is located at the junction of several deep fault lines in the region. Severe earthquakes are bound to happen in this area, although the exact time is difficult to predict. After Tangshan's devastating 1976 earthquake, the best precaution would have been to avoid rebuilding the city at the same location. Unfortunately, the city was rebuilt on the same site (Zhao, 1994), putting millions of people at risk.

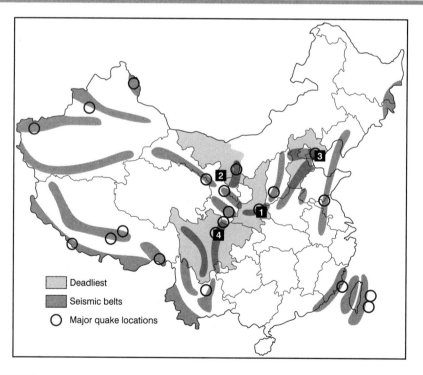

FIGURE 2.2 Major seismic belts in China (darker shading), major earthquake locations in the past (magnitude 8 or higher on the Richter scale) (circles), the four deadliest quakes mentioned in Table 2.2 (numbered black squares), and provinces associated with these deadliest quakes (lighter shading). Based on http://usa.chinadaily.com.cn/epaper/2011-03/21/content_12201556.htm (retrieved July 12, 2016).

TABLE 2.2. The Deadliest Earthquakes in China				
Date	Name of quake (epicenter)	Magnitude[a]	Deaths	Description
January 23, 1556	Shaanxi earthquake (Shaanxi)	8.0 Mw	830,000	The deadliest earthquake of all time occurred during the Ming Dynasty in China. Its epicenter was in the Wei River valley in Shaanxi province, near the cities of Weinan and Huaxian. The earthquake triggered landslides, which contributed to the massive death toll for people living in the cave dwellings in the Loess Plateau. The estimated death toll (likely overestimated) accounted for over 60% of the region's population. It ranks as one of the worst disasters in human history.
July 28, 1976	Tangshan earthquake (Tangshan, Heibei)	7.8 Mw	242,769[b]	The second deadliest earthquake in China was the Tangshan earthquake in 1976. Two factors contributed to the high death rate: first, the earthquake struck the area at around 4:00 A.M., while most people were asleep; second, Tangshan is a region of low risk for earthquakes, so the buildings were not earthquake-proofed.
December 16, 1920	Haiyuan or Gansu earthquake (Haiyuan, Ningxia)	7.8 ML	200,000[c]	The third deadliest earthquake in China caused total destruction in the Lijunbu–Haiyuan–Ganyanchi area. The earthquake was felt from the Yellow Sea to Qinghai province and from southern Neimenggu (Inner Mongolia) to central Sichuan province. Large numbers of landslides and fissures/cracks in the ground occurred throughout the epicenter area. Some rivers were blocked, and others changed courses.
May 12, 2008	Sichuan earthquake (Wenchuan county, Sichuan)	7.9 Mw	69,197, plus 18,222 missing	The Sichuan earthquake was the most recent deadly earthquake in China. The prefecture-level divisions of Mianyang, Ngawa, Deyang, Guangyuan, and Chengdu suffered the greatest loss of lives. Most of the collapsed buildings were in rural areas that did not adhere to building codes. At least 4.8 million people (some estimates were as high as 15 million) were rendered homeless. All highways into Wenchuan, the epicenter, were damaged by the quake, delaying the arrival of relief troops.

[a]Magnitude is based on measurement of the maximum motion recorded by a seismograph. Several scales have been defined, such as (1) local magnitude (ML) (or "Richter magnitude"), (2) surface-wave magnitude (Ms), (3) body-wave magnitude (Mb), and (4) moment magnitude (Mw).
[b]Slightly modified after Dr. George Pararas-Carayannis's report (see www.drgeorgepc.com/Earthquake1976ChinaTangshan.html).
[c]Total casualties were reported as 200,000 or more from multiple sources (see http://research.omicsgroup.org/index.php/1920_Haiyuan_earthquake).

FIGURE 2.3 Effects of the 2008 Sichuan earthquake: (a) a collapsed school; (b) temporary classrooms in use at the collapsed school; (c) a collapsed bridge.

Major Landform Features

Plate tectonic theory provides a plausible explanation for why southwest China has high elevation, relatively rugged terrain, and diverse landscape characteristics. Plate 1 shows the complex and highly varied topography of China. Plate 2 identifies some of the major landform features.

As suggested earlier, China's overall topography can be described as a series of steps increasing in elevation from the southeast coast toward the west. The Tibetan Plateau, at the western end of China, is the highest topographic step. It is an extensive landscape, extending from the Kashmir State of India into China. Two mountain ranges (see Plate 2), the Kunlun Shan (*shan* means "mountain" in Chinese) and the Himalayas, mark the northern and southern boundaries of the Tibetan Plateau. These are examples of mountain ranges with east–west orientations, unlike the predominant north–south orientations of mountain ranges in North America. The Tibetan Plateau is the highest plateau on earth and is commonly known as the "roof of the world." It covers not just the Xizang (Tibet) autonomous region, but also most of Qinghai province. Therefore, the plateau is also called the Qingzang Plateau (combining the Qing of Qinghai and the Zang of Xizang) or the Qinghai–Tibetan Plateau. Due to the high elevation in the plateau, the atmosphere is generally thin, the temperature is low, and permafrost[7] is widespread. Solar radiation is intense, and winds are strong. Because the natural conditions are so unfavorable to human activities, the population density is low, and settlements are sparse and widely distributed.

Going north from the Tibetan Plateau is a steep escarpment, which includes the Kunlun Shan. The land then drops down to the Tarim Basin and the Turfan (or Turpan) Depression in the Xinjiang autonomous region. The escarpment has one of the steepest descents on earth, dropping several thousand meters in altitude over one hundred or so kilometers.

Stepping down from the Tibetan Plateau eastward and northward, the land is composed mainly of plateaus and basins with elevations of 1,000–2000 m (3,280–6561 ft) above sea level. The prominent landscapes include the Inner Mongolian Plateau, the Gobi Desert, the Loess Plateau, the Yunnan Plateau, and four basins or depressions (the Tarim, Junggar, Turfan, and Sichuan). The Turfan Depression is the lowest point in mainland China, extending north toward the borders with Russia and the Mongolian Republic. West of the basins and depressions is the Tian (or Tien) Shan, a mountain range serving as a natural border between China and neighboring countries in Central Asia. East of the basin and depression region is the Gobi Desert, which stretches across Inner Mongolia and the Mongolian Republic. Although oases are occasionally found (e.g., Turfan or Tulufan), this extensive region stretching toward the western border is the most arid part of the country. Inhabitants are either nomads herding cattle and moving around for grassland and water, or urban dwellers who reside in cities. The cities were established to exploit the significant natural resources in the region, as well as for historical and cultural reasons.

All the regions mentioned above may be regarded as western China, according to some regionalization schemes. Central China is characterized by a series of mountain ranges, plateaus, and lowlands. Its topographical changes are not as dramatic as those in the west. Not too far south of the Gobi Desert is the northern edge of the Loess Plateau. It stretches across several provinces: the eastern part of Gansu, Henan, Shaanxi, and much of Shanxi. Much lower in elevation and smaller in area than the Tibetan Plateau, the Loess Plateau is of greater historical significance than most landform features in China, as discussed in Chapter 1. The plateau is loosely bounded by the Yellow River to the north and the Wei River to the south (see Figure 2.4). The plateau was formed by the long-term accumulation of silty sediments picked up by the winter monsoon winds. These winds blow from the Mongolian Plateau southward across the Gobi Desert until they are blocked by the Qin Ling,[8] a major east–west mountain range in southern Shaanxi province. The mountains reduce the wind speed and cause the silt to be deposited in an area north of Qin Ling—the present-day Loess Plateau. Loess is the most highly erodible soil on earth, and yellowish silt gives the Yellow River its name. Overall, the soil of the Loess Plateau region is rich in minerals. Although its climate is semiarid,[9] irrigation water from the Yellow River allows agriculture. This enabled the region to develop into the cradle of Chinese civilization.[10]

The Qin Ling Mountains divide central and eastern China into north and south. To the southwest of Qin Ling is the Sichuan Basin, a low-lying area surrounded by mountains or highlands. It is also known as the Red Basin because the major type of soil in the region is red, which is explained later.

Further south in the central section of China is the Yunnan Plateau (also known as the Yunnan–Guizhou Plateau), with an elevation of about 1,000–2,000 m

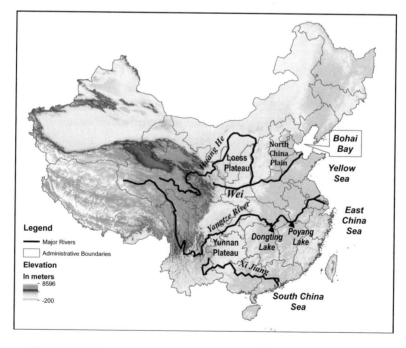

FIGURE 2.4 Major hydrographical features (rivers and lakes) in China.

(3280–6561 ft). Directly west of the plateau, within Yunnan province, the land starts to rise toward the Tibetan Plateau. The Yunnan Plateau is characterized by high, rugged ground surfaces cut by deep gorges and high waterfalls. Limestone strata are widely distributed, and karst topography[11] is well developed in the region.

In northeast China are the Greater Khingan Range and the Taihung Shan (see Plate 2). These two mountain ranges run generally from north to south and separate the Loess Plateau from the Northeast Plain and the North China Plain. These are two major lowland areas ideal for agriculture in terms of topography. The Southeast Uplands, which are not too far from the coast, are moderately rugged, with elevations mostly lower than 1,000 m (3,281 ft); therefore, they do not form a major barrier. Across the Taiwan Strait, the island of Taiwan has a mountain range running from north to south on the eastern side, while the west coast is relatively gentle with low elevation.

Hydrographic Features

Another major element of the physiographic system is the hydrological system, which includes rivers and lakes. Figure 2.4 shows the four major river systems in China. Most river systems have many tributaries with different names, but only the main rivers are shown in the figure. Numerous lakes are found all over China, but only two of the largest and most important lakes are shown here.

The two longest river systems in China are the Yellow River (Huang He) and the Yangtze River. Both rivers are fed by melting snow from the Tibetan Plateau, and both flow from west to east, moving down the topographic steps before entering the seas in eastern China. The Yellow River makes several turns in the Tibetan Plateau, cutting through the rugged terrain. After it comes down from the plateau, it turns north to circumvent the Loess Plateau. After flowing past the plateau, it turns southward and merges with the Wei River, a major tributary of the river system. Then it flows eastward through the North China Plain, out to the Bohai ("hai" in Chinese is sea) and Yellow Sea.

As discussed in Chapter 1, the Yellow River valley and the Loess Plateau are regarded as the cradle of Chinese civilization. Although the river was important to early Chinese settlements, it also brought much grief. The conflux area where the Wei River meets the Yellow River experienced numerous floods historically, forcing people to relocate. In ancient times, a legendary ruler, Yu the Great (大禹), was honored because of his efforts in "taming" the floods. As the flow of river water slows in its lower course, sediment is deposited on the river bed, and the river becomes shallower over time. This makes the river prone to flooding, especially when water level rises after heavy rain or heavy snowmelt. The lower course of the river has changed its channel during floods many times throughout its history. While the flooding caused damage and casualties, it also brought alluvium (river sediment) from the river bed to the adjacent lands, providing fertile soil to support intensive agricultural activities.

The Yangtze River, the longest river in China, originates not too far from the source of the Yellow River on the Tibetan Plateau. Instead of flowing directly eastward after leaving the Tibetan Plateau, the river turns south, cutting through part of the Yunnan Plateau in southwest China before turning back to the north. Then it flows east and enters the East China Sea near Shanghai. Along the lower course of the river are many freshwater lakes, such as Dongting Lake and Poyang Lake. These are two of the largest lakes in China and are part of significant ecological and environmental systems along the lower Yangtze River. Areas around these lakes have attracted significant settlements, in addition to their value for tourism.

The third major river system is the Xi Jiang in southern China, with one of its major sources on the Yunnan Plateau. The Xi Jiang, which means "western river," is the major river of a multiple-river system that covers part of Yunnan, Guangxi, and Guangdong provinces (see Figure 2.4). When this river merges with other tributaries of the same system and flows out to the ocean in the delta region in southern Guangdong near Macau and Hong Kong, it becomes the Pearl River. Although the river basin is not large compared to the other two major rivers, its delta region is very agriculturally productive. One of its tributaries, the Dong Jiang (meaning "eastern river"), is the major source of Hong Kong's freshwater supply.

CLIMATE

A region's landscape characteristics are affected not only by where the region is generally located within the lithospheric system, but also by the region's hydrological features (such as rivers) and the climatic conditions. An understanding of climatic systems is essential to comprehending the interaction between the hydrosphere and lithosphere. As an example, we discuss the monsoon climatic system, which affects the eastern section of China.

The Monsoon System and China's Climate

"Monsoon" refers to the seasonal change in the direction of atmospheric circulation and the associated precipitation patterns. When air is heated up (usually by solar radiation), it rises. Rising air creates a low-pressure center. When air cools, it sinks. Sinking air creates a high-pressure center. As air rises in the low-pressure area, it creates a vacuum near the earth's surface (lower atmosphere). To fill in the vacuum, surface air flows from the high-pressure region into the low-pressure region. The direction of airflow in the upper atmosphere is the opposite. Thus an air circulation system is formed between the earth's surface and the upper atmosphere. The direction of circulation is controlled by the relative locations of the high- and low-pressure centers. The formation of these centers is mainly attributable to the different rates at which continents and oceans absorb and release heat (solar radiation) over different seasons. Solid land masses such as continents absorb heat faster than oceans, but they also release heat, cooling faster than oceans.

In summer, continents absorb heat faster than oceans, and so air masses over continents have lower pressure than those over the oceans. To fill the vacuum created by the low-pressure centers over the continent, wind blows in from the ocean, creating a sea breeze or onshore wind. During winter, the situation is reversed: Air masses over the continents are relatively cool and descend, while air masses over the ocean are relatively warm and rise (oceans still release heat slowly). Thus high-pressure centers are over the continents, and low-pressure centers are over the oceans. Wind blows from the continental interior with cold temperatures toward the ocean, bringing cold fronts to warmer coastal regions intermittently.

Because of its vast territory, the climatic system in China is complex, but it may be divided into two major subsystems. Eastern (or coastal) China is dominated mainly by the East Asian monsoon climate, which also affects Korea and Japan. A small part of southwestern China is affected by the Indian monsoon system. On the other hand, the western part of China lies in the continental interior, which is too far from the oceans to receive their moderating effects. Therefore, western China is not affected by the summer monsoon. Broadly, the two major subsystems of China's climate are the continental (western) climate and the East Asian monsoon, as illustrated in Figure 2.5.

The East Asian monsoon is the main component of the Asian monsoon system. It plays an important role in weather and climate in China. For instance, regional flood and drought disasters in China in summer are closely related to the seasonal anomalies of the major rain belt known as *meiyu* or "plum rain." This rain belt is

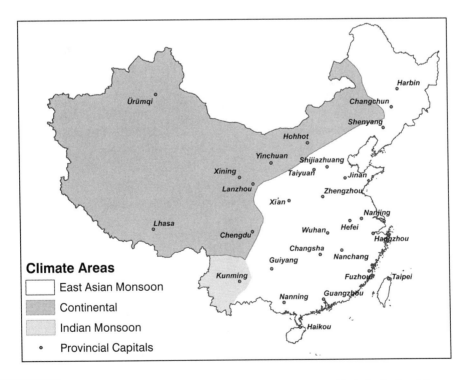

FIGURE 2.5 Areas of China affected by the continental climatic system (dark shading) and the monsoon climatic system. The area affected by the monsoon system is further divided into the East Asian monsoon area (no shading) and the Indian monsoon area (medium shading).

significantly influenced by the East Asian monsoon, and huge floods occurred in
central China during the *meiyu* periods in 1991 and 1998. These floods resulted in
much loss of property and life. The East Asian winter monsoon affects extensive
areas, including southern China, in the form of cold, dry air blowing from the
continental interior. There are sometimes intense cold waves causing sudden temperature drops in southern China. As shown in Figure 2.5, a small part of southwest
China is affected by the Indian monsoon subsystem, drawing moisture mainly from
the Indian Ocean region.

Figure 2.6 shows the directions of the monsoon winds in winter and summer.
In summer, the interior of the Asian continent as well as the northern part of
the Indian subcontinent are relatively hot, and therefore low-pressure zones are
formed in north central China and Mongolia, as well as the northern part of India.
High-pressure zones sit over the oceans surrounding the continent, including the
Indian Ocean, the South China Sea, and the Pacific Ocean, as they have cooler
temperatures. Humid, warm air from the oceans blows toward the continent. In
winter, high pressure sits over the continental interior, and low pressure sits over
the oceans. Frigid, dry wind blows from the continent toward the oceans over the
coastal areas in China and India.

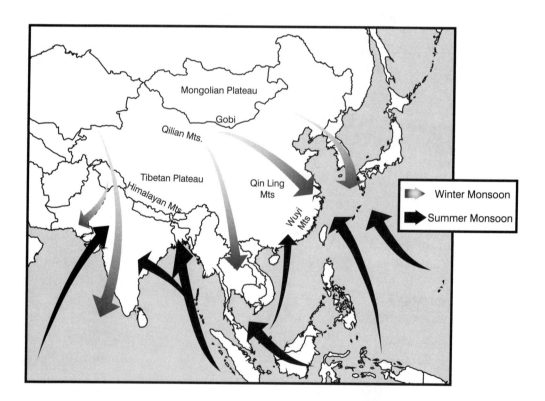

FIGURE 2.6 The dominant wind directions of the monsoon in Asia. Darker arrows indicate the summer
wet season; lighter arrows indicate the winter dry season.

In addition to the monsoon, typhoons in the summer affect the weather and climate of China. A "typhoon" is also known as a "tropical cyclone" or a "hurricane" in North America. It is essentially a system of rotating wind with extreme low pressure at its center. Exactly how a typhoon starts is still not clearly known, but it is believed that during mid- to late summer, ocean water in the region can be very warm, creating low-pressure zones. Fed by the warm water and the global circulation system of the atmosphere, these low-pressure zones start to organize into rotating systems. Typhoons usually form in the eastern parts of the Pacific Ocean, and move across it and the South China Sea toward the coast of China following the onshore wind directions of the monsoon system. The typhoon season in China may start as early as June or July, and may last until October or November. These days, the so-called "supertyphoons" hit the Chinese coast quite frequently.

Climatic Regions

The climatic conditions of coastal and eastern China are affected by the East Asian monsoon system. They can be characterized as humid and hot in summer, and as either dry, cool, or cold in winter, partly depending on latitudinal position. Interior China is characterized by the continental climatic system, hot and dry in summer, and cold in winter. These are very broad characterizations of climatic conditions. There are also more detailed climate classification systems. A common climate classification system is the Köppen system,[12] which defines climate types by temperature (types A, C, D, and E) and dryness or precipitation (type B), although precipitation does not determine aridity entirely (evaporation and soil characteristics also affect aridity). In general, the A type refers to a tropical climate, while the E type has the coldest temperatures. The H type, which was added to the system later, refers generally to highland climate.

Most of China is in the middle latitudes, and so most areas have C and D climate types. For more fine-grained climate classification, subtypes (a, b, c, etc.) are assigned to the main classifications. Due to the relatively mild winter and the effects of the monsoon, most of southeast China, including most of the Yangtze River basin and the southern part of the Yellow River basin, has the Cfa climate type (i.e., a humid subtropical climate, hot in summer with mild winters).[13] In the "Cfa" climate type label, the "C" refers to the temperate climate, meaning that winter is not too cold (usually above –3 degrees Celsius/26 degrees F); the "f" means that precipitation is quite even over the year, without a clear dry season; and the "a" indicates that the warmest summer temperature is 22 degrees Celsius (71 degrees Fahrenheit) or higher. The southeast United States has the same type of climate.

Areas north and west of the region with the Cfa climate type show more climatic variation. Immediately north of the Cfa region is a region dominated by the Cwa climate type, stretching across north central China. It differs from the Cfa type mainly because it has a clear dry season in winter (the "w" in "Cwa"). Further north and west are regions with the Cfb and D climate types. They are characterized by colder and drier winters. Figure 2.7 shows the average annual precipitation levels

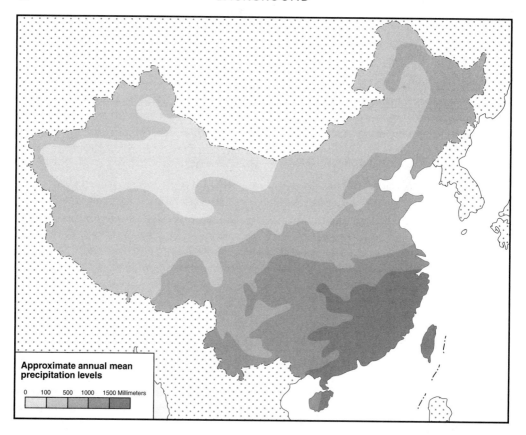

FIGURE 2.7 Approximate annual mean precipitation levels in China. Based on Zhao (1994, p. 13).

over the country. Precipitation is clearly a factor in determining climate types: Most areas with heavier precipitation have the Cfa climate type, and drier areas in the north and west have the Cfb and D climate types. In the northwest region of the country, the precipitation level is relatively low; therefore, this is an arid region with a desert landscape.

Temperature and precipitation are major climatic factors. Their characteristics directly affect human activities, especially agricultural and settlement patterns. Primarily for agricultural reasons, humans have preferred to reside in temperate regions, without extremes of heat or cold. Thus midlatitude regions have been popular for human settlement. Water is critical to human survival and agricultural production; therefore, areas with sufficient precipitation or water supplies, such as rivers and lakes, are usually favorable places for settlement. Areas with mild temperatures and sufficient supplies of water have relatively high population density levels. The following areas all have relatively high population densities: the capital region around Beijing, and the major delta regions of the Yellow River (Hebei and Shandong provinces), the Yangtze River (the municipality of Shanghai and surrounding provinces), and the Pearl River (Guangdong province). The much dryer and colder west and north are relatively sparsely populated. The spatial distribution of population is discussed further in Chapter 3.

Another area with relatively high population density in China consists of Sichuan province and the municipality of Chongqing. This region has unique geographical conditions. The Sichuan Basin is surrounded by high mountains and plateaus.[14] The basin itself is mainly composed of low mountains and hills, with an average elevation of about 500 m (1,640 ft). The fertile, well-irrigated Chengdu Plain lies along the foothills of the western high mountains. Sichuan is drained by the Yangtze River and its tributaries. The famous Three Gorges of the Yangtze are located at the eastern borders of the Basin. The rocks in Sichuan are basically reddish sandstone and purple shale; this is why it is also called the Red Basin. The soil is rich in calcium, phosphorus, potassium, and other nutrients, creating one of the most naturally fertile regions in China. Geographically, the Sichuan Basin is almost completely surrounded by higher lands. However, its diverse and rich resources can support a huge population, making it an almost self-sufficient area and one of the most densely populated regions in China.

NATURAL VEGETATION

The term "vegetation" refers to all of the plant forms in a region. It is a reliable indication of the natural geographical environment. As might be expected from its huge territory and great variety of climates, China has a large number of vegetation types. The animal life associated with the vegetation is similarly diverse. Differences in climate (i.e., temperature and rainfall) help explain why one area is desert while another is grassland or forest. Different combinations of precipitation and temperature lead to the formation of tropical (hot), temperate (moderate), and polar (cold) deserts, grasslands, and forests. Climate and vegetation also vary with elevation, forming vegetation zones at different elevation levels (vertical zonation). Figure 2.8 shows the three broad vegetation zones in China: the Eastern Forest Zone, the Northwest Grassland/Desert Zone, and the Qinghai–Tibetan Plateau Frigid Zone.

Each vegetation zone contains many ecosystems that have adapted to differences in climate, soil, and other environmental factors. Because of China's midlatitude geographical location, and its unique geomorphological settings, it has almost all major vegetation types found on the earth's surface. Before the advent of agriculture, forest probably occupied about 40% of China's total land area. From north to south, major forest types include cool-temperature needle-leaved forest (taiga); temperate mixed needle- and broad-leaved forest; warm-temperature deciduous broad-leaved forest; subtropical mixed evergreen and deciduous broad-leaved forest; tropical monsoon forest; and rainforest.

After forest, the second major vegetation type in China is grassland, accounting for about 30% of total land area. Grassland is mainly found in the Northwest Grassland/Desert Zone and the Plateau Frigid Zone, where the total annual rainfall is less than 400 mm (16 in). Major grassland types include forest steppe, steppe, desert

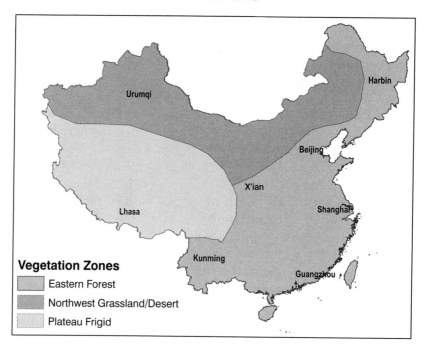

FIGURE 2.8 Major vegetation zones in China: the Eastern Forest Zone, the Northwest Grassland/Desert Zone, and the Qinghai–Tibetan Plateau Frigid Zone.

steppe, alpine steppe, and park savanna. In addition, the area of China affected by the East Asian monsoon subsystem has large patches of secondary-growth grassland scattered in deforested areas.

Deserts are widely distributed in China, especially in the northwest and northern Tibetan Plateau, occupying about 22% of China's land area. They are characterized by sparse vegetation coverage, a poverty of species, and a simple plant community. The land is predominantly covered by drought-resistant shrubs and small, low shrubs. However, in the course of human and economic development, the Chinese people have removed or altered much of the natural vegetation for farming, livestock grazing, mining, and construction of towns and cities.

MAJOR SOIL TYPES

Its vast territory and complicated physical conditions make China rich and varied in soil resources. The Chinese have used the soil for thousands of years to sustain growth and development. A number of factors affect the formation of soil, such as temperature and precipitation, which directly affect the vegetation of a place. Vegetation in turn affects the locations of many types of human activity, particularly agriculture. However, the major factors affecting soil formation are the characteristics of the bedrock, which interact with climate (temperature and precipitation) and the biotic complex (vegetation and fauna). If the temperature is relatively low for extensive periods, organic matter in the soil may not decompose, and therefore the soil may not be fertile. Even if the soil is fertile, crops cannot grow without sufficient moisture.

Soils can be classified at a very detailed level. Since written records were kept, the Chinese have classified soils primarily according to color, which is a good indicator of soil fertility. In this section, we discuss five types of soil found in different parts of China, describe their primary colors, and examine their relationships with the surrounding environment.

Chernozems

The soils in northeast China are black and are predominantly "chernozems," which develop in a temperate subhumid environment (see Figure 2.9). The natural vegetation associated with chernozems is temperate grassland, similar to the prairie in the Central Plain of North America. The darkness of these soils reflects their high humus content. Humus is decayed organic matter in the soil, which is a major constituent determining soil fertility. Variation in temperature between seasons can result in organic matter in the soil that is partly decomposed, adding to the soil's fertility.[15] Usually the darker a soil's color, the richer its humus content and the more fertile the soil. Thus the chernozems found in northeast China, especially in the Northeast Plain, are fertile and can support intensive agriculture. Agriculture in northeast China is described further in Chapters 4 and 11.

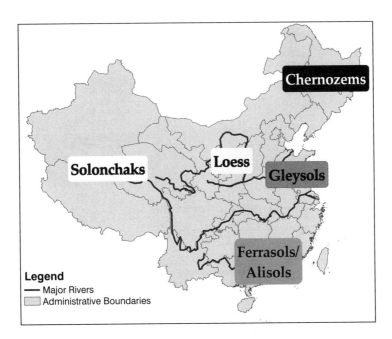

FIGURE 2.9 Geographical distribution of major soil types in China.

Loess

Yellowish soil called "loess" is found mainly in the Loess Plateau region in north central China. The region is drained by the middle course of the Yellow River. As described earlier, wind blowing from the north in winter carries fine dust-like silt from the desert to the Yellow River region. After centuries of accumulation and deposition, the dirt became a plateau, forming very deep soil profiles (see Figure 2.10a). The "yellow earth" is relatively light and easy to work for agriculture. With sufficient supplies of precipitation and water from river tributaries, the region around the Loess Plateau has been a major breadbasket of China for centuries. A major problem with loess is that it is subject to water erosion (see Figure 2.10b).

As described earlier, sediments from the upper and middle course of the Yellow River have caused the river to become shallower over time, leading to frequent floods on the North China Plain. The flooding water has deposited sediments from the river beds on the adjacent lands as fertile alluvium. Therefore, while the flooding of the Yellow River created major disasters over the centuries, it has benefited agriculture by replenishing the rich and fertile soil. Alluvium is also found in the Yangtze River Delta region in the east and the Pearl River Delta region in the south.

Gleysols

The Yangtze River flows out to the East China Sea in the delta region around Jiangsu, Anhui, Shanghai, and Zhejiang, with many tributaries flowing into the Yangtze in the region. Therefore, water is quite abundant, and wetlands are common landscape features in the region. The soils formed in wetlands, saturated with water, are called "gleysols" or "gleyzems" and are characterized by greyish-bluish colors (Figure 2.9). The word "gley" means "clay." These are heavy, sticky, wet clay soils. Their high water content makes the soil along the Yangtze River good for growing paddy rice, which requires a flooded field during part of the growing period. Gleysols are common in lowlands in the tropical and subtropical areas of China.

Ferrasols and Alisols

South of the Yangtze River, the climate is hot and humid. The region receives abundant rainfall from the summer monsoon that carries the moisture from the Pacific Ocean. The hot and humid climate favors the oxidation of minerals—a process that is conducive to the formation of "ferrasols" and "alisols" (see Figure 2.9).[16] Ferrasols have a reddish color because of their rich iron oxide content, while alisols are yellowish because they are rich in aluminum oxide. The abundant rainfall leaches away organic matter in these soils. Therefore, the soils found in this region are acidic and not fertile (more alkaline soil is better for growing crops). Intensive agriculture must be supported by the application of fertilizers. Nevertheless, southern

FIGURE 2.10 (a) Soil profiles exposed after a highway was built, cutting through loess deposition. (b) Massive amounts of loess were eroded, creating escarpments or cliffs. (Photos: Kenneth K. K. Wong)

China sustains a viable agricultural sector with the application of traditional and chemical fertilizers.

Solonchaks

Finally, the western part of China is characterized by a relatively dry (arid) climate. The region in general is located in the continental interior with different levels of aridity. The Tibetan plateau and some basins are not as dry as other areas. "Solonchaks" are soils commonly found in western China. They occur widely in steppe and desert areas where surface evaporation is greater than precipitation. These soils are high in salts, which accumulate near the surface, giving the soils a whitish color (see Figure 2.11). Salts are brought to the surface from the subsoil through capillary action. Irrigation is necessary if these soils are to be used for agricultural production. Because aridity is the norm in western China, this region has relatively low potential for agricultural production.

MAJOR PHYSICAL ZONES

China can be divided into three natural regions, or physical zones, according to their major physical characteristics: Eastern Monsoon China, Northwest Arid China, and the Qinghai–Tibetan Frigid Plateau (see Figure 2.12). A comparison of

FIGURE 2.11 Solonchak (found in western China) with salt accumulated near the surface, giving the soil a whitish color. (Photo: Kenneth K. K. Wong)

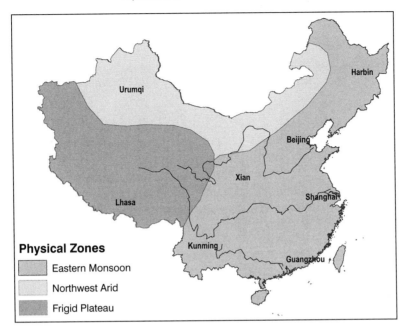

FIGURE 2.12 Three major physical zones of China: Eastern Monsoon China, Northwest Arid China, and the Qinghai–Tibetan Frigid Plateau.

Figure 2.12 with Figure 2.8 indicates that the three physical zones in Figure 2.12 correspond closely to the major vegetation zones in Figure 2.8.

Eastern Monsoon China

Eastern Monsoon China represents about 45% of China's area. Its general topography is lower than 3,000 m (9,842 ft), and the average annual precipitation is more than 380 mm (15 in), the minimum precipitation level to support non-oasis agriculture. Precipitation lower than this demarcates the western boundary of the zone. The region has the following characteristics:

- Its coastal location is strongly influenced by the summer maritime monsoon.
- The climate is humid or subhumid, with forest as the dominant natural vegetation.
- Temperature decreases from south to north due to latitudinal differences, and precipitation also decreases from southeast to northwest due to the distance from the sea.
- Few mountains rise more than 2,000 m (6,562 ft) above sea level. The two largest stretches of alluvial lowlands are the North China Plain and the Northeast Plain.
- Major river systems drain the area, and the surface water is fed mainly by precipitation.

- Both fauna and flora are rich in species, and a reddish, weathering soil crust is widespread.

- Practically all arable land has been cultivated, and almost all natural vegetation has been modified. The impact of human activities is conspicuous.

Northwest Arid China

Northwest Arid China forms the eastern part of the huge Eurasian desert and grassland. It is the second largest physical region in China, occupying about 30% of the total land area. It can be characterized as follows:

- It is made up mainly of plateaus and inland basins, but very high mountains are also common (some of them higher than 3,000 m/9,843 ft) that surround or traverse neighboring plateaus and basins.

- It is affected by the continental climatic system; the influence of the summer monsoons is weak. The climate is arid or semiarid.

- Most drainage is inland, with few rivers fed by the runoffs and melting snow from the surrounding mountainous areas. Lakes are numerous, but most are saline.

- Because of the harsh climate and aridity, both fauna and flora are poor in species and in population.

- Many fertile oases have been developed where water is available. Large tracts of grassland have been used for pasture since ancient times. Overall, the human impact is less conspicuous than that in Eastern Monsoon China.

Qinghai–Tibetan Frigid Plateau

The Qinghai–Tibetan Frigid Plateau is the highest and largest plateau on earth. Its mean elevation is more than 4,000 m (13,123 ft). Its unique features are as follows:

- Because of high elevation, the atmosphere is thin, the temperature is low, permafrost is widespread, solar radiation is intense, and winds are strong.

- Most areas have inland drainage, with numerous lakes in the inland basins.

- The Plateau forms the upper course of major rivers in China and Southeast Asia, such as the Yellow River, the Yangtze River, and the Brahmaputra River (in India and Bangladesh).

- Both fauna and flora are rich in species. Vertical zonation is conspicuous.

- Because of the harsh natural conditions, soil profiles are poorly developed, and soil fertility is low.

- Natural conditions as a whole are unfavorable to human activities. Population is sparse.

NATURAL RESOURCES TO SUSTAIN DEVELOPMENT IN THE 21ST CENTURY

China relies heavily on its rich and varied natural resources. Historically, physical settings determined the spatial organization of people's activities. Over the centuries, environments were exploited and modified for the production of goods and services. Therefore, the types of natural resources and their locations are related to the spatial distribution of human activities utilizing these resources.

The term "natural resources" broadly refers to anything from nature that can be used to meet human needs. Thus water, soil, and natural vegetation can be regarded as natural resources, as long as they are enjoyed or consumed by people. But often "natural resources" refers to a more limited set of materials, such as minerals and fossil fuel deposits. These natural resources are essential to modern human society, and from China's perspective, they are critical to the economic well-being of its people. In this section, we focus on a few natural resources that are critical to China's economic development and to its emergence as a global power in the 21st century.

Energy

Given its huge population, China ranks first or second in the following areas: total energy consumption, coal production, petroleum consumption, and electricity production and consumption.[17] China not only consumes a huge amount of energy, but it also needs to produce significant amounts to meet its current and increasing needs. The economic reform launched in the late 1970s and early 1980s propelled China into an energy-intensive economic system. For China's economy to take off, its industrial sector needed to expand, and so its energy sector had to expand in parallel to support the growing industrial sector. The resulting economic development has been accompanied by improvements in the economic well-being of many, if not all, Chinese citizens. These improvements include change from a simple, in some cases primitive, lifestyle in rural areas to a modern urban lifestyle with many electronic and electrical appliances and higher mobility using public transportation or cars. To support these changes, increasing energy consumption was inevitable. Can China afford to sustain these increases in energy demand and consumption? Increasing energy consumption has been accompanied by environmental impacts, particularly on global climate change. In 2013 China surpassed the United States as the world's leader in carbon dioxide emissions (Central Intelligence Agency [CIA], 2016). Is it possible for China to reduce its carbon dioxide emissions?

In a modern economy, energy is produced from different sources. A major form of energy is electricity, which is generated when a turbine spins. Turbines are typically driven by highly pressurized gas or steam, or by fast-flowing water. The combustion of different types of fossil fuel has been used to generate steam for producing electricity (thermoelectric power), as has nuclear power. Hydroelectric power (HEP) production utilizes water-driven turbines to generate electricity.[18]

Fossil fuels and nuclear power are regarded as nonrenewable energy, whereas HEP is regarded as renewable energy. We consider fossil fuels and HEP in detail below.

Fossil Fuels

China has an abundant supply of various types of energy. Before and during the early years of Chinese economic reform, coal was the major energy source. It was important as a major source of fuel for generating electricity and as an energy source for industrial production. Iron and steel manufacturing, in particular, require large quantities of coal. Since the late 1980s, petroleum (oil) and natural gas have been important sources of energy. These fossil fuels together (mainly coal and oil) have generated approximately 67% of electricity production in China in recent years (CIA, 2016).

China has rich deposits of coal. According to the beta website of the U.S. Energy Information Administration (EIA), China is the world's largest coal producer, at the level of almost 4 billion metric tons (mt) per year in 2013. This compares with almost 900 million mt for the United States and over 600 million mt for India, the second and third largest producers, respectively.[19] Chinese coal production has expanded fourfold since 1990. China is also the world's largest coal consumer; its consumption level is about one-half of the world's total. Coal supplies about 66% of the total energy consumed in China (U.S. EIA, 2015). However, Chinese coal consumption may have peaked. One sign is that coal production has been falling slightly in recent years. While one reason for lowering domestic coal production could be the import of coal from Australia, another reason could be the desire to use cleaner energy; burning coal is a major source of air pollution. There is also an increasing supply of alternate energy sources such as HEP.[20] Over the years, the coal industry in China has been undergoing a series of restructurings and reforms (Woodworth, 2015). Diminishing coal production may be regarded as a promising sign that China is becoming proactive in decelerating climate change.[21]

Although coal deposits and production are quite widely distributed over Chinese territory (23 provinces), its major production sites are mainly in the north, northeast, and southwest. The three major production regions include the Shanxi–Neimenggu–Shaanxi–Xinjiang region in the north and northwest; the Guizhou–Sichuan–Yunnan region in the southwest; and the Liaoning–Hebei–Henan–Shandong–Anhui belt in the northeast and east. Although the first region is the largest producer, the third production region is closest to the main markets along the coast. Coal in China is of varying quality. Lignite in general has higher sulfur content, and therefore releases less energy and has a higher pollution level. On the other hand, bituminous coal is of higher quality. The approximately 12,000 coal mines in China produce primarily bituminous coal, but also a fair share of lignite and other types of coal.

After coal, the second most important fossil fuel in China is petroleum, which accounted for 20% of primary energy consumption in 2012 (U.S. EIA, 2015). Worldwide, China's petroleum consumption level was the second highest after that of the

United States, and it was the largest net importer. Its proven oil reserves are second to Russia's in the Asia–Pacific region. (Many countries in the Middle East, including Saudi Arabia, have the largest reserves.) China's petroleum production level has been increasing tremendously over the past several decades; at this writing, its capacity is ranked fourth in the world. Analysts expect that China's petroleum production will continue to rise, partly to keep coal utilization at least stable, if not at a lower level. The future growth of oil demand in China will be determined by several factors, including future economic growth—particularly the future trajectories of manufacturing industries and the transportation sector. Gasoline consumption by motor vehicles will likely continue to rise, as the number of cars and trucks continues to increase. The increasing popularity of vehicles that run on liquefied natural gas may ease the rising demand for petroleum to a certain degree.

Approximately 80% of crude oil production in China comes from onshore operations, while the reminding 20% comes from shallow offshore oil fields. The offshore oil basin is rather extensive, covering part of the Bohai area, the Yellow Sea, and the coastal area from the East China Sea to the South China Sea. Onshore production is heavily concentrated in northeastern, north central, and western China (U.S. EIA, 2015). There are also significant oil fields in the relatively remote parts of western China. In Xinjiang, the Tarim Basin and Junggar Basin have extensive oil fields; there is also oil in the smaller Qaidam (or Tsaidam) Basin (an area between the Tibetan Plateau and Qinghai Lake) and the Jiuquan Basin, closer to north central China. These are newer fields that have been explored relatively recently, but they have relatively large reserves. In north central China, the Ordos Basin (extending from the south central portion of Neimenggu to Qinghai, Shaanxi, and Shanxi) is another major oil field. This one is closer to the major markets than those in western China. In the Northeast Plain is the Daqing oil field, one of the oldest and largest fields in China. The heavy industries in northeast China (in Heilongjiang and Jilin provinces) benefit tremendously from proximity to this oil field. The area around the Bohai Bay (mentioned above) is another major oil field; however, its proximity to major cities, including Beijing and Tianjin, has produced severe air pollution. Another major oil field is in the Sichuan Basin. Overall, significant petroleum deposits are found quite extensively across the country, but only some of the more desirable sites have been exploited and developed.

Although China produces a large quantity of petroleum, its consumption level well exceeds its production level. Therefore, China has been importing large quantities of oil. Major suppliers of oil to China include countries in the Middle East (Saudi Arabia, Oman, Iraq, Iran, the United Arab Emirates, and Kuwait), as well as China's long-term partner, Russia. China has been expanding its sources to other countries in Africa (e.g., Angola and South Sudan) and South America (e.g., Venezuela and Colombia) (U.S. EIA, 2015).

Among the major types of fossil fuels, China uses natural gas the least. It provided about 5% of primary energy consumption in 2012 (U.S. EIA, 2015). From 2003 to 2013, China tripled its natural gas production. Production and consumption levels are likely to increase, partly to alleviate the use of coal (and associated pollution levels). Natural gas generates less pollution than other fossil fuels. However, increases in consumption levels have exceeded increases in production levels. Therefore, about 32% of China's natural gas consumption was of imported gas in 2013 (U.S. EIA, 2015). Industries account for the majority of natural gas usage, but consumption by the transportation and power sectors has been increasing.

China has extensive natural gas reserves in the onshore and offshore basins. Except for the smaller area in Songliao Basin in the northeast (the Daqing oil and gas field), the majority onshore production sites are in the Tarim, Junggar, and Qaidam Basins (Xinjiang and Qinghai) in the northwest; the Ordos Basin in Shanxi in the north; and the Sichuan Basin in the southwest. A major offshore gas reserve is found in the South China Sea. Natural gas comes from several sources, one of which is shale. China may have the largest shale gas reserves in the world (U.S. EIA, 2015). However, China has just begun exploiting its natural gas reserves, and has had to deal with many challenges as it acquires advanced technological knowledge and skills to extract gas.

Although the market plays a significant role in the Chinese economy, the government still tightly controls essential economic sectors. Energy is one sector almost entirely dominated by government enterprises that control the production and distribution processes. China's national oil companies include the China National Petroleum Corporation (CNPC), the China Petroleum and Chemical Corporation (Sinopec), and the China National Offshore Oil Corporation (CNOOC). In addition to handling domestic petroleum production and distribution, these companies, on behalf of the country, have acquired or invested in foreign energy resources such as oil–gas fields and coal mines. These companies' worldwide acquisitions include coal mines and oil fields in Australia, Africa, the Middle East, Central Asia, South America, and even the United States. The major goal is to secure a long-term supply of energy to support China's future economic development.

Hydroelectric Power

As in most other countries, fossil fuels provide the majority of China's power consumption, but a major concern is the resulting pollution. China has been developing HEP over the past several decades, in part to address environmental issues. In 2013, China was the largest HEP producer in the world, with output accounting for about 18% of the country's total electricity production (U.S. EIA, 2015). A prerequisite for HEP is a steady supply of fast-flowing water. Although China has several major river systems, the lower course of the Yellow River does not provide sufficient water of the right type for HEP. While the potential for HEP development in the middle Yellow River has been exploited to some degree, the greatest HEP potential is in the middle Yangtze River, which has a large flow volume in general. This is where the world's largest HEP project is located.

The Three Gorges Dam project is located in the Yangtze River basin (see Figure 9.7 in Chapter 9) and is one of the world's largest HEP projects. Completed in 2012, it has 32 turbines; it generated 99 terawatt-hours (TWh; 1 TWh = 10^{12}

watt-hours) of energy in 2014 (U.S. EIA, 2015), the highest level ever for a single HEP project. By comparison, the Hoover Dam in Nevada—one of the largest dams in the United States—has 17 turbines, with an average total production level of 4 TWh.[22] The Three Gorges Dam is 2.3 km (1.4 miles) in length, the longest in the world. The dam is about five times wider than the Hoover Dam. On the other hand, the Three Gorges Dam is not very tall—only 185 m (607 ft), compared to over 220 m (726 ft) for the Hoover Dam.[23] These physical characteristics of the Three Gorges Dam may not reflect the significance of the structure. Economically, this project should produce enough electricity to meet a significant level of the country's total demand. In addition, the project should boost the use of the Yangtze River for freight shipments.

However, the Three Gorges Dam project is very environmentally controversial. Erecting the dam regulates the flow of water downstream and has created a huge reservoir in the middle Yangtze River by flooding the area around the three original river gorges: Qutang, Wu Xia, and Xiling. The three gorges cover an extensive area. The reservoir is about 660 km (410 miles) in length, and the project flooded over 600 km^2 of land (255 square miles); it displaced numerous towns and villages, and probably over a million people.[24] Countless historical artifacts and many ancient architectural sites are now under water. In addition, the dam disturbed and destroyed the original ecological systems of the river, and its long-term negative environmental impacts have not yet been fully assessed.

Although the Three Gorges Dam is the most well known to the international community because of the controversy, it is far from the only major dam project in China. Over 86,000 dams are scattered all over the country. They are not as massive in scale as the Three Gorges Dam, and many are in the middle and upper reaches of the Yellow River. Nonetheless, they have significant impacts on the ecology and environmental systems. The long-term sustainability of these projects is also in question because sediment accumulating at the bottom of the dams will eventually threaten their operation. Moreover, the output levels of HEP projects are at the mercy of nature: Water flowing fast and steadily is needed, and the frequency and extent of droughts very much affect the amounts of electricity these plants can produce.

China has developed other energy sources. Given the increasing energy demands created by economic growth, investment in and production from different sources of energy have increased. Among different types of renewable energy, the use of wind power is relatively restricted by China's geography in general. Although China was the world's second largest wind electricity producer in 2013, its utilization relies highly on the efficiency of the transmission system connecting the wind farms to the power grid, although improvements in infrastructure have been gradually increasing the utility usage rate over the past several years (U.S. EIA, 2015).

China is very aggressive in exploiting solar power. All signs show that China is dominating the solar industry. It is among the largest producers of solar energy and photovoltaic (PV) solar or solar-electric panels in the world. The adoption of solar energy technology is widespread in China, as small solar panels and solar water heaters are found on rooftops everywhere, from large cities to rural villages. Apparently, China has set the goal for large-scale use of solar power—bolder than the ideals of many Western countries.[25]

Another alternative energy source that China is aggressively expanding is nuclear power, although it is not a renewable source in the strict sense (since the supply of uranium is finite) and it poses well-known hazards. Currently, most nuclear power plants are located along the coast in the east and south. In 2015, China possessed more than one-third of the world's nuclear power capacity (U.S. EIA, 2015). More plants are likely to be built, some of which are expected to be in inland regions.

Metallic Ores

In the early stages of industrial development under Communist leadership, China emphasized heavy industries and manufacturing, very much following the Soviet development model. Developing the iron and steel industries and the machinery needed for these industries were China's top priorities. Other essential metals such as tin and aluminum were also high on the list of needs for development. Overall, China has significant deposits of most major metallic ores, including uranium. China has the technological capability to refine uranium for both nuclear energy and military uses. However, the country lacks significant deposits of copper and nickel, two other essential metals.

The major problem that China has in utilizing its metallic ore deposits is one of geographical mismatch. Ore deposits are scattered across the country in remote locations (particularly in the far west), away from the population centers. Therefore, many plants and mills for heavy manufacturing, including smelters for metallic ores, are located in peripheral regions.[26] For instance, Baotau in Neimenggu/Inner Mongolia has one of the largest iron and steel mills in China. Most heavy manufacturing centers using metallic ores are in the north and northeast. For instance, some of the large iron and steel mills are in cities in Liaoning and Heilongjiang. A few heavy manufacturing centers are near the south and the east coasts, such as Maanshan in Anhui, another center producing iron and steel.

The supply of energy affects the location of metal manufacturing. Some metallic ores, such as iron and aluminum, require the input of large amounts of energy during the smelting or refining processes. The availability of cheap energy can be a factor in determining the location of a manufacturing plant. North and northeast China have abundant supplies of coal and oil, which is why many iron and aluminum industries are found there. Most of these manufacturing companies are government enterprises, controlling the production and supply of these essential materials, which are then used by other industries.

BOX 2.2. How Smartphones and Hybrid Vehicles Damage China's Environment

New technologies often use rare metals or minerals. When these technologies were first developed, limited supplies of rare minerals were not a concern, as they were used in small quantities per product and as the quantities of those new products were relatively small. When the technologies became widely adopted and the new products were produced in larger quantities, the supplies of these rare minerals became an issue. A set of minerals known as the "rare earth elements" (REEs) are now used in devices ranging from smartphones to wind turbines, electric vehicles, and compact fluorescent lightbulbs. This set of minerals includes 17 elements.[a] Contrary to their names, not all of them are rare. Some are quite abundant, but are found in dispersed locations at low concentrations. Mining them cost-effectively or finding them in large quantities is challenging. Some of them are relatively rare. Today China controls 80–90% of the world's REE production.[b] The major production sites are mostly found in north central China, including Baotou, a major mining and energy center in Neimenggu (Inner Mongolia). Baotou is a center not only of coal and iron mining, but also of REE extraction and processing.

Currently, there is very little mining or production of REEs in parts of the world other than China. Australia has an REE mine at Mount Weld. The Mountain Pass mine in California's Mojave Desert is the only well-known and significant deposit of REEs in North America, but the owner has encountered financial difficulties in keeping the mine operating. Moreover, even when these mines outside China were in full production, they produced relatively small quantities of REEs and did not produce some of the more important of these minerals. For the near future, China will still control the global production and supply of REEs. China has been accused of violating free-trade agreements by setting an export quota on REEs and raising their prices, which may include an export tax. However, the mining and processing of REEs have taken a big toll on the Chinese environment. Some of these elements are toxic and radioactive. Mining and processing them have severely polluted the environment, because China has not had environmental safeguards in place. Abnormally high cancer rates have been found among workers and residents near the mines. In other words, the relatively low prices of REEs that China charged in the past to the global market were subsidized by damage to China's workers and its environment.

The Chinese government has been tightening environmental regulations in the mining and processing of REEs, and these requirements will raise the costs and thus the prices of REEs in the international market. The demand for products that require REEs is expected to continue to grow, and the prices of REEs are likely to increase. How long can China and its people endure the environmental damages associated with the extraction of REEs? And how much longer will China have a monopoly on REE production?

[a]http://minerals.usgs.gov/minerals/pubs/commodity/rare_earths.

[b]How much control China has over REE production is not definitely clear. Different sources have reported different levels of control. See, for example, www.nytimes.com/2010/12/15/business/global/15rare.html?_r=0 versus www.theguardian.com/sustainable-business/rare-earth-mining-china-social-environmental-costs.

• • • • • • • • • • • • • • • **FINAL THOUGHTS** • • • • • • • • • • • • • • • • •

China's natural environment is full of contrasts. It has fertile and accessible low-lands with humid temperate climates, and these lowlands have become densely populated regions. It also has rugged terrains and harsh climates, such as the largest and highest plateau on earth, extensive arid regions in the form of basins and deserts, and a continental climate in the sparsely populated interior and northern parts of the country. However, these highly diverse environments provide suitable conditions for a variety of agricultural practices, different types of settlements and lifestyles, a heterogeneous economic system, and various forms of tourism. "Diversity" is probably the single word that best describes China's physical environment. Do you consider such diversity a blessing or curse?

China's natural resources are diverse and relatively abundant. However, China's natural environment is constantly under pressure to produce more to support its large and growing population. Progress in economic development has also increased pressure on the environment. Thus the physical environment has been modified extensively by various types of human activities. A critical issue facing China today is how to ensure a sustainable physical environment in the long run.

Notes •

1. The tropical region falls between the Tropic of Cancer, at approximately 23.5 degrees North, and the Tropic of Capricorn, at approximately 23.5 degrees South. The polar regions are the Arctic and Antarctic regions, beyond 66.5 degrees North and South, respectively.

2. The elevation of Mount Everest and the lowest point are not reflected on our topographic maps because elevations on the maps are reported in grid cells with 1 km × 1 km resolution, not in points. In addition, map elevations were not derived from survey instruments with high precision and accuracy.

3. For a detailed explanation of plate tectonics, please visit a section of the U.S. Geological Survey website (http://pubs.usgs.gov/gip/dynamic/dynamic.html).

4. West of the Australian Plate is the Arabian Plate. Some studies label the northwestern end of the Australian Plate as the Indian Plate, an interface between the Australian, Arabian and Eurasian Plates. Therefore, the Australian Plate is also known as the Indo-Australian Plate.

5. http://earthquake.usgs.gov/earthquakes/world/10_largest_world.php.

6. Yan Jie reported government efforts in determining fault lines under major urban areas (http://usa.chinadaily.com.cn/epaper/2011-03/21/content_12201556.htm, retrieved July 12, 2016).

7. "Permafrost" is permanently frozen ground, usually found in the sub-Arctic and Arctic regions, but in this case in high-elevation areas.

8. The Qin Ling Mountains provide a natural boundary between northern and southern China. The mountains also form the watershed boundary between the Yellow River basin of northern China and the Yangtze River basin of central China.

9. According to the Köppen climate classification system discussed in the section of this chapter on climate (see note 12, below), the Loess Plateau region has the BSn type of climate.

10. A video/documentary about the Loess Plateau can be found on YouTube (www.youtube.com/watch?v=bjLV_aVRUmQ).

11. https://www.nationalgeographic.org/encyclopedia/karst.

12. See www.britannica.com/science/Koppen-climate-classification.

13. See the climate classification map of Asia produced by the University of Melbourne (http://people.eng.unimelb.edu.au/mpeel/Koppen/Asia.jpg).

14. Geographically, the Sichuan Basin is surrounded by the Qinghai–Tibetan Plateau in the west, the Qin Ling Mountains and Loess Plateau in the north, the mountainous regions in western Hunan and Hubei in the east, and the Yunnan–Guizhou Plateau in the south. It is one of the four largest basins in China (see Plate 2).

15. If the temperature is high all year round (such as in a tropical climate), the decomposition level will be intense for a long period, and all organic matter will be decomposed; as a result, it will not add to the fertility of the soil. If the temperature is too low, chemical decomposition cannot take place.

16. www.fao.org/docrep/003/y1899e/y1899e08a.htm.

17. www.eia.gov/beta/international/country.cfm?iso=CHN.

18. http://water.usgs.gov/edu/wuhy.html.

19. www.eia.gov/beta/international/country.cfm?iso=CHN.

20. www.wsj.com/articles/chinas-coal-consumption-and-output-fell-last-year-1424956878.

21. www.nytimes.com/2015/09/22/world/asia/fading-coal-industry-in-china-may-offer-chance-to-aid-climate.html?_r=0.

22. www.usbr.gov/lc/hooverdam/faqs/powerfaq.html.

23. www.usbr.gov/projects/Facility.jsp?fac_Name=Hoover+Dam&groupName=Overview.

24. http://news.nationalgeographic.com/news/2006/06/060609-gorges-dam.html.

25. China has built the largest floating solar farm. See http://time.com/china-massive-floating-solar-field/.

26. www.britannica.com/technology/smelting.

REFERENCES •

Central Intelligence Agency (CIA). (2016, July 11). China. In *The world factbook*. Retrieved from https://www.cia.gov/library/publications/the-world-factbook/geos/ch.html.

U.S. Energy Information Administration (EIA). (2015, May 14). China: International energy data and analysis. Retrieved from www.eia.gov/beta/international/analysis_includes/countries_long/China/china.pdf.

Woodworth, M. D. (2015). China's coal production goes west: Assessing recent geographical restricting and industrial transformation. *Professional Geographer, 67*(4), 630–640.

Zhao, S. (1994). *Geography of China: Environment, resources, population, and development.* New York: Wiley.

FURTHER READING •

Fang, J.-Y., Song, Y.-C., Liu, H.-Y., & Piao, S.-L. (2002). Vegetation–climate relationship and its application in the division of vegetation zone in China. *Acta Botanica Sinica, 44*(9), 1105–1122. Retrieved from www.jipb.net/.%5Cpubsoft%5Ccontent%5C2%5C2314%5CX020321(PS2).pdf.

Fang, J.-Y., & Yoda, K. (1989). Climate and vegetation in China II: Distribution of main vegetation types and thermal climate. *Ecological Research, 4,* 71–83.

Fu, C., Jiang, X., Guan, Z., He, J., & Xu, Z. (Eds.). (2008). *Regional climate studies of China.* New York: Springer.

Hartmann, R., Wang, J., & Ye, T. (Eds.). (2014). *A comparative geography of China and the U.S.* New York: Springer.

Tse, P. K. (2011). *China's rare-earth industry* (U.S. Geological Survey Open-File Report No. 2011-1042). Retrieved from http://pubs.usgs.gov/of/2011/1042.

Wang, F., & Zhao, Z. (1994). Climate change and natural vegetation. *Journal of Meteorological Research, 8*(1), 1–8. Retrieved from www.cmsjournal.net:8080/Jweb_jmr/EN/Y1994/V8/I1/1.

Wei, S., Gong, P., Liang, L., Dai, Y., & Zhang, K. (2014). Soil diversity as affected by land use in China: Consequences for soil protection. *Scientific World Journal, 2014,* Article ID 913852. Retrieved from www.hindawi.com/journals/tswj/2014/913852.

Zhang, Z. M., Liou, J. G., & Coleman, R. G., (1984). An outline of the plate tectonics of China. *Geological Society of America Bulletin, 95*(3), 295–312.

Zhao, S. (1986). *Physical geography of China.* Beijing: Science Press/New York: Wiley.

CHAPTER 3

Population
Dynamic and Diverse

LEARNING OBJECTIVES

* Compare and contrast the historical growth of the population in China with global population history.

* Relate the recent population growth in China to the demographic transition.

* Recognize the various demographic characteristics of China's population and their spatial variability.

* Understand the ethnic diversity in China and the geographical distributions of major ethnic groups.

KEY CONCEPTS AND TERMS

demographic transition model;
birth rate, death rate, and growth rate;
sex ratio; population pyramid;
dependency ratio;
youth and elderly dependency ratios;
diversity and segregation indices

CHINA'S POPULATION: A DRIVING FORCE BEHIND EVERYTHING?

In Chapter 2, we focused on the physical environment on which human activities are organized. In Chapter 4, we discuss how the Chinese agricultural system produces enough food to support the massive population by adapting to the physical environment. In later chapters, we discuss other aspects of the built environment, including the urban system, economic activities, and transportation. However, population is the driving force behind all changes in both the physical and built environments. Trewartha (1953), who first proposed the subfield of population geography, argued that population is the "pivotal" topic for understanding all aspects of a society. For example, how do we explain the growth of cities and the urban system in many Western countries? The major forces in urban dynamics have included the migration of population from rural areas into cities in the early urbanization era, and population growth in recent history. How do we estimate environmental degradation in the near future? An accurate projection of population size and an understanding of people's behaviors are crucial for developing a reliable estimate of environmental impacts. The major reason for all studies of a society is to determine how people will be affected, and so the study of population is a highly important part of this research. Therefore, studying population is crucial to understanding China, just as it is to understanding other countries.

Moreover, studying the population of China is not just useful for understanding China, but for understanding the whole world. Although China is not the largest country territorially, it is the largest country in terms of population.[1] Within the territory directly or indirectly under the control of the People's Republic of China (PRC), the total population is approaching 1.4 billion. The population of Taiwan, which is controlled by the Republic of China (ROC), is over 20 million, a number dwarfed by the mainland's population size. Chinese emigrants form another subpopulation of Chinese, but residing overseas. Chinatowns or Chinese enclaves are found in most major cities of the world. Although the actual number of overseas Chinese is difficult to determine, it is still relatively small as compared to the population on the mainland.[2] Given that the world's total population is (at this writing) approximately 7.4 billion, the population in China accounts for 18–19% of the world's total population. Therefore, whatever mainland Chinese people do, especially if they do it collectively, will have a tremendous global as well as local impact. China's global influence is found in multiple realms: the world's economy and global markets, territorial disputes, environmental impact, and climate change, just to name a few. Population is thus a driving force and motivation not only behind China's actions, but in how those actions are felt around the globe.

Population may be studied from multiple perspectives. In this chapter, we first describe China's population characteristics from historical and demographic perspectives. Then we elaborate further on selected demographic characteristics, using a geographical perspective to highlight their spatial variability.

HOW DID CHINA'S POPULATION BECOME SO LARGE?

Historical Population Growth

Today's world population, as noted above, is approximately 7.4 billion.[3] However, the world's population was relatively small throughout most of its history (Newbold, 2013). Some studies have estimated that the world's population was about 4 million on the eve of the agricultural or farming revolution,[4] and about 200 million in 1 C.E. (Weeks, 2015). The world's population did not reach 1 billion until the middle of the 18th century, before the industrial revolution. Within the last 250 years or so, the population has increased to over 7 billion (see Figure 3.1a). The population-doubling time[5] (the number of years in which the population will double) shortened from more than 150 years in around 1600 to 37 years in 1960

(Weeks, 2015). In other words, the world's population grew relatively slowly most of the time before the industrial revolution, but it shot upward after the 18th century and is still rising rapidly today, as shown in Figure 3.1a.

Rapid population growth in the Western world was associated with the advent of the industrial revolution. However, China was largely isolated from the influence of Western civilization and technological development. Although Chinese history is well documented, compiling an accurate population history of China is still challenging. One set of historical population estimates show that population in China had been relatively small and stable before 1000 C.E. Between 1000 and 1200, the population surged, but it then declined by 1400 (see Figure 3.1b). While China's population started a growing trend during the Ming dynasty (around the 14th century), the most rapid growth occurred between 1749 and 1851, during which the population more than doubled (Banister, 1987). This resembled the population growth trajectory experienced in the West. Although the effect of the industrial revolution on population growth in China is not clear, the large increase in population put pressure on the agricultural system to expand arable land and develop new

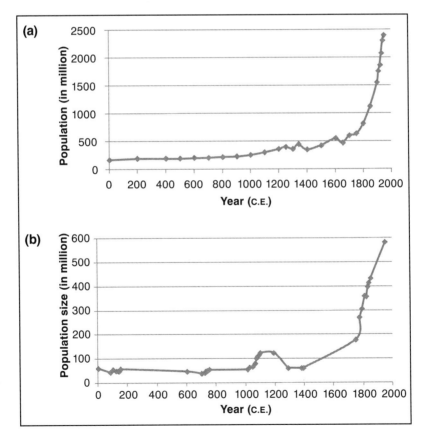

FIGURE 3.1 Historical population estimates for (a) the world and (b) China in selected years between 2 C.E. and 1953. Data from (a) lower estimates from www.census.gov/population/international/data/worldpop/table_history.php, and (b) Banister (1987, p. 4).

BOX 3.1. What's in a Chinese Name?

People's names in English are complicated in terms of structure (first name, middle name, last name, suffix), meaning, and naming traditions. Chinese names are relatively simple in today's China in terms of structure, but they can be confusing for many non-Chinese-speaking people and even for the Chinese. This confusion is partly due to the differences in naming convention between the Chinese and the Western worlds, and partly due to the complexity of the Chinese language system.

As discussed in Chapter 1, the Chinese language is written in characters. Chinese names are usually formed by combining two to four characters. People from some minority groups may have names with more characters than typical, as their native languages are not Chinese, and their names are translated into Chinese characters. Similar to Western names, the two- to four-character Chinese names include an individual's given name and family name. Whereas the Western naming tradition is to place the given name first, followed by the family name, Chinese names are in reverse order: family name followed by given name. For example, the family name of the former Chinese Communist leader Mao Tze-tung (or Mao Zedong) is Mao (毛), and the given name is Tze-tung or Zedong (泽东). In this example, the given name consists of two characters, and the family name of one character. Although most Chinese family names are one-character names, a few surnames, such as Situ (or Seto and Szeto), are compound names, consisting of two characters. The given name for a Chinese person can also be one character or two characters. Traditionally, the Chinese do not have middle names, although some people have alternate names or nicknames.

In English-speaking societies, some common last names include Smith, Jones, Johnson, and Taylor. Different sets of common family names are found in different Chinese societies. In mainland China, the five most common family names are Li (李), Wang (王), Zhang (张 or 張), Liu (刘 or 劉), and Chen (陈 or 陳), accounting for about 28% of the mainland population.[a] However, when these common family names are searched in pinyin (Romanization based on pronunciation; see Chapter 1), not all Chinese communities in the world will recognize them. For instance, Zhang may not be recognized as a common last name in Hong Kong, because most people with the family name Zhang (张 or 張 in Chinese) spell it as Cheung or Chang—a Romanization according to the sound in Cantonese, the local dialect of Hong Kong, Macau, and Guangdong province. Similarly, the family name Wong is not common in mainland China, but is quite common in overseas Chinese communities. This is because Wong is the Cantonese Romanization of two family names, 王 and 黄, that sound identical in Cantonese. However, the names are Romanized as Wang and Huang, respectively, on the mainland, because they are pronounced differently in Mandarin. This difference indicates that the overseas Chinese (including the earlier Chinese migrants to Europe and North America) with Wong as their family name mainly came from Guangdong province and southern China.

---

[a]www.chinawhisper.com/top-10-common-surnames-in-china/

methods to raise productivity—an issue that existed before the Communists took over the country after World War II.

The periods before and after World War II can be characterized as tumultuous and chaotic in China. The era of the Republic, after the fall of the Qing dynasty, gave people a glimpse of hope as the country tried to recover from the repression of the Manchu (Qing). But occupations by foreign powers, the internal political chaos that eventually evolved into battle between the Communist and Kuomintang parties, the invasion of Japan, World War II, and the final phase of the civil war put China's population in flux. Nevertheless, population growth remained on an upward trend (see Figure 3.1b). After the Communist party took over the mainland, demographic data were not well gathered until recently, and statistics reported from different sources are not consistent (e.g., Banister, 1987; Wang, 1999).

The Demographic Transition in China

A major demographic trend experienced by most countries is summarized by the "demographic transition" model. This model describes the changes in "crude birth rate" (sometimes abbreviated as CBR) and "crude death rate" (sometimes given as CDR), and thus the population growth of a country over time. The difference between CBR and CDR is the "rate of natural increase," or RNI. The version of the model presented here has four stages, corresponding to different levels of birth and death rates as shown in Figure 3.2. At stage 1, both the birth rate and death rate are generally high with fluctuations, and therefore population growth is minimal. A decline in death rate, partly due to industrialization and advances in medical technology, marks the beginning of stage 2. The birth rate does not decline much during stage 2, so the difference between the birth and death rates produces a

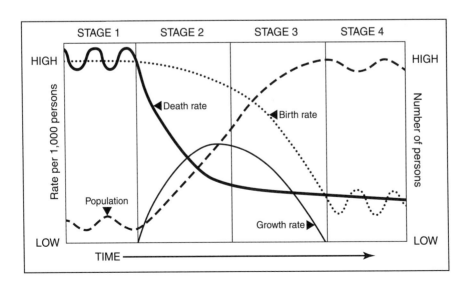

FIGURE 3.2 The demographic transition model, described by changes in crude birth rate, crude death rate, growth rate, and population size.

positive growth rate, and thus population increases. Stage 3 is marked by the gradual decline of birth rate, partly due to the transition from an agriculture-oriented economy to an industrialized economy, reducing the demand for massive labor. However, the birth rate still exceeds the death rate, resulting in continued population growth, although the growth rate is declining. At stage 4, both birth and death rates are relatively low, with slow population growth.

This model describes the demographic experience of many Western countries. Many developing countries, however, did not follow the model closely: They experienced a very sharp drop in the death rate in stage 2, with the birth rate staying at a high level for a much longer time in stage 3. The result was massive population growth for an extended period. This is sometimes called a "population explosion." China was once labeled as a developing country. Have population dynamics in China followed the developing countries' model or the Western model?

Both Banister (1987) and Wang (1999) provided estimates of demographic statistics of China from 1949 to 1984, while Wang included estimates until 1997. In general, the estimates provided by Banister for both CBR and CDR were higher than those provided by Wang. As a result, the total population estimates by Banister were slightly smaller than those by Wang. The major difference is for the period between 1959 and early 1960, during the Great Leap Forward movement. Banister estimated a dramatically higher death rate from this movement than did Wang. Figure 3.3, depicting the demographic transition of China, was constructed with Banister's data for the 1949–1984 period. For the period between 1985 and 1994, the data reported in Wang (1999, pp. 56–57) were used, and data from the National Bureau of Statistics of China were used to cover the period from 1995 to 2014.

After World War II and the Communist takeover, Chinese society resumed functioning normally to a certain degree, and the death rate declined sharply for a short period. About 1960, however, failure in economic production (particularly in farming) during the Great Leap Forward resulted in widespread famine and thus in high mortality, as shown clearly in Figure 3.3. Simultaneously, the birth rate also dropped sharply, resulting in negative population growth—a rare demographic situation that is usually not seen except during major wars. When the Great Leap Forward was over, the death rate dropped to the premovement level, and then further to below 10 deaths per 1,000 (for the first time in 1969)—a level that was somewhat on a par with those in the developed world.

However, after the Great Leap Forward, the birth rate shot up to a very high level, reaching a peak at 49.79 births per 1,000 in 1963. It took about a decade, until 1973, for the birth rate to decline to about 30 births per 1,000—a level resembling that of many developing countries in Africa today. Figure 3.3 also shows that the birth rate fluctuated for a few years after 1965, probably due to the chaotic social environment created by the Cultural Revolution, which included sending urban populations not considered loyal to the Communist party or Mao into rural areas for farm labor. Nevertheless, the combination of a relatively high birth rate for an extended period with a decline in death rate created huge population growth. The birth rate seemed to stabilize at around 20 per 1,000 in late 1970 and early

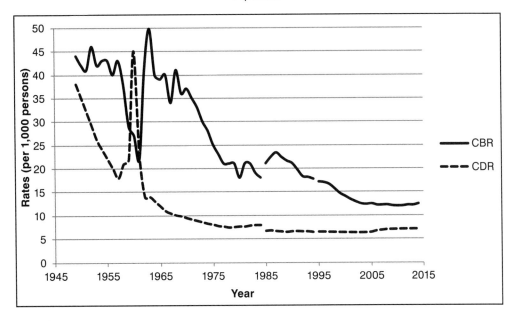

FIGURE 3.3 The demographic transition of China, based on estimated crude birth rates (CBRs) and crude death rates (CDRs), 1949–1984, 1985–1994, 1995–2014. Data for 1949–1984 from Banister (1987, Table 10.1, p. 352); data for 1985–1994 from Wang (1999, Table 3.1, pp. 56–57); data for 1995–2014 from http://data.stats.gov.cn (retrieved April 16, 2016).

1980. Reliable estimates between 1985 and 1994 were not available. The birth rate declined to about 15 per 1,000 around the year 2000 and has been kept around 12 per 1,000 for a period, limiting the RNI to about 5 per 1,000.

The birth and death rates in 1945 and 2000, as shown in Figure 3.3, suggest that population in China seems to have gone through a demographic transition during that period, similar to the typical model shown in Figure 3.2. China went from high birth and death rates to low birth and death rates with a significant population increase between the two terminal stages. The relatively small gaps between the birth and death rates in recent decades were clearly changes from the past. However, the changes in birth and death rates during this period were chaotic, different from the relatively smooth trajectories that Western countries experienced. The unique demographic transition that China experienced was partly attributable to major sociopolitical movements and the population policies enacted during this period. China's population policies are discussed further below.

The current 0.5% rate of population growth (5 per 1,000 in RNI) means that it will take about 140 years for the population to double. This would be a comfortable number for most countries, especially small countries, but a doubling of China's current population will bring it to well over 2.6 billion people—a size that is almost unimaginable. The 0.5 per 1,000 RNI translates into approximately 70 million additional people *each year*. This is more than the population of California and Texas together.[6]

A HISTORY OF CHINA'S POPULATION POLICIES

The discussion above describes the magnitude of population growth in China. In fact, in the early Communist era, Chinese leaders had promoted family planning rather than birth control. Most leaders, particularly Chairman Mao, strongly believed Karl Marx's ideas that only people, not machines, can produce value, and that a larger population would make the country stronger. They thus viewed population growth as beneficial because it would increase the productivity of Chinese society. After Mao's era, Chinese leaders gradually implemented a series of policies to curb population growth. The most controversial of these is the well-known "one-child policy." China has been criticized by Westerners for stringently implementing such an extreme policy and not considering other, less aggressive policies. In fact, China did not jump into the one-child policy immediately. It was chosen after the effectiveness of a series of other policies to control population growth had been tested.

After the famine caused by the Great Leap Forward, Mao's attitude toward a large population seemed to have changed. One of the other leaders, Zhou Enlai, initiated a major propaganda campaign to control population growth in China. The campaign targeting family formation was launched in the late 1960s, with the slogan of "later, longer, and fewer" (*wan, xi, shao;* 晚, 稀, 少); that is, the campaign advocated later marriage, longer spacing between children, and fewer children. The campaign was quite successful in reducing the birth rate between 1970 and 1976 (see Figure 3.3), but the birth rate could not be lowered further. Later leader Deng Xiaoping, who is credited with modernizing China through economic reforms, believed that the enormous, fast-growing population would act as a brake on economic development, and thus a more aggressive population policy was warranted. At first a "two-child policy" was implemented, and the results were impressive. The government's desperation to curb population growth more quickly, however, led to the policy of limiting each couple to one child. Introduced in 1979, the policy was imposed only on the Han majority. Minorities were exempted, due to their relatively small numbers.

The one-child policy included a series of penalties, mostly economic, if people failed to comply. Some penalties included fines and removal of certain entitlements. This population policy has been one of the most controversial policies in contemporary history. It has had many side effects: forced or coerced sterilization, gender-selective abortion, and an unbalanced sex ratio (addressed in detail later), just to name a few. Nevertheless, the policy was very effective in curbing the relatively high birth rate. The CBR of China dropped below 15 births per 1,000 in 1999, and has been around 12 per 1,000 since 2002 (see Figure 3.3). The total fertility rate (i.e., the number of children an average woman would bear during her life) was estimated to be about 1.4–1.6, much lower than the rates in the United States and many other developed nations (CIA, n.d.).[7]

The effectiveness of the one-child policy in suppressing the birth rate for an extended period has created an uncomfortable situation for the Chinese government. The number of children added to the population has been declining over several decades; the resulting demographic structure of China may be characterized as top-heavy, with increasing numbers of elderly persons but shrinking numbers of youth. Such a demographic structure puts a strain on the economy because the labor force keeps shrinking while the retired population keeps rising. Being able to sustain the welfare of the elderly population is a major concern. Thus, at the end of 2013, the Chinese government announced that it was relaxing the one-child policy by allowing partners who were the only children in their own families to have two children.[8]

Although China has thus created a limited "two-child policy," it is unlikely to boost the birth rate quickly to a significant level. Most qualified young couples living in cities do not want to have more children; indeed, many believe that having even one child (let alone two) will impose unbearable economic and financial burdens on them. Raising a child in China has become quite expensive, with the costs of child care, education, and housing all increasing, and the relaxation of the population policy has not been accompanied by any incentives to encourage childbearing.

DEMOGRAPHIC CHARACTERISTICS OF CHINA'S POPULATION

Migration, Infant Mortality, and Life Expectancy

The previous section has touched on some basic demographic characteristics, such as the fertility or birth rate, of the population in China. In this section, we first consider another element in the demographic equation: migration.[9] These days, the movement of people across China's borders is not as tightly controlled as before. Emigration exceeds immigration most of the time, as immigrants to China have been few. The net migration rate (for a definition, refer to note 9) is not high in absolute value; it is ranked 119th internationally (according to the 2017 estimate from CIA, n.d.). The loss of 0.40 person per 1,000 translates to over 0.5 million of the net population lost.[10] But this number is insignificant, given China's large population size.

Other demographic statistics reflect the quality of the population. For instance, the infant mortality rate (IMR) is often used to reflect a country's development level. China's IMR is about 12 deaths per 1,000 live births (2016 estimate from CIA, n.d.)—a number similar to that for Mexico, but much lower than the IMRs for many of the poorest countries. However, it is not quite comparable to those of more developed nations: for instance, 9.40 for Thailand, 6.90 for Russia, 5.80 for the United States, 4.4 for Taiwan, and 2.40 for Singapore.[11] Another health measure is life expectancy at birth (i.e., the number of years that an individual is likely to live if born now). For China, current life expectancy is about 75 years, similar to that for Mexico. This compares to 80 years for the United Kingdom and 85 for Singapore and Japan. China still has some distance to go to catch up.

Gender Imbalance: Difficulties in Finding a Wife

China's one-child policy has had one major undesirable effect on the population structure: an imbalance between the two sexes. As in many cultures, Chinese family names are passed on to future generations through male children. Therefore, in Chinese society, baby boys are more valued than baby girls. The "sex ratio" of a population is the number of males divided by the number of females, multiplied by 100. A sex ratio higher than 100 means more males than females; a sex ratio lower than 100 means more females than males. For most populations, the sex ratio at birth is often slightly higher than 100 (i.e., more baby boys are born than baby girls). But males tend to have a higher mortality rate than females in all age categories. As a result, the sex ratio gradually drops from about 100 to below 100 as a group (a cohort, in demography jargon) ages. The sex ratio is usually quite low in the elderly, since females tend to outlive males.

Figure 3.4 compares the sex ratios of China and three other countries: Ghana, India, and the United States. All four countries exhibit the same general trend: The sex ratios at birth are higher than 100, and they gradually decline across older age groups. However, some of these countries have unique features. Ghana and the United States have about the same sex ratio at birth (slightly over 100), but India clearly has a higher sex ratio than either of these countries. The sex ratio at birth is the highest for China—119 men per 100 women. China, Ghana, and the United States all follow the trend of decreasing sex ratio with increasing age. Whereas

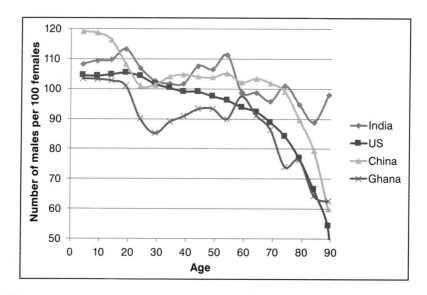

FIGURE 3.4 Sex ratios by age: China (2010), Ghana (2011), India (2011), and the United States (2010). Data for China from www.stats.gov.cn/tjsj/pcsj/rkpc/6rp/indexch.htm (retrieved April 19, 2016); data for Ghana and India from http://unstats.un.org/unsd/demographic/products/dyb/dybcensusdata.htm (retrieved April 19, 2016); data for the United States from http://factfinder.census.gov/faces/tableservices/jsf/pages/productview.xhtml?pid=DEC_10_SF1_QTP1&prodType=table (based on 2010 U.S. census, SF1).

Ghana's sex ratio drops severely for young adult and adult groups, China's sex ratio does not decline with age as quickly as in the United States. In other words, the mortality disparity between males and females in China is not as significant as that in the United States. In fact, China's sex ratio is high at birth and remains above 100 until age 74. The sex ratio in the United States drops below 100 at age 39. Thus, among Americans over 39 years old, there are more women than men, but Chinese men outnumber women up to 74 years of age. The sex ratio in India declines only slightly by age, indicating that both males and females in India survive aging equally well.

Although the sex ratio in China is far from the highest in the world, China does have an imbalance.[12] This creates difficulties in family formation because there are fewer women than men. The number of men who may fail to find a wife is estimated to be 24–30 million by 2020.[13] The competition for wives is extremely keen in China. It is so fierce that some reports have claimed that 2% of gross domestic product (GDP) growth in the past was attributable to the spending of men trying to recruit a wife.[14] Men spend money on big items, including houses, since having a house is regarded as a prerequisite for marriage. Being able to purchase expensive items proves a man's financial strength and qualification. Many men who cannot find Chinese wives seek to import brides from foreign countries, first from Asia and then from Europe.

A Young but Aging China

Still another important demographic characteristic of China is its age structure. Population may generally be categorized into the young (ages 14 and younger), the old (ages 65 and older), and those in the middle (ages 15–64). The young and old may be regarded as dependent groups because they are likely to be economically inactive. Thus a "dependency ratio" can be formulated as the ratio between the combined populations of these two groups and the population between 15 and 64 years old (the economically active population). This ratio may reflect how much of a burden is placed on the economically active population by the young and the elderly. Dependency ratios can also be compiled separately for the young and the old, to quantify the burden from each of these two groups. Figure 3.5 shows dependency ratios for China and a selection of other countries for comparison.

China has an overall dependency ratio lower than those for the United States, Japan, and Ethiopia. The United Arab Emirates (UAE) has the lowest ratio of the countries depicted in Figure 3.5, partly because this nation hosts a large number of migrant workers from Southeast Asia and South Asia. With the exception of Japan, which has a dependency ratio for the elderly higher than that for youth, the burden from the young exceeds that from the elderly in China and all other countries shown in the figure. Therefore, China's situation is typical: Its economically active population does not have to shoulder much burden from the young and elderly population groups. However, this situation is likely to change in the future.

The dependency ratio is based on a demographic structure of three major groups roughly divided by age. A more detailed depiction of demographic structure

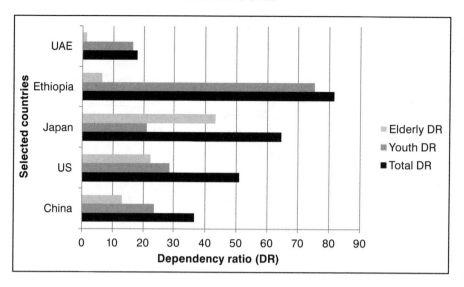

FIGURE 3.5 Dependency ratios (DRs) for China and a selection of other countries. UAE, United Arab Emirates. Data from https://www.cia.gov/library/publications/the-world-factbook/geos/ch.html (retrieved April 18, 2016).

is the "population pyramid." This standard tool for demographic study is a graph that shows the population sizes of the two sexes by age. The vertical axis is for different age groups at 5-year intervals, except the oldest group (the 100+ group). The horizontal axis shows the population size, which can be the actual size or the proportion to the total population. Figures 3.6a and 3.6b show the population pyramids of China for 1990 and 2010, respectively.

The upper portion of the 1990 pyramid is a typical triangular pyramid with a wider base and narrow top, indicating that people died as they aged. However, this pyramid has three distinctive features. The first one is the relatively large size of the population cohorts between 30 and 39 years old. This group was born starting in 1951, after the end of the civil war between the Communist and Kuomintang parties. Another surge in population growth happened after 1960, with the large cohorts between 15 and 29 years old when the Great Leap Forward ended. The return to relative normality provided an ideal environment for increased childbearing. This phenomenon is similar to the "baby booms" experienced by many Western countries, including the United States after World War II.

After this period of rapid population growth, the sizes of the cohorts between 5 and 14 years old shrank quite drastically back to their pre–Cultural Revolution levels. This shrinkage was probably an effect of the early population reduction policies. The youngest cohort (0–4 years old) was the largest in size, but this was not the result of an increase in birth rate; it was mainly because of the large size of the 20- to 29-year-old cohorts, whose members were then becoming parents. Just as the post–World War II baby boomers in Western countries produced a "baby boomlet" when they reached their 20s and 30s, the large size of China's 0–4 cohort in 1990

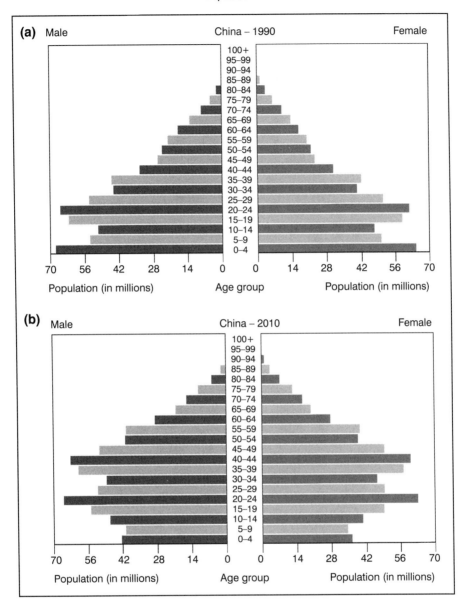

FIGURE 3.6 Population pyramids of China for (a) 1990 and (b) 2010. Data from www.census.gov/population/international/data/idb/informationGateway.php (retrieved April 18, 2016).

was an aftereffect of the size of their parents' generation. After 1990, each successive cohort has become smaller, as shown in Figure 3.6b. This is a clear indication that the birth rate has been declining over time.

The shape of the 2010 population pyramid in Figure 3.6b may be characterized as a "tapered-base" pyramid. This shape is shared by the pyramids for several Western European countries and Japan, which have been experiencing shrinking populations. The proportion of young who make up the population has been declining, and the largest cohort (45–49 years old in 2010) will become elderly in a decade or so. The elderly population, in other words, will keep on growing over time. If the shrinking of the youngest cohort continues, the pyramid will become top-heavy. The large elderly population will impose a tremendous financial burden on a shrinking workforce. This likely trajectory is the reason why the Chinese government relaxed the one-child policy and allowed a second child for qualified couples, as discussed above. The government wants to slow down, if not reverse, the shrinking of the youth population.

ARE ALL CHINESE THE SAME?

China's population is relatively homogeneous, as more than 90% of the population belongs to the Han ethnic group. Less than 10% of the population consists of ethnic minorities, although there are a large number of minority groups. The Chinese government officially recognizes 55 minority groups, but some estimates indicate that the number of ethnic groups not recognized by the government could be more than 200. Note that we have not used the term "Chinese population" in this chapter because who is and isn't "Chinese" is not clearly defined. Is it whoever resides permanently within the Chinese political boundary or holds a Chinese passport? What about the citizens of the ROC (Taiwan)? Among minorities, the term "Chinese" may refer only to the Han population.

Table 3.1 lists the 55 minority groups recognized by the Chinese government and their proportion of the total population according to the 2010 census. The table has 58 entries, which include the Han (numbered 1 in the table), the "unofficial" group (numbered 22), and the "foreign" group (numbered 58). Clearly the Han constitute an overwhelming majority, with over 91% of the total population in China. The "unofficial" group is the aggregate of those minority groups not recognized as individual groups by the Chinese government. Nevertheless, this group has over 600,000 people. The tiny "foreign" group, with only about 1,400 people, consists of foreigners who have become naturalized Chinese citizens. However, the remaining non-Han groups amount to 8.4% of the population, or 110 million people—more than the population of the 13th largest country in the world, the Philippines.[15] Minority populations in China thus cannot be ignored. Table 3.1 lists the ethnic groups in order from the largest to the smallest. The largest minority group is the Zhuang, with almost 17 million people according to the 2010 census. Each of the next three ethnic groups, the Hui, Manchu, and Uyghur, has about 10 million. Each group from the top to the 19th entry (the Dai) in Table 3.1 has a population of 1 million or more. Nevertheless, all these groups are dwarfed by the 1.22 billion Han.

Most of the names of the 55 minority ethnic groups are phonetic approximations of their names in Chinese. The names of quite a few groups may be familiar from history or current global events. The Manchu group (4) is the group that established the Qing dynasty, the last ruling dynasty in Chinese history. The Mongol group (10) is the group that established the Mongol Empire and the Yuan dynasty,

TABLE 3.1. Proportions of Han, 55 Minority Groups, and Two Other Groups in China

	Group	% of total		Group	% of total
1	Han	91.5992	30	Tu	0.0217
2	Zhuang	1.2700	31	Mulao	0.0162
3	Hui	0.7943	32	Xibe	0.0143
4	Manchu	0.7794	33	Kyrgyz	0.0140
5	Uyghur	0.7555	34	Jingpo	0.0111
6	Miao	0.7072	35	Daur	0.0099
7	Yi	0.6538	36	Salar	0.0098
8	Tujia	0.6268	37	Blang	0.0090
9	Zang	0.4713	38	Maonan	0.0076
10	Mongol	0.4488	39	Tajik	0.0038
11	Dong	0.2161	40	Pumi	0.0032
12	Bouyei	0.2153	41	Achang	0.0030
13	Yao	0.2098	42	Nu	0.0028
14	Bai	0.1451	43	Ewenki	0.0023
15	Korean	0.1374	44	Gin	0.0021
16	Hani	0.1246	45	Jino	0.0017
17	Li	0.1098	46	Deang	0.0015
18	Kazakh	0.1097	47	Bonan	0.0015
19	Dai	0.0946	48	Russian	0.0012
20	She	0.0532	49	Yugur	0.0011
21	Lisu	0.0527	50	Uzbek	0.0008
22	"Unofficial"	0.0480	51	Monba	0.0008
23	Dongxiang	0.0466	52	Oroqen	0.0006
24	Gelao	0.0413	53	Derung	0.0005
25	Lahu	0.0365	54	Hezhen	0.0004
26	Va	0.0322	55	Gaoshan	0.0003
27	Sui	0.0309	56	Lhoba	0.0003
28	Nakhi	0.0245	57	Tatar	0.0003
29	Qiang	0.0232	58	"Foreign"	0.0001

Note. Data from 2010 population census, National Bureau of Statistics of China, www.stats.gov.cn/tjsj/pcsj/rkpc/6rp/indexch.htm (retrieved April 19, 2016).

thanks to their famous leader, Genghis Khan. Mongol is also the ethnic group of the people in Mongolia, the northern neighbor of China. Further down the list are the Korean, Kazakh, Kyrgyz, Tajik, Russian, and Uzbek groups. These are minorities who have some of the same language and cultural characteristics as people in China's neighboring countries (see Chapters 1 and 11). Labeling all these people as "Chinese" may be a misnomer. The locations where these minorities are mainly found (i.e., their spatial distributions) are discussed next.

SPATIAL DIMENSIONS OF POPULATION IN CHINA

Population Density

The discussions so far about the demographic characteristics of China's population have not considered their variability across different regions and provinces. In this section, we focus on the spatial variability of these demographic characteristics. Figure 3.7 shows the population density at the provincial level. (Here and hereafter in this discussion, "provincial" is used for brevity's sake to refer not only to the provinces, but to the municipalities and autonomous regions.) It is clear that population density levels are the highest in the four municipalities: Beijing, Tianjin, Shanghai, and Chongqing. Jiangsu, the province next to Shanghai, also has the highest population density, partly due to spillover from the metropolitan growth of Shanghai. Guangdong and Taiwan also have relatively high population density levels. In general, the coastal region has higher population density levels than those in the interior and northeast.

Some interesting facts are not apparent from the map in Figure 3.7. For example, Beijing, Shanghai, and Tianjin (three of the four municipalities) are all shown having the highest population densities, yet there is variation among them. Beijing and Tianjin have population densities of slightly above 1,000 people per square kilometer (km^2). This is still considerably below the 3,600 people/km^2 density of Shanghai. Nevertheless, the high density of Shanghai is dwarfed by the density levels of the two special administrative regions (SARs), Hong Kong and Macau, which have population densities of about 6,500 and 23,900 people/km^2, respectively. The two SARs are cities with little or no rural area, and therefore their population densities are higher than those of provinces or even municipalities, which usually include a significant portion of rural land.

Mortality

Earlier in this chapter, we considered the birth and death rates for the total population. Although we would like to look at variation in those rates by municipalities and province, birth rate data at the municipal and provincial levels are unfortunately not available. The crude death rates (CDRs) reported by provinces and autonomous regions are shown in Figure 3.8. The relatively high death rate found in Yunnan province is not too surprising, as it is one of the less developed regions in China. The high death rates in two of Yunnan's more developed neighbors, Sichuan

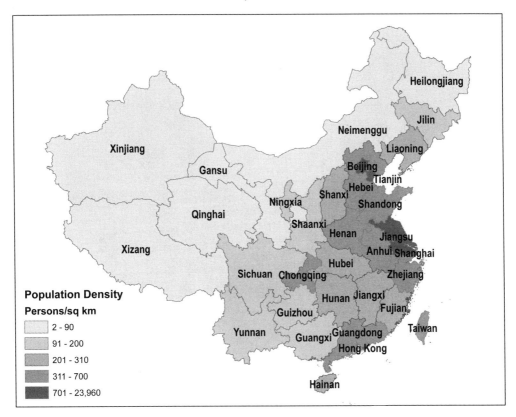

FIGURE 3.7 Population density at the provincial level, 2010 Chinese census. (In this and subsequent figure captions, "provincial" refers not only to the provinces of China, but to the municipalities and autonomous regions.) Data from www.stats.gov.cn/tjsj/pcsj/rkpc/6rp/indexch.htm (retrieved April 19, 2016).

province and Chongqing municipality, are quite surprising. Equally surprising are the relatively high death rates near the North China Plain, including the coastal provinces from Liaoning all the way down to Jiangsu. This is one of the most developed regions in China. However, CDRs do not account for age structure. Areas with higher proportions of elderly persons in their populations tend to have higher CDRs (e.g., the U.S. state of Florida). Later, we show that Sichuan's high CDR is probably due to the relatively high proportion of elderly residents. The relatively high death rates in the northeast coastal region cannot be clearly explained.

Sex Structure

Earlier in this chapter, we also reviewed the history of China's population policies after World War II. These policies eventually led to an imbalance in the sex ratio, with the number of males exceeding the number of females (sex ratios of over 100) in most age groups. Figure 3.9 shows provincial sex ratios, using 2010 census data. Although all of these sex ratios are above 100 (more males than females), the areas with the highest ratios are in the north (Neimenggu) and south (Hainan,

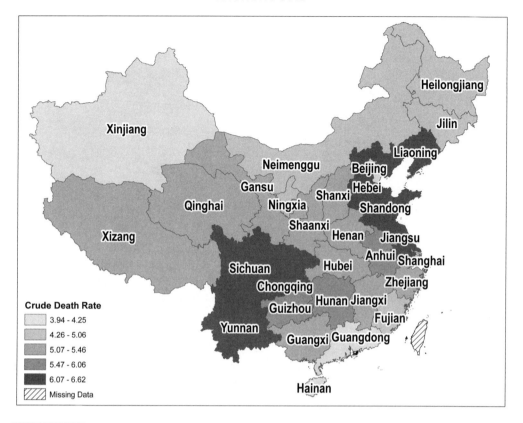

FIGURE 3.8 Crude death rates at the provincial level, 2010 Chinese census. Data from www.stats.gov. cn/tjsj/pcsj/rkpc/6rp/indexch.htm (retrieved April 19, 2016).

Guangdong, Guangxi, and Yunnan). Areas in the east and northeast tend to have the lowest sex ratios. Chongqing, an interior municipality, has one of the lowest sex ratios. The higher sex ratios in selected regions are probably related to a more adverse environment and to the presence of certain types of economic activities (e.g., mining, heavy manufacturing) in those places.

Age Structure

As we also discussed earlier, age structure can be summarized in terms of dependency ratios. China adopts the international definition of the youth dependency group as persons 14 years old and younger. For the elderly dependency ratio, China uses 60 and older as the criterion, since 60 is the general retirement age in China. Figure 3.10a shows the total dependency ratios by province. Guizhou in southern China has the highest total dependency ratio. Guizhou in general is not highly developed, and many places in this province are still quite well preserved with pristine environments. High dependency seems to follow a belt from Tibet in the west toward south and central China, including Sichuan, Chongqing, Guangxi, Hunan, Jiangxi, Anhui, and Henan. These areas have relatively small economically active populations. The northeast (Heilongjiang and Jilin) has the lowest dependency ratios. Other provinces in the coastal area and central region (Shanxi, Shaanxi, and Hubei) also have relatively low dependency ratios. These low-ratio areas are more economically productive and industrialized regions of China, with high concentrations of manufacturing industry and a large service sector. Thus these areas have larger proportions of the economically productive population (ages 15–59).

Figures 3.10b and 3.10c show the youth and elderly dependency ratios, respectively, by province. As it does on total dependency ratio, Guizhou scores highest on youth dependency ratio. In general, the autonomous regions in the west and south have relatively high youth dependency ratios. These are regions with high concentrations of minority populations (which, as noted earlier, have been exempted from the Chinese government's restrictive population policies). The numbers of children in minority families are generally higher than those in Han families. Therefore, it makes sense that areas with a relatively high concentration of minorities also have higher youth dependency ratios than the rest of the country. Henan and Jiangxi are the exceptions: They have relatively high youth dependency ratios, but do not have high concentrations of minorities.

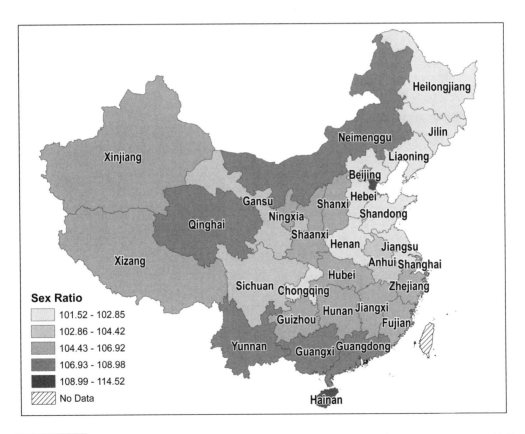

FIGURE 3.9 Sex ratios at the provincial level, 2010 Chinese census. Data from www.stats.gov.cn/tjsj/pcsj/rkpc/6rp/indexch.htm (retrieved April 19, 2016).

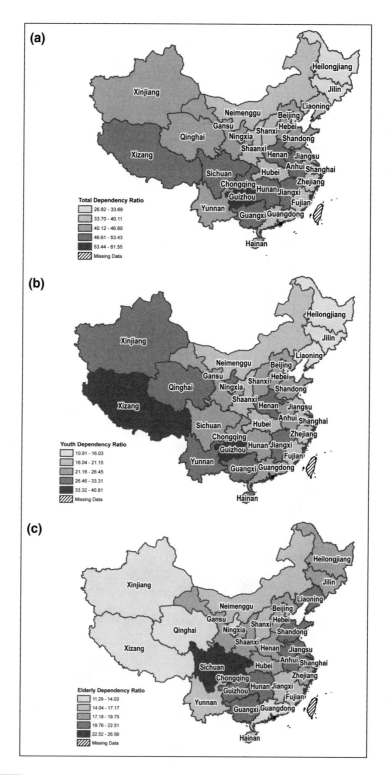

FIGURE 3.10 (a) Total dependency ratios, (b) youth dependency ratios, and (c) elderly dependency ratios at the provincial level, 2010 Chinese census. (Note that for China, the elderly dependency ratio includes those 60 years of age and older.) Data from www.stats.gov.cn/tjsj/pcsj/rkpc/6rp/indexch.htm (retrieved April 19, 2016).

For the elderly dependency ratio, Sichuan province and the neighboring Chongqing municipality stand out from the rest, as shown in Figure 3.10c. Areas southeast of Sichuan and Chongqing also have relatively high elderly dependency ratios. Along the east coast from Liaoning to Shanghai, except for Hebei, Beijing, and Tianjin, there are also relatively high elderly dependency ratios. To some degree, this reflects people's longer lives in areas with advanced economies. On the other hand, the autonomous regions in the west all have low elderly dependency ratios. This partly reflects the lack of longevity in less developed regions. Guangdong may be treated as a special case: Due to the explosion of industrialization during the 1990s, there was an influx of migrant workers into the province. The proportion of elderly residents shrank, and the elderly dependency ratio was lowered, due to the increase in the economically productive population.

Ethnic Diversity

China's ethnic composition is overwhelmingly Han across most of the country, with a few exceptions. Figure 3.11 shows that Xizang (Tibet) has the lowest proportion of Han (8.20%), followed by Xinjiang (40.5%). In all other areas, Han is the majority group. The Han constitute 51–80% of the population in Neimenggu and Ningxia in the north; Qinghai in the west; and Guizhou, Yunnan, and Guangxi in the south. They account for more than 80% of the population in all other provinces.

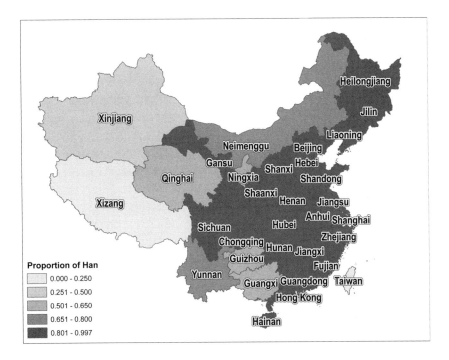

FIGURE 3.11 Proportions of Han by provinces, 2010 Chinese census. (Although Taiwan, Hong Kong, and Macau were labeled as "zeros," racial/ethnic figures of these entities are not included here.) Data from www.stats.gov.cn/tjsj/pcsj/rkpc/6rp/indexch.htm (retrieved April 19, 2016).

BOX 3.2. One Country, "Many Nations"?

Despite the presence of 55 officially recognized minority groups in China, these groups do not have a strong presence in the core area of China (the area defined by the Yellow River, the Loess Plateau, and the North China Plain). With the exception of the Gaoshan in Henan province, and the Hui and Salar in the autonomous region of Ningxia, no other minority group is settled near the center of the country. All other groups occupy the peripheral regions.

Many ethnic groups in the periphery bear the same names as the people in neighboring countries, including Korea in the northeast; Mongolia and Russia in the north; and Kazakhstan, Kyrgyzstan, Tajikistan, and Uzbekistan in the west. These minority groups do not just carry the same names as the citizens of neighboring countries do; many are also racially/ethnically, culturally, and physically similar. Members of some minorities in the western region look more like people in central Asia in facial structure and skin color than like typical Han Chinese. The loyalty of these minority groups to the ruling Chinese has always been an issue for China's rulers, from the emperors of different Chinese dynasties to the current Communist party. As discussed in Chapter 1, China has been expanding its territory throughout its history, conquering neighboring populations and then assimilating them into the Chinese culture. To facilitate cultural assimilation, and to enforce control and oversight, the Chinese government has been relocating Han Chinese to the peripheral regions. For instance, the current proportion of Han in Xinjiang is about 40%. Such a high proportion is primarily the result of massive relocation of a Han population to this autonomous region through official assignments and economic development.

A typical measure of the imbalance between two population groups across different regions (e.g., Chinese provinces or U.S. states) is the "dissimilarity index," D.[16] This measure is also known as the "segregation index," as it is widely used to measure segregation in the social sciences, particularly in sociology, demography, and geography. The index ranges from 0 to 1, with 0 indicating no segregation (i.e., the two groups are distributed across area units in the same manner, not necessarily evenly) and 1 indicating perfect segregation when each unit is exclusively occupied by one or the other group (i.e., populations of the two groups do not co-locate in any unit). When the Han majority is treated as one group and all minorities as another group, the dissimilarity value of the two groups at the provincial level is 0.58. For comparison, the dissimilarity index value for blacks and whites in the United States in 1990 was about 0.46 at the county level and was about 0.27 at the state level.[17] The figure of 0.58 for China at the provincial level seems high. In fact, when county-level data are used, the dissimilarity index between the Han and non-Han groups is above 0.75. Thus the segregation between Han and non-Han in China is quite high. The Han and non-Han groups occupied different places to a large degree.

Figure 3.11 shows a large number of provinces with very high proportions of Han. Obviously, these provinces have low diversity. Quantitatively, the level of diversity can be measured by a standardized "diversity index" with a range from 0, indicating the exclusive dominance by one group, to 1, showing that all groups have the same share of population in the area.[18] Given that over 90% of the population in China is Han, an equal share among all population groups is impossible. Low levels of diversity are expected. In the case of China, the diversity level of a place should be higher when the place has a higher proportion of minority populations. Figure 3.12 shows the standardized diversity index values at the provincial level.

In general, the central and eastern regions have a lower level of diversity, as these are areas highly dominated by Han (80% or higher proportion of Han in the population; see Figure 3.12). The highest diversity levels are found in areas with relatively large proportions or large numbers of minorities. For instance, Guizhou and Yunnan do not have the largest proportions of non-Han groups in their populations (Xizang [Tibet] has the highest), but they have the highest diversity index values. Yunnan has a high diversity index value because it has the largest number of minority groups. Minority groups are usually highly concentrated in certain areas. After we identified the regions where minority groups had the largest concentrations, we created Figure 3.13 and Table 3.2 by tabulating the number of groups with the largest presence in each region. Yunnan is in the highest category in Figure 3.13, since 17 minority groups have their largest concentrations in Yunnan (see Table 3.2). Guizhou has only 6 minority groups with their largest concentrations there, while Guangxi has 5 (again, see Table 3.2). However, Guizhou, with a much smaller number of minority groups, has a diversity index value comparable to that of Yunnan. This is because each of those groups in Guizhou has a large presence, thus raising the province's level of diversity.

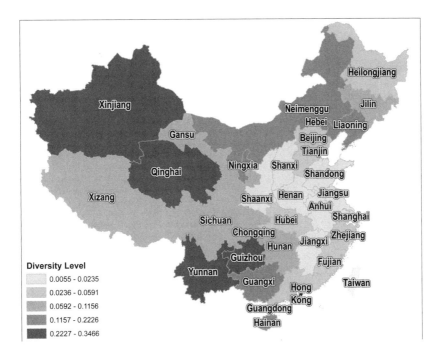

FIGURE 3.12 Diversity index values at the provincial level, using all recognized ethnic groups, 2010 Chinese census. Data from www.stats.gov.cn/tjsj/pcsj/rkpc/6rp/indexch.htm (retrieved April 19, 2016).

Xinjiang is in a similar situation. With 7 minority groups mainly found there (see Table 3.2), the Han account for approximately 40% of its population (Figure 3.13)—but the largest group is the Uyghur, accounting for 45% of the population. With the two largest groups of similar proportions, the diversity level in Xinjiang is relatively high. On the other hand, only one minority group (Tu; see Table 3.2) is mainly found in Qinghai, but only 53% of the population is Han. The relatively large number of minorities makes this province quite diverse. Somewhat surprising is the relatively low diversity level of Xizang (Tibet). In general, areas with large minority populations should have high levels of diversity. However, the situation in Xizang is the opposite of that in areas dominated by the Han: In Xizang, over 90% of the population is Zang (Tibetan). That is, one of the country's minority groups is in the majority in this autonomous region. Table 3.2 shows that Moba and Lhoba are also mainly found in Xizang, but these two are very small minority groups. Their presence does not alter the overwhelming dominance of the Zang. Even the Han have only slightly more than 8% of the population there. Therefore, the overall diversity level in Zang-dominant Xizang is low. The low diversity of a region in China can be due to the dominance of either the Han or a minority group.

Population diversity in China is thus a highly geographical phenomenon. In the central and eastern portions of the country, ethnic diversity is not commonly observed. In the south and part of the north (or northwest), diversity is normal in everyday life. In the extreme southwest, those who are minorities in the country

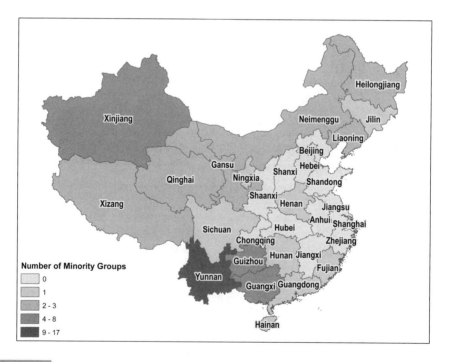

FIGURE 3.13 The numbers of minority groups with the largest concentrations (or of groups mainly found) in the provinces, 2010 Chinese census. Data from www.stats.gov.cn/tjsj/pcsj/rkpc/6rp/indexch.htm (retrieved April 19, 2016).

TABLE 3.2. Provinces, Autonomous Regions, and Municipalities Where the Highest Concentrations of Minority Groups Are Found	
Province, municipality, or autonomous region	**Minority groups with the largest concentration in each area**
Beijing	
Tianjin	
Hebei	
Shanxi	
Neimenggu	Mongol, Daur, Ewenki
Liaoning	Manchu, Xibe,
Jilin	Korean
Heilongjiang	Oroqen, Hezhen
Shanghai	
Jiangsu	
Zhejiang	
Anhui	
Fujian	She
Jiangxi	
Shandong	
Henan	Gaoshan
Hubei	
Hunan	Tujia
Guangdong	Han
Guangxi	Zhuang, Yao, Mulao, Maonan, Gin
Hainan	Li
Chongqing	
Sichuan	Qiang
Guizhou	Miao, Bouyei, Dong, Sui, Gelao, "unofficial"
Yunnan	Yi, Bai, Hani, Dai, Lisu, Va, Lahu, Nakhi, Jingpo, Blang, Achang, Pumi, Nu, Deang, Derung, Jino, "foreign"
Xizang	Zang, Monba, Lhoba
Shaanxi	
Gansu	Dongxiang, Bonan, Yugur
Qinghai	Tu
Ningxia	Hui, Salar
Xinjiang	Uyghur, Kazakh, Kyrgyz, Tajik, Uzbek, Russian, Tatar

Source: Tabulated by the authors based on 2010 Census.

as a whole constitute the majorities at the local level. Fully describing and comprehending the ethnic diversity of population in China will require additional data, analyses, and better understanding of the population history and political development of China.

DYNAMICS AND QUALITY OF THE POPULATION IN CHINA

Another demographic characteristic with a very strong geographical dimension is migration, as mentioned earlier in this chapter. In fact, China has experienced massive domestic migration during the past several decades, particularly the influx of migrant workers (the "floating population")—a topic discussed further in Chapter 6. Internationally, China has been a net exporter of migrants for decades. We have noted earlier that China has a net loss of 0.40 person per 1,000 people, and ranks 119th in the world in net migration.[19]

The Chinese have been emigrating to foreign countries for various reasons and through various channels. Besides reuniting with family members already residing in foreign countries, many young Chinese leaving in the past have sought advanced education. Does this mean that China is not providing sufficient education to its citizens? Although this question is beyond the scope of this book, we can get a glimpse of the geographical variability in education levels as an indication of the quality of the population. Figure 3.14 shows the percentages of provincial populations 6 years

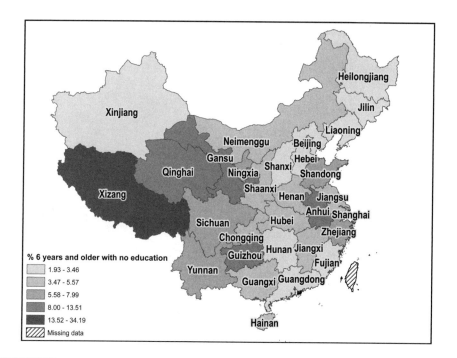

FIGURE 3.14 Percentages of provincial populations 6 years of age and older with no education, 2010 Chinese census. Data from www.stats.gov.cn/tjsj/pcsj/rkpc/6rp/indexch.htm (retrieved April 19, 2016).

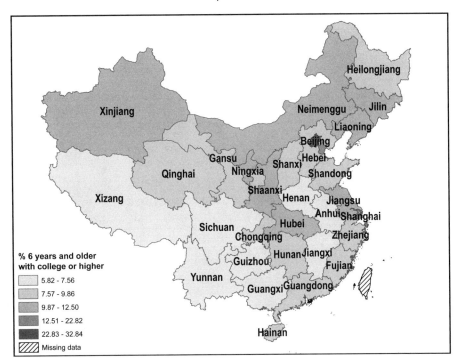

FIGURE 3.15 Percentages of provincial populations 6 years and older with college or higher levels of education, 2010 Chinese census. Data from www.stats.gov.cn/tjsj/pcsj/rkpc/6rp/indexch.htm (retrieved April 19, 2016).

of age and older with no education, according to the 2010 census. In general, the west, particularly Xizang, and the south have the least educated populations. Anhui in the east also has a relatively high percentage of those with no education.

Figure 3.15 shows the percentages of provincial populations 6 years of age and older with college or higher levels of education. Clearly, Beijing as the capital attracts the educated, together with two other municipalities (Shanghai and Tianjin). Although the low percentages in areas of the north (Xinjiang, Neimenggu, Shaanxi, and Hubei) are not surprising, some of the less developed and poorer areas have decent percentages. Well-educated people may be attracted to these regions by such factors as the presence of industries with a demand for engineers. The less industrial economies in the south and southwest may be less attractive to the educated.

• • • • • • • • • • • • • • • • **FINAL THOUGHTS** • • • • • • • • • • • • • • • •

The population of China is vast and still growing, but the rate of growth is slowing down. In the near future, India may overtake China as the country with the largest population. Due to China's long-term enforcement of the controversial one-child policy, the population will encounter challenges associated with slower growth, gender imbalance, and a graying population. Although the Chinese government has been heavily investing in education to raise the quality of human capital, which is of critical importance to future economic development, spatial disparities in education levels clearly persist. Still, the largest persisting spatial disparities are found in the ethnic composition of the population. The Han-dominant eastern/coastal area presents a stark contrast to the minority-dominant west and interior. Such spatial disparities are strongly associated with economic disparities, despite decades of Chinese government efforts to promote economic development in the poorer interior west.

Fully comprehending China's population situation is a major challenge. Recent Chinese censuses have provided invaluable detailed data about this massive, diverse population. However, China probably changes faster than many other parts of the world. Getting timely, comprehensive information about the population of this huge country is costly and definitely challenging.

NOTES ●●●

1. Many studies project that the Indian population may surpass the Chinese population. An example is the world population data sheet provided by the Population Reference Bureau (www.prb.org/pdf16/prb-wpds2016-web-2016.pdf, retrieved September 27, 2016).

2. Some studies have estimated that the overseas Chinese population is about 50 million. See, for example, www.asiapacific.ca/sites/default/files/filefield/researchreportv7.pdf (retrieved April 14, 2016).

3. The U.S. Census Bureau has a "Population Clock," counting the population in the United States and worldwide (www.census.gov/popclock).

4. https://genographic.nationalgeographic.com/development-of-agriculture.

5. Population-doubling time is determined by the population growth rate. A shortcut for estimating the population-doubling time is $70/g$, where g is the population growth rate in percent, usually per year. If the growth rate is 2% per year, the population will double in 35 years—a time independent of the size of the population.

6. www.census.gov/newsroom/press-releases/2015/cb15-215.html (retrieved April 21, 2016).

7. CIA (n.d.).

8. www.theguardian.com/world/2013/nov/15/china-one-child-policy-relaxed-reforms.

9. The "demographic equation" states that the population of a country at time $t + 1$ is as follows: $P_{t+1} = P_t + B - D + I - E$, where P_t is the population at time t, B is the number of births, D is the number of deaths, I is immigration, and E is emigration during that period. "Net migration" is the difference between immigration and emigration, which can be positive or negative.

10. CIA (n.d.).

11. CIA (n.d.).

12. China's sex ratio is far from the highest in the world (CIA, n.d.). Most countries with very high sex ratios are in the Middle East because of large numbers of migrant workers from South and Southeast Asia.

13. One of two news stories retrieved April 21, 2016, reported 24 million (www.bbc.com/news/world-asia-20030681); the other reported 30 million (www.newsweek.com/2015/06/05/gender-imbalance-china-one-child-law-backfired-men-336435.html).

14. http://fortune.com/2013/02/15/how-chinas-lonely-bachelors-are-helping-its-economy-grow.

15. CIA (n.d.).

16. The dissimilarity index is formally defined as

$$D = 0.5 \sum_{i=0}^{n} \left| \frac{a_i}{A} - \frac{b_i}{B} \right|$$

where a_i and b_i are population counts of the two groups in subunit i, and A and B are the total population counts of the two groups in the entire study region.

17. In general, using smaller areal units will produce higher values for the segregation index, as population mix tends to be more uniform (dominated by one group) when the area becomes smaller.

18. The entropy-based diversity of an area or region can be calculated as

$$E = -\sum_{i}^{k} \frac{p_i}{P} * \ln \frac{p_i}{P}$$

where p_i is the population count of subgroup i, P is the total population of the entire study area, and there are k groups in the study area. The ln is the natural logarithm with base e. The index is essentially the proportion of each group multiplied by the log of the proportion, and the sum of the products over all groups. The index has a minimum value of 0, meaning that the area is dominated by one group exclusively, and a maximum value of $\ln(k)$, when all groups have the same proportion (share). Therefore, E is often divided by $\ln(k)$ to derive H, with a range between 0 and 1.

19. CIA (n.d.). The top net gainers of migration were Qatar, the British Virgin Islands, Luxembourg, the Cayman Islands, and Singapore.

REFERENCES ●

Banister, J. (1987). *China's changing population.* Stanford, CA: Stanford University Press.

Central Intelligence Agency (CIA). (n.d.). *The world factbook.* Retrieved from https://www.cia.gov/library/publications/the-world-factbook.

Newbold, K. B. (2013). *Population geography: Tools and issues.* Lanham, MD: Rowman & Littlefield.

Trewartha, G. T. (1953). A case for population geography. *Annals of the Association of American Geographers, 43*(2), 71–97.

Wang, G. T. (1999). *China's population: Problems, thoughts and policies.* Aldershot, UK: Ashgate.

Weeks, J. R. (2015). *Population: An introduction to concepts and issues* (12th ed.) Boston: Cengage.

FURTHER READING ●

Hsieh, C.-M. (2004). Changes in the Chinese population: Demography, distribution, and policy. In C.-M. Hsieh & M. Lu (Eds.), *Changing China: A geographical appraisal* (pp. 192–210). Boulder, CO: Westview Press.

Wong, D. W. S., & Matthews, K. (2004). Population characteristics and ethnic diversity. In C.-M. Hsieh & M. Lu (Eds.), *Changing China: A geographical appraisal* (pp. 211–228). Boulder, CO: Westview Press.

PART II
THEMATIC TOPICS

CHAPTER 4

Agriculture, Food, and Culture

LEARNING OBJECTIVES

- Appreciate the relationship among agriculture, food, and culture in China.

- Recognize the relationship between China's physical environment and agricultural regions.

- Understand major food production systems in China and their relationships with population size, growth, level of economic development, demand for food, and changing diets.

- Comprehend China's food safety, security, and supply problems in a global context.

KEY CONCEPTS AND TERMS

agricultural regions; cropping system; intensive agriculture; economic (land) rent; collectivization; grain-centered, high-protein, and meat-centered diets; terracing; aquaculture; regional cuisines

FOOD CULTURE, POPULATION, AND FEEDING THE MASSES

Eating is an important aspect of Chinese culture. A well-known Chinese proverb is "Citizens are most important to the emperor, while food is most important to the people" (王者以民为天, 而民以食为天). "Have you eaten yet?" is still a common greeting among the Chinese. Chinese restaurants and takeout places are found in many corners of the world, and many non-Chinese believe that those places serve the same types of foods that feed the majority of the Chinese population. Chinese food served in takeout boxes and eaten with disposable chopsticks often appears in TV scenes when friends and coworkers socialize, reinforcing the impression that Chinese food is relatively inexpensive. Contrary to these popular views, Chinese food is also famous for its unusual delicacies. These may include precious items that are difficult to find, items that people in other part of the world would not dare to eat, or common food items cooked in very special ways. Unfortunately, neither the popular Western views nor the special delicacies are truthful reflections of the foods that most Chinese consume daily.

The term "agriculture" carries both broad and narrow meanings in China. In a broad sense, agriculture includes a wide range of activities: farming, forestry, animal husbandry, various sideline activities, and fishery. However, in the narrow sense, agriculture in China just means cultivating land to grow crops, and grain production is of special importance in Chinese agriculture. Historically, the massive Chinese population has mainly been fed by grains. The five main types of grains in the Chinese diet are four cereal crops (rice, wheat, millet, and barley) and a legume crop (soybeans). Many people still look upon grain production as the mainstay of Chinese agriculture.

Ensuring the adequate production and supply of these grains now and in the future is critical to the well-being and security of the country. However, given the improving standard of living and rising affluence among many Chinese, the demand for non-grain food items, particularly meats, has been increasing. The Chinese are gradually switching from grain-based diets to more meat-abundant diets. But the increasing demand for meat does not lower the demand for grains because grains are needed to feed animals. In fact, more grains are needed to produce the same amount of nutrition from animals that is derived from grains directly. Therefore, the demand for grains in China has been increasing (Brown, 1995).

Does China have the capacity to produce more food to meet the increasing demand? This situation seems to fit the centuries-old hypothesis proposed by Thomas Malthus, who claimed that population growth would outstrip the ability to produce enough food, and that eventually humanity would reach a crisis. In Chapter 3, we learned that the growth rate of the Chinese population dropped significantly by about 1980, after the implementation of the one-child policy—but the Chinese population is still growing, although more slowly. Feeding such a huge population is challenging. An answer to the question of whether China can produce enough food is beyond the scope of this chapter. Nevertheless, we can offer a sense of China's agricultural potential and capacity by surveying its agricultural system. Crops cannot be grown everywhere. What a country can grow to feed its population is very much determined by the physical environment and conditions. In Chapter 2, we discussed the topographic landscape of China, the climatic systems dominating China, and the major soil types found within the country. All these are major factors affecting agricultural practices in different parts of the country. To feed the masses, growing food crops is not enough.[1] In recent years, the amounts of Chinese land converted into industrial crops have increased substantially. China also has become more heavily reliant on its animal husbandry and fishery industries; both of these are also strongly influenced by geographical settings.

In this chapter, we discuss the agricultural system in China from a geographical perspective, linking local agricultural practices to local environmental characteristics and physical conditions. Other food-producing systems are also discussed in a geographical context.

THE PHYSICAL ENVIRONMENT
AND CHINESE AGRICULTURAL REGIONS

As described in Chapter 1, Chinese civilization originated on the Loess Plateau and North China Plain in the middle course of the Yellow River (Huang He). One reason China's civilization was able to flourish in this region was that it had a desirable physical environment for settlement, including conditions favorable for growing crops. In Chapter 2, we touched on the physical-environmental characteristics of China as a whole. Here we focus on the specific conditions favorable to certain crops and the emergence of major agricultural regions.

Land Resources and Environment

Agricultural activities are quite widely spread over the country, particularly in Eastern Monsoon China. Farmland stretches from the lower-latitude subtropical region in southern China to the high-latitude temperate region in the northeastern corner. The potential for agricultural development is quite limited in western (continental) China, mainly because of aridity and other extreme weather conditions in some places. The spatial distributions of land devoted to permanent crops and of arable land in China are shown on a map produced by the Food and Agriculture Organization (FAO) of the United Nations.[2] Permanent crops include trees (e.g., fruits and coffee) and shrubs (e.g., flowers) that do not need to be replanted after each harvest. Although arable land in general refers to land with suitable conditions, including climate, soil, and topography, for agricultural practices, in this FAO map, arable land is more narrowly defined as land for temporary cropping.[3] With the adoption of new technologies, some of the agriculture-limiting factors in western China could be remediated to expand arable farmland. Although the absolute amounts of arable land and land for permanent crops in China is quite significant, the per capita amounts are relatively small, given the large Chinese population and in comparison to the amounts in India and the United States (see Table 4.1). However, China has a relatively large percentage of land that can be classified as permanent pasture, particularly in the central and western regions. Compared to the two other countries shown in Table 4.1, China has relatively large land resources to raise animals.

China is a vast country and a land of great diversity. Throughout the country, different combinations of solar energy, water resources, and soil conditions influence local agricultural practices. Even within regions with similar physical-environmental characteristics, Chinese experience in using land for farming varies tremendously. Therefore, no single agricultural regionalization of China will be applicable throughout the country at the local scale (National Committee for Agricultural Regionalization, 1981). Nevertheless, formulating broad agricultural regions is helpful to understanding the agricultural system in China, and one of many regionalization schemes is presented here. As pointed out in Chapter 2, China can be divided into three main physical regions: Eastern Monsoon China, Northwest Arid China, and the Frigid Plateau (see Figure 2.12 in Chapter 2). According to the National Committee for Agricultural Regionalization (1981), the greatest agricultural regional difference in China is found between the eastern and western parts. These largest regions are considered "first-level" zones. The lands in the eastern part have similar combinations of solar energy, water resources, soils, and human conditions that favor the development of agriculture. Therefore, most cultivated land, crops, forestry, fishery, and other farming activities are concentrated here. The western part is arid, and the weather can be harsh in the continental interior. The population is smaller and cropping activities are found in isolated areas, while most of the land is used for grazing. Both the eastern and western parts can be further divided into northern and southern parts. These are considered "second-level" zones. Yang (1991) has further divided the whole country into 10 agricultural regions, creating a "third level" as shown in Table 4.2. The geographical distribution of these 10 regions is illustrated in Figure 4.1. The third-level regions numbered 1 through 6 fall in the Eastern Monsoon Region (Eastern Monsoon China); 7 and 8 fall in the Xinjiang–Inner Mongolia Arid Region (Northwest Arid China); and 9 lies in the Qinghai–Tibetan Plateau Region (the Frigid Plateau). Region 10, the Region of Fishery, lies in the seas off the east coast.

TABLE 4.1. Land Resources for Agriculture in China, India, and the United States

	China		India		U.S.	
	CIA	**FAO**	**CIA**	**FAO**	**CIA**	**FAO**
Total land (km^2)	9,326,410		2,973,193		9,161,966	
Arable (%)	11.30	Arable land (km^2) 1,053,884	52.80	Arable land (km^2) 1,569,846	16.80	Arable land (km^2) 1,539,210
Permanent crops (%)	1.60	Permanent crops (km^2) 149,223	4.20	Permanent crops (km^2) 124,874	0.30	Permanent crops (km^2) 27,486
Permanent pasture (%)	41.80		3.50		27.40	
Population	1,367,485,388		1,125,695,584		321,368,864	
Per capita arable	0.000771		0.012489		0.004790	
Per capita permanent crops	0.000109		0.000993		0.000086	
FAO (2012) arable land in 1,000 Ha		106,521		156,200		155,107
Per capita arable land (Ha)		0.077896		0.124268		0.482645

Note. Ha, hectare. Central Intelligence Agency (CIA) data from https://www.cia.gov/library/publications/resources/the-world-factbook (retrieved September 30, 2015); Food and Agriculture Organization (FAO) data from www.fao.org/faostat/en/#country (retrieved September 4, 2017). The FAO statistics in km^2 are converted from hectares by the authors. The last two rows are statistics from FAO in hectare.

TABLE 4.2. Regionalization of Agriculture in China			
First-level zones	**Second-level zones**	**Third-level regions**	**Physical regions**
Eastern	North	1. Northeast China	Eastern Monsoon Region (Eastern Monsoon China)
		2. North China Plain	
		3. Loess Plateau	
	South	4. Middle and Lower Yangtze River Valley	
		5. Southwest China	
		6. South China	
Western	North	7. Inner Mongolia	Xinjiang–Inner Mongolia Arid Region (Northwest Arid China)
		8. Gansu and Xinjiang	
	South	9. Qinghai and Tibet	Qinghai–Tibet Region (the Frigid Plateau)
		10. The Region of Fishery	

Note. Based on Yang (1991).

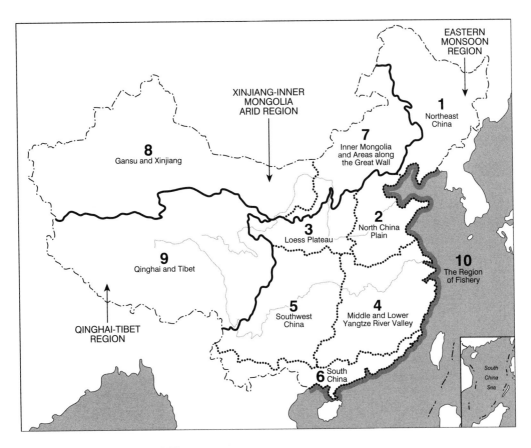

FIGURE 4.1 Agricultural regions of China. Based on Yang (1991).

China's Agricultural Regions

Agricultural Regions in Eastern China

The first-level agriculture zone of eastern China occupies about 45% of the total land area of China. The altitude of most of this zone is lower than 3,000 m (9,843 ft), with average annual precipitation greater than 380 mm (15 in). This corresponds to the western limit of non-oasis agriculture.[4] The cropping system in eastern China is affected by the latitudinal position, which controls the amount of solar radiation received and the length of the growing season. The monsoon determines the rainfall patterns of the region. A great variety of crops can be grown in these broad climatic belts in eastern China (see Figure 4.2).

Geographically, an interesting division seems to occur at the latitude of about 35 degrees North, which corresponds to the Qin Ling–Huai He (Huai River) line that divides China into north and south (refer to Plate 2). To the north of this line are Northeast China, the North China Plain, and the Loess Plateau, where agriculture is dominated by wheat production. To the south of the line are the Middle and Lower Yangtze River Valley (including the Sichuan Basin), Southwest China, and South China, where rice is the dominant crop. Most of the rice produced in China

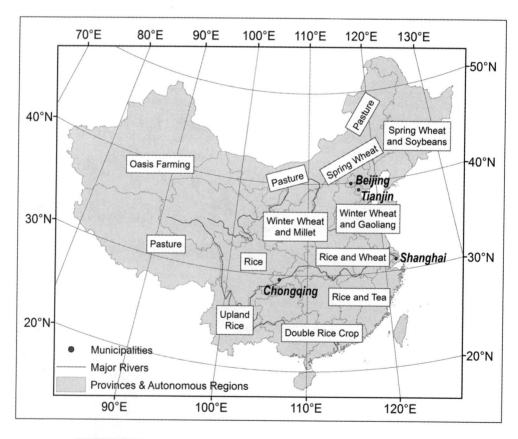

FIGURE 4.2 The spatial distribution of major agricultural systems in China.

is paddy rice, a variety that requires a flooded field over a long growing period. Thus an adequate supply of water is critical for growing paddy rice. In southern China, water is relatively abundant, particularly in the summer when the summer monsoon brings in plenty of moisture from the neighboring seas. In addition, the alluvial plains formed by deposits of river sediment in the delta regions provide water and an ideal growing environment for paddy rice.

Northeast China is the northernmost agricultural region (region 1) in eastern China, including all of Heilongjiang and Jilin provinces and part of Liaoning province. The region is well served by rivers, such as the Heilongjiang (the river) to the north, the Songhua Jiang in the middle, the Liao He to the southwest, and the Yalu Jiang to the southeast of the region. The black soils or chernozems found in this region (see Chapter 2) are rich in organic matter and humus and have high fertility levels. The annual rainfall ranges from 450 to 700 mm (18 to 28 in). The winter is long and cold, with only a short frost-free period. Therefore, only one set of crops can be grown per year in most of the region. Grains are the dominant crops: maize, soybeans, wheat, millet, sorghum, and some rice. In general, cropping in Northeast China is extensive. Little manure or fertilizer is applied, and the yields are comparatively low.

The North China Plain (region 2) is drained by three rivers: the Yellow River (Huang He), the Huai He, and the Hai He. Geographically, it also includes the hilly land of Shandong Peninsula. The region is a flat alluvial floodplain, with elevation declining gently from west to east. The climate is warm to temperate, with cold winters and scorching summers. The annual rainfall is 500–800 mm (20–31 in), brought by the summer monsoon from the sea. The main crops of the region are wheat, maize, and cotton. The other crops include peanuts, sesame, tobacco, millet, sorghum, and soybeans. The region is also the leading producer of temperate-zone fruits, such as apples, pears, persimmons, and jujubes (Chinese dates).

The Loess Plateau (region 3) is situated to the west of the North China Plain. The climate of the region is mild and temperate and possesses more characteristics of a continental climate than region 2 does. The annual rainfall is 400–600 mm (16–24 in), and it can be quite variable, with low water availability most of the time. Water for irrigation is available for those areas adjacent to major rivers and their tributaries. Grains are the main crops grown in this region. Wheat is the dominant crop, with maize (corn) and millet also grown (see Plate 3).

The Middle and Lower Yangtze River Valley (region 4) lies to the south of the North China Plain, and its northern boundary is along the Qin Ling Mountains–Huai He line mentioned above. A dense network of rivers and streams runs across the region, and it has a large number of lakes. The freshwater in the region accounts for one-half of the freshwater in the country. The climate is warm and humid, and the annual rainfall is 800–2,000 mm (31–79 in). Along the coast, typhoons bringing heavy rainfall are common in summer. The majority of cultivated land is in paddy rice, and a large proportion of this land grows two crops of rice a year, together with a winter crop such as wheat, rapeseed, or barley. The region also produces cash crops, such as cotton, tea, silk, jute, bamboo, and subtropical fruits. Moreover, many inland waters (lakes, ponds, reservoirs, rivers, and streams) are habitats for freshwater fish, and have been utilized for aquaculture in recent years.

Southwest China (region 5) has complex topographic features, including mountains, plateaus, and basins. In the south is the Yunnan–Guizhou Plateau, and in the north are many mountains and basins, such as the Sichuan Basin. Much of the cultivated land is on mountain slopes devoted to dryland farming. Terraced farms are common. The climate of the region is warm and humid, except on the Yunnan–Guizhou Plateau, where summer temperatures are relatively lower because of the high altitude. The Sichuan Basin is characterized by cloudy, foggy, and rainy weather; it has the fewest periods of sunshine in the country, and thus is unfavorable for photophilic crops such as cotton. The main crops of the region are rice (see Figure 4.3), wheat, maize, and rapeseed. The major industrial crops include sugar cane and ramie (a fiber plant used for fabrics). The cured tobacco from Yunnan and Guizhou is renowned for both its quality and yield. Other industrial crops include tea from Yunnan and Guizhou, and sugar cane and silk from Sichuan. The major limitations for agricultural development in this region are its mountainous topography and remoteness from the ocean.

South China (region 6) is the southernmost agricultural region of eastern China. It is a tropical and subtropical area bounded by the Nan Ling Mountains in the north. It is characterized by high temperatures and heavy rainfall, which favor the growing of tropical plants. Much of the region is free from frost, ice, and snow. The annual rainfall in most parts of the region is 1,500–2,000 mm (59–79 in).

FIGURE 4.3 Rice growing in lowland Yunnan province in southwest China. (Photo: Kenneth K. K. Wong)

BOX 4.1. What Crops Should Grow Where?: An Economic Land Rent Model

The physical and environmental characteristics of a region provide the necessary conditions to grow certain crops. But farmers often also consider the economic environment in deciding what to grow, particularly in farmland near cities. For instance, under China's economic reforms from the late 1970s onward, growing cash crops has become more profitable. Many farmers have shifted from growing wheat and rice to growing higher-priced agricultural products such as vegetables and fruits. Therefore, the economic rent model proposed in the 19th century by economic geographer Johann von Thünen is highly applicable in China (Clark, 1967). The model determines the "bid rent" of land—that is, what a renter will bid to use a piece of land. von Thünen suggested that higher-intensity crops with higher market prices will be found near cities (the marketplace), while lower-intensity crops with lower market prices will be found farther away from cities.

In the land rent model, the bid rent of land located at distance d from the city center (the market) is $R(d) = y(p - c) - ytd$, where y is the production level per unit of land, p is the price of the commodity, c is the per unit cost of production, and t is the per unit cost of transportation. Therefore, the first term on the right side of the equation is the revenue after production costs. Where the production is located determines the cost of shipping the products to the market (the second term on the right side). Economic rent is the amount left after the costs of production and transportation have been deducted from the revenue, and is the amount that the producer is willing to pay the landlord in order to use the land at that location (distance d from the market). Economic rent decreases with increasing distance from city markets. The landlord will lease the land to the producer who offers the highest bid rent.

Figure 4.4 shows the bid rent functions in a simple hypothetical situation with three types of agricultural activities. Ranching (raising cattle) consumes the most land area, but has the lowest profit and productivity level per unit of land. Gardening (i.e., growing fruits and vegetables) has the highest price and profit per unit of land. Grain production is between the two extremes. The cost of shipping fruits and vegetables is the most expensive (i.e., high t value), because they are perishable; shipping meat products is the least expensive (i.e., low t value), because animals can be herded to the market for sale. Therefore, the bid rent function of gardening is very sensitive to increases in distance (a steep slope in Figure 4.4), and the function for cattle ranching is relatively flat. Gardening offers the highest bid rent when the location is near the market. Therefore, the bid rent function for cattle ranching is relatively insensitive to increases in distance (a relatively gentle slope in Figure 4.4). Ranching cannot offer high economic rent near the city center, but the economic rent for ranching at the fringe is relatively high.

Let's assume that those engaging in the three types of activities bid for all locations to use the land for their respective productions. As land will be allocated to the highest bidder, gardening will outbid the other two activities for locations closer to the city center. Ranching will occupy the fringe, as it offers the highest bid rent for that location. Grain production will take the area between the two. The bid rent principle can be applied to explain agricultural activities in China quite well. Perishable agricultural goods, such as dairy products, are costly to ship. Their production is often located near cities (Figure 4.5). Cattle are usually raised in the more remote areas, far away from cities.

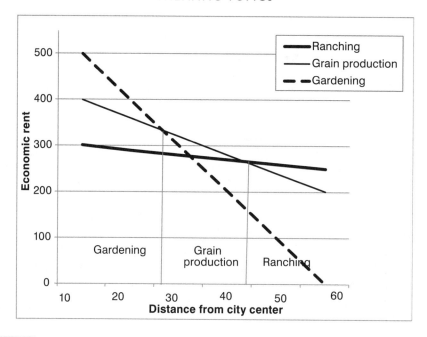

FIGURE 4.4 Bid rent functions for three types of agricultural activities: gardening, grain production, and cattle ranching.

FIGURE 4.5 Dairy farming is another profitable activity near large cities. The Guangming Dairy Farm, Shenzhen, China, supplies fresh milk to brand-name dairy companies that sell to Hong Kong and the entire Pearl River Delta area. (Photo: Kenneth K. K. Wong)

In the coastal deltas and plains in the eastern part of the region, three grain crops can be grown per year. The farming activity is dominated by paddy rice. Sugar cane and peanuts are the other important crops. The region is also the main growing area for China's tropical and subtropical fruits, such as bananas, pineapples, litchi, longan (or dragon eye), oranges, and tangerines. Fishery and aquaculture are common in inland waters. A unique dike–pond agriculture system has been in use for centuries; this is considered to be a typical example of a "circular economy," or one that is restorative and regenerative by design (Zhong, 1990).[5]

The broad north–south division of eastern China into six agricultural regions is partly due to the influence of the monsoon climatic system. The summer monsoon brings abundant precipitation to southern and coastal China. Temperature can occasionally drop close to freezing, but the winter is relatively short; thus, the growing season is quite long. Northern China is significantly colder and drier. The longer winter imposes a shorter growing season in the north. Given these contrasting conditions between the north and south, agricultural practices need to adjust to the local climatic and environmental conditions. As precipitation is relatively abundant in the south, rice is the primary staple crop. With less precipitation and colder climate in the north, wheat is the dominant staple crop. But other crops, such as soybeans, millet, and gaoliang (Chinese sorghum), are often grown in addition to these staple crops.

Agricultural Regions in Western China

The agricultural system in western China is affected by many adverse environmental conditions. The Xinjiang–Inner Mongolia Arid Region is part of the vast expanse of the central Eurasian desert. It covers 30% of China's total area. The climate throughout the region is characterized by its dryness (aridity) due to the great distance from the coast. The region can be divided into two third-level regions: Inner Mongolia (region 7), and Gansu and Xinjiang (region 8).

The eastern boundary of Inner Mongolia (region 7) extends more or less along the line of the Great Wall.[6] Livestock grazing is the main activity in most of the region. The most luxuriant grassland can be found in the Hulun Buir Meng Prairie (near Hulunbuir). The Mongols exclusively raise livestock and follow a nomadic system of husbandry. The livestock are mainly sheep, goats, cattle, and horses; the latter two are used as draft animals. During Mao's era, there was an overemphasis on cropping and not enough emphasis on animal husbandry. This has caused serious problems because rainfall and temperatures in the region are low, and winters are long and bitterly cold because of the high latitude and altitude. Only cold-tolerant crops with a short growing season can grow, and their yield is low. Mao's "grain-first" policy proved to be a great failure, and tilling of the grassland has led to extensive desertification in the region (see Chapter 9).

The Gansu and Xinjiang region (region 8) is located in the northern part of western China. This is a region where many minorities live. Throughout the region the climate is dry, with annual rainfall less than 250 mm (10 in). Cropping is impossible without irrigation. Fortunately, there are many mountains, such as the Tian

Shan and Qilian Shan Mountains, which receive higher precipitation levels (mostly snowfall) than the surrounding regions. The melting snow in summer provides the main source of irrigation water for the local oasis agriculture. Rain-fed cropping is possible only in a few alluvial fans in the foothills of high mountains. Most cultivated land is found in the piedmont plains, where water is available for irrigation. Because of water scarcity, only a few types of crops are grown, such as spring wheat, maize, long-staple cotton, and sugar beets. Normally only one crop a year is grown. Cultivation is extensive, and salinity in the soil is a widespread and serious problem (see Chapter 2). Oasis farming and animal husbandry are the main agricultural activities. The livestock raised in this region are sheep, wool-bearing goats, and camels. However, Xinjiang has a very large fruit industry, producing not just historically famous melons, but also exotic fruits such as kiwi, which are not native to China.[7]

The Qinghai and Tibet region (region 9) is the highest and largest plateau in the world and is known as the "roof of the world." It is a high-altitude alpine area with a vast expanse of land and sparse population. This region constitutes 25% of the country's territory. Most of the region rises 4,000–5,000 m (13,000–16,400 ft) above sea level, making crop growing difficult, if not impossible. Thus large-scale agricultural production is absent in the plateau region. The main domestic animals in the region are the high-altitude-tolerant yak, the Tibetan sheep, and the Tibetan goat; the main crops are naked barley, wheat, peas, potatoes, and rapeseed, all of which are cold-tolerant. Forests are mainly spruce and fir.

In Figure 4.1, region 10, the Region of Fishery, is off the eastern coast of China. This region is discussed later in this chapter (see "Seafood Production and Aquaculture").

GRAIN PRODUCTION

Agriculture has been the economic backbone of China for centuries. After educators (including government officials), farmers had the second highest social status in ancient Chinese society, mainly because farmers produce food to feed the people. Because the Chinese population has been increasing over time, even after the introduction of the one-child policy, the farming system has been under constant pressure to produce more. Much of this pressure has been placed on the grain production sector.

Evolution of the Crop Production System after World War II

Once the Communists took over China after World War II, a major goal was to collectivize the agricultural system, following the Soviet model. About 24,000 communes were created (Lohmar, Gale, Tuan, & Hansen, 2009). Under this communal farming system, the central government determined the prices and production levels of staple crops (e.g., corn, millet, rice, potatoes, sorghum, soybeans, and wheat).

Local quotas were imposed on the farmers by the local state-owned marketing bureaus that coordinated transfers of surpluses and deficits across areas. Production of non-staple crops (cash crops) was limited to small plots. Production levels of staple crops were relatively high, as feeding the population during the postwar era was critical.

At the beginning of economic reform in the late 1970s, the new "household responsibility system" was introduced to partially replace the commune system. Individuals leased land from the collectives for a fixed quota of important crops. Beyond the quota, they could grow whatever they felt best fit their situations. They could consume the surplus—produce or livestock—or sell it in rural markets. As a result, free markets for food were reestablished. Farmers allocated resources more efficiently than under the command system; cash crops and livestock production levels rose. The decollectivization of the agricultural system raised overall food productivity; it also freed excess farmers in rural areas to migrate to urban areas to fuel industrial growth.

From 1978 to 2008, grain production (rice, wheat, and corn) increased from 247 million metric tons (mt) to over 470 million mt, with the largest production increase in corn. Production of pork and eggs increased quickly in the early years; dairy production has increased in recent years. Almost all agricultural production in China still came from small-scale operations, however. In 2007, the average cultivated land per farm household was 0.6 hectare (1.5 acres). Even this small area might be subdivided into noncontiguous parcels, making mechanization difficult (Lohmar et al., 2009). Instead, intensive agriculture was and remains typical.[8]

Many changes have occurred in recent years in Chinese grain production and in Chinese agriculture in general. The overall efficiency and productivity of grain production have improved tremendously. However, the mix of cereal crops has changed over time: Corn production has been on the rise, but the production of wheat and rice has declined. China traditionally has been an agrarian country; the agricultural sector, especially grain production, used to be the largest economic sector. Due to rapid economic development, China has evolved into an industrial and service economy, and the importance of agriculture and grain production is declining. Primary industry, including agricultural production, used to account for more than 50% of the Chinese economy, but recently it accounted for about 10% of economic output (Leipnik, Su, Lane, & Ye, 2014). Finally, due to improved standards of living, the Chinese diet has shifted from a grain-centered diet to a more high-protein and meat-centered diet. Thus the demand for non-grain foods has increased tremendously, changing the mix of food production. However, the pressure to produce more food continues.

Expanding the Amount of Arable Land

There are at least two general ways to raise the level of grain production: expand the amount of arable land, and adopt new farming methods to raise the productivity level per unit of farmland. One of the major limitations in producing more grains in China is the limited amount of arable land. Among the three largest countries in population, China has the smallest amount of arable land (see Table 4.1), but the largest population size. Ideally, farmland should have sufficient topsoil (not barren rock), fertility level, and moisture, and be located in an area warm enough to grow crops. Land meeting all these conditions is limited in supply. Often land cannot meet all these conditions, and therefore improvement is needed.

As urban areas in China have expanded toward rural areas, prime agricultural land has been converted to nonagricultural uses, and this process accelerated in the early 1990s (Wong & Zhao, 1999). Preserving existing farmland and expanding arable land are among the major challenges in today's Chinese agricultural system (Leipnik et al., 2014). One way to expand arable land that the Chinese have been practicing is to convert forest into agricultural land use. An example was the "grain-first" campaign during Mao's era, in which the government urged farmers to cultivate as much grain (the staple foods) as possible to feed the rising population (Ho, 2003). The campaign mobilized the masses to clear forests in the humid south, to reclaim lakes, and to use grasslands in the arid west to grow crops. As a result, Smil (1991) argued, the early 1960s saw the beginning of an accelerated degradation of China's soils, grasslands, forests, and wetlands. The campaign's activities indeed increased the amount of arable land, but at the expense of ecological damage—a devastating problem in contemporary China, which we address more thoroughly in Chapter 9 on environmental concerns.

Even if a land parcel has sufficient fertility, topsoil, and moisture, and is at a location with suitable weather for agriculture, the land may still not be arable if it is hilly. Steep slopes not only create challenges in daily farming activities; they also often trigger erosion, carrying away topsoil. In addition, hilly areas cannot retain water, which is essential for paddy rice fields in southern China. In order to grow crops in rugged terrain, and even on steep slopes, the Chinese have been practicing terracing. This allows farming to take place even on mountain slopes and hilly areas (see Figure 4.6).

Terracing essentially creates leveled "steps" along slopes, making room for relatively flat farm plots. Steeper slopes require more but smaller steps, while gentler slopes can use larger but fewer steps. When these terraces are created, they are often filled with water and used as paddy rice fields. Growing other crops is also feasible. Given China's tremendous pressure to feed the massive population, even tiny paddy rice fields created from terracing are valuable. Thus the supply of farmland in China has increased significantly with this rather simple method of modifying the natural landscape.

Land too dry for agriculture can be modified by irrigation. Irrigation is essential for the Chinese agricultural system, as the growing of paddy rice in the south requires water to flood the fields for an extended growing period. Thanks to the large river systems and tributaries covering the eastern section of China, irrigation ditches and dikes have been used by Chinese farmers to channel water from rivers into the fields. Land in arid locations with little rainfall, including some desert areas, may still be used for agriculture when an irrigation system is built. Thus, the amount and boundary of land that can be farmed is greatly extended with irrigation.

Another factor affecting the arability of land is climate. Due to its latitudinal position, southern China has a long growing season, and "double-cropping" (growing two crops per year) is feasible in many locations. Farther north, the growing season becomes shorter because winters are longer and the temperatures are colder. To extend the growing season artificially, greenhouses and related technologies have been adopted in recent decades. Building greenhouses to augment production is expensive. Crops growing in greenhouses need to have relatively high market values in order to recoup the costs; therefore, greenhouses are often used to grow vegetables, fruits, and seedlings, but not less expensive crops (see Figure 4.7). Instead of rigid greenhouse structures, plastic and canvas have been used to trap solar radiation during the daytime (even when the temperature is relatively low during the day) and to protect the crops from frost at night.

FIGURE 4.6 Long, narrow terraced fields filled with water on very steep slopes in Longsheng (Longji), north of Guilin, Guangxi autonomous region. (Photo: David W. S. Wong)

FIGURE 4.7 A greenhouse producing high-value agricultural products (mainly fruits and vegetables) as part of the operation of Guangming Farm, Shenzhen, China. This is a showcase for integrating an agricultural landscape with new town development for the "Green City," Guangming, in Shenzhen city. (Photo: Kenneth K. K. Wong)

Raising the Intensity of Land Use

Irrigation not only turns areas otherwise too dry for agricultural production into arable land, but it also raises the agricultural productivity per unit of land. For instance, rice can be grown in paddy fields, in highlands, or in dry land. But when plenty of water is available, paddy fields produce more rice per land unit because grains of rice can be planted closer together. In dry land or upland where water is relatively scarce, rice must be planted sparsely, so that the plants can draw moisture from a larger surrounding area. Thus the production level per land unit of this extensive type of farming is relatively low. Irrigation can be regarded as a method to enable intensive agriculture, increasing the crop yield per unit of land. Given the constant pressure to produce more to feed a massive population with limited farmland, Chinese farmers practice intensive agriculture whenever possible. In North America, extensive farming is more common.

When a land parcel has a reasonable amount of topsoil, sufficient moisture, and suitable climatic conditions, but low fertility, the land can still be used to grow crops. However, the yield (productivity) per land unit is likely to be low. In general, fertile land is difficult to find. Even if the land is fertile, the fertility of the soil will decline after prolonged cultivation. Traditionally, natural mechanisms such as flooding, which brought fertile alluvium from rivers to riverbanks and floodplains, replenished the fertility of Chinese soils. However, flood control projects (especially huge modern dams and other efforts) prevent this natural replenishment of soil fertility. As a result, fertility and hence productivity continue to decline over time. Chinese farmers have been dealing with this issue since ancient times; applying animal and even human manure as organic fertilizer has been a common practice. More recently, applying nitrogen-based chemical fertilizers has not only enabled stronger crops, but has also supported more crops per land unit, thus raising the intensity level of agriculture. Some have argued that nitrogen fertilizer was the single most important factor in raising agricultural production levels during the reform era (e.g., Smil, 2004).

Intensive farming remained the norm in Chinese agricultural practice even after the Communist revolution because farm machinery was not widely available (or practical, since each farmer managed a small plot). However, increasing urbanization has drawn farmers away from their farms and into cities. Farms have been consolidated in rural areas, and using farm machinery has thus become more feasible and appealing. Even when plots were too small for farmers to acquire their own machines, the farmer-initiated Transregional Operation of Farm Machines arranged for farmers over an extensive region to share machines such as combine harvesters (Leipnik et al., 2014). The government sponsors the machine-sharing method now by providing information and transportation to move agricultural machines around farming areas, so that even small-plot farmers can have temporary access to the machines. Although the intensity of farming may not increase when machinery is adopted, per capita productivity is increased.

The pressure to produce more food, not just grain, is felt throughout Chinese society. Given the already intensive farming practices across China, putting more crops into the fields may not be possible. However, when the paddy rice fields are filled with water, they literally become ponds, which can be used to raise fish. Therefore, a specific type of mixed or hybrid farming practice is to combine paddy rice farming with aquaculture (fish farming). This is an example of extremely high-intensity land use practice: The same plot of land produces both rice and fish, combining different food production systems in an innovative manner.

ANIMAL HUSBANDRY

Livestock Production Systems

Grains, the staple food crops for the majority of the population, dominated the traditional Chinese diet.[9] As the majority of the population was poor, people treated other foods as "auxiliary." While auxiliary foods help make a good meal, they are not essential. Vegetables, meat, eggs, milk, and bean curd (from soybeans) are all considered auxiliary foods. It has been a tradition for many Chinese families to grow vegetables, raise poultry, and domesticate other animals to produce auxiliary food for their own consumption.

Archaeologists have found the bones of pigs, cattle, dogs, goats, and poultry in the Peiligang Ruin (裴李崗遺址) in Henan province (Chen, 1991). Carbon dating revealed that animal husbandry was practiced in this part of China for at least

8,000 years.[10] While these food sources provide higher protein levels, poorer people historically regarded these food items as treats. Now animal husbandry operates on a large scale to produce a wide variety and large quantities of livestock products to satisfy increasing demand, due to the increasing standard of living of China's population. The livestock population increased from 833.7 million in 1999 to 954 million by 2004 (Hu & Zhang, 2006). Livestock products are of great commercial value. Between 1996 and 2005, the increase in the output of major livestock products ranged from a low level of 34% for sheep's wool to almost 290% for cows' milk. Other major livestock products include pork (61% increase), beef (91% increase), sheep and goat meat (140% increase), and milk (248% increase).[11] Among different types of livestock, pigs accounted for almost 50% of the total, followed by goats and sheep, and then cattle and buffalo. Per capita meat availability in 1999 was about 47 kg, which was above the world's average.

Different types of livestock are raised in different environments and systems. Herbivores such as cattle and sheep can be raised in an extensive grazing system in the western part of China, which constitutes the "pastoral region." Minority populations in western China raise sheep and cattle for their own consumption, and also keep horses, donkeys, and camels for transportation. In eastern China, on the other hand, the Han people are peasant farmers who keep pigs and poultry in pens to provide meat and eggs, in addition to staple foods of rice or wheat.

In extensive grazing practice, or nomadic herding, animals move over a large territory without any planned route. Saddle horses and dairy cows are usually raised in a fenced or controlled environment. A more intensive environment is often used for raising pigs, and therefore the productivity (per unit of land) is also higher. During the past several decades, China has been taking different approaches to integrate livestock into farming systems throughout the country. The objective is to utilize the farming resources fully on the one hand, and to produce enough to feed the livestock on the other hand. These integrated farming operations include growing grass and fodder, feeding cattle with maize silage, and feeding sheep with ammoniated straw. All these approaches help increase the productivity of livestock while utilizing the farming systems more fully.

Livestock systems vary geographically. Areas with little pasture are not suitable for raising cattle or sheep. Therefore, six provinces and autonomous regions in western China with abundant pasture land have a high concentration of pastoral industry—namely, Neimenggu (Inner Mongolia), Xinjiang, Xizang (Tibet), Qinghai, Sichuan, and Gansu. These pastoral provinces and regions accounted for 70% of sheep, almost all camels, 44% of horses, and 39% of donkeys in China in 1999 (Hu & Zhang, 2006). However, they accounted for only about 15% of pigs, 23% of cattle, and 25% of goats, as these animals are more often found in eastern China, where they are raised in more intensive land use settings. These uneven distributions of livestock types are partly attributable to differences in environmental conditions (e.g., availability of pasture) and partly to differences in the cultures and ethnic/religious affiliations of the areas' populations (see Chapter 3). For instance, many minority groups in western China, such as the Uyghur, are mostly Muslim; therefore, raising pigs is out of the question for them. Sheep are their major meat source.

Poultry

A major type of food consumed by the Chinese people is poultry, which includes mainly chickens, ducks, geese, and smaller birds such as quail. Similar to the general trend in livestock production, there has been an increase in poultry production, partly due to the growing population and partly due to increasing per capita demand because of rising affluence levels. In 2000, the amount of poultry raised in China was over 12 million mt, which was dwarfed by the over 40 million mt of pork, the largest amount among all types of meat (FAO, 2005a). The amounts of beef and buffalo, and of mutton and goat, were in the ranges of 5 million and 3 million mt, respectively. However, China did not reach such high levels of production until recent decades. For poultry production, the levels were 1.3 million and 3.2 million mt in 1980 and 1990, respectively. The annual growth rate was 8.8% between 1980 and 1990, and 14.3% between 1990 and 2000 (FAO, 2005a). These are impressive numbers.

The geographical distribution of poultry production is strongly aligned with population distribution patterns. Areas with high densities of poultry production are concentrated in the eastern part of the country. However, the southern parts of Guangdong and Hainan provinces are among the areas with the highest concentrations. Parts of Sichuan province, the municipality of Chongqing, the East China Plain, and a narrow strip in the northeast from Liaoning to Jilin and Heilongjiang provinces also have relatively high levels of poultry production (FAO, 2005a). In general, poultry production is intensive in terms of land use, and therefore poultry producers have traditionally been located not too far from their markets (population centers). However, today, refrigeration can keep poultry fresh despite long-distance shipment. Poultry production can thus move farther away from cities, paying less for land and lowering the costs of production.

With increasing levels of poultry production, there has been an increase in egg production. In fact, egg production experienced double-digit annual growth from 1980 through 2000, and the amount rose from 2.8 million mt in 1980 to over 24 million mt in 2002. These are impressive figures, although the per capita growth is not that impressive, due to the increasing population.

Overall, China's diet has improved tremendously in the past several decades. However, Chinese animal husbandry (including poultry production) is facing many problems. According to Chen (1991), there is a shortage of feed, as well as a problem of poor feed quality. The grass in the western pastoral region is poor and has been getting worse as the number of animals raised there has increased in recent years. Desertification is a major problem confronting the entire region (see Chapter 9). Providing sufficient feed of adequate quality for pig and poultry production in eastern China is also problematic. The quality of the breeding stock for poultry and many other animals is poor, and productivity is low. Huge investments are needed to modernize the production system, so that sufficient poultry and meat of good quality can be raised to meet the needs of the market. However, this could lower the profit margin for the farmers, and therefore their motivation to invest.

Finally, although China has a long history of animal husbandry, the activity has almost always been confined to individual families and has always been treated as a "minor" activity. This attitude toward animal husbandry needs to change. China needs to develop modern animal husbandry to meet the increasing demands of its population, in terms of both quantity and quality.

SEAFOOD PRODUCTION AND AQUACULTURE

China's supply of seafood comes mainly from two sources: wild-caught seafood, and seafood raised via aquaculture. Note that "aquaculture" is generally defined as the raising of aquatic animals and even plants; it is not limited to fish, as we explain below. Seafood can be farmed along freshwater rivers or lakes, or along coastal waters. The Chinese have a long tradition of both catching and raising fish; methods of raising fish and principles of catching fish were recorded 2,000 years ago. China is fortunate to have a long coastline with an extensive continental shelf. The coastal waters span the temperate, subtropical, and tropical zones of the ocean. Therefore, in addition to the nine terrestrial agricultural regions discussed above, China has a 10th region—the Region of Fishery, extending from the Bohai Sea and the Yellow Sea in the north, to the East China Sea, the South China Sea, and the Pacific Ocean east of Taiwan (see Figure 4.1 and Chapter 1).

Throughout its history, China's marine fishery has been an important part of its fishing industry; it accounted for about 35% of all its fish production in 2003 (FAO, 2005b), and about half of it more recently. The other half comes from inland waters, such as lakes, ponds, reservoirs, rivers, and streams; this half includes both wild-caught fish and aquaculture products. The fishing methods used in marine fishery include trawling, purse seining, gill netting, and line fishing. However, the increasing mechanization and motorization of these fishing operations mean that Chinese fishing fleets can go farther and farther away from their country's coast. Starting in the 1980s, China formed a "pelagic fleet" for fishing in the waters west of Africa, in the Bering Sea, and in the Gulf of Alaska.

Overfishing is an important problem. Many species of marine fish, particularly those near the coast, are exhausted, and this seriously affects the future development of China's marine fishery. In recent years, the government has started to impose strict limits on areas fished and to establish seasons when fishing is prohibited. Also restricted is the use of harmful fishing methods. However, international organizations and foreign countries are well aware of the illegal fishing practices of many Chinese fishermen and their fleets beyond China's coastal region.

As mentioned above, aquaculture is more than just farming fish; any marine animal or product can be included—prawns (shrimp), mollusks, and seaweed, for example. Thus aquaculture systems are highly diverse. In general, the aquaculture industry in China can be divided into marine and freshwater aquaculture (Netherlands Business Support Office [NBSO], 2010). More than 70% of output from marine aquaculture in 2007 was shellfish, followed by algae. The total was over 13 million mt (NBSO, 2010). Some of the major species were shrimp, scallops, oysters, mussels, crabs, abalone, sea cucumbers, urchins, and clams. These creatures are farmed in shallow seas, mudflats, and bays, by means of floating rafts and cages. From freshwater farms, fish accounted for almost 90% of output, and the total output was over 19 million mt (NBSO, 2010). Among the fish species, carp is dominant. Tilapia and eel are also quite popular. They are raised in ponds, reservoirs, lakes, and river channels.

Clearly, marine aquaculture has to be located along the coast; freshwater aquaculture is widely spread across the country wherever a suitable water supply exists. Geographically, aquaculture activity can be divided into three regions. The first region, including the Bohai and Yellow Seas, is in the northeast and includes Liaoning, Hebei, Shandong, and Tianjin. Marine aquaculture in these locations is dominated by large government-owned corporations. The second region is in the southeast, including Zhejiang, Fujian, Guangdong, Guangxi, and Hainan. This region includes a significant proportion of marine farms operated by small private enterprises. The third region is along the Yangtze River, running from Jiangsu and Anhui in the east to Chongqing and Sichuan in the middle Yangtze River Valley. These are freshwater farms using ponds, lakes, reservoirs, and channels. The provinces with the largest aquaculture outputs in 2007 were Shandong, Guangdong, Fujian, Zhejiang, and Jiangsu (NBSO, 2010).

According to a World Bank (2013) report, China's emerging middle class is expected to lead the world's growing demand for fish (the World Bank used the term "fish" to cover all seafood). China is likely to have an increasing influence on the global fish market. According to the World Bank's model projection (see Table 4.3 for some results of this projection),[12] China will account for 37% of fish production and 38% of global consumption of fish in the year 2030. Fish have always been

TABLE 4.3. Summary Results (in Thousands of Tons) under Baseline Scenario of Fish Production (Capture and Aquaculture) and Consumption

	Total fish supply		Food fish consumption	
	Data for 2008	Projection for 2030	Data for 2006	Projection for 2030
World				
Capture	89,443	93,229	64,533	58,159
Aquaculture	52,843	93,612	47,164	93,612
Total	142,286	186,842	111,697	151,771
Selected regions				
China	49,224	68,950	35,291	57,361
Japan	4,912	4,702	7,485	7,447
Southeast Asia	20,009	29,092	14,625	19,327
India	7,589	12,731	5,887	10,054

Note. "Fish" in this table refers to all seafood. Data from World Bank (2013).

an important source of protein for the Chinese. Fisheries, both inland and marine, should continue to play an important part in agricultural production in China. Ensuring these fisheries' sustainability in the future to meet the upsurge in fish demand is a great challenge.

FOOD PRODUCTION TRAJECTORIES, FOOD SECURITY, AND FOOD SAFETY

As described throughout this chapter, China has increased its production levels of various types of food. Although grain production has historically been the most important, the increase in the amount of grain directly consumed by humans may level off in the future, as Chinese population growth continues to slow and the Chinese diet shifts to being more meat-oriented (Fukase & Martin, 2014). The livestock production level is likely to increase, but the production of grain used to feed animals will also probably increase. As Brown (1995) has argued, eating more meat does not reduce the demand for grains. The production of vegetables, fruits, and other non-staple crops will also increase due to the growing market, both domestic and international.

While agricultural production levels have been rising, or at least staying on a par with population growth, sustaining or increasing current levels poses serious challenges. One of the major challenges is the loss of agricultural land to economic development. Such pressure comes from at least two directions. Like most developing countries, China has become more urbanized, with an increasing proportion of the population living in urban areas (see Chapter 6). More than 50% of China's population currently lives in urban areas, and that proportion is likely to increase. To accommodate the rising urban population, urban areas have expanded mostly through annexation, converting rural land into urban land (see the discussion of spatial restructuring in Chapter 5). This conversion lowers the capacity for agricultural production.

It can be argued that even if agricultural land is annexed by cities, this land can still be used for agricultural production. However, due to industrial expansion, large quantities of farmland have been converted to industrial land use. The conversion of agricultural to industrial land use has been especially prominent in industrial regions, such as the Pearl River Delta region in Guangdong province and the Yangtze River Delta region. These are also traditional agricultural regions in China. As these regions lose agricultural resources, northeast China has expanded its agricultural sector, producing more grain than ever; it is now regarded as the new "breadbasket" of China (Zader, 2013). Thus a spatial restructuring of the agricultural system has occurred in China in response to economic and spatial forces.

Despite the pressure to feed its massive population, China has been self-sufficient in grain production thus far (Fukase & Martin, 2014; Smil, 2004). There has been little pressure for China to import agricultural products in large quantities, although grain imports since economic reform in 1978 have fluctuated over time. After China joined the World Trade Organization in 2001, imports of agricultural products, especially soybeans and cotton, have increased significantly, while exports have increased more modestly (Lohmar et al., 2009). China has thus opened itself up to the international market for agricultural products. Maintaining its ability to produce sufficient staple food for the population is a national security issue, and China is unlikely to forgo this capability easily.

Among the various problems that China has to deal with in its agricultural sector is food safety. Agricultural products are mostly produced by small-scale production units, as noted earlier. This approach to production makes quality control and assurance processes difficult to implement nationwide. As a result, the Chinese market is notoriously flooded with substandard agricultural products, even ones that may be harmful to human health. Such products include counterfeit food items, as well as food products that are contaminated with impurities, contain toxic ingredients, or pose other health hazards. One scandalous incident was the discovery of a hazardous chemical in powdered baby formula.[13] Dealing with counterfeit or tainted products in a business environment of aggressive short-term profit seeking has proven to be extremely difficult, if not impossible.

Partly due to profit seeking, and partly due to the pressure to produce large quantities of food, China's agriculture has been relying on all possible methods to boost production levels. Nitrogen-based fertilizers, insecticides, and other chemicals are known to help raise productivity levels. However, the proper use of such chemicals is essential, and Chinese farmers are often lax in following protocols, resulting in food contamination. Packing chickens in a crowded setting is another example of raising productivity levels, but doing so increases the chances for disease outbreaks. Chicken farms in southern China have experienced outbreaks of avian flu almost every year. Although consuming fully cooked chickens, even if infected, may not be harmful to humans, the flu can pass to humans through the handling of live chickens (which are preferred by many Chinese in southern China, including Hong Kong). Food safety is no longer just a matter of eating or not eating certain foods; it has now become a major public health concern.

Due to such an insecure food safety system, many Chinese who can afford to purchase more expensive imported products of assured quality prefer to buy such products. For China to sustain its expanding agricultural system and to increase its exports to the international market, the country needs to take the food safety problem seriously by working to ensure that its foods do no harm to consumers, domestic and abroad.

AGRICULTURAL PRACTICES, DIET, AND FOOD CULTURE

The traditional grain-oriented agricultural system in China was strongly influenced by regional variations in climatic conditions. The cooler, drier north and northeast were dominated by wheat production, while the warmer and wetter south and southeast were dominated by rice growing. This geographical variation in wheat and rice growing affected the diets of the local populations. Diet in northern China has traditionally been wheat-based, including noodles and buns, while (white) rice or rice-derived food items are consumed in most meals in the south. Besides this general north–south differentiation, local regions also have favorite diets—partly to take advantage of the local produce, and partly to assist the local residents in coping with the local environment. As a result, there are many regional Chinese cuisines, with different dishes and flavors reflecting local facets of Chinese life and agriculture.

While it is impossible to describe all major regional Chinese cuisines in this chapter, the following discussion provides a quick overview of the food landscape in China. There are many ways to define different regional cuisines. A rather simple but probably misleading one is to label anything that is not Cantonese as "north Chinese" (Anderson, 1988). Anderson (1988) suggested a geographically logical classification of regional cuisines based on regional environmental characteristics and the food sources available regionally. This classification divides Chinese cooking into the following categories: eastern, western, far southern, northern, and minority group cuisines.

Eastern Cooking

In Anderson's (1988) classification, the eastern region covers the coastal region north and south of the lower Yangtze River Valley. The cooking in this region was developed in an environment where freshwater and saltwater mix, and therefore anything that lives in such water (such as crabs, shrimp, water plants, and seaweed) is important. Food is cooked with much oil, vinegar, sugar, sweet bean paste, and rice ale. Eastern cooking involves both simple and complex dishes; the wide variety is made possible by access to all kinds of ingredients. Residents of all cities in the Yangtze River Delta use their own variants of the basic style to create their own special dishes. These cities include Suzhou, Hangzhou, Shanghai, and Ningbo. Cooking in Shanghai, for example, uses ingredients from across the country and even from all over the world. Due to the establishment of international settlements by foreign powers in Shanghai during the Republican era (see Chapter 10), Shanghai played an important role in introducing Western foods to China, such as bread, cakes, pies, candy, and many others. Today's Shanghainese restaurants do not have a distinctive style. To the north of the delta region, today's Shandong is known for its wheat products, such as dough-wrapped dumplings filled with meats or vegetables. The cooking style is a mix of the eastern and northern styles.

The cooking of other provinces around the delta region is not well known. However, farther south, the cooking in Fujian province and surrounding areas is much better known. A distinctive aspect of Fujianese cooking is an emphasis on soup or soupy dishes, including those with shark fins and birds' nests. Rice is often eaten in the form of porridge or congee. Using lard for cooking was common in Fujian in the past; as the region is relatively hilly, growing oilseeds was more challenging than raising pigs. Thus, deep-frying is popular. Today, using lard for cooking is a matter of local or individual preference only. Slow cooking is another characteristic of Fujianese cooking. Soups and stews are simmered slowly, and even steamed and roasted Fujianese foods are often regarded as overcooked by the Cantonese.

The ingredients of Fujianese food are similar to those of other cuisines in eastern China, except that coagulated blood from pigs and poultry is used as a special addition. Blood originally began to be used as a food mainly to avoid waste because Fujian province was relatively poor. Although Fujian is south of the Yangtze River, wheat and rice noodles of different varieties cooked in soup or stir-fried are very popular. A special type of noodle is a hair-thin wheat noodle.

Farther south of Fujian is Guangdong province. One of the most distinctive Guangdong cuisines is Chaochow (Chaozhou or Teochew) cooking, developed by the people around the present-day cities of Chaozhou and Shantou. Compared to Fujianese cooking, Chaochow cooking is faster, lighter, and spicier. This area's location along the coast allows people to use seafood extensively. Famous dishes include fried fish and cold fish, shellfish balls, turtle stews, and marinated roasted goose. Their cooking combines eastern and southern cooking.

South of the mainland is Hainan province, where Hainanese chicken rice is a distinctive dish. The entire chicken is poached in simmering water, resulting in stock. Rice is first fried and then cooked in the stock, which makes the rice tasty and slightly oily. Ironically, Hainanese chicken rice is now most famous in Singapore, partly due to the migration of Hainanese there in the past.

Across the Taiwan Strait from Fujian is Taiwan. Many early Taiwan residents were speakers of Hokkien ("southern Min"); these people migrated from what is now Fujian province on the mainland. Therefore, cooking in Taiwan is similar to that of mainland Hokkien speakers, except that Taiwan has been significantly influenced by Japan because of previous Japanese occupation. Thus cooking in Taiwan is relatively light, delicate, and heavily oriented toward seafood. Taiwan also produces high-quality tea and a variety of fruits (particularly citrus), due to the warm climate and diverse landscape. Another famous Taiwanese food item is dried bean curd, an important ingredient in Buddhist cuisine.

Western Cooking

The west is the spicy zone in China. Although some have claimed that the spicy style was a result of influence from India, archeological evidence and ancient literature suggest that western Chinese cuisines were spicy from the start. Chili pepper, garlic, brown pepper, cassia, star anise, five-spice powder, and coriander leaves are commonly used. Ingredients of western cuisines include rice, noodles, pork, cabbages, radishes, and river fish. Ingredients found in the mountains include bamboo shoots, mushrooms and other fungi, game, wild roots, and herbs. Fruits (particularly citrus) and varieties of nuts are commonly used in their dishes.

Some scholars claim that Changsha, the capital of Hunan province, is the heart of western cuisine. Hunan cuisine is world-famous, and is often regarded as the "hottest" Chinese cuisine because of its intensive use of hot chili pepper. In neighboring Sichuan province, the year-round moisture also favors the use of spices, and spicy food is synonymous with Sichuan cuisine. Sichuan produces a wide range of foods because of the diverse agricultural system and mountainous environment. Access to aquatic foods is limited, and so Sichuan cuisine relies more heavily on

BOX 4.2. Some Famous Chinese Foods

To Westerners, the term "Chinese food" may be associated with two extremes. One extreme consists of inexpensive Westernized dishes, such as "General Tso's chicken" and "Hunan beef," offered by fast-food and take-out restaurants. The other extreme consists of unusual food delicacies, involving precious, often rare items (e.g., bears' paws, sea horses); weird items (e.g., shark fins, snakes, bird saliva, fried scorpions, pig brains); or common foods prepared in special ways (e.g., fish fried with their heads still alive, "thousand-year-old" eggs).

Some Westerners are unaware that many of the inexpensive "Chinese" takeout foods in the first group described above are not authentic Chinese foods. For example, General Tso's chicken is often associated with Hunan cuisine, although it did not originate in Hunan and was not invented by or associated with anyone called General Tso. Chop suey now has recipes, but originally it was prepared with whatever was leftover or readily available, and it did not have any fixed set of ingredients.

Nevertheless, some famous or popular Chinese foods are quite authentic. "Dim sum," as noted in the chapter text, refers to small portions of bite-sized steamed or baked foods. When Cantonese have dim sum, they often say they are going "to drink tea" because serving Chinese tea is typical in restaurants providing dim sum. Peking duck originated in Beijing, which used to be known as Peking. This special roasted duck dish is believed to have been one of the main dishes in the imperial menu, and it has been served to foreign dignitaries, including former U.S. Secretary of State Henry Kissinger. Today many Chinese restaurants in the west offer versions of Peking duck on their menus, but few are authentically prepared.

Some of the foods in the second group described above are abundant (such as the eggs used for "thousand-year-old" eggs) and are part of the daily Chinese diet. But most people, even in the relatively affluent portions of today's Chinese society, cannot afford many of these delicacies. In the old days, these dishes were often reserved for the rich, the famous, and the aristocracy, but not for average citizens. In addition, the use of some of these foods is problematic today. For example, some exotic foods are made from threatened or endangered species, and consuming them conflicts with environmental conservation. Eating certain animals is considered inhumane because they are not usual food sources, or unsanitary because of how they are eaten. The exotic dish of (raw) monkey brain, for instance, is both inhumane and unsanitary. Dogs are not a typical food source in the West, but eating dogs used to be quite common in southern China, as their meat is tender. Eating snakes is less controversial. Shark fin soup (i.e., shark fins cooked in chicken broth) is a premier and expensive dish. Ordering it at a restaurant reflects one's economic status to a certain degree. Due to global conservation efforts to protect sharks, however, the United States and other Western countries have recently banned the import of shark fins. They continue to be available in China, although the consumption of shark fin soup has declined.

bean products than Hunan cooking (hot, spicy fish heads are a Hunan delicacy). Sichuan dishes also use more mountain products, such as bamboo shoots, mushrooms and fungi, and seeds. Finally, Sichuan foods rely more on pickling; sausage, smoked meat, and dried meat are very common.

Two famous Sichuan dishes are hot-and-sour soup and Ma Po bean curd (tofu). Ingredients for the soup include rice vinegar, different types of peppers, pork, bamboo shoots, other vegetables, and coagulated duck's or pig's blood. But the hot-and-sour soups served in Chinese restaurants in the Western world are toned-down versions. As Anderson (1988) put it, the real thing "should be as thick as stew and as potent as firecrackers, but extremely subtle" (p. 205). Ma Po bean curd is mashed-up bean curd and minced pork stir-fried with sesame oil and hot bean paste or chili. Although the origin of the dish's name is unknown, Ma Po may mean "hemp old lady." A more likely explanation is that a woman with Ma as her family name invented this dish. Another famous Sichuan–Hunan dish comparable to Peking duck is camphor-and-tea-smoked duck, which is smoked and fried.

Yunnan's cooking is partly influenced by neighboring Sichuan and partly by the local minorities. The cooking uses fewer spicy, hot flavorings. Meat preserving is a common practice. Yunnan produces the finest ham in China; it is similar to the salt-cured hams of Virginia and is sold by the entire leg. The "boneless pigs" made by minorities are wind-cured after the bones are removed. A difference from the cooking of other provinces in the region is that Yunnan dishes use yogurt. Proximity to India and the influence of the Tibetan people are factors. A special way to cook noodles in Yunnan is to put noodles that are not fully cooked into hot soup or broth to finish the cooking; this variation is called "crossing-the-bridge noodles."

Cooking in the Far South

Southern cooking in China essentially refers to Cantonese food, but some popular or famous southern dishes are Hakka dishes. The Hakka ethnic group moved from central China to the south more than a thousand years ago, and intermingled with other minority groups in the mountainous areas of Guangdong, Jiangxi, and Fujian. These days, the Hakka people are scattered throughout southeast China. Somewhat distinct from Cantonese dishes, Hakka cooking is simple and straightforward. For instance, in salt-baked chicken, salt literally covers the chicken, sealing in flavor and juices as it cooks slowly and evenly. Hakka cuisine is also famous for the use of animals' organs (tripe, livers, kidneys, etc.). A famous dish uses the marrow from the spines of cows, stir-fried with vegetables. Beef balls and fish paste are other famous Hakka foods.

There is a popular old Chinese saying: "Live in Hangzhou, marry in Suzhou, dine in Guangzhou, and die in Liuzhou." Hangzhou in Zhejiang province has the best scenery, and so it is considered the best place to live. Suzhou in Jiangsu province has the most beautiful women, and so it is considered the best place to find a woman and get married. Because Cantonese food tastes the best, and Guangzhou (formerly Canton) is the capital of Guangdong province, Guangzhou is viewed as the best place to eat. Liuzhou produces the best wood for coffins, and so it is believed to be best to die there. Cantonese cooking has several characteristics: the freshness of the food, the precision of cooking time, the quality of the ingredients, the wide range of ingredients, a variety of cooking techniques, and a large variety of dishes. Soups and desserts are not strengths in Cantonese cuisine; Chinese food in general does not favor desserts. Spices and wheat products are rarely used. The cooking involves few beans, but uses more tropical fruits and local produce.

Simplicity is a distinctive feature of Cantonese cooking, and so steamed fish, boiled shrimp, stir-fried vegetables, fried oysters, and boiled chicken are popular dishes. The key factors, again, are the timing of the cooking process and the quality of the ingredients. Seafood is an important ingredient in Cantonese cooking. Besides fish, various types of shellfish, sea cucumbers, squid, and octopus are highly regarded, especially if they are alive before cooking. Poultry was traditionally reserved for special occasions and religious rituals; pork is the standard meat. The whole pig is roasted slowly with brown sugar and spices to make roast pork. The skin becomes golden-red and crunchy, with tender, juicy meat under the skin. Barbecued pork consists of baked lean pork strips that have been marinated with honey, soy sauce, and other flavorings. The Cantonese also like to cure meats—not only pork (sausages and bacon), but also duck. The variety of Cantonese food is best manifested in "dim sum," which are small portions of steamed or baked dishes, including different types of dumplings, buns, and desserts (see Plate 4). Other popular small dishes in dim sum are fried chicken feet, rice wraps in soy sauce, and squid. The number of dishes, depending on the chef's knowledge, experience, and skill, can be as many as several dozen.

Cooking in the North

Except for food from Beijing, cooking in the north is generally unimpressive. Although every northern province has its own distinctive style, none of them stands out. On the other hand, Beijing was the imperial capital for many centuries and was the birthplace of many fancy dishes including exotic ingredients, such as bears' paws, which are far from being everyday favorites. However, rinsed lamb or mutton, which is also called "Mongolian firepot," is popular (especially during winter). Mongolian barbecue is a way to cook a variety of meats. It allows customers to select their own flavors and ingredients, which are then tossed onto a brass grill to cook. Beijing is also famous for its dumplings or "pot-stickers," which are often lightly pan-fried to become crispy. Another famous Beijing food is stretchy noodles. In a process similar to tossing pizza dough, a rope of dough is stretched repeatedly so that it forms very thin, chewy noodles. In some restaurants, the stretching process becomes an attractive show, like the tossing of pizza dough.

Minority Cuisines and Cross-Fertilization of Cuisines

The north, including Gansu and Ningxia, has a significant Hui population (a Muslim minority group), and so Muslim cooking is found in localized areas in the region. Because of this area's proximity to Sichuan, chili pepper is used by the locals—who also favor garlic, which was in turn adopted into Sichuan cooking to a degree. This is an example of cross-fertilization among regional cuisines. Mutton stir-fried with onions and garlic is a popular dish.

Anderson (1988) also provided detailed discussions of the cuisines of minorities around the periphery of the country—from the indigenous mountain people in Taiwan, to the minority populations in the south and southwest, the Tibetans in the plateau, the nomads in the northwest, and the Koreans in the northeast. Space limitations do not allow us to explore the cooking in those regions here.

The distinctiveness of local regional cuisines and the variations among them reflect the richness of Chinese food culture. Using the term "Chinese food" to label all of these cuisines ignores the differences and complexity of the food systems in China. In the past, regional cuisines were served only in their respective local areas. But due to high population mobility and migration, regional cuisines are no longer restricted to local areas. Today versions of Peking duck are served in many parts of China and abroad, although authentically prepared ones can only be found in selected places. Cantonese cuisines are found in many major Chinese cities, while dim sum is still mainly served in southern China and Hong Kong. The ethnic Uyghur cuisine can be found in southern China and the coastal area. Thus regional cuisines have been adopted by other areas. In fact, Chinese cuisines have been internationalized to a large degree, as Chinese restaurants worldwide serve various regional cuisines.

• • • • • • • • • • • • • • • • FINAL THOUGHTS • • • • • • • • • • • • • • • •

It is a daunting task to produce enough food to feed China's massive and growing population. Recent Chinese history shows that the Communist party's early "command economy" failed to handle this task efficiently and effectively. Although the freer market of more recent years may not be working perfectly, it has been helping the country to raise its food production level. In fact, given its limited agricultural resources, China has been producing disproportionately large amounts of food (Lohmar et al., 2009). Although China still has the capability to raise its production level, the trajectories of food production may hinge upon the country's future economic development and the international trade atmosphere.

Nevertheless, the Chinese agricultural sector is facing many challenges, including constraints imposed by environmental conditions, as well as deficiencies in the infrastructure supporting the food production systems. Clearly, many deficiencies are institutional issues that have evolved over time. Local agricultural systems and practices also affect local cuisines and food cultures. Given China's diverse physical and environmental characteristics, diverse food production systems have been developed, and thus a variety of local/regional cuisines have evolved. Despite China's opening up to the Western world and adopting some Western cooking, many Chinese cuisines not only have maintained their distinctiveness but have spread to foreign countries—a sign of the globalization of Chinese culture.

NOTES •••

1. Crops may be classified in many ways. One classification scheme categorizes crops into "food," "feed," and "industrial" crops according to their use (Singh, 2010). Food crops are mainly for human consumption; feed crops are mainly for animal consumption; and industrial crops are commercial crops of little value for food and feed, but important for industrial production. However, these narrowly defined categories are economy/society-dependent and fail to reflect that some crops have multiple uses. For example, corn or maize is a food crop in many countries, but in the United States it is used as a food, a feed, and an industrial crop.

2. www.fao.org/countryprofiles/maps/map/en/?iso3=CHN&mapID=612 (retrieved June 16, 2016).

3. www.fao.org/ag/agn/nutrition/Indicatorsfiles/Agriculture.pdf.

4. "Oasis agriculture" refers to the agricultural practices found in the oases of deserts or arid regions. "Non-oasis agriculture" thus refers to the agricultural practices outside such regions. Irrigation may still be needed for drier areas.

5. See also www.i-sis.org.uk/DykePondSystem.php (retrieved July 5, 2016).

6. The Great Wall of China, in addition to being China's best-known cultural icon, has always been considered as a cultural boundary between the nomadic herders (Mongols) to the north and west and the agricultural settlers (Han) to the east.

7. A different but highly detailed map and description of China's farming systems have been used by the FAO (www.fao.org/countryprofiles/maps/map/en/?iso3=CHN&mapID=601, retrieved June 16, 2016).

8. "Intensive agriculture" or "intensive farming" refers to the practice of investing large amounts of capital and labor in order to increase the productivity per unit land. For example, paddy rice requires large capital inputs in the form of building the paddy and irrigation system. The number of seeds planted per unit of land is also very high. In addition, fertilizer is routinely used.

9. Rice, wheat, and maize are the three main grain crops; the other most important grain crops are barley, millet, sorghum, and beans. Sweet potatoes are an important staple crop as well.

10. The Peiligang settlement practiced agriculture in the form of cultivating millet, and animal husbandry by raising pigs, cattle, and poultry. The settlement was also one of the oldest in ancient China to make pottery.

11. We computed these percentages, using data from Table 7 in Hu and Zhang (2006).

12. The model results reported here and in Table 4.3 are from the baseline model, in which it is assumed that the current situation will continue to a large extent.

13. www.usnews.com/news/world/articles/2008/10/09/the-story-behind-chinas-tainted-milk-scandal (retrieved July 4, 2016).

REFERENCES •••

Anderson, E. N. (1988). *The food of China*. New Haven, CT: Yale University Press.
Brown, L. R. (1995). *Who will feed China?: Wake-up call for a small planet*. New York: Norton.

Chen, R. (1991). The components of agriculture. In G. Xu & L. J. Peel (Eds.), *The agriculture of China* (pp. 73–107). Oxford, UK: Oxford University Press.

Clark, C. (1967). Von Thunen's isolated state. *Oxford Economic Papers, 19,* 370–377.

Food and Agriculture Organization (FAO) of the United Nations. (2005a). *Livestock sector brief: China.* Rome: Author, Livestock Information, Sector Analysis and Policy Branch. Retrieved March 13, 2016, from www.fao.org/ag/againfo/resources/en/publications/sector_briefs/lsb_CHN.pdf.

Food and Agriculture Organization (FAO) of the United Nations. (2005b). *National aquaculture sector overview: China.* Rome: Author, Fisheries and Aquaculture Department. Retrieved March 13, 2016, from www.fao.org/fishery/countrysector/naso_china/en.

Fukase, E., & Martin, W. (2014, September 29). *Who will feed China in the 21st century?: Income growth and food demand and supply in China* (Policy Research Working Paper No. 6926, World Bank Development Research Group, Agriculture and Rural Development Plan). Washington, DC: World Bank. Retrieved March 21, 2016, from https://arefiles.ucdavis.edu/uploads/filer_public/2014/10/09/fukase_-_martin.pdf.

Ho, P. (2003). Mao's war against nature?: The environmental impact of the grain-first campaign in China. *China Journal, 50,* 37–59.

Hu, Z., & Zhang, D. (2006). *Country pasture/forage resource profiles: China.* Rome: Food and Agriculture Organization of the United Nations. Retrieved March 11, 2016, from www.fao.org/ag/AGP/AGPC/doc/Counprof/PDF%20files/China.pdf.

Leipnik, M., Su, Y., Lane, R., & Ye, X. (2014). Agriculture and food production in China and the U.S. In R. Hartmann & J. Wang (Eds.), *A comparative geography of China and the U.S.* (GeoJournal Library No. 109, pp. 117–158). Dordrecht, The Netherlands: Springer.

Lohmar, B., Gale, F., Tuan, F., & Hansen, J. (2009). *China's ongoing agricultural modernization: Challenges remain after 30 years of reform* (Economic Information Bulletin No. EIB-51). Washington, DC: U.S. Department of Agriculture, Economic Research Service. Retrieved July 12, 2017, from www.ers.usda.gov/publications/pub-details/?pubid=44386.

National Committee for Agricultural Regionalization. (1981). *[A comprehensive regionalization of China]* (in Chinese). Beijing: Agricultural Publishing House.

Netherlands Business Support Office (NBSO). (2010). *An overview of China's aquaculture.* Dalian, China: Author. Retrieved March 13, 2016, from http://china.nlambassade.org/binaries/content/assets/postenweb/c/china/zaken-doen-in-china/import/kansen_en_sectoren/agrofood/rapporten_over_agro_food/an-overview-of-chinas-aquaculture.

Singh, B. P. (Ed.). (2010). *Industrial crops and uses.* Wallingford, UK: CAB International.

Smil, V. (1991). Land degradation in China: An ancient problem getting worse. In P. Blaikie & H. Brookfield (Eds.), *Land degradation and society* (pp. 214–222). London: Routledge.

Smil, V. (2004). *China's past, China's future: Energy, food, environment.* New York: Routledge.

Wong, K. K., & Zhao, X. B. (1999). The influence of bureaucratic behavior on land apportionment in China: The informal process. *Environment and Planning C: Government and Policy, 17,* 113–126.

World Bank. (2013). *Fish to 2030: Prospects for fisheries and aquaculture* (World Bank Report No. 83177-GLB, Agriculture and Environmental Services Discussion Paper 03). Washington, DC: Author. Retrieved June 16, 2016, from www.fao.org/docrep/019/i3640e/i3640e.pdf.

Yang, S. (1991). The ten agricultural regions of China, In G. Xu & L. J. Peel (Eds.), *The agriculture of China* (pp. 108–143). Oxford, UK: Oxford University Press.

Zader, A. (2013). China's agricultural regions. *Chinese Studies*. Retrieved from http://oxfordindex.oup.com/view/10.1093/obo/9780199920082-0054.

Zhong, G. (1990). The types, structure and results of the dike–pond system in South China. *GeoJournal, 21*(1-2), 83–89.

FURTHER READING ●

Dixon, J., Gulliver, A., & Gibbon, D. (2001). *Farming systems and poverty: Improving farmers' livelihoods in a changing world.* Rome/Washington, DC: Food and Agriculture Organization of the United Nations/World Bank.

Fu, Q., Liu, Y., Li, L., & Achal, V. (2014). A survey on the heavy metal contents in Chinese traditional egg products and their potential health risk assessment. *Food Additives and Contaminants: Part B: Surveillance, 7*(2), 99–105.

Sun, H. (1994). *[Agricultural natural resources and regional development of China]* (in Chinese). Nanjing: Jiangsu Science & Technology Press.

Xu, G., & Peel, L. J. (Eds.). (1991). *The agriculture of China.* Oxford, UK: Oxford University Press.

CHAPTER 5

China's Changing Economic Geography

State, Space, and Market[1]

LEARNING OBJECTIVES

* Understand how China's economic development has evolved from a planned economy to a market economy with strong government interventions.

* Understand the use of spatial restructuring of administrative units (cities) to transform the economy and stimulate economic growth.

* Recognize how regional planning policy shifted among different types of industries, before and after the economic reforms, and the resulting regional disparity.

* Comprehend the connections between Chinese economic development and the global economic system.

* Examine the spatial concentrations of selected economic sectors.

KEY CONCEPTS AND TERMS

planned economy; spatial fix; administrative zone economy; special economic zones (SEZs); prefecture-level cities; urban districts; comparative advantage; neoliberalism; foreign direct investment (FDI); state-owned enterprises; mobility of factors of production; location quotient; e-commerce; "one belt, one road" plan

CHINESE-STYLE ECONOMIC REFORM: A PLANNED VERSUS MARKET ECONOMY

Economic geography concerns the relationships between space or location and economic activities. Consider these questions: How do the geographical characteristics of a location affect its manufacturing and retail activities? How do processes

125

associated with specific economic activities, such as the financial and entertainment industries, create distinctive patterns in a region? How does the globalization process, which fuels an increasingly connected and interdependent world, affect regional and local economic development? Our conventional understanding of these relationships is dominated by mainstream economic theories and geographical concepts. Do non-Western or noncapitalist economies, such as China (or Cuba), conform to the typical structures and operations of the market economy as discussed in the literature?

The Chinese Communist party took power in 1949 and introduced a planned economic system in China. A planned economy embraces state ownership of production factors and economic entities; centralized economic control; and collectivization of economic production. By contrast, a market economy is characterized by the private ownership of property (especially land), a relatively free flow of production factors (e.g., labor and capital), and the interaction of demand and supply. Whereas efficiency and profit maximization are considered the primary goals of a market system, a planned economic system adopts egalitarian goals to ensure that the poor are taken care of (this is, at least, the original intent of launching such a system). The central allocation of resources is a means to achieve such goals. Politically, a planned economy often features one-party rule, whereas a market economy typically features majority rule.

The planned economic system in China gave rise to an economic logic in the country very different from that of previous eras, and hence a new economic geography was developed. Adoption of a planned economic system suggests that many relationships between space and economic activities that are common in a market economy were not applicable to China. The roles of location/place, distance, and region in shaping economic activities and patterns in a planned economy are different from those found in typical market economies.

People think that today's China is a market economy because economic reform since 1979 has opened the country to certain free-market principles. This understanding does not entirely match reality. Since the country introduced economic reform, there have been heated debates on whether the reforms have transformed the country into a capitalist/market economy. While some former socialist countries in Eastern Europe dismantled their planned economic systems and embraced the market economy swiftly, China's reform process is characterized by gradualism, best described by the saying "Cross the river by feeling the stones." The reform has progressed in a step-by-step manner, despite the poor efficiency of the new systems and incompatibility between the old and new systems. Numerous studies have shown that the country has become increasingly engaged in free-market principles such as privatization and corporatization of state-owned enterprises; deregulation of the housing and human services sectors (services such as health care, education, and welfare were previously monopolized by the state); and the commodification of land. At the same time, these studies reveal the active roles played by the Chinese government in economic development (He & Wu, 2009; Liew, 2005; Walker & Buck, 2007). Indeed, the newly introduced market principles have been superimposed on the older, planned economic system, creating a mixed economy in which market and government regulations are juxtaposed.

The political reality of a single party makes the Chinese government the default promoter of economic growth. The Chinese government's leading role in promoting economic growth, its close connection with business firms, and its employment of capitalist tools to achieve economic and political goals indeed suggest that the economic geography of China is shaped by both liberal market forces and authoritarian central regulations. In other words, although market reform and the opening up of the economy have led to new relationships between space and economic activities, these processes do not necessarily mean that spatial and economic relationships in China are equivalent to those in a market economy.

At another level, China's market reform has been facilitated by global economic transformation. In the 1980s, the political leadership of Margaret Thatcher in the United Kingdom and Ronald Reagan in the United States brought about a significant paradigm shift from a government-led approach in the promotion and protection of economic and social well-being to one driven by free-market principles. This resurgence of the market is known as "neoliberalism." The success of Anglo-American neoliberalism has affected virtually all industrialized countries, inducing the global shift of manufacturing industries (Dicken, 2011), the intensification of global trade, and the proliferation of intercountry economic blocs. China's economic reform and opening of its markets proceeded in conjunction with these global economic processes. The joint impact of global and domestic forces, as well as the coexistence of the old (i.e., state planning) and new (i.e., market) systems, produced a new form of economic geography in China.

It is worth mentioning that in China, where authoritarian central regulations are common, space is generally used as a tactic to stimulate economic growth instead of just being a product of economic activities. Indeed, a large-scale spatial restructuring process lay behind the country's economic reform. This is the topic of the next section.

MAKING SPACE FOR ECONOMIC GROWTH

Economic growth is a process of capital accumulation whereby assets are created for production and the accumulation of wealth and profit. Once started, this process is unlikely to stop because owners of the factors of production want to create more assets and make more money. In his analysis of capital accumulation, David Harvey (1975, 1982) suggested that space is a key component in this process. Why is space important? Space provides a "self-repairing mechanism" for the process of capital accumulation; it can overcome crises stemming from productivity decreases, increases in production costs, and losses of efficiency. This mechanism is known as a "spatial fix," because space is used to fix economic problems.

How does a spatial fix work? It works through geographical expansion, such as the opening of new overseas markets, as well as the development of new regions within a country to generate demand and investment opportunities. These extra dynamics can sustain the process of economic growth. The cycle of economic growth—decreases in productivity, followed by geographical expansion—can be repeated, creating more and more wealth. Therefore, the relationship between economic growth and space suggests that economic development needs an expandable and sizable geographical space to sustain the growth. This geographical space can be regarded as the "economic hinterland." It is often an area that can be served by a city and falls within its sphere of influence. Expansion of urban areas toward rural farmland, for instance, is a good illustration of such a relationship.

The description above articulates the role of space in a market economy in the context of economic development. In China, the role of space has been formulated under a different rationale. In Mao's era, market forces were replaced by the operations of a planned economy, executed by bureaucrats who coordinated the allocation of factors of production. In other words, the market's lateral channels across sectors based on demand and supply were replaced by vertical ones that relied on commands and orders. To facilitate this allocation method, the Chinese government nationalized all factors of production, including land and capital. An administration system was then established to allocate factors of production (including labor) to various sectors and regions through production plans. Relationships between industries and the state, among factories, and among regions were administrative and vertical in nature. The lack of lateral connections suggests that there was no collaboration among provinces or cities. Each region and sector was a closed cellular system.

The administrative hierarchical relationships created a unique form of spatial economy—an "administrative zone economy" (Liu, Jin, & Zhou, 1999). An "administrative zone" refers to the territory of a government unit (be it a province, city, or county). Such a territory is a bounded geographical area over which a government has control and to which government services are provided. An administrative zone is different from an economic hinterland or geographical region that supports economic growth. Whereas an economic hinterland is flexible and subject to change according to market forces such as population dynamics, an administrative zone is fixed and rigid. In a planned economy controlled by bureaucratic directives, the administrative zone of a province, city, or county is always the same as its economic hinterland. This means that expansion into an economic hinterland is restricted by the boundaries of its rigid administrative territory. Furthermore, as the factors of production are allocated by the administration, administrative boundaries act as "invisible walls" between localities, limiting the lateral flow of production factors and stripping away opportunities for collaboration based on market forces. Such an arrangement demonstrated the absolute power (i.e., authority, domination, and coercive power) of the Chinese government in the original command economy. It created a closed, cellular, spatial economic structure, which was designed for the allocation and control of resources in a "top-down" direction. It did not favor the networking of economic activities and efficient allocation of resources based on demand and supply (Figure 5.1a).

The role of space in economic growth suggests that for China to increase the efficiency of its economy, its cellular spatial economic structure had to be changed. In other words, China needed to remove the restrictions on capital circulation, flows of production factors, and expansion of economic hinterlands imposed by administrative boundaries. Therefore, when Deng Xiaoping decided to open up the country

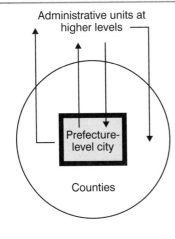

(a) Spatial structure of a planned economy.

The administrative boundary of the prefecture-level city restricts
(1) expansion of economic hinterland of the prefecture-level city; and
(2) lateral links with its adjacent counties.

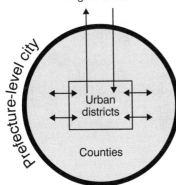

(b) Spatial adjustment of the "city-led counties" system.

The administrative boundary of a prefecture-level city is adjusted to include adjacent counties in the city's administrative territory, favoring lateral connections between city and counties.

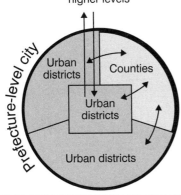

(c) Spatial adjustment of the designation of the counties as urban districts.

The administrative boundary of urban districts is adjusted, creating a bigger economic hinterland for the prefecture-level city. City's function as an economic center is strengthened.

FIGURE 5.1 Spatial adjustments in China.

to the world economy, the country employed the logic of restructuring spatial organizations to facilitate the accumulation of wealth—that is, economic development. Such territorial adjustments have occurred in two waves at the city level.

The first round of territorial adjustment was initiated in the 1980s, featuring the implementation of the "city-led counties" (*shi guan xian*) system. This system did not merely restructure administrative territories by subsuming counties under cities; it also redrew the boundaries of cities. The objective was to strengthen the position of cities as centers for economic activities, so that the circulation of capital, commodities, and labor would be accelerated. Spatial concentration of economic activities was also aimed at generating cost savings through the collective use of urban infrastructure and services such as transportation facilities. "Prefecture-level cities" were the targets of such restructuring (see Chapter 6 for a discussion of this and related administrative entities). Existing prefecture-level cities were expanded by including rural counties in their jurisdictions (see Figure 5.1b). New prefecture-level cities were created through (1) "promoting" lower-level prefecture administrative units to become prefecture-level cities; and (2) merging several adjacent counties to form new prefecture-level cities. After this restructuring, territories (which were also the economic hinterlands) of existing prefecture-level cities expanded, and additional territories were designated as prefecture-level cities, thereby providing these cities with a larger geographical space for capital circulation and hence economic growth. This restructuring was associated with a decentralization of economic decision-making power, so that prefecture-level cities were given more power to introduce local policies to intensify the flow of factors for local production.

The second wave of spatial adjustment came in the 1990s. With the aim of further consolidating the economic and administrative positions of cities, this round of adjustment sought to expand the "urban districts" of the prefecture-level cities. Such expansion could be considered as an advancement of the city-led counties system by focusing on the subcity level (Figure 5.1c). Note that the term "urban district" in China does not refer to loosely built-up areas inside a city, as it does in the West. Rather, the administration of a Chinese urban district is directly under the control of the prefecture-level city government. The judicature, public finance, urban planning, and construction rights within the district are controlled by the prefecture-level city. To expand the urban district, therefore, implies an expansion of the territory directly under the city's control. The expansion of urban districts is pursued through redesignating counties/county-level cities as urban districts. Under this arrangement, the territory of a county is given to the city as part of its urban district. The original county is hence dismantled, at the same time as the city is empowered and its position as a center for economic activities is consolidated.

The change to city-led counties, and the redesignation of counties as urban districts, have been implemented gradually from the coastal region to the central and interior regions. Generally, during the reform era, the state preferred the coastal region over other regions as the major base for spatial restructuring. When the system of city-led counties began to be implemented in 1982, it was concentrated in coastal provinces such as Jiangsu and Guangdong. Table 5.1 shows that between 1985 and 1992, frequent territorial adjustments were recorded for the coastal

TABLE 5.1. Changes in the Number of Prefecture-Level Cities in Three Regions, 1985–2010

Year	Eastern region No. of cities	Eastern region GR	Central region No. of cities	Central region GR	Western region No. of cities	Western region GR	Total
1982	39	n.a.	42	n.a.	28	n.a.	109
1985	65	66.6	58	38	39	39	162
1988	79	21.5	65	12	39	0	183
1990	81	2.5	65	0	39	0	185
1992	84	3.7	67	3	40	2.6	191
1995	89	5.9	75	12	46	15	210
1998	94	5.6	82	9.3	51	10.8	227
2000	98	4.2	100	21.9	61	19.6	259
2002	98	0	100	0	77	26.2	275
2005	98	0	101	1	84	9	283
2008	98	0	101	1	84	0	283
2010	98	0	101	1	84	0	283

Note. The eastern region includes Beijing, Tianjin, Hebei, Liaoning, Shanghai, Jiangsu, Zhejiang, Fujian, Shandong, Guangdong, and Hainan; the central region includes Shanxi, Jilin, Helongjiang, Anhui, Jiangxi, Henan, Hubei, and Hunan; the western region includes Neimenggu (Inner Mongolia), Guangxi, Chongqing, Sichuan, Guizhou, Yunnan, Xizang (Tibet), and Shaanxi. GR, growth rate since the last reporting year; n.a., not available. The shaded areas represent periods of rapid growth in comparison to growth in the other regions. Data are compiled by the authors from multiple years of the *China Statistical Yearbook,* published by the State Statistical Bureau (SSB).

region, with a rapid increase of prefecture-level cities. Major territorial adjustments then shifted to the central regions during the late 1990s, and to the western region after 2000. By 2005, all cities except those in Hainan province had undergone a certain degree of spatial restructuring through the establishment of city-led counties. The redesignation of counties as urban districts followed a similar geographical trend, starting in the coastal region and then continuing to the central and western regions. The system was first implemented in the city of Shanghai, and then spread to coastal cities such as Guangzhou, Shenzhen, and Hangzhou. The process reached its peak at the beginning of the new millennium (Table 5.2). Between 2000 and 2004, 32 prefecture-level cities were restructured, and about 75% of the adjustment took place in the Pearl River and Yangtze River Delta regions (Cheng, 2011).

Spatial adjustment has successfully restructured the urban system, creating a favorable environment for economic growth revolving around an urban setting. This development is vividly illustrated by the substantial increase in the urban population in general and in prefecture-level cities in particular (Chan, 2010; Chan & Hu, 2003). The increases are associated with a shift in China's labor force from agricultural to industrial sectors (Pannell, 2002). Cities have become the catalysts for development and centers of modernization (Wu & Gaubatz, 2013; Yeung & Xu,

1992). Large cities clearly stand out as the centers of domestic and foreign capital investment and industrial production (Gu, Shen, Wong, & Zhen, 2001; Lin, 2002). Furthermore, cities adjacent to each other have developed different kinds of interactions and cooperation, forming what scholars consider to be "city-regions" (Sit, 2005; Zhao, Chan, & Sit, 2003; Zhou, 1991). All of these developments suggest that territorial adjustments have effectively developed a spatial structure that favors economic growth.

BOX 5.1. "Making Space" Globally for Economic Development

Domestically, China has attempted to sustain economic growth through spatial restructuring at various geographical scales. Globalization provides another vehicle of economic development for China by expanding its "economic territory" beyond its political borders. China has been investing significantly in mines and land in South America, Australia, and Africa, securing more natural resources elsewhere (see Chapter 2). Associated with these foreign acquisitions is foreign direct investment (FDI) on China's part—that is, setting up production entities in other countries. These foreign production establishments provide job opportunities for Chinese people overseas, facilitating the flow of capital within China and across other countries.

To sustain further economic development, China has launched the "one belt, one road" initiative. Under this proposed plan, China will build transportation infrastructure, including highways, railroads, and ports, to form better trade connections between China and the rest of the Eurasian continent through different corridors or routes. Each route (the "one road") transverses trade partners, forming a trade belt (the "one belt"). The formation of the "road" will leverage existing transportation infrastructure, but new transportation systems may be built when it is necessary and existing systems may be enhanced to create an efficient transportation network along the "road." Although various specific routes have been proposed, the general idea is to follow the historical "Silk Road" from Xi'an westward to central Asia and Europe, and to create a new maritime "Silk Road" involving ports in southeast China, Southeast and South Asia, the Middle East, and Africa.[a] While the plans for the maritime "Silk Road" are fluid, the revival of the old "Silk Road" land route is quite clear. China's immediate neighbors to the west, including Kazakhstan and Kyrgyzstan, are likely to reap the most benefits from this revival. The long-term objective is to promote trade between China and countries along the route; the immediate benefit of this infrastructure-building initiative is to create jobs for the Chinese both in China and abroad. These job creation activities serve as vehicles through which China can sustain economic development when other sectors in the economy, such as the manufacturing and home construction sectors, have been sluggish.

The "one belt, one road" plan is a vision that some Chinese leaders would like to achieve because they believe it will be beneficial to China. The process of building this infrastructure can help China generate jobs and thus keeps capital flowing in the economy. This initiative is another example of how government can use space as a means to facilitate economic development.

[a]Different versions of the scheme are shown in online maps with different routes, for example, www.clsa.com/special/onebeltoneroad (retrieved June 8, 2016).

TABLE 5.2. Number of Urban Districts in Chinese Cities		
Year	Number	Growth rate (for every 2 years)
1982	527	n.a.
1984	595	12.9
1986	629	5.7
1988	647	2.8
1990	651	0.6
1992	662	1.6
1994	697	5.2
1996	717	2.8
1998	737	2.8
2000	787	6.8
2002	830	9.2
2004	852	2.6
2006	856	0.4
2008	856	0
2010	853	−0.3

Note. n.a., not available. The shaded areas represent periods of rapid growth in comparison to growth in the other years. Data were extracted from multiple years of the *China Statistical Yearbook,* published by the State Statistical Bureau (SSB).

BUILDING A NEW REGIONAL GEOGRAPHY OF INDUSTRIAL LOCATIONS

Spatial planning has been used to facilitate economic growth at the regional scale. Regional planning is not a new idea in a centrally planned economy like China. It has been used to allocate industrial projects and state investments at the regional scale since the establishment of the People's Republic of China (PRC). Despite this, China's regional plan during Mao's era did not conform to any conventional market logic. Initially, Mao's utopian vision of building an egalitarian society resulted in a development strategy that favored inland regions. His intention was vividly announced in a major party speech that criticized the agglomeration of industries, both light and heavy, in the coastal regions; Mao, taking the perspective of development equity, advocated a change from such an "irrational" pattern.[2] To correct such uneven regional development, the lion's share of state investment was injected into the central and inland regions of China. For example, two-thirds of the 700 major industrial projects in the first Five-Year Plan (1953–1957) were located inland. The three northeast provinces—Liaoning, Jilin, and Heilongjiang—alone received

58 projects and over 20% of the country's total fixed investment in infrastructure (Liu & Feng, 2008).

In the 1960s, the breakup of the China–Soviet Union alliance, on top of the intensification of the Cold War between the United States and the Communist bloc, resulted in more radical regional policies. Industries, particularly military-related ones, were relocated to "mountains, caves, and dispersed locations" (*shan, dong, san*). State investment and resource allocation also followed this direction, pouring into the inland regions of China. This radical pattern of industrial location suggests the lack of connections between regional economies (Friedmann, 2005). Regions in Mao's era, like cities as noted earlier, remained isolated and closed. This spatial fragmentation demonstrated a cellular structure at the regional scale.

From Heavy to Light Manufacturing Industries

Under China's central planning system, industrial development and location did not follow any market logic, such as considerations of cost, supply–demand, efficiency, and profit. The Chinese economy was basically an agricultural one when the Communist party took power in 1949. Industrialization was therefore a top priority of the new government. Taking the Soviet Union's experience as a model, China intensified the utilization of the country's resources in high-priority sectors such as machinery, metallurgy, chemicals, and military hardware, hoping to become industrialized and modernized through the development of heavy industries. This model of industrialization, unfortunately, meant forgoing light industries. "Production first, livelihood second" was the slogan promoted across the country at the time, to advocate the sacrifice of material affluence for national development. Although the strategy emphasizing heavy industries increased China's per capita gross domestic product (GDP) from 119 to 379 yuan between 1952 and 1978, light industries shrank significantly. Between 1950 and 1960, the contribution of heavy industries to the nation's gross industrial output value increased from 29 to 66% (State Statistical Bureau–Department of National Economic Integrated Statistics [SSB-DNEIS], 1999). Although the gross output value of heavy industries dropped in the following years, the proportion remained over 50% throughout the pre-reform period. In 1979, the output value of heavy industries still accounted for 57% of the country's total industrial output value (SSB-DNEIS, 1999). This imbalance contributed not only to the dislocation of the country's various industrial sectors and low efficiency in production, but also to low standards of living and serious shortages in consumer products. Food availability remained below the minimum standard suggested by the World Bank.

Not until China initiated economic reform in 1979 did light industries have a chance to revive. Such a revival was the result of a paradigm shift and the adoption of a new development strategy. The shift from Mao's egalitarianism to Deng's "Let a small number of people get rich first" has led to a new understanding about the relationship between economic development and regional disparities. A "ladder-step" doctrine was adopted; this doctrine advocated a more gradual process of development, moving from the prosperous coastal region to the less affluent interior regions.[3] The ladder-step doctrine not only suggested an attitude of greater tolerance toward inequality and uneven development, but also offered new opportunities for the country's shrinking light industries. Associated with this doctrine was a coastal development strategy, which embraced "comparative advantage" as the guiding principle to promote export-oriented industries and foreign trade in the coastal region. Comparative advantage is a common economic concept in a market economy. It refers to the economic strength of a country that can produce a good or service at a lower cost than other countries. Usually the country will produce and export more such products to achieve larger potential gains. Increasing economic efficiency through foreign trade is the concept behind the principle of comparative advantage. To pursue this principle in China, four "special economic zones" (SEZs) were established, and 14 coastal cities were opened to foreign investment (see also Chapter 6 on urban geography). Preferential policies allowed the local governments of these cities and zones to create a favorable environment to attract foreign direct investment (FDI) and promote trade. These preferential policies included greater fiscal autonomy for local governments; greater freedom with credit, loans, and currency circulation; and a higher foreign exchange retention ratio. These policies successfully consolidated the comparative advantage of the coastal region, resulting in a massive influx of FDI and hence a boom in light manufacturing industries. These four SEZs were allowed to experiment with the new policies before the policies were widely adopted (see Chapter 8 for a description of this practice in regard to transportation policies).

FDI and Local Ingenuity

If there was any specific feature in the boom of light manufacturing industries in China, it was probably its reliance on FDI. A substantial share of FDI was injected into the light manufacturing sector, including industries in textiles, communications, electronic equipment, chemical products, pharmaceuticals, and chemical raw materials. Hong Kong played a very important role in this development. At the beginning, Hong Kong investors provided capital, raw materials, machinery, and technical and marketing know-how to small factories across the border in Shenzhen and to neighboring towns and cities in southern Guangdong province. Throughout the 1980s, FDI from Hong Kong accounted for over half of the country's total FDI (Li, 2009). The high proportion of Hong Kong investment (over 53%) was maintained at that level during the first half of the 1990s, but decreased to about 38% on the eve of the new millennium (Li, 2009). FDI from Hong Kong has resumed its strength in recent years, however (Table 5.3). In 2010, it accounted for 57% of the country's total FDI, and it went up to 60% in 2011 (State Statistical Bureau–Department of Trade and External Economic Relations Statistics [SSB-DTEERS], 2012).

Most FDI was poured into Guangdong province, particularly the Pearl River Delta region (Table 5.3). The high concentration in the region was the result not only of geographical proximity to Hong Kong, but also of the Chinese government's decision to set up Guangdong as the national showcase for FDI promotion.

TABLE 5.3. Foreign Direct Investment (FDI) in China and Guangdong, 1979–2011

Year	FDI in nation (U.S. $, billion)	FDI in Guangdong (U.S. $, billion)	FDI in Hong Kong (U.S. $, billion)
1979–1982	1.77	0.49	n.a.
1985	1.96	0.51	0.45[a]
1990	3.49	1.45	1.25
1995	37.52	10.18	8.99
2000	40.72	12.23	7.44
2005	60.33	12.36	5.82
2010	105.74	20.26	12.90
2011	116.01	21.79	14.03

Note. FDI represents the amount of foreign capital actually utilized. Data from SSB-DTEERS (2012); GDSB and SSB-GDSO (2012); GDSB (1992, 1996).
[a]Macau included.

Between 1979 and 2005, over 86% of the country's FDI was concentrated in the coastal region (Yao, Wei, & Liu, 2010). At the city level, Shanghai, Suzhou, Wuxi, and Nanjing together received over 72% of the total FDI flowing into the Yangtze River Delta; in the Pearl River Delta region, Guangzhou, Shenzhen, and Dongguan took the lion's share of the FDI (Tuan & Ng, 2008). In contrast, the central and western regions received only a small share (14%) of the total FDI inflow to China.

Evidently, this uneven distribution of FDI was the result of the country's post-1979 spatial strategy and prefectural policies favoring the development of coastal regions, as noted earlier. Coastal localities were highly innovative in developing a dynamic non-state sector, flexible organizations, and thus rapid market reform. For instance, in the Pearl River Delta, a specific type of production arrangement known as *sanlaiyibao* was introduced to facilitate exports. *Sanlaiyibao* refers to four different forms of export-oriented manufacturing: (1) bringing in raw materials for processing; (2) bringing in finished and semi-finished parts for assembling; (3) providing product samples or design layouts for manufacturing; and (4) compensation trade.[4] Many factories involved in *sanlaiyibao* manufacturing were "township and village enterprises" (TVEs). These were small factories located outside the urban, state-run industrial system (both geographically and institutionally; see Chapter 7 for a fuller discussion). In other words, unlike their urban counterparts, they were free from strict state regulations and had "soft" budget constraints. These positions allowed the TVEs to facilitate production and competition by (1) using production factors according to market principles; (2) setting labor wages at competitive levels to attract, and to keep, skilled workers; and (3) adopting suitable organizational structures to improve production efficiency. In addition to favorable policy environments, such as tax exemption and inexpensive government loans, TVEs' production incentives were raised. Competition among themselves for lower costs and higher profit levels made them the most dynamic part of the country's economy between 1978 and the mid-1990s (Jefferson, Xu, & Zheng, 1994; Naughton, 2007). Not only did their share of production in the manufacturing sector increase from 28 to 40% between 1988 and 1995 (Otsuka, Liu, & Murakami, 1998), but TVEs' output also soared from less than 6% of GDP in 1978 to 26% in 1996 (Naughton, 2007). Despite their small-scale production, TVEs were more efficient than state-owned enterprises in terms of productivity and labor efficiency (Otsuka et al., 1998). The robust development of TVEs, a non-state sector, demonstrated what Naughton (1995) considered as "growing out of [the central] plan" in the era of economic reform.

Dynamics and Regional Disparity in Development

The growing importance of market forces is further illustrated by the flow of labor—an important factor of production that was strictly controlled during Mao's era by the household registration (*hukou*) system (see Chapter 6). The higher mobility of labor has not entailed the abolition of this system. Although using the household registration system to control population flow is no longer effective, the system still affects the allocation of social goods such as housing, medical care, and pensions. The weakening of control over population flow has led to massive influxes of rural populations to cities and to the coastal region because of job opportunities and the potential for higher income. As a result, interprovincial migration has increased substantially. Between 1990 and 2010, Guangdong and Zhejiang provinces were consistently the most popular destinations for migrants (the so-called "floating population"; see Chapter 6), receiving over 30% of all interprovincial migration (Chan, 2012). In contrast, provinces located in the central and western regions, such as Sichuan, Anhui, Henan, and Hunan, recorded large amounts of out-migration during the same period (Figure 5.2).

Nevertheless, the reach of market forces is uneven among sectors. Whereas sectors like low-end manufacturing, retail, and service industries are engaged in intensive market competition, strategically important sectors, such as finance, oil/other energy, and infrastructure, are still controlled by the Chinese government. Not only do these sectors have a low level of FDI utilization, but they are dominated by state-owned enterprises, in spite of the wide-ranging reforms in these enterprises in the 1990s. In the oil industry, for example, PetroChina Ltd. and Sinopec Ltd. are two major oil companies listed on the Hong Kong Stock Exchange and involved in international oil trading, but they are held by the state-owned enterprises China National Petroleum Corporation (CNPC) and China Petroleum and Chemical Corporation (Sinopec), respectively (Andrews-Speed, 2012). Furthermore, although the prices of oil products are in principle linked to international prices, they are adjusted by the government at the wholesale level and are tightly controlled at the retail level (Kong, 2010). Market forces and state controls thus coexist.

Therefore, the geography of industrial production in the reform era is determined by the joint forces of market mechanisms and state planning. In the labor-intensive manufacturing sector, the uneven distribution of FDI suggests an uneven development of the manufacturing industry, creating relatively high concentrations

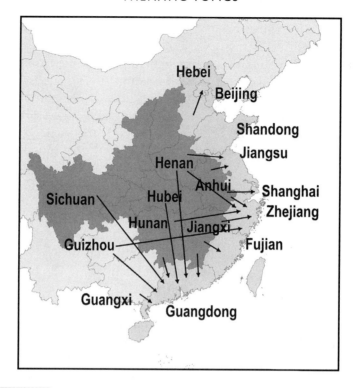

FIGURE 5.2 Major sources and destinations of labor flow. Based on Chan (2012).

of manufacturing in a few areas in the coastal region, such as the Pearl River and Yangtze River Deltas. Manufacturing industry in the coastal region as a percentage of the national total output rose from 52% in 1990 to 73% in 2003 (Wang & Wei, 2007). Within the coastal region, the Pearl River Delta demonstrated a substantial growth rate, from 6 to 19%, followed by a 5% growth rate in the Yangtze River Delta and a mild increase in the Bohai Bay area (Wang & Wei, 2007). Among the manufacturing industries that recorded more than 5% growth, 18 were concentrated in the Pearl River Delta, 13 in the Yangtze River Delta, and 7 in the Bohai Bay area (Wang & Wei, 2007). Within the Pearl River Delta, the three major cities—Guangzhou, Shenzhen, and Dongguan—contributed over 70% of the area's industrial output (Tuan & Ng, 2008). In the Yangtze River Delta, Shanghai, Suzhou, and Nanjing consistently shared about one-half of the area's total output. Thus the emphasis on comparative advantage has attracted manufacturing industries to the coastal region, creating coastal manufacturing belts. Using worker population as the variable, Figure 5.3 shows the location quotients (LQs) of manufacturing industries. The LQ compares the proportion of the worker population in a particular industrial sector in a region to the same proportion in the entire country. The higher LQs in the coastal provinces, such as Guangdong, Fujian, Zhejiang, and Jiangsu, demonstrate a high concentration of manufacturing industries in these provinces—a geographical pattern in line with the high FDI in the region.

The "Invisible Hand" versus the "Visible Hand" in Industrial Locations

Classic regional development theories and the principle of comparative advantage suggest that when production costs in a region increase, industries will move to areas with lower production costs. In China, a shift in labor-intensive industries started in the mid-2000s, but this change was not entirely determined by changes in production costs. Chinese governments at the central and local levels have always used a "visible hand" (as opposed to the notion of the "invisible hand" of the market, a term coined by 18th-century economist Adam Smith) in regulating industrial development. At the national level, regional policies like the Western Development Program, the Rising of Central China, and the Northeast Revitalization Program have provided policy, fiscal, and infrastructure support for industrial developments in the interior regions. Local governments in the inland regions also provide favorable conditions and incentives to attract industries and investors, although labor costs, the capital–labor ratio, labor productivity, and outputs do not have any comparative advantage in these interior regions for industrial development (Cai, Wang, & Qu, 2009). At the same time, during the downturn of the world economy in 2008, local governments in the coastal region began to view labor-intensive and heavily polluting industries as unattractive, due to the deterioration of environmental

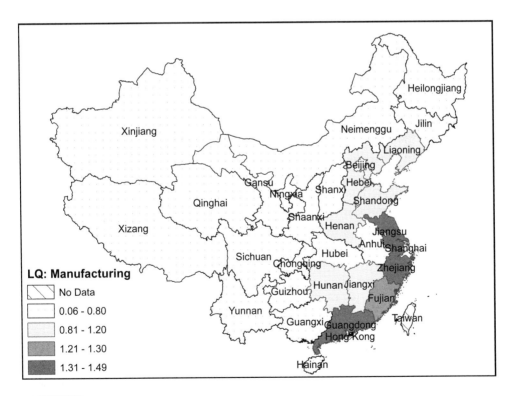

FIGURE 5.3 Location quotients (LQs) of manufacturing industries. Data from State Council Economic Census Leading Group (SC-ECLG) (2010).

quality as well as the decrease in productivity (which in turn was due partly to reaching the point of diminishing returns in large-scale production). The local governments have introduced policies to relocate these industries to the country's less developed regions. These polices include tax incentives for high-value, high-technology, and innovative industries, and at the same time tough measures for pollution control and labor insurance. This strategy is known as "emptying the cage for new birds," and demonstrates the local governments' determination to upgrade and restructure industry from a labor-intensive emphasis to a high-tech and capital-intensive one.

It is almost certain that this restructuring was crafted by careful planning at various levels and supported by appropriate economic policies. Chinese leaders understood that the restructuring was not just a shift or an upgrade of economic activities, but was also intended to stimulate creativity, build technological capacity, and encourage investment in research and development (R&D)—an important step for China to join the ranks of developed countries. Naughton (2007) summarized various approaches that China has adopted to acquire technology since the market reform. The strategy started with simply importing commodities, trading market access for technology, and opening the country to FDI; it then changed to hiring and training domestic personnel and encouraging domestic spinoffs. Government spending on R&D in proportion to GDP increased from less than 1% in 1989 to 1.3% in 2005 (Naughton, 2007). The emphasis on training local scientists, engineers, and research personnel and on adopting new technologies explains why the country's R&D industry has been concentrated in the central region, where about one-third of the country's tertiary education institutions and technical schools are located (Liu & Feng, 2008). This pattern is also supported by the LQs of the R&D industry, which demonstrates a high concentration of workers in the R&D industry in the central and western provinces (Figure 5.4).

As mentioned earlier, the impact of China's market reform is highly uneven across different industrial sectors. Some industries are still dominated by the state. Generally, these are heavy industries such as mining, petroleum, iron/steel, metallurgy, and machinery. These heavy industries are located in the central and northeast regions of the country. This locational pattern is demonstrated by an LQ analysis of energy industries—a major group of heavy industries in China (Figure 5.5). The northeast is considered China's traditional industrial region (see Chapter 11). It was initially developed in the 1930s during the Japanese occupation and was developed further under Mao's strategy to prioritize heavy industries. The concentration of heavy industries in the central region was a result of central planning. Market forces have not had a substantial impact on the location of heavy industries. The northeast region maintains its position as the country's heavy industrial center and supplies up to 50% of the country's production equipment and machinery (Liu & Feng, 2008). Industrial cities such as Shenyang, Dalian, Anshan, Fushun, Jilin, and Changchun have agglomerated different types of specialized industries and are connected by different production and supply chains. Both central and local governments' fixed investment is the major source of capital for heavy industries in this region.

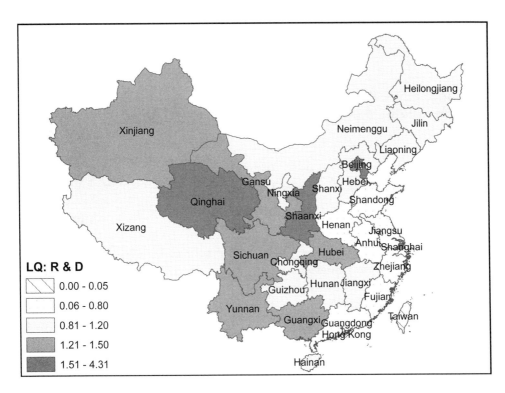

FIGURE 5.4 LQs of the research and development (R&D) industry. Data from SC-ECLG (2010).

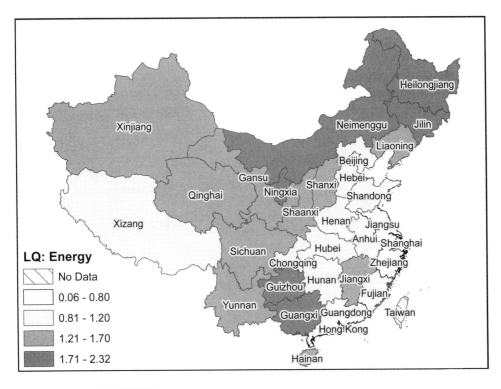

FIGURE 5.5 LQs of energy industries. Data from SC-ECLG (2010).

GOING GLOBAL

Economic reform and the opening up of the Chinese economy have not only connected China to the world economy, but transformed the country into a global trading power. Before 1979, China's total trade volume never exceeded 10% of its GDP (Naughton, 2007). In the 1960s, the country's major trading partners were the Soviet Union (as it was then) and other socialist countries. However, the breakup of the Sino–Soviet relationship, as well as the domestic economic hardships stemming from the Great Leap Forward and the Cultural Revolution, significantly affected the country's trading profile. In 1970 and 1971, China's trading volume dropped to 5% of GDP, with Hong Kong as its major export market (Naughton, 2007). The later 1970s witnessed a gradual recovery in international trade. However, attempts to expand imports of machinery and other technological items to raise production were hindered by the lack of foreign exchange, not to mention the rigid trading system monopolized by the state-owned enterprises. These difficulties demonstrated the incompatibility between the planned economic system and the liberal market economy. China's domestic economy and the world economic system were very much separated.

With almost no trade with foreign countries, China began its export-led industrialization. Such an industrialization strategy significantly increased China's trade volume at a rapid pace. Between 1985 and 2000, the value of China's exports increased from $808.9 million to $20,634.4 million, and imports expanded from $1,257.8 million to $18,638.8 million (SSB-DTEERS, 2012). (All dollar values given in this discussion are U.S. dollars.) During the same period, the export volume as a proportion of the country's GDP expanded from 9 to 21%, which accounted for 3.9% of world exports in 2000 (SSB-DTEERS, 2012).

China's admission to the World Trade Organization in 2001 was a milestone in the country's processes of economic reform and greater openness. Since then, not only have the country's trade opportunities expanded, but transaction and import costs have been reduced. In 2005, China became the third largest trading country in the world, after the United States and Germany. It took China only 2 years to overtake Germany as the second largest. In 2009, China became the country with the largest trading volume in the world. In 2011, Chinese exports totaled $18,983.8 million, which accounted for 26% of the country's GDP (SSB-DTEERS, 2012) and 10.4% of the world's total trade volume (SSB-DTEERS, 2012). The "Made in China" label became globally known, due to the boost in China's export industry. The country's major trading partners include both developed and developing nations. In 2011, China's top five trading partners were the European Union, the United States, Hong Kong, the Association of Southeast Asian Nations (ASEAN),[5] and Japan (SSB-DTEERS, 2012).

Despite the powerful global reach of the "Made in China" label, the effects and benefits of international trade are uneven across China. The coastal region, where a substantial share of FDI and factories are found, is a major player in the country's international trade. In 2005, Guangdong, Zhejiang, Jiangsu, and Shanghai shared about 66% of China's international trade volume—a big leap from their

22% share in 1979 (Tuan & Ng, 2008). Guangdong outperformed Shanghai and Jiangsu and achieved the biggest share in international trade, with a share 4.5 times greater than in 1979 (Tuan & Ng, 2008). In addition to its position as the major destination of FDI and the champion of economic growth, Guangdong and the Pearl River Delta in general have earned the titles of the "fifth little dragon of Asia" (Hong Kong, Singapore, South Korea, and Taiwan being the other four) and the "regional powerhouse" (Enright, Scott, & Chang, 2005; Sung, Wong, & Lai, 1995). Thus, although the concentration of FDI and export activities in the coastal areas has facilitated new industries and economic activities, it has led to uneven regional growth.

BOX 5.2. What Does "Made in China" Mean?

Sara Bongiorni (2007), an American journalist, conducted an innovative experiment to test the impact of "Made in China" on people's everyday lives. She and her family decided to go for 1 year without buying any products that were made in China. They found that their lives were very difficult. Not only did they need to pay more for non-Chinese-made products, but they had difficulty in finding substitutes for them. The experience led them to conclude that in the context of the United States' growing imports from China, "[s]wearing off Chinese products forever seems impractical" (Bongiorni, 2007, p. 225).

Although Chinese products have flooded the world market, not all of them have a good reputation. In 2006, a special report in *Urban China (Chenshi Zhongguo)*—a Chinese magazine about urban issues—exposed a few aspects of the "Made in China" phenomenon that were little known to many Chinese people. In addition to brand-name and franchise products, China produces a large number of counterfeit and inferior products. Many of these products are exported to Africa, South America, and other less developed countries through illegal channels involving tax evasion and smuggling. These counterfeit products are also exported to markets in developed nations, including shops in Chinatowns globally. Chinese products thus include both high-end and cheap merchandise, and are shipped to every corner of the world through both legal and illegal channels.

Within China, "Made in China" may mean products of inferior quality, or (even worse) fakes. These "fakes" are not just inferior merchandise carrying specific famous brand names, but products (including foods and health care items) that are manufactured using substitutes that may be harmful for human consumption. This problem has become so pervasive that finding some types of authentic products in China is becoming difficult. Thus Chinese tourists traveling to foreign countries will try to buy all kinds of brand-name merchandise, from high-end handbags and watches to daily consumer items such as baby formula powder (see Figure 5.6).

Chinese's global manufacturing status has been challenged recently. As Chinese wages have increased and other costs of doing business in China are rising, firms have started moving their manufacturing operations to less costly areas, including Southeast Asia (e.g., Vietnam) and South Asia. Such a global restructuring of industrial geography implies that the "Made in China" label will become less common among low-cost consumer items, and that the shift to the Chinese's economy to more information- and technology-intensive sectors has already begun.

FIGURE 5.6 Shoppers from mainland China lined up (a) outside a "dispensary" (pharmacy) in Hong Kong for health care and baby products, and (b) outside a Gucci store in Hong Kong. (Photos: David W. S. Wong)

Industrial sectors dominated by the Chinese government have joined the global economy in another way. For instance, restructuring the companies' traditional organizations and building subsidiary companies have enabled state-owned oil companies, such as PetroChina, to be listed in overseas stock markets; in turn, this enables them to raise funds to augment their production capacities, grow larger in scale, launch overseas production projects, and attract new investment. In 2013, PetroChina spent 10.6 billion yuan to purchase a mining project in the state of Western Australia from the country's resource giant, BHP Billiton (PetroChina, 2014). A few months later, the company spent $2.6 billion to purchase an energy company from the Brazilian national oil company (PetroChina, 2014). Purchases like these are only the tip of the iceberg: Chinese state-owned companies are aggressively engaging in global economic activities and pursuing valuable global resources through FDI.

These Chinese state enterprises have used the same practices and strategies in Africa. The African continent is resource-rich, but its nations are economically desperate to develop and acquire investment. To a large extent, Chinese overseas investment strategy is similar to that of developed nations several decades ago: heavily investing in the resource sectors in the less developed nations, in order to secure a stable supply of natural resources and raw materials. This strategy is also similar to imperialism or colonialism, in which imperialist nations took control of foreign land and resources to support their domestic economies. Whereas in the old days imperialists relied on military power, economic means (in effect, economic imperialism) are now used. Thus China has transformed itself from a major recipient of FDI into a major investor.

SERVING OVER 1.3 BILLION PEOPLE

The early stages of the Chinese economic reform emphasized manufacturing industries and energy production. The heavy concentration of manufacturing activities in the two delta regions discussed above may offer an impression that China's economy is entirely dominated by the secondary sector (manufacturing, construction, and energy). According to the 2008 China economic census, slightly more than 54% of the labor force was in the secondary sector. The Chinese economy cannot just produce commodities; its huge population needs to be served. Therefore, slightly more than 41% of the labor force was in the tertiary or service sector in 2008. (The remaining 4.37% of the labor force was in agriculture and mining industries—the primary sector.)

The service sector involves a large variety of economic activities (Stutz & Warf, 2012). "Consumer services," or services geared toward individual consumers, include entertainment, food, and tourism. Wholesale and retail activities can be treated as a group, as they bring commodities from producers to consumers. Another type of services is geared toward corporations or producers. These are known as "producer services," which include finance, insurance, real estate, and other business services. Other categories in the service sector include transportation, communication, and services offered by government and nonprofit organizations. Activities related to production and management of information and knowledge are often grouped separately into a quaternary sector, but they may be grouped with the service sector to a large degree.

Figure 5.7 shows the distribution of the labor force across the primary and secondary sectors, and the subgroups under the tertiary or service sector. Although the figure shows that only about 9% of labor was in government, this proportion may be too low. In the 2008 economic census data, there was no category for the

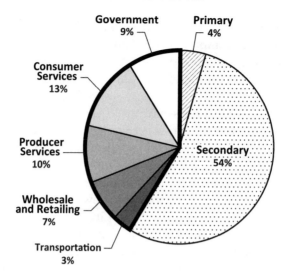

FIGURE 5.7 Distribution of the labor force (the number of employees in registered legal entities) across major sectors and subsectors in services. Data from SC-ECLG (2010).

government labor force. The government labor force includes only those in the "resources and public management" and "public administration and organizations" categories. Other activities, such as education, health/welfare, community services, and education, are lumped under the "consumer services" category, which has the largest percentage among all services. The relatively large sizes of these service categories are not surprising. Despite the potential undercount as noted, China's human services sector has experienced a substantial degree of liberalization since economic reform; it is engaging a growing number of new players, including both local and foreign investors. Furthermore, producer services as defined above are growing: They accounted for almost 10% of the entire economy, about as much as the government and consumer services sectors. In other words, the sector of business that serves other businesses is now a significant component of the Chinese economy.

As these industries are intended to serve the population, their geographical distribution should resemble the spatial distribution of the population. In other words, more services should be found in more densely populated areas, such as cities and urban areas. In terms of LQ, the spatial distribution of wholesale and retail services combined is quite similar to the overall distribution of the population: Most provinces and autonomous regions have LQs close to 1, indicating that the concentrations are close to the national average (0.8 < LQ < 1.2) (Figure 5.8). The region stretching along the Yangtze River has a slightly below-average concentration of wholesale and retail activities. On the other hand, we do expect large cities, such as Beijing and Shanghai, to have much higher concentrations of retail activities than the average.

We cannot discuss the spatial distributions of all subcategories of services here, but we can describe a few with unexpected spatial patterns. The 2008 Chinese economic census provided separate counts of labor for the public administration and organizations sector. This sector may be interpreted as a government sector, while other sectors, such as education and health/welfare, may be also partially government-operated. The employee numbers of the public administration and organizations sector were analyzed via LQs to indicate the sector's varying degrees of concentration over China, and the results are shown in Figure 5.9a. Clearly, there is a relatively large presence of this sector in the peripheral regions, probably related to the management of minority populations or border issues. Figure 5.9b shows the LQs for the finance sector. Quite unexpectedly, the coastal region does not have relatively high concentrations of financial employment; the interior, particularly Ningxia and Gansu, has the highest concentrations. Note that these concentration levels are not dramatically higher (the maximum is only around 2.0) than those for the rest of the country.

A word of caution is needed here, so that we do not interpret these maps beyond what the data can support. The economic census data were tabulated at the provincial level, and service activities, as mentioned before, are highly concentrated in cities. Thus the patterns observed at the provincial level reflect the provinces overall and are unlikely to reflect the situations in particular cities. Another factor is the recent explosive growth of e-commerce, which is part of the service sector. The geography of e-commerce and the logistical aspects of the online marketplace are discussed in the chapter on transportation (Chapter 8).

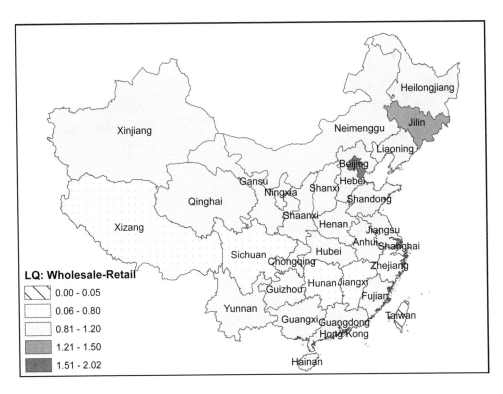

FIGURE 5.8 LQs of wholesale and retail industries. Data from SC-ECLG (2010).

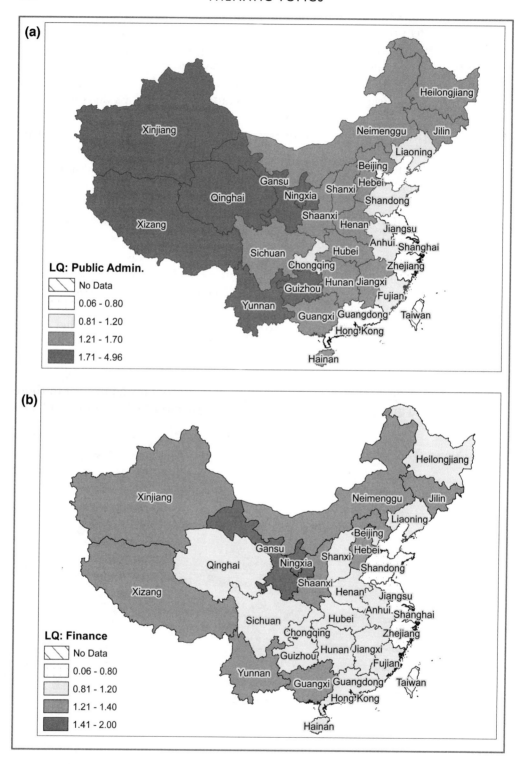

FIGURE 5.9 LQs of the (a) public administration and organizations sector and (b) finance sector. Data from SC-ECLG (2010).

• • • • • • • • • • • • • • • FINAL THOUGHTS • • • • • • • • • • • • • • • •

The current economic geography of China has developed within the context of the country's economic reform and globalization. Unlike the reform experience of the former socialist countries in Eastern Europe, the strong directives of the Chinese government in steering and regulating the country's economic activities have produced a different and relatively successful track record in raising China's overall productivity level and its people's living standards. In this chapter, we have illustrated the role of the government in the two waves of spatial restructuring: the implementation of the coastal development strategy, and preferential policies favoring coastal cities and SEZs. Space has been discussed as a tactic that facilitates capital circulation and capital accumulation, rather than merely an outcome of economic activities.

Understanding the active role of government produces useful insights into the debate over China's seemingly neoliberal trend and the benefits of globalization. First, the way that space is used to facilitate economic growth has demonstrated the Chinese government's efforts to retain its control over the economy. Unlike the typical command system, which was hostile to the market, a new, more flexible architecture that incorporates market mechanisms is under construction. This architecture allows the market to operate within the framework defined by the state. In this case, although the country's economic activities are increasingly guided by neoliberal principles, China will not become a pure market economy equivalent to those in the West. Chu and So (2010) call China's distinctive model of development "state neoliberalism."[6]

At another level, the active role of the Chinese government has echoed the arguments of Dicken (2011) and others that government power is consolidated, rather than weakened, through globalization. In his book, Dicken suggests four important roles for governments: as containers, regulators, competitors, and collaborators. This chapter does not address all of these roles, but the Chinese government's role as a regulator in controlling the spread of capital flows across space, formulating industrial strategy, and regulating the inflow of FDI has been vividly illustrated. In the context of China's party–state politics, economic success will consolidate the Chinese Communist party's ruling position and its role as the necessary force leading the future development of the country. China's economic geography has been shown to be crafted by government actions, rather than purely by market forces.

NOTES •

1. Preparation of this chapter was partially supported by the General Research Fund of the Research Grants Council of Hong Kong (project code: HKBU242111).

2. The speech, titled "On the Ten Major Relationships," is available online (www.marxists.org/reference/archive/mao/selected-works/volume-5/mswv5_51.htm).

3. The ladder-step doctrine is considered the Chinese version of the inverted-U model, which suggests that regional inequality is inevitable at the earlier stage of economic

growth; it will disappear when economic efficiency increases. See Fan (1997) for a detailed explanation.

4. "Compensation trade" is a form of trade in which foreign investors provide equipment and technology and are committed to buyback from the local government after a certain period of time.

5. For more information about ASEAN, see its website (http://asean.org).

6. Conceptually, "state neoliberalism" is not identical to "state capitalism"; please refer to Chu and So (2010) for details.

REFERENCES ●

Andrews-Speed, P. (2012). *The governance of energy in China: Transition to a low-carbon economy.* New York: Palgrave Macmillan.

Bongiorni, S. (2007). *A year without "Made in China."* Hoboken, NJ: Wiley.

Cai, F., Wang, M. Y., & Qu, Y. (2009). Zhongguo gongye chongxinpeizhi yu laodongli liudong chushi [Industrial relocation and trends of labor flows in China]. *Zhongguo Gongye Jingji [China Industrial Economics], 8,* 5–16.

Chan, K. W. (2010). Fundamentals of China's urbanisation and policy. *China Review, 10*(1), 63–94.

Chan, K. W. (2012). Migration and development in China: Trends, geography and current issues. *Migration and Development, 1*(2), 187–205.

Chan, K. W., & Hu, Y. (2003). Urbanisation in China in the 1990s: New definition, different series, and revised trends. *China Review, 3*(2), 49–71.

Cheng, G. (2011). *Zhongguo chexian Jianqu de xintansuo [Probe into the re-designation of counties as urban district].* Beijing: Jinji Kexue Chubanshe.

Chu, Y., & So, A. Y. (2010). State neoliberalism: The Chinese road to capitalism. In Y. Chu (Ed.), *Chinese capitalisms: Historical emergence and political implications* (pp. 46–72). New York: Palgrave Macmillan.

Dicken, P. (2011). *Global shift: Mapping the changing contours of the world economy* (6th ed.). New York: Guilford Press.

Enright, M. J., Scott, E. E., & Chang, K. (2005). *Regional powerhouse: The greater Pearl River Delta and the rise of China.* Singapore: Wiley (Asia).

Fan, C. C. (1997). Uneven development and beyond: Regional development theory in post-Mao China. *International Journal of Urban and Regional Research, 21*(4), 620–639.

Friedmann, J. (2005). *China's urban transition.* Minneapolis: University of Minnesota Press.

Gu, C., Shen, J., Wong, K.-Y., & Zhen, F. (2001). Regional polarization under the socialist-market system since 1978: A case study of Guangdong province in south China. *Environment and Planning A, 33*(1), 97–119.

Guangdong Statistics Bureau (GDSB). (1992). *Guangdong tongji nianjian 1992 [Guangdong statistics yearbook 1992].* Beijing: Zhongguo Tongji Chubanshe.

Guangdong Statistics Bureau (GDSB). (1996). *Guangdong tongji nianjian 1996 [Guangdong statistics yearbook 1996].* Beijing: Zhongguo Tongji Chubanshe.

Guangdong Statistics Bureau (GDSB) & State Statistics Bureau–Guangdong Survey Office (SSB-GDSO). (2012). *Guangdong tongji nianjian 2012 [Guangdong statistics yearbook 2012].* Beijing: Zhongguo Tongji Chubanshe.

Harvey, D. (1975). The geography of capitalist accumulation: A reconstruction of the Marxian theory. *Antipode, 2,* 9–21.

Harvey, D. (1982). *The limits to capital.* Oxford, UK: Blackwell.

He, S., & Wu, F. (2009). China's emerging neoliberal urbanism: Perspectives from urban redevelopment. *Antipode, 41*(2), 282–304.

Jefferson, G. H., Xu, W., & Zheng, Y. (1994). Productivity changes in Chinese industry: A comment. *Chinese Economic Review, 5,* 235–241.

Kong, B. (2010). *China's international petroleum policy.* Santa Barbara, CA: ABC-CLIO.

Li, S. (2009). The Pearl River Delta: The fifth Asian little dragon? In K. K. Wong (Ed.), *Hong Kong, Macau and the Pearl River Delta: A geographical survey* (pp. 178–207). Hong Kong: Hong Kong Educational.

Liew, L. H. (2005). China's engagement with neo-liberalism: Path dependency, geography and party self-reinvention. *Journal of Development Studies, 41*(2), 331–352.

Lin, G. C. S. (2002). The growth and structural change of Chinese cities: A contextual and geographic analysis. *Cities, 19*(5), 299–316.

Liu, J., Jin, R., & Zhou, K. (1999). *Zhongguo Zhengqu Dili [Geography of China's administrative zone].* Beijing: Kexue Chubanshe.

Liu, Y., & Feng, J. (2008). *Zhongguo jingji dili: Bianhuazhong de quyu geju [Chinese economic geography: Changing regional patterns].* Beijing: Suoduo Jingjimaoyi Daixue Chubanshe.

Naughton, B. (1995). *Growing out of the plan: Chinese economic reform 1978–1993.* Cambridge, UK: Cambridge University Press.

Naughton, B. (2007). *The Chinese economy: Transitions and growth.* Cambridge, MA: MIT Press.

Otsuka, K., Liu, D., & Murakami, N. (1998). *Industrial reform in China: Past performance and future prospects.* Oxford, UK: Clarendon Press.

Pannell, C. W. (2002). China's continuing urban transition. *Environment and Planning A, 34*(9), 1517–1589.

PetroChina. (2014). PetroChina Company Limited 2013 annual report. Retrieved February 24, 2015, from www.petrochina.com.cn/ptr/ndbg/201404/2e04894eb74141488c1c192 5bf13411d/files/40615da8916144309bc9f4960ba35739.pdf.

Sit, V. F. S. (2005). China's extended metropolitan regions: Formation and delimitation. *International Development Planning Review, 27*(3), 297–331.

State Council Economic Census Leading Group (SC-ECLG). (Ed.). (2010). *Zhongguo jingjipucha nianjian 2008 [China economic census yearbook 2008].* Beijing: Zhongguo Tongji Chubanshe.

State Statistical Bureau–Department of National Economic Integrated Statistics (SSB-DNEIS). (1999). *Xin Zhongguo 50 Nian Tongjiziliao Huibian [Collection of statistics for the 50th year of the new China].* Beijing: Zhongguo Tongji Chubanshe.

State Statistical Bureau–Department of Trade and External Economic Relations Statistics (SSB-DTEERS). (2012). *Zhongguo maoyiwaijin tongji nianjian 2012 [China trade and external economic statistical yearbook 2012].* Beijing: Zhongguo Tongji Chubanshe.

Stutz, F. P., & Warf, B. (2012). *The world economy: Geography, business and development.* Upper Saddle River, NJ: Pearson.

Sung, Y., Wong, Y., & Lai, P. (1995). *The fifth dragon: The emergence of the Pearl River Delta.* Singapore: Addison-Wesley.

Tuan, C., & Ng, L. F. (2008). China's FDI inflows and manufacturing structural adjustments: Inter-city competition in the globalized delta economies. In H. G. Blaine (Ed.), *Foreign direct investment* (pp. 85–121). Hauppauge, NY: Nova Science.

Walker, R., & Buck, D. (2007, July–August). The Chinese road: Cities in the transition to capitalism. *New Left Review, 46,* 39–66.

Wang, Y., & Wei, H. (2007). Chanye tezheng, kongjian jingzheng yu zhizaoye dilijizhong [Sectorial characteristics, spatial competition and geographical agglomeration of manufacturing industries: The Chinese experience]. *Guanli Shijie [Management World], 4,* 68–77, 171–172.

Wu, W., & Gaubatz, P. (2013). *The Chinese city.* London: Routledge.

Yao, S., Wei, K., & Liu, A. (2010). Economic growth, foreign investment and regional inequality in China. In G. Greenaway, C. Milner, & S. Yao (Eds.), *China and the world economy* (pp. 194–225). New York: Palgrave Macmillan.

Yeung, Y.-M., & Xu, X. (Eds.). (1992). *China's coastal cities.* Honolulu: University of Hawaii Press.

Zhao, S. X. B., Chan, R. C. K., & Sit, K. T. O. (2003). Globalisation and the dominance of large cities in contemporary China. *Cities, 20*(4), 265–278.

Zhou, Y. (1991). The metropolitan interlocking region in China: A preliminary hypothesis. In N. Ginsburg, B. Koppel, & T. G. McGee (Eds.), *The extended metropolis: Settlement transition in Asia* (pp. 89–112). Honolulu: University of Hawaii Press.

FURTHER READING ●

Enright, M. J., Scott, E. E., & Chang, K. (2005). *Regional powerhouse: The greater Pearl River Delta and the rise of China.* Singapore: Wiley (Asia).

Harvey, D. (2005). *A brief history of neoliberalism.* Oxford, UK: Oxford University Press.

Rawski, T. G. (2006). Social capabilities and Chinese economic growth. In W. Tang & B. Holzner (Eds.), *Social change in contemporary China* (pp. 89–103). Pittsburgh, PA: University of Pittsburgh Press.

Wei, H. (2014). Regional economic development in China: Agglomeration and relocation. In H. Wei, M. Bai, & Y. Wang (Eds.), *The micro-analysis of regional economy in China: A perspective of firm relocation* (pp. 1–27). Singapore: World Scientific.

CHAPTER 6

Chinese Cities
Growing in Size and Number

LEARNING OBJECTIVES

★ Learn how the word "city" and related terms are defined and used in China.

★ Understand the role of the government's economic development policy in China's urbanization history.

★ Learn about the size of the Chinese city system and its geographical extent.

★ Understand the internal structure of some Chinese cities.

★ Learn about the recent developments in Chinese cities.

KEY CONCEPTS AND TERMS

urbanization;
city system and urban hierarchy;
hukou system; rank–size distribution;
primacy; ethnocentric view of city design;
land leasing; new city centers;
megalopolis

HOW URBANIZED IS CHINA?

In Chapter 3, we pointed out that China's population is not just large; it is also very unevenly distributed, with a relatively high concentration in the east (especially along the coast) and a relatively sparse settlement in the west. The spatial disparities of population distribution are exhibited not only at the national level, but also at the regional and local levels. The population is clearly concentrated in cities. According to the Population Reference Bureau, an estimate of 57% of China's population in 2017 resided in urban areas.[1] The Population Reference Bureau also reported that 47% of the population lived in urban areas in 2010, and that the rate had been increasing by 10% in the 7 years since 2010.[2] Given that China's population is close to 1.4 billion, then almost 800 million Chinese reside in cities or urban environments. According to the 2010 U.S. census, the New York City urban cluster, including parts of the states of New York, New Jersey, and Connecticut, had more than 18 million people.[3] To accommodate the urban population in China, therefore, would require more than 40 cities equivalent to the size of the New York City urban cluster.

In this chapter, we review China's current urbanization level and city systems. In brief, "urbanization" refers to the process that leads to the growth of urban areas and that is due to the migration of population from rural to urban areas. By "urbanization level," we mean the proportion of the nation's population found in urban areas or cities. Urban areas do not emerge haphazardly. Their existence and growth are related to history, the dynamic forces in the surrounding areas, and their functional relationships. Therefore, we also provide an account of the historical development of Chinese cities. Moreover, cities within a country are interdependent; their relationships can be perceived as the functioning of a system of cities. This chapter discusses the relationships among cities in terms of their population sizes. Each city also can be treated as a system, as its different elements are functionally related and exhibit a certain spatial organization. The internal structure of "typical" Chinese cities is thus reviewed. Finally, recently developed Chinese cities have been formed differently from typical Western cities. We highlight some of these features, which are the results of urbanization in "Chinese style."

CITIES IN CHINA

An urban area is usually characterized by its high population density. Therefore, some countries use population density level as the criterion for classifying an area as urban or not. However, different countries use different density levels as their criterion, and population size is also often used. In the United States, 1,000 people per square mile (386 people per square kilometer, or km^2) is the general criterion adopted to determine if an area is urban. Places with more than 2,500 people can be defined as urban clusters or urbanized areas. In Argentina, for instance, populated centers with 2,000 people or more may be regarded as an urban area (United Nations Statistics Division, 2013). In China, the general criterion is 1,500 people per km^2, but there are other administrative criteria (United Nations Statistics Division, 2013).

What's in a Name?: The Word "City" in China

In many countries, cities are expected to be urban; areas beyond cities are often classified as rural. Unfortunately, the word "city" in Chinese is *shi* (市), and it doesn't necessarily mean the same thing as "city" (城市) in the English-speaking world. Figure 6.1 (based on Chan & Hu, 2003) shows the geographical administrative hierarchy of China. The provincial-level units were discussed in detail in Chapter 1. Below the provincial level are prefecture-, county-, and township-level units. Some units have clear urban designations (darker shading in Figure 6.1), and some are clearly rural (lighter shading). Some units can be either urban or rural (no shade).

At the provincial level, the two special administrative regions (SARs) of Hong Kong and Macau are cities, and they can be regarded as urban units. (Small portions of the two SARs are regarded as rural, but their subcity-level units do not fit into this national geographical hierarchy.) The four autonomous municipalities are also regarded as "cities" (e.g., "Shanghai" in Chinese is literally the city of Shanghai), but a municipality can include urban districts (at the county level) and rural townships (at the township level). At the prefecture level (地级), the term "cities" (in Chinese, *shi* or 市) is again used, but cities do not necessarily mean urban areas. Within the prefecture-level cities, some areas may be designed as urban districts, but some counties under the prefecture-level cities may have rural townships. Cities also exist at the county level. Again, these cities are not necessarily urban. Cities can be rural towns or townships coexisting with urban towns and urban streets.

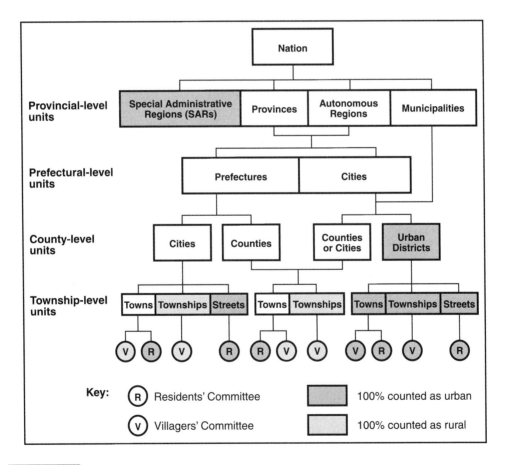

FIGURE 6.1 The Chinese geographical administrative hierarchy, and definitions of cities and urban areas. Based on Chan and Hu (2003).

As Figure 6.1 indicates, "urban" or "rural" is defined mostly at the township level. If all towns, townships, and streets are urban, then they can form an urban district under a prefecture city or municipality. The term "city" (市) used in China is not equivalent to "urban"; it is a purely administrative term that has nothing to do with the density of population or the spatial layout of the area. Cities at different levels of the hierarchy enjoy certain privileges and special treatment in terms of power and access to resources, and so local jurisdictions would like to achieve the status of cities. Thus the number of "cities" in China has been increasing over time, partly due to the desirability of the designation. This issue was briefly addressed in Chapter 5.

How Large Are Chinese Cities?

According to the United Nations *2008 Demographic Yearbook* (United Nations Statistics Division, 2010), China had 656 cities with a population larger than 100,000.[4] These cities accounted for more than 580 million people, about 45% of the nation's 2005 estimated population of 1.3 billion. According to the World Bank, more than half the Chinese population lived in cities in 2013.[5] Among these cities, 162 had a population over 1 million. The largest city was Shanghai with over 14 million, followed by Beijing with 11.5 million. The 10 largest cities have a total population of about 83 million. The 20 largest Chinese cities are listed in Table 6.1, together with their population sizes. The largest is the municipality of Shanghai, a "city" with the political status of a province; the last city on the top-20 list is Qingdao in Shandong province, with a population of over 2.7 million. Its size is very close to that of 19th-ranked Zibo, another city in Shandong province. In fact, the sizes of cities after the 12th-ranked city decline quite gradually—a phenomenon that we explore in greater detail later in this chapter.

The locations of these 20 largest cities are shown in Figure 6.2. All these cities are found in the eastern half of the country. In fact, most of these cities are in the coastal provinces, with the exceptions of Wuhan in Hubei province; Xi'an in Shaanxi province; Chengdu, capital of Sichuan province; Chongqing, an independent municipality; Guiyang in Guizhou province; and Kunming in Yunnan province. No other noncoastal provinces have very large cities, even in the eastern part of the country.

As Table 6.1 indicates, many of these large cities are also provincial capitals, but no provincial capitals west of Sichuan province are among the largest cities in the country, although they may be the largest in their respective provinces (see Figure 6.3). Many of these large cities also served as the historical capitals of unified China or kingdoms within China during its long history. For instance, Guangzhou was the capital of the South Han kingdom during the Five Dynasties and Ten Kingdoms period (五代十國). Thus, a city's having been a capital at one time has a lingering effect on its importance and growth. This should not come as a surprise, as these cities were probably chosen in the past because of advantages in their locations. These locational factors may transcend time and have political and economic uses in more recent eras.

TABLE 6.1. The 20 Largest Cities in China			
Rank	Cities	Population	Status
1	Shanghai	14,348,535	Municipality
2	Beijing	11,509,595	Current capital of China; municipality
3	Chongqing	9,691,901	Historical capital; municipality
4	Guangzhou	8,524,826	Historical capital; provincial capital of Guangdong
5	Wuhan	8,312,700	Historical capital; provincial capital of Hubei
6	Tianjin	7,499,181	Municipality; "treaty port" (see text)
7	Shenzhen	7,008,831	Special economic zone (SEZ)
8	Dongguan	6,445,777	SEZ
9	Shenyang	5,303,053	Historical capital; provincial capital of Liaoning
10	Xi'an	4,481,508	Historical capital; provincial capital of Shaanxi
11	Chengdu	4,333,541	Historical capital; provincial capital of Sichuan
12	Nanjing	3,624,234	Historical capital; provincial capital of Jiangsu
13	Harbin	3,481,504	Provincial capital of Heilongjiang; "treaty port"
14	Dalian	3,245,191	
15	Changchun	3,225,557	Provincial capital of Jilin
16	Kunming	3,035,406	Provincial capital of Yunnan
17	Jinan	2,999,934	Provincial capital of Shandong
18	Guiyang	2,985,105	Provincial capital of Guizhou
19	Zibo	2,817,479	
20	Qingdao	2,720,972	"Treaty port"

Note. Data (for the latest available year, ranging from 1989 to 2008) from United Nations Statistics Division (2010).

CHINESE URBANIZATION

The current relatively high rate of urbanization in China is in stark contrast to the low levels of urbanization in China during the 1960s and 1970s. While the current urbanization rate (57%) is slightly above the global average, it is lower than those in developed countries such as the United States and Canada (81%), but higher than in poorer developing countries.[6] India, the second largest country in terms of population size, has an urbanization rate of only 31–32%. For developed countries, including many in Europe, the rates of urbanization gradually rose over about a century, from very low levels in the early 1900s to the current high levels. By contrast, China has experienced dramatic increases in its urbanization rate in just a few decades.

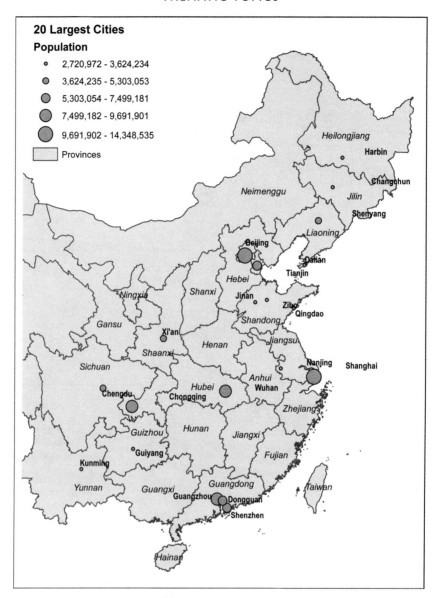

FIGURE 6.2 Locations of the 20 largest cities in China. (In this figure, "provinces" include autonomous regions.)

Emergence of Ancient Chinese Cities

In industrialized countries such as those in Europe and the United States, the emergence of cities was often associated with the establishment of economic activities, such as the presence of raw materials for manufacturing or transshipment. Although economic factors have played an overwhelming role in the growth of certain Chinese cities in recent decades, many large Chinese cities were established mainly for political and administrative reasons. As noted above, many of the largest

FIGURE 6.3 Provincial capitals in China.

cities in China (including the current capital, Beijing) have been capitals of the nation for many dynasties (see Table 6.1). The cities of Chongqing, Xi'an, and Nanjing, for example, have all served as the nation's capital. Some other large cities have been or currently are provincial capitals, such as Guangzhou, Wuhan, and Haerbin (Harbin) (Huang, 2007). From a geographical perspective, these cities were not selected randomly, but for some geographical or strategic reasons. For instance, Xi'an, China's capital for several dynasties, has the locational advantage of being near the confluence of the Huang He (Yellow River) and the Wei River. Because of this location, the region has fertile soil and thus had a strong economic base, from the perspective of the ancient economy. Much more recently, Chongqing, which was part of Sichuan province before 1997, was selected as a temporary capital during wartime (World War II and the subsequent Chinese civil war)—partly because of its distance from the Japanese occupation in the northeast, and partly because of the region's relatively robust food production capacity. To a large degree, Sichuan province and Chongqing could be self-sufficient if they were cut off from the rest of the country.

Traditional Chinese cities performed primarily political and administrative functions, but they also supported other associated activities—serving, for instance, as military bases, transportation hubs, and/or religious/cultural centers. However, their roles as centers of economic activity were limited because the Chinese economy was dominated by agricultural production. Cities served as centers for the exchange of food and products. The urban–rural dichotomy was not obvious in traditional Chinese cities. Industries were not a prominent urban feature in most cities (with the exception of selected cities in the northeast and "treaty cities" like Shanghai; see below) until the Communists took over the country. The economic base of traditional Chinese cities was very different from that of today's urban areas.

The sizes of Chinese cities were often associated with their status in the administrative hierarchy and the rank of the assigned officials. The importance of economic activities, particularly trade and commerce, did not gain ground in Chinese cities until the Song dynasty, when port cities experienced significant growth. The growth of urban centers was also associated with the influence of foreign powers. When the Qing dynasty was defeated in several wars in the mid-19th century, China was forced to sign many treaties. The terms of these treaties included the opening of ports for foreign trade and the concession of special districts to Western powers. Some cities were opened to foreign occupation, including Shanghai, Tianjin, Nanjing, and Qingdao (Table 6.1). Many of these "treaty cities" became major urban centers and have continued to flourish in post–World War II China until the present day. The historical legacy of these foreign occupations in these cities can still be seen by visitors. The German occupation of Qingdao, for example, brought German beer-brewing technology and skill to China; Tsingtao beer is now a world-class beer from China.[7]

Urbanization before Economic Reform

A major difference from Western cities is that the growth and decline of Chinese cities have been strongly affected, if not altogether determined, by the economic development policy of the Chinese central government. That policy has evolved from the one based on extreme socialist ideology for achieving equality to the more recent capitalistic economic policy of letting some people get rich first (see Chapter 5). Different stages of these policies have influenced the growth and decline of cities in different ways.

Europe's early urbanization history was closely tied to the industrialization process. Cities served as centers of manufacturing industries and thus offered employment opportunities. Rural populations migrated to cities to become city dwellers and factory workers, creating waves of urbanization. When the Communists took over China after World War II and the civil war, defeating the Kuomintang party (國民黨), the government inherited a relatively unbalanced urban system: large and prosperous cities in the eastern and coastal regions of the country, but a relatively deserted interior. Governed by Communist ideology, the government invested heavily in heavy manufacturing industries in cities away from the coastal region, with the intent of achieving a more balanced urban system. On the other hand, the Chinese government was very cautious, not letting industries in cities become magnets for a massive rural–urban migration that would create an urban population explosion.

Concomitant with the industrialization of smaller interior cities was the creation of the household registration (hukou, or 戶口) system. The system's explicit purpose was to keep track of where individuals lived. However, where people lived affected the welfare services, other services, and rights they might be entitled to. The system was rigid and deterred individuals from moving from rural areas to cities in search of industrial jobs. In order to be employed, individuals often had to obtain certificates from the local governments where they intended to reside. For rural residents moving to cities, obtaining such certificates was often very difficult, if not impossible. Thus rural–urban migration was discouraged in the early decades of Communist rule. Given the level of industrial development in major cities, higher levels of urbanization should have occurred, but the *hukou* system held back the urbanization process in China, resulting in a situation known as "underurbanization."

Two movements during the 1960s countered the attraction of cities due to industrial development. The Great Leap Forward (1958–1960) led to disastrous failures in agricultural production, which pushed many urban dwellers back to rural areas to engage in agricultural activities. During the Cultural Revolution in the late 1960s, many urban dwellers—young and old, educated professionals and unlettered laborers—were sent to rural areas to be "reeducated" ideologically and to participate in manual labor, including agricultural production. Both these movements lowered the level of urbanization occasionally (the so-called "deurbanization") and held the level of urbanization to about 17% at the beginning of the 1970s (Huang, 2007).

Modern Urbanization, Open-Door Policy, and Globalization

The new economic development policy adopted by the Chinese leadership at the end of the 1970s shifted the focus of urban development from social equality to economic growth. However, this shift did not alter the ideology that the government should play a critical role in the evolution of the entire economic system. Instead of investing heavily in industries in interior and small to medium-size cities, the government turned toward the coastal areas, and locations were chosen strategically. The new policy was clearly manifested in the creation of the special economic zones (SEZs; see Chapter 5). Four zones were created in 1979: Shenzhen, which is north of Hong Kong; Zhuhai, which interfaces with Macau to the south and east; Shantou; and Xiamen. The first three of these are in Guangdong province, while Xiamen is in Fijian province. All these SEZs are coastal seaports in the south and southeast, in close proximity to Hong Kong and Taiwan. The zones were very successful in attracting massive amounts of foreign direct investment (FDI), with a significant portion coming from overseas Chinese and from Hong Kong and Taiwan (see Chapter 12). Following the success of SEZs, more cities were opened up to FDI during the mid-1980s. The existing SEZs were expanded, and new ones were added.

Some of these SEZs were originally small towns or villages. They were chosen to be developed for specific geographical and strategic reasons. Being a seaport along the coast was definitely a critical factor for export industries and the import of raw materials. Forty years ago, no one knew where some of these SEZs were, but now they are among the largest cities in China. Many manufacturing industries from Hong Kong and Taiwan have relocated to these SEZs and other cities in China. The Greater Pearl River Delta region—which includes the provincial capital of Guangzhou, the SEZs of Shenzhen and Zhuhai, and the city of Dongguan—forms the largest and most important manufacturing belt in China, if not the world. These cities together are home to more than 20 million people, and still more live in some of the medium-size to large cities in the vicinity. Whereas industrial growth has been the major force for urban growth in most small to medium-size cities during the past one to two decades, the urban growth of larger cities has been associated with financial and commercial activities. The continuing expansion of Shanghai city proper into the new district of Pudong to the east is an example. Overall, the urban economy of Chinese cities of different sizes has been closely tied to the global economy, with foreign investment playing a critical role in the Chinese economic system.

The arrival of FDI in cities created many job opportunities. But if people were not allowed to move into the cities because of the strict operation of the *hukou* system, then these jobs would not be filled, and cities would not be able to grow. As the Chinese government adopted an open-door policy to fuel the economic growth of cities, the government also relaxed, reformed, or (to a large extent) abandoned the *hukou* system. Starting in 1984, farmers were allowed to move into towns and cities to work in non-state sectors only. However, these sectors were growing and generated plenty of light manufacturing jobs, such as in consumer goods and services. People thus moved into cities, were employed in many industrial jobs, and raised the level of urbanization first to 30% and then to 40% (Huang, 2007). The influx of farmers and other members of the rural population into towns and cities provided cheap labor to fuel the expansion of industries. This occurred despite the fact that workers in the non-state sectors were often denied various types of benefits, such as housing, pensions, and medical care. These rural–urban migrants constituted the so-called "floating population," which amounted to over 100 million, according to some studies. The massive supply of cheap labor was also a major competitive factor attracting FDI. Industries relocated from overseas to the mainland, especially to the SEZs and other cities in the coastal region.

The increase in China's urbanization level during the past several decades is unprecedented. Many developed European countries, such as England, took almost a century to raise their level of urbanization from about 20% to over 50%. Latin American countries such as Mexico took about the same time to reach their current urbanization level. China reached an urbanization level of over 50%, comparable to that of many Western nations, in about 50–60 years (McGee, Lin, Marton, Wang, & Wu, 2007, p. 204). Obviously, such a massive and rapid influx of the rural population into cities imposed huge pressures and created many urban ills, which we discuss later in this chapter.

CITY SYSTEMS, SIZE DISTRIBUTION, AND URBAN HIERARCHY

It has become a tradition in modern China to favor cities in the east and along the coast. However, the emphasis on developing small to medium-size interior cities between 1960 and 1970 has also had an impact. In studying an urban system, a standard approach is to evaluate the distribution of city sizes. The "rank–size rule" has served as a benchmark for comparing city size distributions across countries and over time. The rank–size rule refers to the statistical relationship between the rank of a city in population (compared to other cities) and its population size. Specifically, the rank–size rule states that after cities are ranked from the largest to the smallest by population, the size of the city at a given rank (say, r) should be about the size of the largest city ($r = 1$) divided by r. Let's denote the size of the city at rank r as P_r, and the size of the largest city as P_1. According to the rank–size rule, $P_r = P_1/r$. For instance, the population of a city ranked 10th in the system (i.e., P_{10}) should have a population of $P_1/10$. Many urban systems across different countries at different stages of economic development exhibit this general rank–size regularity. However, minor deviations from the regularity are quite common, as discussed further below.

Figure 6.4a shows a hypothetical rank–size distribution of 20 cities, with the largest city having a population of 100,000. This rank–size distribution follows the

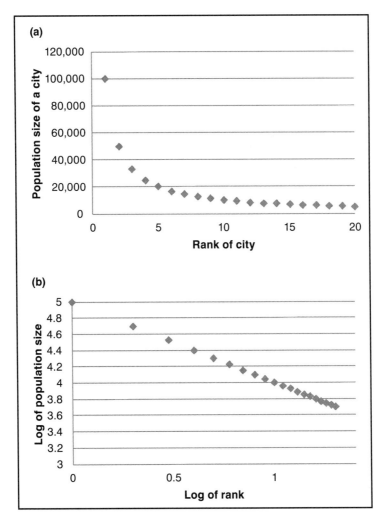

FIGURE 6.4 Rank–size relationship of a set of hypothetical cities, in (a) normal scale and (b) logarithmic scale.

rank–size rule exactly; for example, the population size of the second-ranked city is 50,000, or 100,000/2. Such a distribution always has an interesting characteristic: If both the rank and the population size are in logarithmic scale, the distribution will be linear, or a log-normal distribution. In Figure 6.4b, both the ranks and sizes are in logarithmic scale, and therefore the rank–size distribution follows a straight line. The log-normal distribution of the rank–size relationship has been discussed thoroughly in both the theoretical and empirical literature. Some have argued that the regularity indicates that the optimal city size distribution follows a natural power law (Gabaix, Gopikrishnan, Plerou, & Stanley, 2003). Empirical studies show that city systems in many countries follow the log-normal distribution closely, although not exactly, and that many of those countries are the more developed nations. Rank–size distributions in developing or poorer countries and countries of former European colonies tend to exhibit a "primacy" situation, in which the largest city is much larger than the second or third largest cities in the country, and it dominates the entire urban system (Carroll, 1982). Primacy is found in many countries in Africa that have been strongly influenced by colonialism, and in some Asian countries, such as Thailand. In all these nations, the largest cities are much larger than the other cities (Moomaw & Alwosabi, 2004).

In the case of China, we have analyzed 656 cities with populations of more than 100,000.[8] The actual rank–size distribution is shown in Figure 6.5. Shanghai had

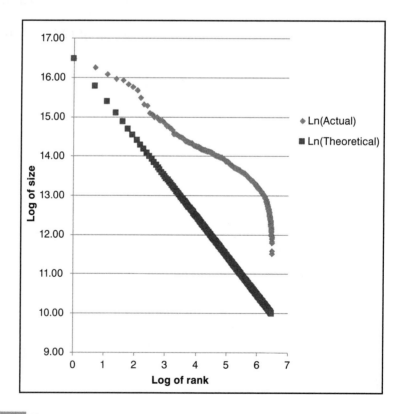

FIGURE 6.5 Theoretical and actual rank–size distribution of Chinese cities with populations over 100,000. Ln, natural log.

the largest population in 2008. Using its population, we have also derived the theoretical distribution ($P_r = P_1/r$) and plotted this in Figure 6.5. As we have used the logarithmic scale for both axes, the theoretical distribution forms a straight line. The actual rank–size distribution does not follow the rank–size rule represented by the theoretical distribution. Cities at all ranks, except Shanghai (the largest), had population sizes larger than those estimated according to the rank–size rule. As the city size distributions of many developed countries follow the rank–size rule quite closely, the log-normal distribution is sometimes interpreted as the optimal city size distribution when the development of the cities is due to a large number of factors within the market mechanism and is not dominated by one or just a few factors. Deviations from the log-normal distribution may indicate the presence of a few dominant factors (Carroll, 1982). The significant deviation of the actual rank–size distribution from the theoretical one strongly suggests that city system development in China has been influenced by one or only a few factors.

This conclusion should not be surprising. Before the adoption of the open-door economic policy, the growth of large and coastal cities in China had been suppressed to favor the growth of small to medium-size inland cities to achieve a more balanced city distribution. The implementation of this policy diverted resources from larger cities to smaller cities and boosted the growth of smaller inland cities. Thus larger cities were not as large as they might have been without government intervention, and small to medium-size cities became larger than would be expected without government assistance.

The convex shape of the actual rank–size distribution of Chinese cities is not the result of a recent phenomenon. City systems before 1990 already exhibited a certain degree of convexity in their distributions, indicating that the Chinese city systems had more large cities than predicted by the rank–size rule (Chen, 1991). Despite the government's focus on developing coastal and large cities in the eastern region, the growth of small and medium-size cities continued after 1990 to create a more balanced system of cities (Xu & Zhu, 2009).

INTERNAL STRUCTURE OF CHINESE CITIES

Besides studying the relationships among cities as a system, it is important to understand the spatial organization within a city. Each city is itself a system with interrelated elements. The literature in urban geography has thoroughly discussed the internal structure of cities in the Western world. Some of the typical models of cities include the concentric-zone model, characterized by several concentric rings of socioeconomic classes; the sector model, reflecting the development of different types of land use along major transportation routes; and the multiple-nuclei model, highlighting suburban development and the emergence of a polycentric city (Knox & McCarthy, 2011). Regardless of the differences among these models, the general structure of Western cities is characterized by a central business district, surrounded by high-density residential and commercial areas, with residential suburbs and heavy industries in the periphery. A somewhat reversed general city layout can be found in many Latin American cities, with high-socioeconomic-status residential areas at the center and slums or squatters' homes in the periphery (Ford, 1996; Griffin & Ford, 1980).

These models, however, do not generally describe the internal structure of many Chinese cities. This is partly due to the unique historical development of these cities in China, and partly to the recent economic development policy. Earlier in this chapter, we pointed out that many ancient Chinese cities were, or still are, political centers primarily performing administrative functions. The internal layouts of these cities tend to be different from those of newer cities, especially the cities in the SEZs created by the recent economic policies. The newer cities inherit little political legacy, and therefore their internal structures are driven primarily by current political and economic processes, as we discuss later in this chapter in more detail. Therefore, a single model of a city's internal structure is unlikely to fit all Chinese cities. Nevertheless, some general principles of city layout can be identified and are discussed here. Understanding the policies and processes of urban land development in Chinese cities will also provide some insights into the cities' current structure.

The internal layout of traditional Chinese cities was strongly influenced by the world view and cosmology of Chinese civilization. While an ethnocentric view is not unique to the Chinese, the Chinese cosmology put the country at the center of the world ("China" in Chinese is 中國 or *Zhong-guo,* meaning "the central kingdom"), surrounded by successive rectangular zones instead of a circular pattern (Tuan, 1974). The successive zones represented decreasing levels of culture from the imperial center. This world view was used as part of the model for the layout of many older Chinese cities serving as capitals or administrative centers at different levels of the political geography. The city centers were often occupied by administrative buildings, including palaces, such as the Forbidden City in Beijing. Layouts of the royal cities possess certain symbolic characteristics. The cities follow the cardinal north–south–east–west orientation, with a square or rectangular shape defined by walls. The walls have 12 gates representing the 12 months. The inner section, symbolizing the center of the world, was exclusively for the royals, surrounded by a buffer zone for interaction between royals and others. Markets were outside the royal palace, often in the north; sacred and religious places, such as altars or ancestral temples, were to the south. A principal street usually led from the south gate of the palace to the south gate of the city wall. The layout of inner Beijing exemplifies some of these characteristics, as well as the interface between an historical urban legacy and recent political and economic forces.

Figure 6.6 is a schematic layout of present-day Beijing, showing the Forbidden City, which was the imperial palace, at the center of the city. Again, the imperial palace or the residence of government officials has traditionally been at the center of Chinese city development (Tuan, 1974). The Forbidden City is surrounded by several layers—first the Imperial City, and then the Inner City, which is the administrative area of the government. The palace faces south; the road from the palace forms the principal axis of the city, and was also the road by which the emperor exited the palace to enter the city. In the south, on one side, is the area for religious rituals. In the case of Beijing, the Temple of Heaven, located southeast of the palace,

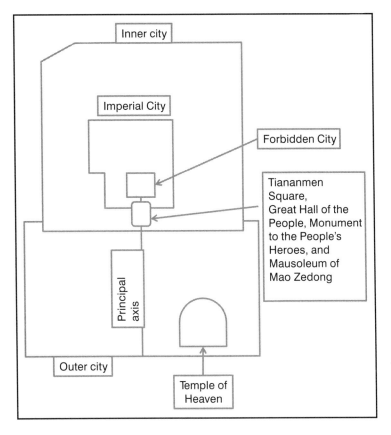

FIGURE 6.6 Schematic layout of the center of Beijing. Based on Tuan (1974, p. 165).

was designated for that purpose. Although other royal cities—such as Ch'ang-an (the current city of Xi'an), the capital of the Tang dynasty—did not strictly follow these layout principles, the overall internal structures of these cities express these principles to a certain degree.

Residential areas are distributed around the center, and commercial activities intermingle with residential structures. Communist rule has modified the centers of former royal cities by creating large monuments and public squares, such as Tiananmen Square (south of the Forbidden City), for large-scale public gatherings to glorify the socialist state. Industrial establishments, both light and heavy manufacturing, have been placed at the edges of the cities. Whereas a central business district forms the center of many North American and European cities, the center of Beijing (and many other older Chinese cities) is dominated by historical landmarks and government offices. In Beijing, business establishments are scattered around the city, with no clear central location. Most businesses are at the intersections of major ring roads (beltways) and arteries radiating from the city center.

The general layout of these historical Chinese cities is usually not the same as that of the newer cities, where city development has been strongly influenced by economic activities. Economic forces have even transformed the layout of some older cities like Nanjing, which was the capital during part of the Ming dynasty and served as the capital of several other dynasties for relatively short periods. Imperial structures or government buildings are not at the center of Nanjing's layout, partly because the palace of the Ming dynasty was destroyed by the Qing dynasty. The center of today's Nanjing is the Drum Tower district; the adjacent district is the administrative district for the municipal government. To understand the development of newer cities, we need to understand land market operations and land transaction processes adopted after the open-door policy was initiated in 1978.

THE CHANGING AND GLOBALIZING CHINESE CITIES

The internal structure of cities is strongly affected by social forces and economic development (Bourne, 1982), and economic development is closely tied to land development policy. The primary economic function for Chinese cities before 1949 was consumption. Cities were places where people could buy or exchange goods and merchandise (Skinner, 1964). Agricultural products were brought from the surrounding rural areas into city marketplaces for purchase. Places with relatively small population sizes might be able to support a market only a few days a week rather than every day. These so-called "periodic markets" were common in cities and towns in the less populated parts of China (Skinner, 1964). After 1949, the primary economic function of cities shifted from consumption to production. Factories were distributed within cities without being concentrated in specific areas. Because production was geared toward serving the domestic local or regional markets, a relatively undifferentiated urban landscape was typical. There were no clear specialized districts for industries or commercial functions, and thus a central business district was absent from most traditional Chinese cities at that time. Even after the start of economic reform in 1978, production in most cities was still oriented toward the local or regional markets. Some larger cities expanded their scope to the national market level, supported by better transportation infrastructure and logistics. Production serving the global economy was limited to the SEZs, however.

After 1980, the open-door economic policy fueled the notion that China could be a major player in the global economy. This national aspiration was put into practice at the city level as production shifted toward the global market. The shift in production orientation was particularly apparent in the larger cities in the east. Many of these cities positioned themselves to enter the world city system over the decade. In the 1990s, China's effort to join the World Trade Organization, and its bids to host the Olympic Games and other international events, began putting the largest Chinese cities (such as Beijing, Shanghai, and Guangzhou) into the international spotlight. To become international cities, they had to become more like other global cities in terms of layout and structure. However, most of these cities were traditionally laid out, as described above: They did not have a clear central business district, and the land-use patterns were somewhat unorganized. Thus, the role of municipal planning has increased. Its goals include developing specialized land-use areas, such as the commercial area of Nanjing Road in Shanghai; relocating old and low-quality residential areas and industrial areas to city peripheries; and improving and modernizing the infrastructure, including transportation (Gaubatz, 2005). The overall intent is to redevelop these traditional cities into modernized cities with organized city layouts, while preserving the historical Chinese characteristics of the urban landscape.

Land Tenure Systems and Urban Development

Broad plans for urban development were made, but executing those plans was not straightforward; numerous obstacles were in the way. One obstacle was the land tenure system in Chinese cities. Before 1988, all land in China was owned by the central government, but was allocated to administrative or local units without charge. The policy adopted in 1988 marked the beginning of land reform. It allowed the land-use rights to be temporally transferred for payment; in other words, a land-leasing system was introduced. Local jurisdictions were also empowered to collect land-use taxes, ending the era of free land use. However, most land that was allocated in the past through the administrative process is still allocated administratively; that is, the earlier process continues. Therefore, a dual-land-market system emerged, with both leased and administratively allocated land. Under this dual-market system, three main types of land ownership exist: collective ownership (farmland in rural areas is owned by farmers collectively); government ownership (land owned by central or local governments is allocated to various administrative units); and lease (land-use rights for land the government owns are obtained by paying the government). Rural land owned collectively cannot be leased to individuals, but the state or local governments can acquire the land through the administrative allocation process. Eventually, governments can then lease the land to individuals.

Under this system, city governments monopolize the supply of land available for leasing. Leasing land provides a major stream of revenue, which can be used to improve urban infrastructure. Essentially, through the leasing process, the market mechanism determines the price of land. Despite the existence and popularity of the land-leasing system, however, most of the land is still allocated through the administrative channel. With this dual-market system, land redevelopment in traditional cities is affected by two types of processes. Leasing land allows city governments to redevelop the city centers with office buildings and other high-value land uses. FDI has been attracted to city centers to play a role in the urban renewal process. Redevelopment through the land-leasing system has usually resulted in a more organized urban structure because planning usually precedes the redevelopment. Redevelopment of land under administrative control is more haphazard; it tends to be rapid, without thorough planning. Government owners of this type of land may work with other users through the land-leasing mechanism in the redevelopment process. Large-scale relocations of residential and business areas from city centers to the suburbs are now feasible with the market mechanism in place.

The dual-market system has transformed the traditional, relatively compact city layout into a dispersed metropolitan structure with intense redevelopment around the city center, rapid suburbanization, and "leapfrog" sprawl toward rural areas.

Thus, it is not uncommon to have commercial or modern residential high-rises adjacent to one- or two-story slum-like shacks near city centers. Because redevelopment near the city center is usually based on land parcels, and the parcels are usually not large, the developers of large-scale new development projects (e.g., housing complexes, economic zones, or technology parks) are unlikely to find suitable land near the city proper. These large-scale developments are usually launched by municipal governments or departments of governments, and take place in the urban fringe through acquiring land from farmers. "Economic and technology development zones" (ETDZs) have been established to attract such investment projects, particularly from foreign investors. Such development projects and associated large-scale residential developments contribute to urban sprawl in many Chinese cities.

Given such complex land tenure systems, and the dynamics of the processes involved, developing a general model of city land use is quite challenging, although models of some specific cities like Guangzhou have been suggested (Wu & Yeh, 1999). From a planning perspective, ideal urban forms for Chinese cities have been proposed (Gaubatz, 1999). How long it will take Chinese cities to make the transition into a more organized and stable urban layout may be difficult to predict, but the pace should be closely tied to the pace of the overall development of the Chinese economy.

A "New Deal" in Chinese Cities

The Chinese urbanization process is part of the economic development process. In other words, cities that are bigger and more modern, and can attract a lot of businesses, are the fruits of economic development. If local governments and officials are able to achieve this, they will be rewarded. A universal indicator of successful economic development is gross domestic product (GDP) or, more specifically, per capita GDP. The measure of GDP reflects the value of goods and services, which may include infrastructure. Given that the country is entirely focused on economic development with GDP growth as the goal, local governments have leveraged all resources to boost GDP increases, regardless of whether the growth is sustainable.

Led by the central government to a large extent, local governments have invested in various types of infrastructure projects, particularly in the transportation sector. There have been massive spending sprees by local governments in large and small cities across China. Because Chinese inner cities are often old and compact, redevelopment there would be slow and costly. Therefore, many new transportation-related projects are not close to the old city centers. A high-speed rail system is expanding throughout the country (see Chapter 8 on transportation), but building the new high-speed rail stations in old city centers has not been considered. Instead, new stations are being built in the suburban fringes or city outskirts. These outlying new facilities have supported the development of new cities adjacent to the old cities. Aviation infrastructure is also expanding. New, gigantic airports have been and are being built for most of the first-tier cities in China, but they are generally far away from the city centers. Building subway systems is another typical infrastructure project in various large and medium-size (first- and second-tier) cities. Improving the urban infrastructure not only enriches the life of its residents, but also boosts the GDP and employment levels. Various types of transportation investments have a "multiplier effect" by attracting businesses and industries.

For cities to grow and expand spatially, they need to accommodate an influx of migrants from rural areas—and, more importantly, to house new and relocated business establishments. Erecting high-rises and commercial complexes in old city centers is difficult both socially and financially, as the old residents and businesses are usually displaced, and it is economically expensive to relocate them. Instead, a widely adopted development strategy championed by some cities and high-ranking government officials is to build brand-new city centers or central business districts outside the old cities. Essentially, farmland along the urban fringe is used by the local governments to build new cities with modern high-rises, for both commercial and residential uses. Town plans are developed to determine the layouts of the new cities, with the objective of attracting various types of businesses, industries, and services. The Pudong district, built next to the old city of Shanghai, is one of the earliest and largest new towns. Many smaller new towns are being developed outside the old cities (den Hartog, 2010).

Figure 6.7 shows an example. Zhengzhou, the capital of Henan province, is a relatively old city. However, because it lies at the intersection of two major

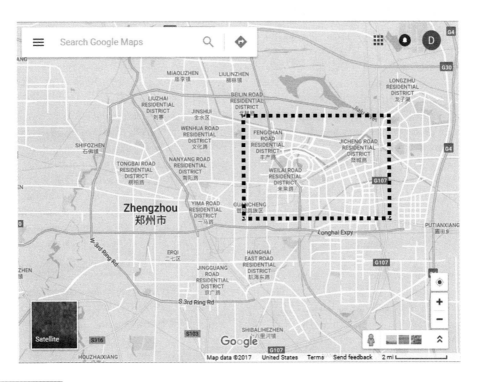

FIGURE 6.7 A Google map showing the old city of Zhengzhou (indicated by the label at left) and the new district of Zhengdong (in which the new central business district is indicated by the dashed-line rectangle). Map courtesy of Google Maps.

BOX 6.1. Ghost Towns and Ghost Cities

A major part of the history of North America is westward development—driven, among other things, by the California gold rush and the expansion of the railroad into the "Wild West." Many Western mining towns flourished for a time, until the natural resources were depleted or the market crashed for the ore being mined (as happened with silver). Once the economic basis of these towns eroded, the population moved away, and the towns became deserted—ghost towns.[a] Other ghost towns emerged because of natural disasters, or alterations in major transportation routes such as highways or railroads.

On the other side of the world, the emergence of ghost towns or cities in China is a relatively recent phenomenon. Unlike North American ghost towns, which were once populated and have been left to deteriorate, Chinese ghost cities have rarely or barely been inhabited. They consist of new or unfinished buildings (see Figure 6.8), standing on their own or as part of an existing large city. They are the results of aggressive, and perhaps overambitious, Chinese urban planning and development.

These cities were built from scratch, with residential apartments, commercial complexes, supporting facilities, and infrastructure, all in advance of populations that may never arrive. Local governments claimed the land from farmers and then sold the rights to developers. Such massive projects were intended to address the fast pace of urban growth experienced by many Chinese cities by diverting immigrants from existing cities into the new cities. Unfortunately, the "build it and they will come" approach has not been effective for many of these new cities. They have failed to attract migrants, and few or no new residents have arrived. Most of the newly built apartments are not occupied, although some might have been purchased by well-off investors. The buildings and grounds are deserted but quite well maintained. An often-cited example of a Chinese ghost city is Kangbashi. It is actually a subregion inside the city of Ordos, Neimenggu (Inner Mongolia), but it is sometimes labeled as a city itself. The plan was to have it accommodate 1 million residents, but today almost no people are visible in the area.

Why would such an unrealistic urban development plan be executed? Remember that China is still a centrally planned economy and that central planning still arguably plays the most important role in urban development, more so than market mechanisms. The motive for launching such massive development projects was to stimulate the economy through construction spending. The hope was that such expenditure would boost the GDP of the city or region, which would then be rewarded by the central government. These huge development projects are by-products of the government policy of economic development, although the policy does not specifically encourage the development of new cities.

What is the future of these ghost cities? The government must hope that eventually people will move into them. The Ordos city government has moved to Kangbashi to boost the daytime population; it is difficult to tell how likely the nighttime population is to increase. Many vacant housing units in these new cities do have owners who bought them as investments. However, many of them may not be able to hang on to their investments much longer without renters. If the situation does not improve, then sooner or later some Chinese cities may see a version of the 2007–2008 collapse of the housing bubble in the United States, resulting in massive numbers of foreclosed housing units and a large drop in real estate values. Recently, however, the Zhengdong new district seems to be making a turnaround, with very high occupancy rates in many commercial buildings. The occupancy rates for residential buildings are somewhat difficult to determine, but vacancies may still be high.

---

[a] Many websites about North American ghost towns can be found (e.g., www.ghosttowns.com).

FIGURE 6.8 Unfinished high-rise buildings unlikely to be completed, in Zhengdong, the new area east of the old city of Zhengzhou in Henan province. This picture was taken in the spring of 2015. (Photo: David W. S. Wong)

high-speed rail routes, it has a locational advantage over other second-tier cities. The old city of Zhengzhou, just left (west) of the center of Figure 6.7, is a typical Chinese city with old low-rise buildings and compact street layout. To redevelop the city center to attract new businesses, investors, or residents from other cities would be quite difficult and costly. The city officials therefore launched a development strategy to develop what is, in effect, a new city: Zhengdong new district, or "Xinzheng" ("xin" in Chinese means "new," and, therefore, the new Zheng city), east of the old city. This new district has a central business district, indicated in Figure 6.7 by the dashed-line rectangle. At the heart of the new central business district is a circular zone with a road network radiating from the center. This new district was built from scratch and includes canals and man-made lakes, as well as numerous commercial and residential high-rises, an exhibition center, and entertainment complexes.

The Zhengzhou–Zhengdong model has been promoted by some government leaders as one of the most successful economic development projects, according to China's GDP-based criteria of economic and urban development. Other, mostly second-tier cities are considering copying it. Together with the relatively new high-speed railroad station, a new but expanding airport in the southern part of Zhengdong, and an SEZ around the airport, Zhengdong shifts the activity and development center of the region toward the east and away from the traditional city center of Zhengzhou. To a large degree, residents, businesses, and the cultural heritage of the old city are now marginalized in this sprawling urban landscape. Saying that the government has abandoned the old city center is not an understatement. At the same time, the Zhengdong new district has its own problems, such as significant underuse of the new buildings and infrastructure.

• • • • • • • • • • • • • • • FINAL THOUGHTS • • • • • • • • • • • • • • • •

Modernization, economic development, and urbanization all go together in China. Although the simultaneity of these processes has been experienced by other countries, the Chinese situation is unique in that governments, both central and local, play an important role in all aspects of urban development. The governments have been using urbanization as a means to restructure space to fuel economic growth (see Chapter 5). In other words, much of China's economic growth is attributable to the physical expansion of cities, massive construction projects, and business growth in urban areas. Although the market plays a key role in determining the prices of many commodities, governments steer the development and execution of land-use policy, massive infrastructure building, and overall economic policy toward goals set by the governments. One may question whether some of these accomplishments, such as building new central business districts out of nowhere, are real successes or not. As governments bear many of the costs for development strategies, one may ask how long governments can financially support those strategies and policies. This is a question of sustainability. Yet the costs of development are often not fully accounted for in the Chinese economy and society. For example, compensation provided to residents who need to be relocated because of new development projects is often not at the level of the property's true market value. Thus the success of certain segments of the urban economy has been obtained at the expense of some people.

Does the level of urbanization in China have an upper limit, a ceiling? China is still the most populous nation in the world, and maintaining the capacity to feed its massive population is a national security issue. A substantial proportion of the Chinese population has to be kept in the countryside in the agricultural sector, but how large should that proportion be? The Chinese government has already launched a plan to reform the household registration (*hukou*) system (Tiezzi, 2016). Although the reform is not drastic and to a large degree maintains the status quo, the effects it will have on the mobility of the population between rural and urban areas are far from clear, and thus the level of Chinese urbanization in the near future is difficult to predict.

A recent trend in urban and economic development is to reinforce the growth of cities within a region by developing an economic "megaregion"—a concept similar to "megalopolis," a term introduced by geographer Jean Gottmann (1957). A megalopolis is the agglomeration of a number of adjacent cities, such as the cities in the northeast United States along I-95 from Boston, Massachusetts, to Washington, D.C., and in southern California from San Diego to Santa Barbara. In China, the spatial agglomeration of cities in the Yangtze River Delta around Shanghai, and the Pearl River Delta around Shenzhen and Zhuhai, have already formed two economic megaregions. Beijing–Tianjin–Hebei is clearly a third one. Developing these megalopolises helps China sustain economic growth and become more competitive internationally. One may even argue that the strategy of developing systems of large cities is a more efficient approach of urban development than its predecessors.

NOTES

1. www.prb.org/pdf17/2017_World_Population.pdf (retrieved September 7, 2017).
2. www.prb.org/pdf10/10wpds_eng.pdf (retrieved September 7, 2017).
3. www.census.gov/geo/reference/ua/uafacts.html (retrieved March 9, 2017).
4. Although more recent versions of the United Nations *Demographic Yearbook* are available at the time of writing, the data on Chinese cities have not been updated since the 2008 version.
5. http://data.worldbank.org/indicator/SP.URB.TOTL.IN.ZS (retrieved June 22, 2015).
6. http://data.worldbank.org/indicator/SP.URB.TOTL.IN.ZS (retrieved June 22, 2015).
7. See the Tsingtao website (www.tsingtaobeer.com).
8. We used the data provided by the United Nations *2008 Demographic Yearbook* (United Nations Statistics Division, 2010) in our analysis.

REFERENCES

Bourne, L. S. (Ed.). (1982). *Internal structure of the city: Readings on urban form, growth, and policy.* New York: Oxford University Press.

Carroll, G. R. (1982). National city-size distributions: What do we know after 67 years of research? *Progress in Human Geography, 6,* 1–43.

Chan, K. W., & Hu, Y. (2003). Urbanization in China in the 1990s: New definition, different series, and revised trends. *China Review, 3*(2), 49–71.

Chen, X. (1991). China's city hierarchy, urban policy and spatial development in the 1980s. *Urban Studies, 28*(3), 341–367.

den Hartog, H. (2010). *Shanghai new towns: Searching for community and identity in a sprawling metropolis.* Rotterdam, The Netherlands: 010 Publishers.

Ford, L. R. (1996). A new and improved model of Latin American city structure. *Geographical Review, 86*(3), 437–440.

Gabaix, X., Gopikrishnan, P., Plerou, V., & Stanley, H. E. (2003). A theory of power law distributions in financial market fluctuations. *Nature, 423,* 267–270.

Gaubatz, P. (1999). Understanding Chinese urban form: Contexts for interpreting continuity and change. *Built Environment, 24*(4), 251–270.

Gaubatz, P. (2005). Globalization and the development of new central business districts in Beijing, Shanghai and Guangzhou. In L. J. C. Ma & F. Wu (Eds.), *Restructuring the Chinese city* (pp. 98–121). New York: Routledge.

Gottmann, J. (1957). Megalopolis or the urbanization of the northeastern seaboard. *Economic Geography, 33*(3), 189–200.

Griffin, E., & Ford, L. R. (1980). A model of Latin American city structure. *Geographical Review, 70*(4), 397–422.

Huang, Y. (2007). Urban development in contemporary China. In G. Veeck, C. W. Pannell, C. J. Smith, & Y. Huang, *China's geography: Globalization and the dynamics of political, economic, and social change* (pp. 233–262). Lanham, MD: Rowman & Littlefield.

Knox, P. L., & McCarthy, L. (2011). *Urbanization: An introduction to urban geography* (3rd ed.). Boston: Pearson.

McGee, T. G., Lin, G. C. S., Marton, A. M., Wang, M. Y. K., & Wu, J. (2007). *China's urban space: Development under market socialism.* New York: Routledge.

Moomaw, R. L., & Alwosabi, M. A. (2004). An empirical analysis of competing explanations of urban primacy evidence from Asia and Americas. *Annals of Regional Science, 38,* 149–171.

Skinner, G. W. (1964). Marketing and social structure in rural China: Part I. *Journal of Asian Studies, 24*(1), 3–43.

Tiezzi, S. (2016). China's plan for 'orderly' *hukou* reform. *The Diplomat.* Retrieved February 16, 2017, from http://thediplomat.com/2016/02/chinas-plan-for-orderly-hukou-reform.

Tuan, Y.-F. (1974). *Topophilia: A study of environmental perception, attitudes, and values.* Englewood Cliffs, NJ: Prentice-Hall.

United Nations Statistics Division. (2010). *2008 demographic yearbook.* New York: Author.

United Nations Statistics Division. (2013). *2013 demographic yearbook.* New York: Author. https://unstats.un.org/unsd/demographic/products/dyb/dyb2013.htm (retrieved September 7, 2017).

Wu, F., & Yeh, A. G. O. (1999). Urban spatial structure in a transitional economy: The case of Guangzhou. *Journal of the American Planning Association, 65*(4), 377–394.

Xu, Z., & Zhu, N. (2009). City size distribution in China: Are large cities dominant? *Urban Studies, 46*(10), 2159–2185.

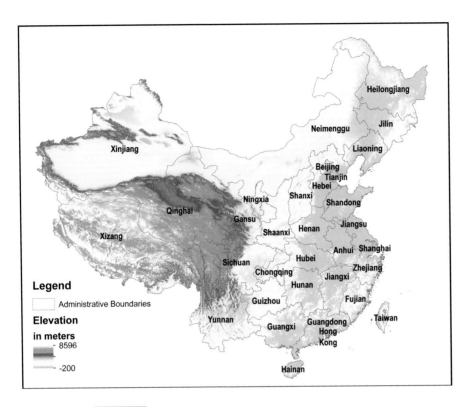

PLATE 1 Topography of China, with provincial boundaries.

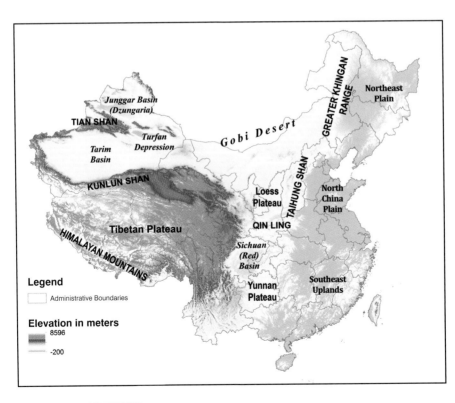

PLATE 2 Major landform features in China, with elevations.

PLATE 3 Farmers growing crops in the Loess Plateau region. (Photo: Kenneth K. K. Wong)

PLATE 4 Some typical dim sum items (clockwise from upper left): egg custard tarts, rice wraps with soy sauce, steamed shrimp dumplings, radish cakes, and fried chicken feet. (Photo: Kenneth K. K. Wong)

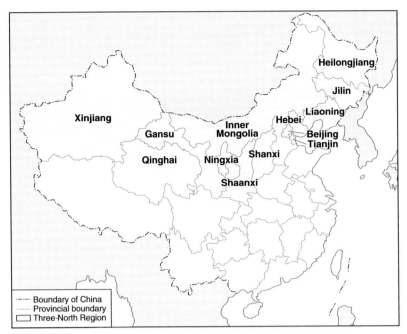

PLATE 5 The area included in China's Three-North Shelterbelt Program. The "Three-North" in the program's name refers to northeast, north, and northwest China.

PLATE 6 The coastal region of China, showing it in relation to other provinces/autonomous regions, municipalities, and special administrative regions (SARs), and to neighboring countries.

PLATE 7 Shanghai's Bund at night. (Photo: David W. S. Wong)

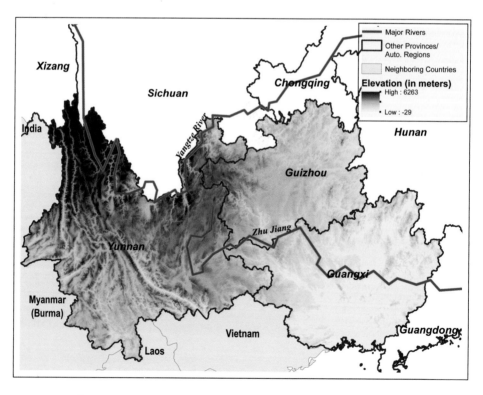

PLATE 8 Topography of the south–southwest peripheral region.

PLATE 9 Limestone landscape features in Guilin: Elephant Trunk Hill (upper left); a saddle (upper right); steep rocks cut through by waters (lower left); and stalactites, stalagmites, and pillars inside a cave (lower right). (Photos: David W. S. Wong)

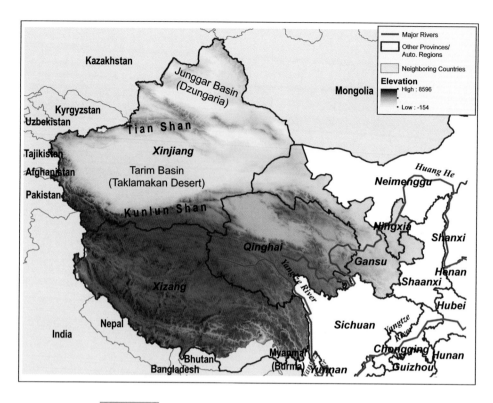

PLATE 10 Topography of the western peripheral subregion.

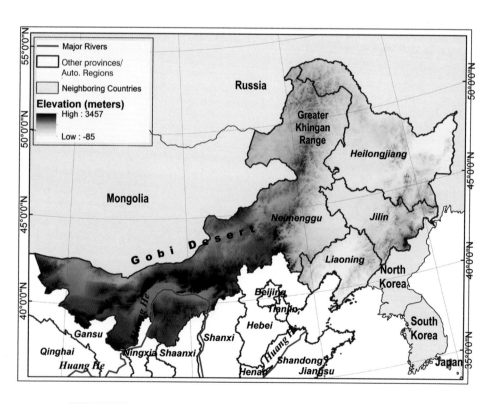

PLATE 11 Topography of the north–northeastern peripheral subregion.

(a)

第22届中国·哈尔滨太阳岛国际雪雕艺术博览会

(b)

PLATE 12 Two views of the Snow and Ice Festival in Harbin, Heilongjiang: (a) sculptures in the snow, and (b) ice structures illuminated at night. (Photos: David W. S. Wong)

PLATE 13 European/Russian-style buildings in Harbin at night. (Photo: David W.S. Wong)

PLATE 14 (a) Demonstrators in the Occupy Central/Umbrella Movement blocked off major thoroughfares and skyways in the Admiralty district. Admiralty, the core zone of the occupied areas, has many government buildings. (b) Police moved into the occupied areas to clear the tents on December 11, 2014. (Photos: Kenneth K. K. Wong)

PLATE 15 An Arayal tribal food store in the Wulai hot spring resort area in southern New Taipei City. (Photo: Kenneth K. K. Wong)

CHAPTER 7

Beyond the Cities
The Chinese Countryside

LEARNING OBJECTIVES	KEY CONCEPTS AND TERMS
★ Comprehend the various meanings of "rural" in China.	peasant; rural poverty; dual economy; collective systems; spatial practices; self-reliance; township and village enterprises (TVEs); urban–rural segregation; villages-in-the-city; modern values
★ Examine distinctive rural practices and their persistence.	
★ Articulate the disparities between China's urban and rural areas, and the prolonged dualism between the two regions.	

HOW IMPORTANT IS RURAL CHINA?

The Chinese countryside carries a very special meaning within the country as a whole. It had previously accommodated over half of the country's population, but by 2011, China's urbanization level had climbed to 51% (State Statistical Bureau [SSB], 2013). Politically, the Chinese countryside is the "root" of the Chinese Communist party; the success of the Chinese revolution was based on Mao Zedong's strategy of "surrounding the cities with rural areas." In Mao's era, national leaders were proud of this tradition. Not only were many socialist experiments initiated in the countryside, such as the redistribution of farmland and the building of collective farms, but intellectuals, students, and urban dwellers were sent to the countryside to learn from the farmers during the Cultural Revolution. In 1978, the country's economic reform was kicked off in the countryside with the introduction of the household farming responsibility system. Some people considered this the "second land reform," after the first land reform in which the government distributed land to farmers in 1952.

The change from a socialist countryside to a market-driven one has been long and painful, accompanied by a shift in government rhetoric from "revolutionary glory" to the tough realities of poverty and underdevelopment. Li's (2002) description of the countryside—the difficult lives of peasants, poor rural areas, and a suffering agricultural sector—shone a light on the hardship of Chinese farmers. Unlike country life in the Western tradition, life in the Chinese countryside is definitely not characterized as a rural idyll. In this chapter, we examine the dramatic developments in rural China, the distinctive features of rural China, and the impact of the country's economic reform on rural life. If urban China, in a broad sense, represents the prosperity and achievement of the country's economic reform, the rural areas present a different picture. Let's begin with a typical textbook question: What is "rural" China?

WHAT DOES "RURAL" MEAN IN CHINA?

The word "rural" has many meanings. It may refer to a territory with specific socioeconomic characteristics, a society with distinctive values, a process that creates distinctive spatial practices, or a state of mind (social representation). In China, "rural" means, among other things, a livelihood, a tradition, and a specific economic structure. Some people consider "rural" primitive and inferior, while others see it as the root of Chinese culture. From an administrative perspective, rural means the levels of the county, township, and the villagers' committee in the administrative hierarchy (see Chapter 6, Figure 6.1). There is clearly no single, standard definition of "rural."

As we've seen in other situations in China, the diversity of rural characteristics and activities challenges the notion that rural areas exhibit uniformity. Halfacree (2006) suggests that the functional and ideational (e.g., belief-based) definitions of "rural" are interwoven rather than disconnected or contradictory. This argument has led to the contention that rural space is socially produced rather than something waiting to be discovered. In other words, rural space exists when people give it an identity by attributing particular economic, social, and cultural characteristics to it in their everyday lives. A multidimensional view of rural space is therefore proposed, suggesting that rural space includes (1) formal representations, (2) actual rural localities, and (3) the everyday lives of rural residents (Halfacree, 2006, 2007).

The formal representations of rural space are the formal images and descriptions of "rural" that are conceived by bureaucrats, politicians, or capitalists. These formal descriptions are usually produced in a top-down manner, demonstrating the logic of the market and the views of government or technical bureaucrats such as town planners and engineers. Rural localities are the spaces that feature distinctive practices, such as thoughts, ideas, and actions, associated with production and consumption. These practices may or may not conform to the formal image, but they spring from people's real lives. The everyday lives of rural residents comprise the individual actions (flows and interactions) that produce or reproduce the material forms of everyday rural reality. These three facets of rural life are interwoven, and each cannot be understood fully without referring to the other two. The three dimensions together capture the diversity and complexity of rural space.

It is worth mentioning here that the term "peasant" (*nong min*) is commonly used to describe Chinese farmers. As used by scholars, the term carries a sense of these farmers' traditional self-reliant livelihood, but also their inequality and vulnerability as a social group under the country's urban–rural dichotomy. Peasants, in comparison to urban workers and city dwellers, are viewed as relatively weak, vulnerable, and powerless. Since the 1950s, the Chinese peasant has been officially defined by the household registration (*hukou*) system, discussed in Chapters 5 and 6. Over 80% of the country's population was classified as "peasants" between 1949 and 1980 (SSB, 2013). In 2012, there were 934 million peasants, but the number dropped to 624 million when residency was used in place of the *hukou* system in classifying someone as a peasant (SSB, 2013).

Rural Areas as China's Traditional and Revolutionary Base

In China, formal representations of the term "rural" are created by the Chinese state. They include rural areas as the source of revolutionary glory; the socialist ideal of a prosperous collective economy; and the current economic reality of rural poverty. These different descriptions are not contradictory (Chung, 2014). In fact, they show the state's intention to modernize the poor countryside and, at the same time, to provide justification for its rural development policies. These formal images have affected the everyday lives of rural residents and the production and reproduction of distinctive rural practices.

In China, the family-based farming system, known as the "small peasant economy," has persisted over thousands of years. Within a highly stable society and a rich, deep-rooted culture, the "rural" area in the past may be regarded as a society of its own, separated from cities. In the 20th century, the Chinese countryside inspired Mao Zedong and the Communist party to search for possible ways to bring about a national revolution. Historians have generally agreed that Mao's personal experience in rural areas, as well as the party's survival needs, solidified the peasants' role in China's socialist revolution. As early as the 1920s, Mao had recognized that the key to the success of the revolution lay in the countryside. Not only did he closely examine peasants' demands and complaints, but he also implemented experimental measures, such as land redistribution, to win the poor peasants' support (Fairbank & Goldman, 1998). At the same time, Marxist–Leninist ideas were incorporated into the country's agricultural production and social relationships, such as landlord–tenant relations, to produce a theoretical framework for the Chinese socialist revolution (Wylie, 1979). Peasants were the leading actors in the Chinese revolution, in contrast to the Soviet Union, where the Marxist–Leninist leadership gave the urban proletariat (workers and urban leaders) a key role in the socialist revolution. The successful revolution in 1949 thus created the image of the Chinese countryside as a place of revolutionary glory—a laboratory that made the country's socialist dream come true. This image became the formal representation of the Chinese countryside throughout Mao's leadership. In general, China during

Mao's era was a relatively egalitarian society in terms of income, although everybody was poor. Mao's egalitarian view was replaced by Deng's pragmatic view when economic reform kicked off.

Rural Areas as Poor and Underdeveloped Regions

The description of rural hardship given by Li (2002) has become the new image of the Chinese countryside. He has conceptualized rural poverty as an accumulation of urban–rural disparities, an ailing agricultural sector, and low peasant incomes. Broadly speaking, these issues stemmed from the economic reforms instituted in China from 1978 onward, which brought inequality as well as prosperity to the country. The advocacy of "letting a small number of people get rich first" has brought substantial changes to the lives of all Chinese people, including farmers. Generally, a rural family's income growth since the initiation of the reforms was rapid at the beginning, but then slowed and has stagnated in recent years. On the eve of reforms in 1978, an urban family's disposable yearly income was 343 yuan, compared to 133 yuan for a rural family (SSB, 2012). The rural-to-urban income ratio was thus 1:2.6. Two decades later, in 2000, the ratio had increased to 1:2.8. In 2010, the gap further expanded to 1:3.2; urban households had three times the disposable income of their rural counterparts. Figure 7.1 shows growing urban and rural income inequality between 1979 and 2011.

How is poverty defined in China? The World Bank has developed an international poverty standard for cross-country comparison. In 1990, a poverty line was set at the level of $1 per day. (As in Chapter 5, all dollar values given in this chapter are U.S. dollars.) This was the minimum amount of money needed to secure minimum nutrition to subsist. In 2008, the level was adjusted to $1.25.

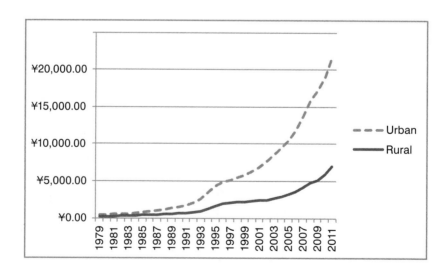

FIGURE 7.1 Urban–rural income gap (in yuan, or ¥), 1979–2011. Data from State Statistical Bureau (SSB, 2012, p. 103).

China, however, has developed its own poverty line. A World Bank (2001) report on China's poverty suggested that the standard China used at the end of the 20th century was equivalent to $0.66 per day. Chinese official materials suggest that the poverty line changes almost every year (see Table 7.1). Although these Chinese versions of the poverty line allow flexibility and take the specific Chinese situation into consideration, some believe that poverty in China has been underestimated (World Bank, 2001). Nevertheless, the different standards for estimating poverty do not prevent a common conclusion: The prevalence of rural poverty is high. In 1986, the Chinese government compiled a list of 331 poor counties (i.e., rural areas) that were eligible for development assistance at the national level. On top of this list, another 368 counties were categorized as poor counties at the provincial level, which made them eligible for funding support at the same level. In 1993, the two lists were combined into one national list, with 592 counties (over 200 million rural residents) designated as "national poor counties," eligible for central government funding for poverty reduction activities. Geographically, many of these counties were located in the southwestern provinces of Yunnan and Guizhou, with two-thirds located in mountainous and remote highland areas (World Bank, 2001).

The country's poverty has been significantly reduced by remarkable economic growth in the past 30 years. However, economic growth has been unequal across the country, and the effects of poverty alleviation have also been uneven. Generally, the reduction of rural poverty has been the greatest in the coastal region. Between 2000 and 2010, the proportion of rural poor in the coastal region fell from 10 to 5% (State Statistical Bureau–Household Survey Department [SSB-HSD], 2012). Conversely, the proportion of rural poor in the western region increased from 60 to 65% (SSB-HSD, 2012). In 2010, the Chinese countryside was home to 27 million poor people, with 1.2 million (4.6%) in the coastal region, 8.1 million (30%) in the central region, and 17.5 million (65%) in the western region (SSB-HSD, 2012). Furthermore, the largest share of rural poverty was still found in the mountainous areas. In 2000, 48% of the country's rural poor lived in mountainous areas; the proportion increased to 49% in 2005 and to 53% in 2010 (SSB-HSD, 2012). Rural poverty has thus increasingly become concentrated at the regional level.

TABLE 7.1. China's Official Poverty Line (in Yuan)

Year	Poverty line	Year	Poverty line
1985	206	2001	630
1987	227	2002	627
1991	304	2003	637
1993	n.a.	2004	668
1995	530	2005	683
1997	640	2006	693
1999	625	2007	785

Note. n.a., not available. Data from State Statistical Bureau (SSB, 2012, p. 105).

The 592 "national poor counties" have experienced substantial reductions in poverty, due to strong government financial and policy supports. In these counties, state investment improved the basic infrastructure (such as water supply, electricity, irrigation, and roads). A protection system has also been gradually developed, providing basic social goods to poor people in these counties. In addition to poverty relief measures, new strategies and measures have been introduced to rebuild and modernize the countryside. For example, agriculture taxes and major levies were eliminated in 2005. New strategies such as the construction of a "new socialist countryside" and "rural planning" have been implemented, aiming to increase agricultural production, improve peasants' incomes and living standards, and build neat and clean living environments.

BOX 7.1. Being Rural as "a Way of Life"

Sociologist Louis Wirth (1938) argued that "Urbanism is a way of life." In China, is being rural "a way of life"? As stated earlier, slightly less than half of the Chinese population can be classified as rural. This group is typically found in the interior and less developed parts of the country, characterized by an agriculture-oriented economy and relatively low socioeconomic status. Some of the physical and visible manifestations of these characteristics include extensive farmland with interspersed villages, villagers engaged primarily in agricultural activities, and village houses in traditional style with limited modern amenities. However, these characteristics do not describe all of rural China.

Rural villages are not immune to the forces of modernization and urbanization. In fact, these villages are facing historically unprecedented pressure to change. From a population perspective, these villages are competing for residents with cities, as villagers in general have a strong incentive to move to cities to seek higher-paying nonagricultural jobs. Villages near urban areas face especially keen competition in trying to hold onto their original residents. For instance, a village in southern Guangdong province (Figure 7.2a) has more than 25 housing units, but only 6 of these are still occupied. Most people have left for cities, including Taishan, the medium-size city closest to the village.

From an economic perspective, agricultural activities are no longer the primary economic activities in some of these villages. Although farmland still exists near the villages, some villagers leave their parcels idle or just plow small plots for their own use. Young people now pursue nonagricultural jobs elsewhere and move away either temporarily or permanently. Many of the remaining villagers are elderly and therefore do not possess the physical strength required for large-scale agricultural work. These villages do not utilize the surrounding farmland to a large degree.

From a structural perspective, these villages still maintain some aspects of the traditional rural lifestyle, such as the use of woodstoves for cooking (Figure 7.2b). However, they have also been extensively modified by modern technologies. For instance, many villages have electricity and landline telephone connections. Many villages in rural areas have cellphone coverage. While the exteriors of some village houses still look the same as in the old days, the interiors may have been remodeled with modern-day amenities. In fact, some units have been rebuilt entirely in a bungalow style with concrete; Figure 7.2c shows one such unit, juxtaposed with a traditional brick structure with tile roof. Rebuilding or remodeling these old structures incurs hefty financial burdens, but apparently these villagers have resources other than their earnings from the fields.

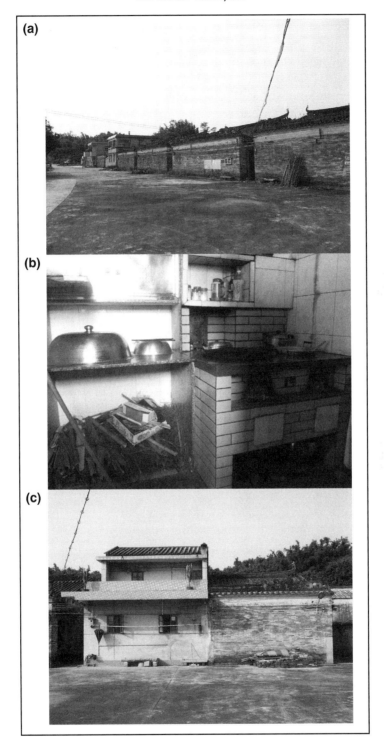

FIGURE 7.2 (a) Village houses in southern Guangdong near the city of Taishan; (b) the wood-burning stove used in a village house; and (c) remodeled and traditional structures juxtaposed with each other. (Photos: David W. S. Wong)

Despite these improvements, the number of rural poor in these designated poor counties still accounted for 63% of the national's total in 2010 (SSB-HSD, 2012). In 2010, the poverty rate in these counties was three times higher than the national average (SSB-HSD, 2012). The net household income of these families was only 34% of the national level. While people in the coastal region and in urban areas enjoy the fruits of economic reform, many in the Chinese countryside are still struggling.

SEGREGATION OF URBAN AND RURAL

The rural–urban income gap and rural poverty are signs of two worlds in China: The modern urban sector is connected to the global system in many ways, while the traditional rural sector has relatively low capital investment, low productivity, and surplus labor. Economists call this pattern of development a "dual economy," and it is commonly found in developing countries. The classic theory of structural change (Lewis, 1954) explains the development of many of these dual economies. The theory suggests that the rising demand for labor in the modern sector will eventually absorb all surplus labor in the traditional sector and modernize it, with living standards improving to above subsistence levels. This argument is based on the assumption that factors of production, including labor, can move freely across regions. In other words, the economy operates toward consolidating resources and increasing the economic scale of production to boost development and prosperity. Economic growth then trickles down to the less developed areas and eventually eliminates the development gap between the two sectors.

Given China's unique development, however, the structural change model does not provide a satisfactory explanation of the country's disparities, and the Chinese situation also challenges the applicability of the trickle-down effect. China established a planned system to replace market forces and determine resource allocation. In other words, market mechanisms were eliminated, and therefore factors of production did not flow freely within the economy. Generally, production factors, such as labor, land, and capital, were allocated through plans in a top-down manner. Under Mao's strategy to prioritize industrial development, plenty of resources were poured into the urban sector to build heavy industries. Associated with this development strategy were various administrative measures and procedures, including the *hukou* system, collective land ownership, local financial and welfare systems, and the food rationing system—all of which favored urban residents instead of rural farmers. The farmers stayed in rural areas and engaged in agricultural production to provide the necessary food and raw materials for cities, the centers of industrialization. These administrative measures soon created an "invisible wall" that separated urban from rural life and the industrial sector from the agricultural sector.

Economic reform has done little to change this institutional structure. It continues to serve as an "invisible wall," which continues to constrain the flow of production factors between urban and rural sectors and to hinder their integration. Land is a case in point. In cities, economic reform has made land a commodity

BOX 7.2. Villages-in-the-City

Villages-in-the-city (*cheng chong cun*) are common features in Chinese cities experiencing rapid urbanization. These villages were rural settlements known as "production brigades" in Mao's era. Residents were involved in agricultural activities, and the assets, production, and distribution of commodities were organized through the collective framework. Urban expansion fueled by economic reform has engulfed parts of these villages (mostly the farmland), but has left considerable parts untouched (mainly the peasants' residences and the collective structures). As a result, a distinctive landscape has gradually formed—irregular, shabby buildings surrounded by a modern, well-planned urban landscape. Figure 7.3 illustrates the typical stages in which a village-in-the-city develops.

Institutionally, the intact part of a village that becomes a village-in-the-city retains the old village system and has not been reconciled with the urban system of planning and management. In Shenzhen, China's most successful special economic zone (SEZ), there were 241 such villages in 2005 (Ding, 2005). Guangzhou, the provincial capital of Guangdong province, which sits 100 km to the northwest of Shenzhen, had 139 villages-in-the-city in 2000 (*Yangcheng Wanbao,* 2000). Based on their locations, Li (2001) grouped villages-in-the-city into three types: (1) villages that have completely lost their farmland and are located in the city core; (2) villages retaining a certain amount of farmland and located in suburban areas; and (3) villages still with much farmland located on the outskirts of a city. Among the 139 villages-in-the-city in Guangzhou, 45 were located in the city proper (*Yangcheng Wanbao,* 2000).

Because they are areas where cities' planning prescriptions and management have not been implemented, villages-in-the-city are considered disorderly spaces in the urban landscape (Chung, 2009). Adding to the sense of disorder is the prevalence of illegal constructions and indiscriminate land use in these villages (Tang & Chung, 2002). Houses are often built bigger and higher than cities allow, usually at the expense of public space and social facilities such as parks and playgrounds. Villagers call this high-density style of development "shaking-hand buildings" or "kissing buildings," because one can often literally shake hands with or kiss neighbors in the next block through windows. Many of these villages have buildings on over 90% of their land (Lan, 2005). This high building density suggests population density, and the latter is indeed very high in villages-in-the-city—120,000 people/ km^2, as suggested by Tan (2005). The chaotic environment has made villages-in-the-city eyesores. They are often described as "slums" with connections to various kinds of illegal activity, such as gambling, prostitution, and drug trafficking.

Despite this negative image, villages-in-the-city have played a very important role in China's recent economic development. With many rural migrants swarming into cities for opportunities, heavy pressure is being put on housing in urban areas. The supply of housing for migrants, especially affordable housing, has been very limited. Taking advantage of their exclusion from formal regulations, native villagers of villages-in-the-city have been leasing out rooms and floor space in their houses (Zhang, Zhao, & Tian, 2003). This is particularly common in villages located in city centers, with good public transport connections. Field investigations in Guangzhou reveal that this rental business has boosted the population of one village to 100,000, with 80% of the residents being rural migrants. Rental activities provide native villagers, who are now landlords, with a golden opportunity to survive in the urban economy after losing agricultural land and income from farming. At the same time, their actions have provided an informal solution to the lack of affordable housing in Chinese cities—an issue not anticipated by city governments.

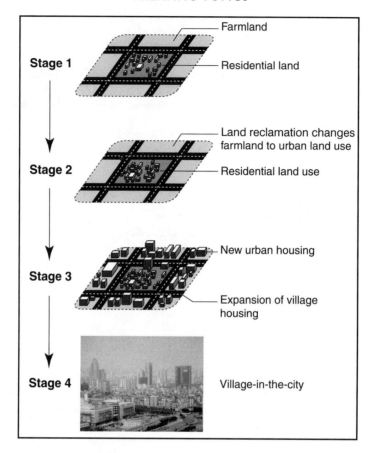

FIGURE 7.3 Formation of villages-in-the-city.

for the first time since 1949. Urban land is state-owned, but land use rights can be transferred, creating a "paid-use" system of property markets in cities (see Chapter 6). In contrast, rural land is collectively owned by villages, and it has remained welfare-in-kind, with free use. Rural land use rights are not transferable; buying, selling, and leasing land for nonagricultural purposes are not allowed. The different property rights associated with urban and rural land have thus engendered different land management and planning systems in urban and rural areas. In this case, the disparities between urban and rural represent a genuine dichotomy—a continuing reproduction of disparities by incompatible institutions. In other words, unequal development and rural poverty are structural problems in China. The dichotomous view also suggests that the Chinese countryside cannot be reconciled with urban China, despite the rapid pace of urbanization since 1978. The rural areas, therefore, have remained a distinctive system, apart from the urban system. A distinctive manifestation of this is the "village-in-the-city," a unique landscape commonly found in Chinese cities with rapid urbanization. This distinctiveness is not entirely explained by landscapes and functions, but rather by distinctive spatial practices and institutions. These are discussed in the following sections.

DISTINCTIVE RURAL PRACTICES

Two important practices found in rural China are the collective system and self-reliance (Chung, 2014). These specific practices were developed in rural China, are considered aspects of the country's traditional and revolutionary base, and are keys to understanding the current development of rural areas. These practices have evolved during the era of economic reform, and new institutions have been formed to support these evolving rural practices.

The Collective System

The collective system is a socialist legacy in the Chinese countryside. In Mao's era, the loyalty of peasants encouraged Mao to carry out his ambitious socialist experiments in the countryside. After the return to peace from the civil war between the Communist and Kuomintang parties, Chinese peasants restored production by quietly launching the campaigns of "cooperativization" and "collectivization." As early as 1953, mutual aid teams and cooperatives of a semisocialist type were formed in the Chinese countryside. The nationwide campaign of cooperativization began in 1955; it was followed in 1958 by the building of people's communes, commonly known as collectivization. It was argued that large collective farms would be able to consolidate land, personnel, and other resources; this would permit the introduction of better farming methods, would encourage a higher level of investment, and hence would raise outputs. This practice was particularly used in areas with poor natural endowments. Given the experience of the Soviet Union, Chinese leaders believed that only large-scale collective farming would facilitate mechanization. Traditional small-scale, family-based farming did not have the necessary conditions, such as farm size, outputs, and savings, for such a process. The intention to mechanize was linked to pursuing a strong growth rate to support the country's industrialization.

People's communes were organized under the principle of "big and collective." How big was a people's commune? In 1956, a commune generally comprised 100–300 households; it was thus much bigger than a cooperative, which only included 30–40 households (Walker, 1968). A detailed investigation of a commune in Guangdong province in 1978 revealed that it covered 11,900 households, or a population of 57,934, with a total area of 115 km^2; it was divided into 21 production brigades and 187 production teams, with average memberships of 2,759 and 504 people, respectively (Lee & Lau, 1980).

Collective ownership was another principle of a people's commune. Private ownership of production means, particularly land, was eliminated. Arable land, fish ponds, large groups of trees, livestock, draft animals, large farm equipment, and irrigation works were all collectivized. Chinese farmers who were granted land ownership immediately after the Communists took power had their property taken away during collectivization. Only a small private plot of arable land was given to each collective member to grow vegetables for personal consumption. Although government regulations for collectives suggested that farmers' participation was voluntary, in many cases they were ordered to contribute their land, cattle, and tools (Zhou, 1996). The state's procurement policy, established in 1955, unified purchases and sales at fixed prices, and farmers lost their control over production and harvest. Income allocation was also controlled by the state through the people's communes, and a "work points" system was introduced for income distribution among commune members. In principle, the calculation of work points was based on days of labor and the value of the labor day—both the quantity and quality of work (Walker, 1968). Thus collectivization turned Chinese farmers back into farm laborers.

Obviously, farmers were unhappy with the collectivization movement, as their land, animals, and large farm tools were nationalized with very little (or no) compensation. Those with better land and higher incomes were especially unhappy. In the early days of collectivization, farmers expressed their discontent with the system by leaving the countryside and moving to cities. The Chinese state responded to this by implementing strict measures between 1956 and 1957 that effectively banned rural-to-urban migration. Not only were factories in cities instructed not to employ rural migrants, but a large number of rural migrants were sent back to the countryside. The state urged police departments and transportation workers to work together to keep farmers from moving to the city (Guo & Liu, 1990). In 1958, Chairman Mao signed a document titled *Regulation for Household Registration of the People's Republic of China,* and the household registration (*hukou*) system was legitimized. The primary objective of the system was to stop rural-to-urban migration. Through the control of mobility, jobs, food supply, and social goods and services, the *hukou* system anchored Chinese farmers to the countryside, and a closed society was created.

In the period before economic reform, the collective system was not unique to the countryside. Collective work units (*danwei*) were also established in cities. These urban collectives were state-owned. Through this institution, the state organized production and redistributed foodstuffs, jobs, housing, and other social goods to urban dwellers. Like their rural counterparts, urban dwellers had to depend on the urban collectives for their everyday necessities. Nevertheless, reform of state-owned enterprises, the abolition of job allocation, housing reform, and the commodification of social services during economic reform gradually detached urban dwellers from their work units. Individuals' needs—for jobs, food, housing, medical services, education, and other social services—are now supported by specific market-driven service sectors. Workers' dependency on collectives has thus been significantly reduced. This transformation shifted the identity of an urban resident from a "work unit" person to a "societal" person who relies on market and social resources in everyday life (Jin, 2003). The urban collective and its control over the circulation of production factors and goods had come to an end.

Unfortunately, such changes have not occurred in rural areas. The collapse of collective farming in the 1980s did not dismantle the rural collective system. Table 7.2 shows the transformation of rural collectives after the abolition of the people's communes in the 1980s. These changes were like the proverbial process of putting old wine into new bottles because the fundamental idea of collective ownership was not touched. In fact, collective ownership has been retained, and rural residents still depend on their collective units for production, housing, and basic welfare. In

TABLE 7.2. The Transformation of Rural Collectives since the 1980s

Before 1980s	After decollectivization	Since mid-1990s
People's commune	Town/township (town/township government)	Town/township (town/township government)
Production brigade	Administrative village (villagers' committee)	Shareholding company (board of directors)
Production team	Natural village (villagers' group)	Group either merges with a shareholding company or becomes a subsidiary of the shareholding company

the coastal region, where economic development is more advanced, rural collective units use their land, trucks, and other assets to develop a robust collective economy. Such an economy is no longer related to cultivation; instead, the units lease their land and storage facilities to foreign investors who set up their manufacturing factories in China (Chung & Unger, 2013). Corresponding to this new economic activity is the new name of these rural collectives—"shareholding companies."

The persistence of a collective system is further demonstrated by the persistence of internal distribution. Under the new structure of a shareholding company, all of a village's assets are converted to shares and distributed to native villagers. Villagers thus become shareholders of the collective unit. Each shareholder receives a certain number of shares, and dividend income is allocated annually. In the southern part of China, where rural collectives can earn hundreds of millions of dollars from leasing their land to overseas investors, members may receive a handsome dividend income (Chung, 2014; Unger & Chung, 2012). Furthermore, these new shareholding companies substantially support the daily operations of the neighborhood of native villagers, their shareholders. According to Chung's (2014) case studies, such involvement can include setting up neighborhood security guards, hiring cleaners to clean the streets in the neighborhood and collect garbage, providing funding for children's education and a senior center, paying for electricity to light public areas, providing scholarships for outstanding students, and funding extra teachers for the community school.

The close involvement of rural collectives in the daily operations of village neighborhoods demonstrates the persistence of the close relationship between rural residents and their collectives. Indeed, under the new shareholder structure, the collective identity of rural residents has been strengthened despite the collapse of collective farming. The collective unit has developed into a welfare state, which has substantially taken over the social responsibility of government (Chan, Madsen, & Unger, 2009). These developments confirm the continuation of the collective system. The closed nature of this system also leads us to consider the persistence of self-reliance.

Self-Reliance

Self-reliance has been a distinctive practice in the Chinese countryside for thousands of years. The traditional family-based farming system relied on local resources for production; most of the farm's output was consumed by the family, with only a small portion sold or exchanged. It was a self-reliant and self-sufficient farming system. This small but self-contained system was a highly stable one because the low level of specialization and product exchange reduced risks from price fluctuation and market failure. Therefore, even the Communists went to tremendous lengths to restore this traditional system (and hence its productivities) when they took power in 1949. These efforts included land reform, which included the confiscation of land held by landlords and its redistribution to landless farmers, including farm laborers. This reform principally targeted landlords; small portions of land owned by rich farmers were basically untouched (Kuo, 1976). Moreover, workers who owned land in the countryside were not counted as landlords in order to secure worker political support.

In 1952, 2 years after the nationwide promotion of land reform, more than 90% of rural farmers in China were granted land. In regions like the Yangtze River Delta, land reform was completed as early as 1950. Kuo (1976, p. 10) gives an account of this achievement:

> By the end of 1952, some 700 million mou (120 million acres), or 44 percent of China's total cultivated area of about 1,650 million mou (274 million acres), 50 million draft animals, 39 million agricultural implements, 5 million tons of food-stuffs, surplus houses containing about 38 million rooms, and other properties owned by landlords had been confiscated and redistributed to some 300 million poverty-stricken peasants who had little or no land and other means of production.

In 1953, the country basically completed the land reform. Not only did all farmers own land, but the amount of land that each rural family held was not more than double the national average (Kuo, 1976). Although former landlords had their land confiscated, they were allowed to retain small parcels so that they could count on their own labor to make a living. Thus the landlord class, as well as the traditional land tenure system, was eliminated by the reform. Moreover, the differences among rich farmers, poor farmers, and former farm laborers were reduced significantly. Chinese peasants now owned land, livestock, and other means of production; their debts to landlords were canceled; and their sociopolitical power was strengthened once the landlord class was eliminated. They might have had no idea what the concept of the "socialist countryside" meant, but they were grateful to the new government. Production incentives increased, and outputs were restored to peacetime production levels (Walker, 1966).

The implementation of the collective farming system was an attempt to develop a new type of organization for agricultural production, but it did not change the self-reliance of farming. Although the building of a planned economy eliminated the role of the market, the idea of self-sufficiency had not been challenged. The practice of self-sufficiency was consolidated by the national development strategy, which prioritized industrial development in urban areas. Since most of the country's resources were poured into cities for industrialization, the agricultural sector relied on the collective farms to consolidate the limited local resources for production. This consolidation effort included farmers themselves, who were organized to work in "production brigades" and teams. Furthermore, Mao's desire to maintain a high level of local production of grains and other food reinforced the need for agricultural production to be self-sufficient. Given the controls on rural-to-urban migration, peasants were anchored in the countryside in agricultural production without having other choices. In return, all members of the rural collective were provided with food and basic welfare. Since each collective unit organized its own production and redistribution, the Chinese countryside remained closed and self-reliant.

China's economic reform began with the restoration of the family farming system, in the form of the household farming responsibility system mentioned at the start of this chapter. Chinese farmers recovered control over production and sale of their outputs, but the collective system was left intact. The persistence of the collective system has consolidated the practice of self-reliance in two ways. Initially, it provided "local citizenship" for rural residents (Smart & Smart, 2001). In the context of China's urban–rural segregation, peasants are not eligible for social goods (such as social security, education, and health care) provided by cities, even if they have moved to work and live in cities. This segregation has forced peasants to rely on their rural collectives for resources and social benefits—a form of local citizenship. Land is the basic resource provided gratis to peasants. This explains why peasants consider it an entitlement and would never give it up. Moreover, in regions where collectives are robust, local benefits are redistributed to their members. Thus local citizenship has tightened peasants' allegiance to their collectives by allowing them to use the latter's resources and share the benefits. Rural collectives demonstrate self-reliance as local resources are utilized, allocated, and redistributed. While the rural collective claims ownership of the land, an individual peasant has the right to use it for cultivation and housing purposes only. Rural residents still heavily depend on their land for livelihood, and so self-reliance has persisted. In the coastal region, where farmland has disappeared as a result of rapid industrialization and urbanization, former farmers lease out land and residential space (both legally and illegally) for rental income.

The restoration of family farming did not restore private land ownership. Land is still owned collectively by a village (formerly known as a production brigade) and allocated to each rural family for farming and housing purposes according to family size. Owing to population change, farmland is reallocated regularly, and each allocation changes the size, location, and quality of land. The insecurity of land tenure has restricted the development of large-scale, extensive agricultural production. At the same time, the growing costs of agricultural production and the associated profits and losses have discouraged farmers from expanding the scale of production and investing in specialized and commercial farming. Nevertheless, they have neither abandoned agriculture nor given up the right to use land, which they consider the only benefit they have from the country. Since farmers are prohibited from using land for nonagricultural purposes, they have shrunk their agricultural production to a self-sufficiency level in response to the stagnant agricultural economy (Chen & Ran, 2012).

Rural Industrialization

Generally, industrialization in the Chinese countryside has tried to take advantage of traditional self-reliance. The policy framework of rural industrialization seeks to keep rural surplus labor in the countryside. The resources for industrialization (such as labor, land, initial capital, institutional support, and innovations) have all been locally based, coming from the countryside. This development started with the relaxation of government control over agricultural production, pricing, and circulation in 1979, when the link was restored between agricultural production and nonagricultural activities such as food processing. Although these changes created a very favorable economic condition for rural industries, their growth, particularly in the early years of economic reform, was constrained by (1) political bias against privatization and (2) a lack of capital funding and resources. Small enterprises collectively owned by villages or townships, known as "township and village enterprises" (TVEs), played a very important role. Not only did they enjoy access to local resources, but their collective status also saved them from criticisms over political and ideological correctness. When TVEs were allowed to begin generating alternative income, they were eager to take advantage of the multiple opportunities.

These rural enterprises pooled their collective resources to facilitate production. For example, some collective teams utilized their trucks and tractors to provide transport services; others changed their farm machinery workshops to produce small household appliances, such as fans, radios, and televisions. In response to the lack of funds, these enterprises raised money from their workers. Common practices included selling bonds to their workers (including managers) or asking new workers to pay cash deposits (Oi, 1999). Interest was paid to the workers, and the funds were used exclusively for the factories' own operational or other purposes, such as buying new machines (Oi, 1999). Some rural enterprises were owned by village or township governments, and they had the governments serve as guarantors for loans from rural credit cooperatives and other credit institutions. Government support to these rural enterprises was later extended to providing producer services, exploring new markets for the products, and attracting investment. Local governments had strong incentives to support these rural enterprises because the latter not only boosted tax revenue, but also provided alternative sources of funds for local construction—not to mention the jobs that they created for rural residents.

TVEs experienced a golden age between 1978 and the mid-1990s (Naughton, 2007). They demonstrated the innovation of Chinese peasants and the dynamics of the countryside in the context of resource and political constraints. The TVE approach was able to keep the benefits within the countryside, unlike Mao's national industrialization strategy, which also emphasized self-reliance but in fact damaged rural areas. Nevertheless, the results of rural industrialization have been geographically uneven. The success of TVEs in southern Jiangsu province, Wenzhou, and the Pearl River Delta transformed the rural economy and made these the most prosperous regions in the country. However, a large number of rural areas have experienced little or no TVE development, adding to the growing gap between coastal and inland regions and between the populations of peasants in these regions.

CHINESE PEASANTS AND RURAL LIFE

Peasants were the most significant source of power for the Chinese Communist party. Land reform and Mao's attempts to lift peasants' social status and political power by emphasizing their class purity earned him their loyalty. Although they felt despondent under Mao's radical agricultural policies, they made significant contributions to the country's self-contained industrialization. It is estimated that through state control of agricultural production and prices, Chinese peasants contributed over 600 billion yuan to the country's industrial sector between 1954 and 1978, whereas their annual income growth in the same period was only 1 yuan (Su, 2009). On the eve of the country's economic reform, agricultural production was stagnant, if not paralyzed. Peasants were living a life of deprivation; in some areas, they were actually suffering from famine. Rural areas were in despair, and peasants' discontent intensified despite their revered status.

At the institutional level, market reform since 1978 has not provided Chinese peasants with basic political, social, and economic rights, or with opportunities equal to those of their urban counterparts. Although the country's *hukou* system is no longer used by the government to control population flows, it still serves as a major institution for benefit entitlement for both urban residents and peasants. The differences in privileges between registered urban dwellers and peasants have thus persisted. Inequality is most evident when peasants move to a city to work and are excluded from the concessions enjoyed by city dwellers. Such exclusion is considered a prime reason why rural-to-urban migrants have become a new urban underclass in Chinese cities (Chan, 2004, 2010; Solinger, 2006).

Market reform earned only a brief round of applause from Chinese peasants. Between 1978 and 1986, the revival of the household farming system, the dismantling of the agricultural product procurement system, the opening up of market channels, and price reforms for agricultural products boosted rural production as well as peasants' real income and consumption expenditure (Kueh, 1993; Li, Davis, & Wang, 1998). However, the boost was not sustained, as the increases in production costs, fluctuation of produce prices, and insecurity over land tenure significantly reduced the peasants' incentives to expand, commercialize, and specialize in rural production. As noted earlier, peasants consider land an entitlement that they will not give up, but many have shrunk their farm production to a self-sufficiency level.

At the same time, many peasants move to cities to work to increase their income, creating a unique social group known as "peasant workers" (*nong min gong*). Wage income has become a major part of rural families' net incomes. In 1990, wage income accounted for 50% of a rural family's annual net income; the proportion increased to 60% in 2000 and 70% in 2010 (SSB, 2013). Rural-to-urban migration has also changed the demographic composition of the countryside. Rural-to-urban migrants are mostly young, physically strong people; older family members and children are usually left behind. The growing dependence on wage income and the unwillingness to give up farmland and farming activities constitute an increasing dilemma for Chinese peasants.

Peasants who are lucky enough to live in villages close to cities are finding alternative ways to make a living. Unlike peasant workers who move to cities from more distant areas, local peasants have a locational advantage in developing a business renting housing. The massive influx of rural migrants to coastal cities has fueled a great demand for affordable housing in urban and suburban areas. In 2012, there were 236 million migrant workers nationwide (SSB, 2013). As peasants, these workers are not eligible for social housing in cities, and formal rental housing appears to be unaffordable for them. Local villages, therefore, have become the only housing source for these "outsiders." The demand provides precious economic opportunities for peasants in villages near cities. The following case illustrates the development.

Mr. Chan is a peasant who lives in a suburban area near the city of Guangzhou. He started to rent his farm shed to migrant workers in the early 1990s, when more and more "outsiders" came to Guangzhou to look for work. A few years later, he used the income he had made, together with a loan from relatives, to rebuild his house with five stories. Each story was further divided into two to four small units. Mr. Chan and his family occupy the top floor, and the rest of the house is leased out. The rent from each unit is about 700–1,000 yuan per month, for a total of about 20,000 yuan per month. Many of Mr. Chan's neighbors have similar businesses. Rental activities have not only offered these former farmers a comfortable way to tap into the urban economy, but they have also allowed them to attain respectable income levels, much better than any blue-collar workers in the cities (Chung & Unger, 2013). Rental income soon becomes a major source of income for these former farmers. Despite this, their status as peasants has not changed. However, unlike peasant workers, they are among the "small number of people getting rich first." Housing is not in high demand in villages farther away from major urban areas, and so those peasants are out of luck. Location matters.

Infiltration of Modern Values

China's rural society is undergoing profound transformation. As in many developing countries, economic development derived from the country's economic reform and opening up to the world market has generated enormous social and cultural changes, from growing social inequality to changing gender roles. Industrialization and other economic activities have led to the emergence of some types of "modern values" while the traditional ones have declined. It is common to hear rural residents appreciating the improvements resulting from greater material affluence, while at the same time lamenting the decline of social cohesion, trust, and other traditional values among fellow villagers.

Among the most radical changes in the Chinese countryside over the past four decades has been the rapid growth of consumption. Although this change has occurred in both urban and rural areas, it is particularly evident in the latter. Under the planned economy and the overarching principle of "production first, livelihood second," the Chinese countryside was considered as a base for agricultural production. Under the state rationing system, standard products at set prices were allocated in rural markets, with no consideration of consumers' preferences and choices. The supply of consumer goods, such as bicycles and watches, was very limited if not nonexistent in the countryside.

The dismantling of the state rationing system, the removal of controls in production, and the increase in rural household income as a result of the country's economic reform have stimulated new demands and thereby greater consumption. In the Pearl River Delta, for instance, rural families' consumption has expanded from basic home appliances (such as televisions, refrigerators, washing machines, and air conditioners) to high-end personal items (such as motor vehicles, cellphones, tablets, and personal computers). Young country folks have given up their plain traditional clothes and wooden clogs, and put on colorful, trendy fashions and sports shoes. They are no longer satisfied with affordable imitations and are conscious of brand names (Guldin, 2001), which are often considered key indications of wealth. The acquisition of these goods is usually associated with an influx of new values and other cultural changes. These processes are intensified by the wide spread of television and the internet in the countryside, providing rural residents with new windows into the world. Young people eagerly watch foreign films and listen to pop music from Hong Kong and South Korea. Other aspects of the "modern" lifestyle, such as dancing, karaoke, traveling, and other leisure activities, are becoming increasingly prevalent. This cultural shift has caused the West in particular, and cosmopolitan global society in general, to be more positively perceived.

The emergence of the consumption-centered lifestyle is associated with another important change in Chinese society—the rise of individualism. In the countryside, a major reason for such a change is the collapse of collective farming, which has prompted a shift in social ethics from an emphasis on collective values to individual values. The loosening (although not complete elimination) of the *hukou* system's restrictions on people's mobility has further disembedded individuals from traditional social/collective institutions such as families and communities. Millions of rural youth have left their families and looked for opportunities in cities. Through the mass media, the influence of urban lifestyles and popular culture has inspired individuals to seek individual rights, greater freedom, and more fulfilling lives. This is vividly illustrated by the wide spread of ideas like free love, personal development, independence, and freedom among young people in rural areas (Yan, 2009). Not only do they have more control over their lives, but they are developing a different set of life expectations (Guldin, 2001).

The rise of individualization in the Chinese countryside does not contradict our previous arguments about the persistence of collective institutions there. Researchers have revealed that individuals are indeed constantly moving in and out of the collectives. This indicates that even when young persons have developed individual choices and a sense of independent agency, they still rely on traditional collective institutions for support. In particular, family continues to play a key role in the Chinese countryside. Not only does it serve as a key resource to support an individual in different stages of life, but it also plays a key role in identity building. This is particularly the case for rural migrants who live and work in cities. Since they are excluded from most of the resources available to urban residents, they depend on their families or neighbors in their home villages to look after their children and have them educated in the local schools. Because not every village has developed a robust collective economy, family is often the only collective institution that an individual can rely on. Thus, despite modernization theory's emphasis on the discontinuity of rural practices and traditional culture with the process of industrialization, the Chinese countryside has demonstrated a condition of "in-betweenness" (Kipnis, 2013). This development, once again, suggests the uniqueness of the Chinese experience.

• • • • • • • • • • • • • • FINAL THOUGHTS • • • • • • • • • • • • • • • •

From land reform and collectivization in the 1950s to the restoration of the family farming system in the 1980s, the Chinese countryside has shifted from representing the country's revolutionary glory to poverty and underdevelopment. At the same time, some villages in certain regions have successfully boosted their economic conditions under the framework of collective ownership. Villages such as Huaxi, which is known as "the number one village in China," have created a new model of rural development. Secondary and tertiary industries have replaced agricultural activities, and native villagers enjoy affluent lives comparable to those of the urban middle class.

There is, however, unequal development in the countryside. In most parts of China, the word "rural" still means agriculture and farming, but rural areas in the coastal region are experiencing new types of development. Despite the loss of farming, distinctive rural practices such as self-reliance and the collective system have persisted. Given the urban–rural dichotomy, it is likely that China will not become a totally urban landscape (as most urban geography textbooks have suggested), but will retain a mix of urban and rural features.

REFERENCES

Chan, A., Madsen, R., & Unger, J. (2009). *Chen village: Revolution to globalization* (3rd ed.). Berkeley: University of California Press.

Chan, K. (2004). *Cities with invisible walls: Reinterpreting urbanisation in post-1949 China.* Hong Kong: Oxford University Press.

Chan, K. (2010). The household registration system and migrant labour in China: Notes on a debate. *Population and Development Review, 26,* 357–364.

Chen, S., & Ran, G. (2012). Chuantongnongye gaizao de shangpingluzhixiao yanjiu [A study of the commodity rate of traditional agriculture during transformation]. *Nongye Jingji Wenti [Issues in Agricultural Economy], 7,* 19–25.

Chung, H. (2009). The planning of 'villages-in-the-city' in Shenzhen, China: The significance of the new state-led approach. *International Planning Studies, 14*(3), 253–273.

Chung, H. (2014). Rural transformation and the persistence of rurality in China. *Eurasian Geography and Economics, 54*(5–6), 594–610.

Chung, H., & Unger, J. (2013). The Guangdong model of urbanisation: Collective village land and the making of a new middle class. *China Perspectives, 3,* 33–41.

Ding, S. (2005). Shenzhen de chengzhongcun wenti yu wenti de jiejue [The problem of villages-in-the-city in Shenzhen and resolutions]. *Kaifang Daobao [China Opening Herald], 3,* 39–42.

Fairbank, J. K., & Goldman, M. (1998). *China: A new history* (enlarged ed.). Cambridge, MA: Belknap Press/Harvard University Press.

Guldin, G. E. (2001). *What's a peasant to do?: Village becoming town in southern China.* Boulder, CO: Westview Press.

Guo, S., & Liu, C. (1990). *Shiheng di Zhongguo [China in disparity].* Hebei: Renming Chubanshe.

Halfacree, K. (2006). Rural space: Constructing a three-fold architecture. In P. Cloke, T. Marsden, & P. Monney (Eds.), *Handbook of rural studies* (pp. 44–62). London: SAGE.

Halfacree, K. (2007). Trial by space for a "radical rural": Introducing alternative localities, representations and lives. *Journal of Rural Studies, 23,* 125–141.

Jin, X. (2003). Chengshi "danweizhi" de shuailuo yu "shequren" de jianshe [The demise of the "work-unit" system and the building of the "community person"]. *Shehuixue [Sociology], 1,* 24–27.

Kipnis, A. B. (2013). Urbanisation in between: Rural traces in a rapidly growing and industrializing county city. *China Perspectives, 3,* 5–12.

Kueh, Y. Y. (1993). Food consumption and peasant incomes. In Y. Y. Kueh & R. Ash (Eds.), *Economic trends in Chinese agriculture* (pp. 229–271). Oxford, UK: Oxford University Press.

Kuo, L. T. C. (1976). *Agriculture in the People's Republic of China: Structural changes and technical transformation.* New York: Praeger.

Lan, Y. (2005). *Doushi lide cunzhuang [A village within city].* Beijing: Sanlun Shudian.

Lee, P., & Lau, S. (Eds.). (1980). *Renmin gongshe yu nongcun fazhen [People's commune and rural development].* Hong Kong: Chinese University Press.

Lewis, A. (1954). Economic growth with unlimited supplies of labour. *The Manchester School, 22*(2), 139–191.

Li, C. (2002). *Wuxiang zongli shuoshihua [I tell the premier the truth].* Beijing: Guangming Ribao Chubanshe.

Li, D., Davis, J., & Wang, L. (1998). Industralisation and the sustainability of China's agriculture. *Economics of Planning, 31,* 213–230.

Li, L. (2001). *Guangzhou chengzhongcun xingchen he gaizao jizhi yanjiu [A study on the formation and reform mechanism of villages-in-the-city in Guangzhou city].* Unpublished doctoral dissertation, Zhongshan University, Guangzhou, China.

Naughton, B. (2007). *The Chinese economy: Transitions and growth.* Cambridge, MA: MIT Press.

Oi, J. C. (1999). *Rural China takes off: Institutional foundations of economic reform.* Berkeley: University of California Press.

Smart, A., & Smart, J. (2001). Local citizenship: Welfare reform urban/rural status, and exclusion in China. *Environment and Planning A, 33*(10), 1853–1869.

Solinger, D. (2006). The creation of a new underclass in China and its implication. *Environment and Urbanization, 18,* 177–193.

State Statistical Bureau (SSB). (2012). *China statistical abstract 2012.* Beijing: Zhongguo Tongji Chubanshe.

State Statistical Bureau (SSB). (2013). *China statistical yearbook 2013.* Beijing: Zhongguo Tongji Chubanshe.

State Statistical Bureau–Household Survey Department (SSB-HSD). (Ed.). (2012). *Zhongguo nongcun pinkun jiance baogao 2011 [Poverty monitoring report of rural China 2011].* Beijing: Zhongguo Tongji Chubanshe.

Su, M. (2009). *China's rural development policy: Exploring the "new socialist countryside."* Boulder, CO: First Forum Press.

Tan, G. (2005). Chengzhongcun jingjizhuti, jingji huodong ji zhuyao tijin [Major characteristics of economic entities and activities in villages-in-the-city]. *Kaifang Daobao [China Opening Herald], 3,* 51–56.

Tang, W. S., & Chung, H. (2002). Urban–rural transition in China: Illegal land use and construction. *Asia Pacific Viewpoint, 43*(1), 43–62.

Unger, J., & Chung, H. (2012). Guangdong: Collective land ownership and the making of a new middle class. *East Asia Forum.* Retrieved from www.eastasiaforum.org/2012/05/18/guangdong-collective-land-ownership-and-the-making-of-a-new-middle-class.

Walker, K. (1966). Collectivization in retrospect: The 'socialist high tide' of autumn 1955–spring 1956. *China Quarterly, 26,* 1–43.

Walker, K. (1968). Organisation of agricultural production. In A. Eckstein, W. Galenson, & T.-C. Liu (Eds.), *Economic trends in Communist China* (pp. 397–358). Chicago: Aldine.

Wirth, L. (1938). Urbanism as a way of life. *American Journal of Sociology, 44*(1), 1–24.

World Bank. (2001). *China: Overcoming rural poverty.* Washington, DC: Author.

Wylie, R. F. (1979). Mao Tse-tung, Ch'en Po-ta and the "sinification of Marxism," 1936–38. *China Quarterly, 79,* 447–480.

Yan, Y. (2009). *The individualization of Chinese society.* Oxford, UK: Berg.

Yangcheng Wanbao [Yangcheng Evening Post]. (2000, September 6). There are 139 "villages-in-the-city" in Guangzhou [Guangzhou "chengzhongcun" gong 139 tiao]. p. A5.

Zhang, L., Zhao, S. X. B., & Tian, J. P. (2003). Self-help in housing and *chengzhongcun* in China's urbanization. *International Journal of Urban and Regional Research, 27*(4), 912–937.

Zhou, K. X. (1996). *How the farmers changed China: Power of the people.* Boulder, CO: Westview Press.

FURTHER READING •

Kojima, R. (1988). Agricultural organization: New forms, new contradictions. *China Quarterly, 116,* 706–735.

Zou, B. (2003). Zhishi chengxiang yitihua guanli mianlin de tiaozhen ji duice [Challenges and measures for the implementation of urban–rural integration management]. *Guihua Guanli [Planning Management], 8,* 64–67, 85.

CHAPTER 8

Transportation Geography and E-Commerce Logistics in China

LEARNING OBJECTIVES

- Understand how different transportation systems have developed in China over the past several decades.

- Comprehend the competition among different modes of transportation in relation to new technologies and changes in laws and regulations.

- Recognize the roles that transportation systems play in regional and local economic development policies.

- Understand the development of e-commerce, online shopping, and delivery services, and their present relationships.

KEY CONCEPTS AND TERMS

hierarchical structure of multimodal transportation; transport connectivity and accessibility; mobility; competition between high-speed rail (HSR) and air transport; containerization; density of transport demand; e-commerce, online shopping; courier services

WHEN MANY PEOPLE MOVE AT THE SAME TIME

In previous chapters, we described how China has experienced rapid urbanization and fast economic growth, and has rejoined the global market through expanding international trade. These are major changes that have occurred since economic reform began in 1978. These changes have been supported by a huge investment in transportation systems. China is among the largest economies in the world; it has a territory similar to that of the United States (see Chapter 1); and its population is more than four times as large. As this vast, densely populated country becomes wealthy, the demand for transportation services has also increased dramatically.

Imagine the difficulties that China has in handling the transportation needs of its huge population.

If a journey involves switching the mode of transportation once (e.g., from bus to rail), then the journey is counted as two "mode-trips." On average, a worker working outside his or her home province needs to make four mode-trips to complete a round-trip journey between workplace and hometown. About 900 million Chinese moved around, or temporarily migrated, during the month of the 2015 Chinese New Year holiday. They made 3.6 billion mode-trips at 4 mode-trips per person. Most importantly, this temporary migration, or *Chunyun* ("spring move"), (春运), takes place every year![1]

A major reason so many Chinese take this annual long-distance trip is that more and more young people have left their homes in the inland provinces to work in the coastal cities. The clustering of export-oriented industries in the Pearl River Delta region gave the region the nickname "the world's factory." Transnational corporations took advantage of the low rent and labor costs. Thus the concentration of manufacturing industries in coastal China put pressure on transportation systems in two ways. First, more seaports and airports had to be built to facilitate imports of raw materials and semifinished products, and exports of finished products such as mobile phones. Second, more railways and highways had to be built to connect places and regions within the country. In general, the past three decades have seen very rapid growth of transportation systems to cope with the economic development. This growth has been spatially unbalanced, reshaping the country significantly from a geographical configuration that supported an underdeveloped command economy.

In this chapter, we take a close look at how improvements in transportation have changed China's internal and external connectivity, as well as the daily life of the Chinese. We also discuss how the progress in transportation interacts with and reinforces the country's economic reforms.

A SHIFT IN TRANSPORTATION NETWORK DEVELOPMENT: FROM RAILWAYS TO HIGHWAYS

Up to the mid-1980s, railways constituted the backbone of China's economic development, as well as a political instrument for national unity (Leung, 1980). There were two major reasons for this. First, the railway was the best-developed means of transportation for large territories at the time. Second, like other countries with vast territory (such as the United States, India, Russia, and Canada), China regarded the rail system as the most economic means for moving low-value bulk staple products, such as ores, coal, and lumber, for the daily necessities of its people and industrialization. The major reserves of these key raw materials are located far away from the most populated regions in the east. Railways had been planned and constructed even during the World War II Japanese occupation for plundering China's resources. For three decades after the founding of the People's Republic in 1949, China insisted on a self-reliant economic policy that limited international trade and thus reduced the need for port development. The policy also led to huge increases in consumption and transportation, largely by rail, of raw materials and industrial products within the country. The role of highways was highly restricted during the central planning era (the 1950s to 1970s), as the leaders and planners believed that trucking was economically feasible only for short distances (within 150 km).

For this reason, as well as the poor economic conditions, the highway sector received very limited resources in comparison with rail. Until the 1970s, the national goal was to connect every city and county by low-grade, conventional highways. Not a single mile of expressway was built during that time. To achieve the national goal of industrialization, the manufacturing and use of trucks were prioritized, but not those of automobiles. Between the 1950s and 1970s, not a single individual in mainland China owned a private car. Only two brands of cars, Hongqi ("Red Flag") and Shanghai, were produced for use by government officials and as taxis in a few major cities such as Beijing and Shanghai. These domestic cars replaced imported cars from the former Soviet Union and other Communist bloc countries, such as Poland.

The priority of industrialization meant a focus on moving goods rather than people, and it also seriously affected the establishment of the aviation industry in China. Prior to the formal separation of the Civil Aviation Authority of China (CAAC) from the Chinese air force in 1987, ordinary Chinese were not allowed to fly, nor could they afford to fly. Anyone traveling by air had to get special approval from his or her working unit, and a round-trip ticket would cost an ordinary worker 6 months' salary. Limited routes and airports, and very low service frequencies, also meant that such an expensive air trip would seldom send the passenger directly to his or her destination unless it was one of the largest cities.

However, economic reform and marketization brought about a substantial increase in the importance of highways and air transportation in the 1980s. Both the interprovincial migration of workers and cargo movements created huge demands that railways alone could no longer handle. Two critical changes led to a boom in the construction of highways and expressways. First, policies and regulations changed to allow the charges for long-haul highway trucking to be regulated according to market principles. The second change allowed foreign capital investment in expressways through joint ventures. Prior to the economic reforms, all transportation services (i.e., the movement of cargo by shipping, trucking, railways, and air transportation) were tightly regulated in a unified pricing scheme set by the national government. Prices were based on (1) the weight of cargo, (2) the mileage shipped, and (3) the mode of transportation. Since 1978, these tight controls on pricing have been greatly relaxed, first for highway trucking and then for road charges. Individuals or non-state-owned enterprises were allowed to own and operate trucks, and to charge according to market demand.

International trade through maritime shipping began to boom due to the open-door policy. In regions such as the Pearl River and Yangtze River Deltas, private investors from Hong Kong started to set up joint ventures with state-owned firms (often subsidiaries of the provincial governments) to build toll expressways. These expressways often linked seaports with nearby cities and counties. Production sites for export were built along these highways. Toll roads were new to Chinese drivers, and the prices were set high to give the highway investors a return. By contrast, the national or regional highways are free to use because they are considered necessities.

Figure 8.1 compares the growth of different modes of transportation in China. It shows that highways and expressways grew faster than railways in terms of total length. They were also more concentrated in the coastal provinces in the east. The unique marketization process of China's economy affected the rapid growth of expressways. Unlike railways, which require integrated infrastructure (a network of standardized tracks) and synchronized operations among components (e.g., trains and stations), express highways can be constructed section by section in a piecemeal manner. Thus the joint ventures between private investors from outside the mainland and the local government subsidiaries constructed a few, often lucrative expressways connecting major cities first, such as between Guangzhou and Shenzhen in the Pearl River Delta and between Shanghai and Nanjing in the Yangtze River Delta. Other expressways followed in the same fashion until the market began to be saturated. The geographical diffusion of toll expressways since 1980 was very different from that of the free national highway system constructed between the 1950s and 1970s, as the latter system was considered a necessity for meeting basic needs.

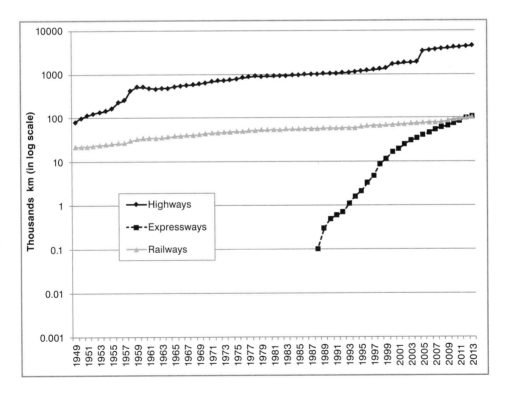

FIGURE 8.1 Growth of highways, railways, and expressways in China, 1949–2013. Data from State Statistical Bureau (SSB), *China Statistical Yearbook*, various years.

BOX 8.1. What Do Those Highway and Railway Numbers and Letters Mean?

Knowing the rules of how a nation's highways and railways are numbered is interesting and helpful. In the United States, interstate highways with even numbers go east and west. For example, I-10 stretches from Jacksonville, Florida to Santa Monica, California, while I-90 connects Boston, Massachusetts with Seattle, Washington. Odd-numbered interstate highways go north and south. For instance, I-5 stretches from the U.S.–Canadian border in Washington state to the U.S.–Mexican border in California. Another example is I-95 along the east coast, which goes from Maine to Florida.

Knowing the labeling system of highways and railroads is also useful for those traveling in China. According to the Chinese Ministry of Transportation, National Highway Lines (国道 or Guodao) are numbered in three ways: (1) lines radiating from the capital city, Beijing; (2) north–south vertical lines; and (3) east–west horizontal lines. The radiating lines are coded as G1 plus a number from 01 to 99. For example, the ring road (the equivalent of a U.S. beltway) around Beijing is included in the category of radiating lines and is numbered G112. North–south lines are coded as G2 plus a number from 01 to 99, and east–west lines are coded as G3 with a number from 01 to 99. For example, G205 links Qinhuangdao, a coastal city in north China, with Shenzhen in south China; G325 goes from Guangzhou, the provincial capital of Guangdong, to Nanning, the capital of the autonomous region of Guangxi. Currently there are 12 national highway lines radiating from the capital, 47 north–south lines, and 60 east–west lines, as well as 81 connection lines, which connect one city to another. The intercity connection lines are coded as G5 plus a number from 01 to 99. For example, G525 is the Pinghu–Hangzhou line within Zhejiang province.

For railway routes, the numbering is associated with the direction and type of train, according to the Central Railway Bureau. For each train route, the identification number consists of an alphanumeric prefix followed by one to three digits. Trains that go toward Beijing or join the main lines from branch lines are called "up-trains," whereas trains that go away from Beijing or split from the main lines to branch lines are regarded as "down-trains." Up-trains are labeled with even numbers, while down-trains use odd numbers.

The alphabetic prefix represents the types of passenger trains based on their distance and speed. Here are the classes by their prefixes:

- G (stands for Gao [高], which means "fast"): High-speed train (HSR), traveling at 300–350 km/hour—the fastest trains in China.
- C (stands for Cheng [城], which means "cities"): Intercity electric multiple-unit (EMU) train, also HSR, traveling at 200 km/hour or above.
- D (stands for Dong [动]): EMU train that runs at +160 km/hour—faster than a train of the T or K classes, but slower than the G and C HSR classes.
- Z (stands for Zhi [直]): Direct express train, mostly nonstop.
- T (stands for Te [特]): Express train, with stops at major cities.
- K (stands for Kuai [快]): Fast train, with more stops but operating across jurisdictions of multiple railway bureaus.
- N (stands for Nei [内]): Fast train that operates within one railway bureau.
- L (stands for Lin [临]): Train temporarily operated, with availability subject to certain circumstances.
- Y (stands for You [游]): Train temporarily operated for tourists.

Trains numbered between 751 and 5998 without an alphabetic prefix are various types of cargo trains.

The geographical areas covered by conventional highways and by expressways overlap to a certain extent, but these roads do not serve the country evenly. Some cities have higher levels of connectivity and accessibility than others. The two highway systems are also mismanaged in an important way: the failure to implement a synchronized charging scheme. Thus trucks overload conventional highways because no tolls are charged on these roads; this overloading creates congestion and overuse, while the toll expressways are underused.

About 90% of cargo for export is put into internationally standardized containers, while domestic goods are still carried by conventional trucks. This is largely due to different domestic standards of living across regions, as well as to the road-pricing system. For example, in the inland provinces, due to the relatively low standard of living, goods delivered via container trucking may cost too much and make the goods unaffordable. Thus the majority of container trucking is associated with ports in the coastal cities and provinces.

THE RAPID DEVELOPMENT OF PORTS
FOR INTERNATIONAL TRADE

Since the 1980s, China has witnessed unprecedented growth in its ports. It has gone from a country that had little international trade through maritime shipping to having the largest ports in the world. According to the World Shipping Council,[2] seven Chinese ports were ranked among the world's 10 largest in 2013 by annual container throughput: Shanghai (1st), Shenzhen (3rd), Hong Kong (4th), Ningbo (6th), Qingdao (7th), Guangzhou (8th), and Tianjin (10th). These rankings illustrate the intensive trade relations between China and the rest of the world. The economic development process has also tremendously altered the physical landscape of the port cities. When these ports were being revitalized, they all lacked deep-water docks nearby that could accommodate the huge and increasing size of ocean-going vessels (Wang, 2014). Therefore, many port cities such as Shanghai, Dalian, Qingdao, Guangzhou, and Ningbo have had their working ports moved to distant locations.

The "big-ship effect" refers to the trend of container ships' increasing in size about every decade from the 1970s to 2010s (Wang, 2014). This effect has made many older ports obsolete because they cannot meet the new requirements for vessel draft. In other words, the water is too shallow to accommodate the larger ships. The largest ocean-going container vessels today are as large as 400 m long and 30 m wide. When fully loaded with 19,000 "twenty-foot-equivalent unit" (TEU) containers, a ship requires 15.5 m of depth at berth and channel, as well as a large maneuvering diameter of deep-water space for turning around. Again, these new standards have forced cities to relocate their working ports to new sites, lest they fall out of competition. For example, the original port area of Shanghai has been relocated to Yangshangang (洋山港 or "Port of Yangshan"), which is located in Hangzhou Bay, 100 km southeast of the Shanghai city center (Figure 8.2). Such port relocations have had mixed consequences. Producers that rely on the ports to ship their products find themselves farther away, and the cost of trucking rises. At

FIGURE 8.2 The Shanghai Yangshangang container terminal, the world's largest single shipping terminal, 2015. (Photo: James J. Wang)

the same time, a more remotely located port may help improve a city's environment by lowering the concentration of emissions and congestion brought by both trucks and vessels.

The consequences of the big-ship effect are not limited to port relocation. They have been felt by provinces and cities along the Yangtze River, such as Wuhan, which became less competitive in attracting investors and manufacturers to set up their factories for the global market. Inland water transport has to use much smaller vessels. Adding up the transshipment cost (the cost of transferring shipment from one carrier to another) and time, these investors and manufacturers find that river transportation along the Yangtze is more expensive and slower than trucking from locations that are near major seaports. To improve this situation, Jiangsu province has dredged the lower reach of the Yangtze to a depth of 10 m to allow ocean liners to come farther inland. Although this effort was successful, it works only up to Nanjing or the lower stream of the Yangtze. Most inland provinces are not able to compete with the coastal ones in the global market. These inland provinces therefore do not need to use internationally standardized containers at all, as long as conventional trucking with conventional packaging is still cheaper for the domestic market.

As long as this divide in the use of containerization remains, the coastal and interior regions of China will continue to fulfill their own roles in the economy. They have separate roles since they differ so significantly in the cost of moving containers, which is a key factor in determining the location of manufacturing for the global market. As shown in Figure 8.3, shipping a container from Shenzhen, a Chinese coastal city in the south, to Hamburg, Germany (18,537 km away), is much

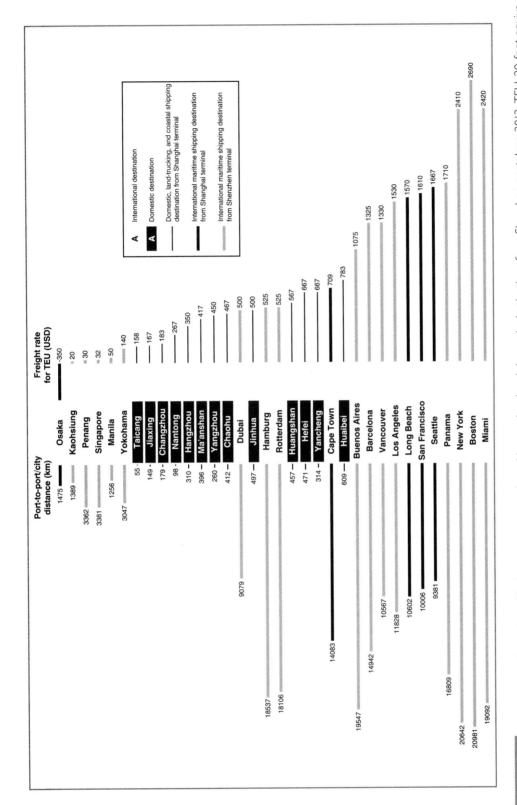

FIGURE 8.3 Comparison of container shipping rates among selected international and domestic destinations from Shenzhen port, June 2013. TEU, 20-foot equivalent unit (a common unit of measurement for internationally standardized containers); USD, U.S. dollars. Data compiled from online quotations given to us by various transport service providers in China.

less expensive than shipping it from Shenzhen to Hefei, an inland provincial capital in China (only 471 km away). This example illustrates how difficult it is for inland China to join the international trade business.

TRAVELING BY AIR OR BY HIGH-SPEED TRAINS?

So far, we have discussed transportation of cargo and ways in which the transportation systems can affect or be affected by industrialization and global trade. Passenger transportation is a different story.

By international standards, China's aviation industry is still in its infancy. For example, there were only about 200 airports in commercial operation by the end of 2014, compared to about 5,500 in the United States. The Chinese civil aviation industry only began moving toward its present status in about 1987, when the Civil Aviation Authority of China (CAAC) was reformed. The CAAC is a ministry-level, quasi-military government authority for air transportation. Before this reform, there was only one airline, also called the CAAC, and civil aviation was in fact operated by the air force. The reform had two major outcomes. First, the CAAC was split into six airlines as independent state-owned enterprises: Air China (home-based in Beijing, mainly for international routes); China Southwest Airlines (based in Chengdu, Sichuan province); China Eastern Airlines (based in Shanghai); China Northwest Airlines (based in Xi'an, Shaanxi province); China Southern Airlines (based in Guangzhou, Guangdong province); and China Northern Airlines (based in Shenyang, Liaoning province). Second, each airport became independently operated, and most airports became subsidiaries of local government authorities. In the 1990s, there was a period of "deregulation" in China's airline industry, when as many as 39 airlines were in operation and competition. For many reasons, including immature markets and poor management, bankruptcies and mergers followed. In 2002, the airlines were systematically reorganized into three major airline conglomerates: China International Airlines (Air China Group), China Eastern Airlines, and China Southern Airlines. Beside these three major airline groups, the fourth largest is Hainan Airlines, a non-state-owned company established in 1989. The trend toward conglomeration has also been seen in airport operation. Capital Airport Holdings, which is the largest airport holdings company, now operates more than 20 airports, including those in many metropolises such as Beijing, Tianjin, Chengdu, Wuhan, Guiyang, Nanchang, Changchun, and Harbin.

This new market for air transportation had a remarkable 17% annual growth rate for 26 years (1987–2013). The market, however, is spatially uneven. In 2014, 95% of the air passenger traffic was geographically concentrated in 63 cities, or one-third of all airports. Beijing, Shanghai, and Guangzhou, the hub airports for the three largest airlines, have 28% of total passenger flights and 51% of air cargo flights in the country. The uneven distribution of air transportation reflects the uneven economic development of China. It also reveals the fact that fewer than one-third of airports are profitable, and these are located largely in coastal regions. Local governments still heavily subsidize their air transportation operations.

Since 2008, high-speed rail (HSR) has challenged the prosperous air transportation market, particularly in cities with profitable but often congested airports. The central government considered HSR a key part of its stimulus program to keep the economy going after the global financial crisis of 2008. An aggressive plan and impressive speed in implementing that plan have quickly made China the world leader in HSR, with an HSR network totaling 12,183 km in length in operation (as of October 2014). This is longer than the total HSR network for the rest of the world, and China plans to have more than 50,000 km of HSR (capable of supporting train traffic at speeds higher than 250 km/hour) completed by 2020 (Bullock, Jin, Ollivier, & Zhou, 2014).

People are more willing to travel by HSR than by air if the travel time is within 4 hours from door to door. If the average HSR speed is 300 km, the maximum distance that most travelers would prefer to travel by HSR would be up to 1,200 km (Figure 8.4a). The ideal distance for HSR at that speed would be around 200–800 km, taking into account travel time from home to the departure HSR station and from the arrival station to the destination. Distances between many major cities in China fall within this range, such as those between Beijing and Nanjing, Nanjing and Shanghai, Guangzhou and Wuhan, Wuhan and Xi'an or Shanghai, and Xiamen and Hangzhou. After HSR started operating, many airlines stopped or significantly reduced service to cities served by HSR. For those flights that remain, the profitability has been greatly reduced because of competition from HSR.

From a national perspective, China has gained from the development of HSR in several ways. First, in comparison to air transportation, HSR is more environmentally friendly in term of per capita energy consumption per kilometer traveled. Second, HSR's carrying capacity is much larger than that of airlines, and HSR is most suitable for countries like China with a relatively high population density. By 2050, China will be the country with the largest number of megacities (i.e., cities with over 10 million residents) and megacity regions in the world (see Chapter 6). The HSR system should link these cities most effectively. Third, China has long suffered from the lack of railway capacity for long-haul freight (i.e., the movement of goods) because the conventional railway system has been largely used for passenger transportation. Limited capacity has been allocated to freight, and most of that has been for basic staples for the national economy, such as coal and crops. A major barrier to long-haul shipment of containerized cargo has been the limited capacity of the railway system, although it is supposed to be more economical and is certainly more environmentally friendly than using trucks. The newly built HSR system will shift passengers away from the old railways and release a reasonably large capacity for freight.

Aside from these advantages, the HSR system in China presents some other geographical features worth noting. Among the effects of HSR development are the spatial disparities in HSR access. The Chinese HSR system will be similar to HSR systems elsewhere, in that only selected cities will be connected with frequent service. A threshold of 1.5 million in population was set in the national HSR development plan in China for the cities to be connected by the year 2020. As a result of this threshold, a large number of cities and places will be bypassed by the HSR

FIGURE 8.4 (a) Platforms of the Wuhan HSR station with some of the high-speed trains, and (b) the walkway to the bus terminus, 100 m away from the Guangzhou South HSR station. The photo in (a) shows the sleek aerodynamic shape of the trains, which is necessary for the high speed. The photo in (b) illustrates that the connections between other transportation systems and the HSR stations are not too efficient in some cases. (Photos: James J. Wang)

network—forming a spatial polarization of rail connectivity, which may lead to the spatial polarization of development opportunities.

Another noticeable feature, one rarely seen in other countries' HSR systems, is the relative remoteness of station locations from the cities they serve (see Figure 8.4b). Many HSR stations in China are constructed in suburban areas or "new districts." There are many reasons for choosing such remote locations for the stations: (1) It is too costly or difficult to find locations in the inner cities; (2) the process of land acquisition to relocate existing stations in the urbanized areas is tedious and may be related to possible delays in completion; (3) HSR stations should act as core businesses or "growth poles" for developing new suburban districts and raising the land value in nearby areas (to increase the government's revenue from development); and (4) it is necessary to keep the railway lines as straight as possible, to reduce the distance required for acceleration. Consequently, travelers using HSR have to pay extra to get to and from the trains in the remote suburban stations (Wang, Xu, & He, 2013). Such a problem may be solved partly by providing efficient light rail or subway systems to link suburban stations with city centers, and partly by the passage of time until these new districts develop successfully as planned. However, for many cities, neither of these solutions is easy.

To respond to the threat from HSR, the three major domestic airlines (China Southern, China Eastern, and China International [Air China]) have formulated a unique strategy for their most popular routes between major cities, such as Shanghai–Beijing and Beijing–Guangzhou. The practice is called "bus-in-the-air": Travelers with a ticket from any one of these airlines may take the next available flight operated by any of the three, regardless of which airline sold the ticket.

The rapid expansion of HSR in China help shortens the travel time for its riders, particularly those traveling between major cities. However, China, with its great geographical diversity, needs to rely on other modes of transportation—air and road, in particular—to provide access to its remote cities, towns, and villages. Smaller airlines, such as some budget airlines, have begun services for tourist attractions not accessible by HSR within China and for some overseas destinations, particularly in Pacific Asia. In general, however, the development of budget airlines is still in its infancy, compared to those in Europe, the Americas, or even Southeast Asia and India. This is due largely to the lack of proper institutional and regulatory environments in China to nurture the entrepreneurship.

DRIVING OR TAKING PUBLIC TRANSIT IN A CHINESE CITY?

In 2013, China became the world's largest market in automobile sales. All major car manufacturers (General Motors, Ford, Volkswagen, Toyota, Honda, Mitsubishi, Fiat, Volvo, BMW, etc.) have assembly lines in China. The number of cars registered in Chinese cities has skyrocketed in the past few decades (see Figure 8.5).

The car ownership rate in the United States was 797 motor vehicles per 1,000 people in 2010,[3] compared with the rate of 152 per 1,000 in China in 2015.[4]

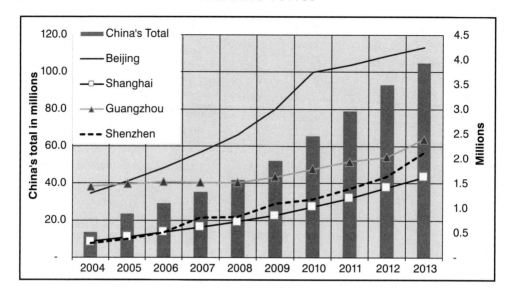

FIGURE 8.5 Rapid growth of private motorized vehicle ownership from 2004 to 2013: Beijing, Shanghai, Shenzhen, and Guangzhou against China's total. Data from SSB (2014).

Considering that the population of China is four times that of the United States, car manufacturers expect the Chinese figure to triple in the next two or three decades. However, anyone who lives in any major Chinese city today would agree that such an increase in car ownership rate should not happen. But it is happening—not only because the Chinese have become wealthier in general, but also because China's urbanization process has been different from that of other countries. For example, in the United States, most wealthy and middle-income families moved to the sub-urbs to enjoy large houses and yards while driving to work in downtowns or central cities. Many of their Chinese counterparts tend to have two residences: high-rise condominiums in inner cities for weekdays, and suburban residences with a more "Western" lifestyle for the weekends. Owning cars allows them to commute within urban areas during the week, but to retreat to the suburbs during the weekend.

The blue-collar working class constitutes the majority of those living in the high-rises in suburbs. As a result, the public transportation system in fact provides quite adequate service at reasonable prices (usually subsidized heavily) for ordinary citizens. For example, Shanghai's metro (subway) system has expanded rapidly. Between 2005 and 2010, this city added more than 400 km of subway lines in order to reduce the surface congestion. In many Chinese cities, about 40% of residents use transit for commuting, another 40% use automobiles, and 20% use nonmotorized modes of transport (including cycling and walking). A trend toward higher percentages of people using both private automobiles and public transit (including the metro and buses) is found in Beijing (see Figure 8.6). The trend toward private auto use, however, indicates that those who have opted to own a car and drive may not shift back to public transportation.

Commuting times by public transit in most Chinese cities are not satisfactory. There are many reasons for this. First, many subway stations were constructed far away from both residential areas and stops for other modes of transportation, such as buses or trolleys. A couple of interrelated reasons contributed to this peculiar spatial misalignment. The most important reason is that subways were always planned and constructed in a rush, since city leaders wanted to see the metros completed within their terms. Related to this is the second major reason: Stations had to be constructed in sites owned by the government, and relocation of any existing activities or residences had to be kept to a minimum. As a result, stations tend not to be located under existing buildings, and commuters have to take long walks to access the subways. Third, many Chinese who live in high-rise buildings should theoretically have better transit accessibility and affordability than many Americans who live in sprawling suburbs with low residential densities, which are detrimental to transit survival. However, many high-rise Chinese neighborhoods are large gated communities (they vary from 5 to 50 buildings or from 600 to 10,000 flats or households). These communities do not allow buses or any other forms of public transportation to set up access points, such as stops or terminals, within the communities. This restriction makes access to transit difficult. Many new districts in large cities, such as Pudong in Shanghai, Xinzheng in Zhengzhou, and Binhai in

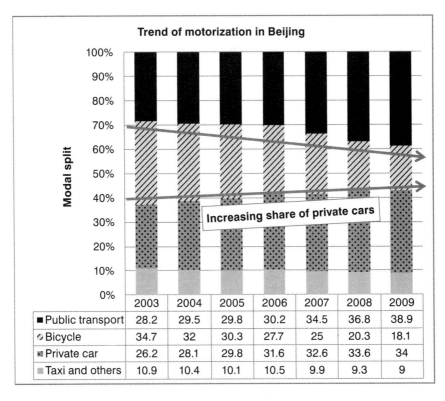

Trend of motorization in Beijing	2003	2004	2005	2006	2007	2008	2009
■ Public transport	28.2	29.5	29.8	30.2	34.5	36.8	38.9
⊘ Bicycle	34.7	32	30.3	27.7	25	20.3	18.1
▧ Private car	26.2	28.1	29.8	31.6	32.6	33.6	34
▨ Taxi and others	10.9	10.4	10.1	10.5	9.9	9.3	9

FIGURE 8.6 Trend of motorization in Beijing. Data from SSB (2014).

Tianjin, have car-oriented rather than walking-oriented street and block designs. A large-scale survey conducted by the Shenzhen city government in 2013 found that the newer residential buildings, whether in the inner city or the suburbs, provided more parking space for each flat than the older buildings did. Such provisions not only facilitate car ownership and usage, but also greatly compromise the effectiveness of public transportation.

Some Chinese cities have found a tough way to control car ownership. By the end of 2014, six cities had implemented a monthly car-purchasing cap system, conducted as a lottery. The right to purchase an automobile is given to the lucky winners each month. Table 8.1 shows that by the time the restrictive measures were put into effect, the car ownership levels of these cities were not very high in comparison to a typical U.S. city. However, when we consider the total numbers of cars, as well as the sizes and population densities of these cities, the problem is serious.

As we emphasized in Chapter 6, China is a large country with more than 460 cities of different sizes, geography, and levels of development; its various modes of transportation thus coexist as outcomes of local history and diverse solutions for the future. By 2015, 36 cities had mass transit rail (MTR) systems built or planned. In the United States and many Western countries, building a new railway line normally requires more than a decade from plan approval to construction. The process is much quicker in China, due to the role of strong and powerful city governments. In addition to MTR, new concepts have been widely introduced, discussed, and actually adopted in China, such as "bus rapid transit" (BRT) from Curitiba, Brazil; "transit-oriented development" from Portland, Oregon; and "free urban bicycles" from Paris, France. The Guangzhou BRT (GBRT) system is now seen as one of the best public transport systems in Asia. An interesting feature of the GBRT is to have free urban bicycles as the feeder system, to overcome the accessibility problem with the large high-rise gated communities not located close to the GBRT.

It is no surprise that in many cities, there are conflicts of interest over land use and among different groups, such as car drivers versus transit riders, each

TABLE 8.1. Implementation of Monthly Cap Schemes for Car Ownership Control in Selected Chinese Cities since 2010

	Beijing	Guiyang	Guangzhou	Tianjin	Hangzhou	Shenzhen
Starting date for car purchasing restriction	12/23/2010	7/12/2011	12/15/2013	12/16/2013	12/27/2010	12/29/2014
Ownership of motorized vehicles (thousands)	4,497.2	786.4	2,695	2,150	2,520	3,140
Population (millions)	19.61	4.39	12.7	14.72	8.84	10.63
Number of motorized vehicles per 1,000 population	229	172	212	146	285	295

Note. Data compiled from various sources, including the regulation announcements from individual city governments, and statistics yearbooks for the corresponding years from the statistics departments of the same cities.

fighting for their share of commuting space and privileges. Urban planners as well as city governments may have ideal sustainable objectives to be achieved through low-carbon transportation projects and programs, but the misconception that owning cars means modernization has deeply affected many Chinese. For these reasons, there may not be any substantial changes in the near future in contradictory regulations and policies—which encourage buying and using automobiles on the one hand, and subsidize and promote public transportation and a nonmotorized lifestyle on the other hand. Change may only come when environmental issues (addressed in Chapter 9) and social inequality concerns become unbearable.

BOX 8.2. Bus Rapid Transit in Guangzhou

Guangzhou Bus Rapid Transit (GBRT) is a system that integrates bike lanes, bike sharing, and metro (subway and bus) stations. GBRT started operating in February 2010, and it consists of 31 bus routes and 26 bus stations. The GBRT system stretches east and west, with a total length of 22.9 km. Figure 8.7 shows a line of GBRT buses waiting for passengers.

The innovative GBRT system was created as the centerpiece of a multimodal transportation network with integrated urban design elements. The GBRT corridor has fully segregated rapid bus lanes, with more than triple the capacity of any other BRT system in Asia. GBRT carries 800,000 daily passenger-trips, which is more than all of the city's five metro lines combined. It boasts a one-way peak passenger flow of 27,000 passengers per hour per direction, which places it second in the world (after Bogota, Colombia). Its passenger flow is higher than that for any of mainland China's metro lines, with the exception of line 2 and possibly line 1 in Beijing.

The GBRT system also has the world's highest BRT bus volumes, with 350 buses per hour in a single direction, or roughly 1 bus every 10 seconds. It is the first to provide direct access to metro stations, with station bridges connecting directly to adjacent buildings. A total of 113 bicycle stations with bike-parking and public bike-sharing systems are installed along the GBRT lines and in adjacent neighborhoods, providing Guangzhou citizens with over 5,000 bikes. A greenway on either side of the GBRT corridor combines dedicated bike lanes and walkways with recreational spaces like parks and plazas.

Other features of GBRT include the flat-rate bus fares and discounted smart cards for frequent users. These are components of the subsidized citywide low-fare program that has reduced the cost of a bus trip by nearly 50%. Polluted waterways were reclaimed as public space as part of the integrated process to build bicycle lanes with trees on the sides.

Since its commencement, GBRT has won many national and international awards for its extensive applicability and efficiency. GBRT received the Sustainable Transport Award from the Institute for Transportation and Development Policy (ITDP) in 2011. It is regarded as the first "metro-replacement-level" BRT system outside South America, with its significantly high passenger flows. In 2012, GBRT was the only Chinese project to win the Lighthouse Award under the United Nations Framework Convention on Climate Change. In recognition of its excellence, GBRT has also been awarded "Gold Standard" status by the ITDP. It is the first and only BRT system in Asia to be given this status, according to the BRT Standard criteria.

FIGURE 8.7 GBRT route 1: A long line of buses in the morning rush-hour direction, waiting for passengers to board, 2014. (Photo: James J. Wang)

THE COEVOLUTION OF ONLINE SHOPPING AND EXPRESS PARCEL DELIVERY

A new way in which transportation is shaping urban life in China is the coevolution of express parcel delivery and online shopping. Before 1994, China had only one domestic entity that was allowed to handle mail and packages—China Postal. Like many state-owned postal systems in the world, China Postal covers the entire country as required by its mission, but it had little incentive to improve the efficiency of parcel delivery because of the lack of competition. Its monopoly was broken by two major changes: (1) the regulatory change that allowed private and foreign operations to enter the express parcel delivery industry and (2) the emergence of e-commerce, which triggered huge business-to-consumer (B2C) sales and hence greatly increased the need for B2C express delivery service. In many developed countries, such as the United States and Japan, express parcel delivery appeared more than 50 years before e-commerce and online shopping; in China, by contrast, the two types of businesses grew hand in hand, coevolving in time and space.

In 2003, a firm named Alibaba (founded in 1999) established its e-marketplace, Taobao, in China as a platform like eBay in the West for consumer-to-consumer (C2C) trade. Then some small firms clustered around Zhejiang province began B2C businesses using Taobao. At the about the same time, a few small express delivery companies in the same province discovered that their business-to-business

(B2B) services for the deliveries between Zhejiang and Shanghai might be extended to B2C as well. In a few years, with delivery provided by these small express service companies, the B2C business on Taobao spread from Zhejiang to the Yangtze River and Pearl River Deltas, then to other parts of the coastal region such as Fujian province, and eventually to all of China.

How Low-End Express Deliveries Are Free

China is now the most rapidly growing market for e-retailing. This growth is driven primarily by the popularity of computers and mobile phones in China. Indeed, among developing countries, China leads in the ownership of mobile and internet-accessible devices. China has 129 million home broadband users, compared to 81 million in the United States (Dobbs et al., 2013). Statistics also indicate that China has the largest number of smartphone users, growing to 519.7 million in 2014 (eMarketer, 2014). By 2020, China's e-commerce market is forecast to be larger than those of the United States, Britain, Japan, Germany, and France combined (*The Economist,* 2013). Buying online is now just a click away. The Chinese, young or old, tend to spend more time online through their devices—not only at their homes or offices, but everywhere and all the time. A rational deduction is that the more time they spend online, the more likely they are to do some internet shopping. However, a survey in Europe reveals that two-thirds of people stop processing their online purchases when the delivery cost is shown (Copenhagen Economics, 2013). This is not the case in China because most of the items on major e-marketplaces such as Taobao or JD.com provide free delivery—or, in Chinese, *baoyou* (包邮) (see Figure 8.8).

Of course, delivery is not free to the sellers, but its cost is included in the price of the merchandise. However, some low-cost express parcel couriers charge much less than one might think. For example, a total of 9.2 billion parcels were delivered in China in 2013, with an average charge of 15.69 yuan (about $2.50 in U.S. dollars) per piece. The profit margin was as low as 12 U.S. cents per piece. This situation is possible because most delivery workers in major cities are members of the "floating population" from poor provinces (see Chapter 6). They work very long hours on a commission basis, but they pay little income tax, and thus they may still earn more than they otherwise could in their home counties.

Moreover, *baoyou* represents a cross-space subsidy, such as when a flat price system is implemented in a large country. A study (Wang & Xiao, 2015) shows that *baoyou* is most popular in the coastal region, where most online shops, online shoppers, and medium-size express parcel companies are concentrated. To get more business from the online retailers, express parcel companies compete fiercely with each other by offering package deals based on the quantity of the deliveries rather than the real delivery cost of each item. The e-retailers offer *baoyou* to increase the total sales. These commercial strategies work together as a price-flattening mechanism, benefiting those shoppers who live near the periphery of but still within the service area. Such spatial concentration does not appear in the United States because when eBay and Amazon.com started their businesses, FedEx and United

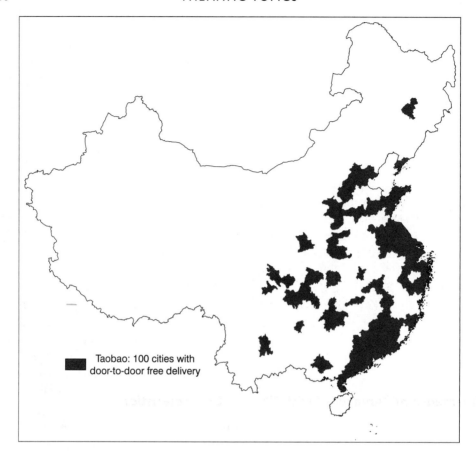

FIGURE 8.8 *Baoyou* in China favors the coastal regions: 100 cities with door-to-door free delivery by Taobao, using low-end express services, 2015. Based on Wang and Xiao (2015).

Parcel Service (UPS) had already well-established national oligopolies and global networks.

Once an e-shop appears in the e-marketplace, it becomes "placeless" in the sense that consumers anywhere in the country may place an order, regardless of the real location of the shop. However, the physical location of the shop or warehouse matters to the seller. The e-business has to find a courier, or a group of them, to cover the entire country. This demand has fostered a young express parcel industry for B2C e-commerce activities. The industry began with (1) regional delivery companies that covered a province or two with their own fleets of trucks and (2) many local delivery partners (LDPs, or *luodipei* [落地配]), which are responsible for the deliveries within their own cities. For example, Mail World (猫屋) was founded in Shenzhen in Guangdong province in 2012. It is now a national franchise with more than 700 chain stores, which serve as LDPs for Alibaba's TMall. Once product orders are delivered to a city with Mail World stores, these stores serve together as a local distribution network and are responsible for providing the last mile of delivery, or serve as a pickup point for residents living within 500 m of a store. These LDPs are also responsible for collecting payments when cash-on-delivery is selected, and for returns when purchases are canceled. Some regional couriers eventually grew into integrated, high-end national logistics firms, such as Shunfeng (SF Express), similar to UPS in the United States. Many other companies contracted franchisees that work in different cities. They fit into low-end markets by employing many people, forming a special informal sector. These couriers use their own motor-tricycles or motorbikes to deliver online-purchased parcels. They appear everywhere in China, from Beijing and Shanghai to smaller cities, counties, or even the countryside (Figure 8.9).

Both the high and low ends of the express parcel delivery industry have been evolving rapidly since 2003 with the growth of e-retailing sales. A positive sign is that purchases from remote regions and from medium-size and small cities are increasing quickly, due to the rapid expansion of express delivery. The spatially progressive effect of e-retailing may indicate that online shopping at e-marketplaces plus the low-end delivery can be a more effective retail solution for the remote and inland areas than the conventional wholesale and retail format. However, at the peak time for e-retailing, November 11 (the so-called "Bachelors' Day" in China), there has been serious congestion at almost every step in the multiple-subcontracting systems. This congestion reveals a serious defect of the system: unreliability for timely delivery.

Emergence of "Amazons" with Chinese Characteristics

A new form of e-retailing appeared around 2008—"channel-based" e-merchants (i.e., merchants carrying a single type of merchandise). They are represented by Jingdong (JD.com) and Yihaodian (YHD). The former sells electronic products and home appliances such as mobile phones, TV sets, and microwave ovens; the latter

FIGURE 8.9 Low-end express service providers with their motor-tricycles quasi-legally parked outside a university campus in Beijing, waiting for university students to pick up the products they bought online, March 2015. (Photo: James J. Wang)

is an online supermarket, selling everything available in a supermarket. Although they carry different types of goods (different "channels"), they have implemented a similar strategy by focusing first on one major city (Beijing for JD.com, Shanghai for YHD) and then gradually expanding to other metropolises. They internalize all logistical and transportation arrangements, from operating regional fulfillment centers and city distribution hubs to providing last-mile delivery to every customer. For orders originating from other regions, they contract out the delivery to third-party logistics (3PL) companies. Thus the delivery of JD.com and YHD goods is time-sensitive within and beyond each major city these e-merchants serve. For example, JD.com (see Figure 8.10) has its regional fulfillment center located in Wuhan, the capital city of Hubei province at the center of China. The center offers four different delivery ranges: within 12 hours, within 24 hours, within 48 hours, and longer than 48 hours.

The strategy has worked extremely well. The success of these channel-based e-merchants has led to a few spatial consequences that may affect the future of retail geography, or even urban development as a whole. On the one hand, online shops stimulate the young express parcel industry to penetrate regions that are otherwise less accessible. This logistical expansion helps the retailers, the manufacturers, and the consumers in these less developed regions to enjoy a generally enlarging

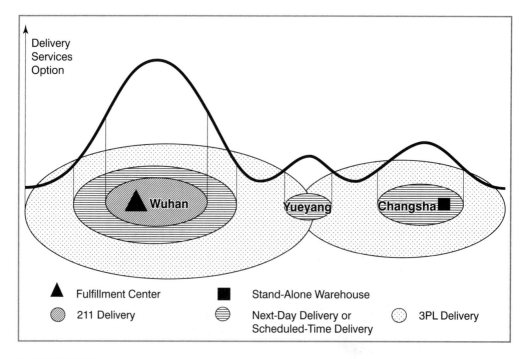

FIGURE 8.10 Illustration of the zonal delivery strategy of JD.com in central China. "211 delivery" refers to the policy that orders placed before 11:00 A.M. will be delivered before 6:00 P.M. on that day, and orders placed after 6:00 P.M. but before 11:00 P.M. will be delivered by 11:00 A.M. the next day; 3PL delivery, third-party logistics delivery. Data from www.jd.com.

market. On the other hand, the channel-based e-merchants are substantially changing buyers' behaviors, as well as retail geography in general. Compared with the conventional retail chains, these e-merchants pay zero rent in expensive urban shopping areas or shopping malls, can send merchandise to consumers' homes in a very short time, and offer attractive discount prices for the same products that are available in conventional stores. All these changes have brought new challenges to urban planners as well as urban transportation management. Where should these e-firms locate their distribution centers? What is the impact of such online shopping on the space requirements for, and roles played by, regional shopping malls or downtown shopping centers? How can planners facilitate a large demand for small vehicles moving around and into gated communities in a safe and environmentally friendly manner?

The impact of e-commerce on transportation is complicated further when firms shift their customer interface from the internet to mobile smartphones—a shift called "online to offline" (O2O). There are more than 500 million people in China using smartphones today. Local positioning system technology, QR codes, and online payment systems together create a new virtual environment that allows people to place a purchase order whenever and wherever they are, as long as they can find the product on their phones. This kind of virtual environment has already appeared in a few major Chinese cities.

Future Trends in Cross-Border E-Commerce

Another way that e-commerce will shape China is through recasting both the transportation and logistics systems to enable cross-border online shopping. Statistics show that China and the United States are the two countries that have the largest cross-border shopping and sales through the internet. The top three categories of cross-border goods purchased by the Chinese are foods and health care products for children (such as milk products from Germany and Australia), cosmetics for women, and brand-name clothing and accessories. Asymmetrically, the items exported from China through e-retailing sales are non-brand-name items and relatively reliable low-priced electronics such as Wi-Fi routers.

Cross-border e-retailing differs fundamentally from domestic e-retailing. It involves not only the language and cultural issues involved in setting up and designing online shops, but also all the issues of global trade, such as tariff and nontariff barriers, which may vary from country to country. Cross-border e-retailing also faces a transportation dilemma: online shoppers' high expectation of speedy, low-cost, direct point-to-point shipment versus expensive, intercontinental, intermodal transportation, by air wherever possible. A practical strategy for online retailers to overcome this dilemma is to purchase popular items based on demand forecast, and ship them as small bulk shipments by maritime transportation or normal flights before orders are placed. These imports of foreign products should ideally be stored in a place free of import duty until the orders are placed. In China, such ideal places are free-trade zones or duty-free zones. These zones have been established only in selected cities approved by the national government. By the end of 2014, only seven cities (Shanghai, Ningbo, Hangzhou, Chongqing, Guangzhou, Zhengzhou, and Shenzhen) were designated as "cross-border e-commerce trial cities" by the central government. In the duty-free zones of these trial cities, foreign consumer goods such as cookware imported from Germany are treated as untaxed products for sale. They can be purchased online as not yet "cross-border" products, and hence they become "personal goods" when they are sold to the buyers. The buyers themselves may actually come to this zone to buy, or ask a logistics firm to pick up and pay the import tax for, the products. The difference is that since the products are bought "abroad" and become "personal goods," the tax to be charged is much lower (if the purchase is within a limited amount for personal use and is made with the buyers' real IDs) than the import tax for foreign "products for trade."

Establishing "trial cities" has been a typical model in China's economic reform since 1978. Some institutional changes toward marketization were first tested in a few trial cities. Once the changes were tested and found to be progressive and constructive to the economic reform, they would be adopted with some necessary modifications on a larger geographical scale for multiple cities or for the entire country. It is difficult to know how long the cross-border e-commerce trials in these seven cities will take. It is clear, however, that these cities are taking advantages of the policies and regulations in the trial that favor global online retailing, and they are trying their best to become transportation and logistics hubs for such retailing. Geographically, it is interesting to note that three of these seven cities (Shanghai, Ningbo, and Hangzhou) are located in the Yangtze River Delta, where most of the e-commerce firms are located, and that this region has the highest percentage of online purchases in China. Two of the other cities (Guangzhou and Shenzhen) are in the Pearl River Delta, which is the second most popular region for online purchase and e-commerce. The two metropolises in inland provinces (Chongqing and Zhengzhou) have the largest international air connections and best surface transportation connections in their regions.

• • • • • • • • • • • • • • • FINAL THOUGHTS • • • • • • • • • • • • • • •

In this chapter, various modes of transportation have been discussed in relation to the overall economic development and reforms in China. Most of the changes we have discussed have taken place within the past three decades or so. They reveal a few key points that deserve our special attention here.

First, marketization and globalization are two major driving forces that have greatly stimulated the movement of people and the demand for goods in China, which in turn have brought huge investments in transportation infrastructure. From the 1980s to the turn of the century, these investments included highway networks for the domestic market and ports for international trade. From the year 2000 onward, they included the national HSR and urban MTR networks. Some of these investments provided stimuli to keep China's economy going after the world financial crisis in 2008 (see the discussion of economic development in Chapter 5).

Second, China followed a unique path in developing its transportation systems. Most developed countries such as the United States experienced peak growth for each separate mode of transportation in order: first canals, then railways, highways, maritime shipping, air transport, and now planning for HSR. China experienced the almost simultaneous booming of several major modes of transport—namely, highways/automobiles, air transportation, and HSR. Together, they have increased the connectivity of most Chinese cities within a very short period. However, major cities and core economic regions have gained much more in connectivity than other cities and regions in almost every mode of transportation, leading to a disparity of accessibility that favors the more developed regions.

Third, new information and communication technologies have been major factors facilitating new transportation arrangements and logistics for unconventional economic activities, such as online shopping and e-commerce. These improved transportation and logistical services for e-commerce also favor major cities and core economic regions.

Last, central and local governments have been playing critical roles in these transportation developments, even though marketization has now proceeded for four decades. In this chapter, we have pointed out that many critical decisions by the national government have set the directions for future transportation development. For example, a city population of 500,000 has been set as the threshold for cities to be connected by HSR by 2020. The planning and construction of MTR or an airport in any city must be approved by the central government. The central government has selected the cities that may experiment with innovative policies and regulations, and hence may gain from cross-border e-commerce shipments.

The strong and visible hand of the state seems to be effective in making things happen fast, but one should never underestimate the unwanted outcomes of these hasty decisions. In the transportation sector, unwanted outcomes may appear immediately, or soon after. For example, the rapid increase in automobiles in many cities is totally inconsistent with the massive investment in MTR and sustainability goals. Other examples are the many HSR stations built far away from city centers with poor local transit connections to them. The remote station locations not only make HSR users waste a tremendous amount of time to access the service, but prevent cities from using HSR stations to revitalize run-down areas in inner cities.

A few possible future directions in Chinese transportation deserve attention. The first is an increase in intercity railway connections within individual provinces. With environmental and economic concerns, provinces such as Guangdong and Jiangsu have started their own railway development plans to facilitate intercity HSR travel, which may be regarded as the second phase of China's HSR network development. This phase is driven not by the central government's stimulus plan, but by local needs. The second possible direction is to open up more airspace for civilian aviation. Currently, only about 20% of the total airspace in China is available for civilian aviation; the remaining 80% is limited to military use. These proportions of civilian and military airspace are the opposite of the situation in the United States. No one knows when the tight control of airspace in China may be relaxed. However, pressure has been building because of serious congestion and delays at major airports. Demand will grow in the future. In 2014, the annual frequency of air travel per capita was 0.3 times for the average Chinese, compared to 2 times per year for the average American. The potential market for general aviation (i.e., small private aircraft operating below 1,000 m in airspace) is huge. Some Chinese individuals and companies have become wealthy enough to have their own aircraft, and the demand for small jet services (e.g., for emergency rescues in mountain areas) is also high. The third direction for future development in transportation is to implement policies and regulations that favor sustainable cities. For example, the encouragement of nonmotorized modes of transportation (such as cycling and walking) as ways of connecting to MTR services or commuting for short distances should go along with tightening control of automobile usage. Indeed, the policies favorable to automobile ownership make sustainable development measures extremely difficult to implement, if not impossible. The "trial city" model discussed earlier in this chapter should be considered; as a Chinese saying goes, "A fine example has boundless power" (榜樣的力量是無窮的).

NOTES ●●●

1. Interested readers may watch two videos about *Chunyun* in China: www.youtube.com/watch?v=wwFNyOVH9hs (produced by a Chinese network, CCTV+) and www.youtube.com/watch?v=r6rILEiocQk (produced by CCTV+ and CNN) (both retrieved June 1, 2016).

2. www.worldshipping.org/about-the-industry/global-trade/top-50-world-container-ports.

3. https://web.archive.org/web/20140209114811/http://data.worldbank.org/indicator/IS.VEH.NVEH.P3 (retrieved June 26, 2016).

4. http://auto.people.com.cn/n1/2016/0126/c1005-28086267.html (retrieved June 26, 2016).

REFERENCES ●●●●●●●●●●●●●●●●●●●●●●●●●●●●●●●●●●●●●●●

Bullock, R., Jin, Y., Ollivier, G. P., & Zhou, N. (2014). *High-speed railways in China: A look at traffic* (China Transport Topics No. 11). Washington, DC: World Bank Group. Retrieved July 20, 2017, from http://documents.worldbank.org/curated/en/451551468241176543/High-speed-railways-in-China-a-look-at-traffic.

Copenhagen Economics. (2013). E-commerce and delivery: A study of the state of play of EU parcel markets with particular emphasis on e-commerce, a report for DG Internal Market. Retrieved from https://ec.europa.eu/futurium/en/content/e-commerce-and-delivery-study-state-play-eu-parcel-markets-particular-emphasis-e-commerce.

Dobbs, R., Chen, Y., Orr, G., Manyika, J., Chui, M., & Chang, E. (2013). China's e-tail revolution: Online shopping as a catalyst for growth. McKinsey Global Institute. Retrieved June 1, 2016, from www.mckinsey.com/global-themes/asia-pacific/china-e-tailing.

The Economist. (2013). The Alibaba phenomenon. Retrieved March 23, 2013, from

https://www.economist.com/news/leaders/21573981-chinas-e-commerce-giant-could-generate-enormous-wealthprovided-countrys-rulers-leave-it

eMarketer. (2014, January 16). Smartphone users worldwide will total 1.75 billion in 2014. Retrieved June 1, 2016, from www.emarketer.com/Article/Smartphone-Users-Worldwide-Will-Total-175-Billion-2014/1010536#sthash.Zdxd1uYw.dpuf.

Leung, C. K. (1980). *China: Railway patterns and national goals* (Department of Geography, Paper No. 195). Chicago: University of Chicago.

State Statistical Bureau (SSB). (2014). *China statistical yearbook 2014.* Beijing: Zhongguo Tongji Chubanshe.

Wang, J. J. (2014). *Port–city interplays in China.* Aldershot, UK: Ashgate.

Wang, J. J., & Xiao, Z. (2015). Co-evolution between etailing and parcel express industry and its geographical imprints: The case of China. *Journal of Transport Geography, 46,* 20–34.

Wang, J. J., Xu, J., & He, J. (2013). Spatial impacts of high-speed railways in China: A total-travel-time approach. *Environment and Planning A, 45*(9), 2261–2280.

FURTHER READING ●

China Internet Watch. (2013). China e-commerce market to reach 30 trillion yuan in 2020. Retrieved June 1, 2016, from www.chinainternetwatch.com/2007/china-e-commerce-market-2020.

Dong, J., Jin, F., Wang, J., & Liu, D. (2013). Game of high-speed rail and civil aviation and its spatial effect—a case study of Beijing-Shanghai high-speed rail. *Economic Geography* (in Chinese), *33*(5), 104–110.

Hughes, C., & Shu, X. (2011, May). Guangzhou, China Bus Rapid Transit: Emissions impact analysis. Institute for Transportation and Development Policy. Retrieved June 1, 2016, from www.itdp.org/wp-content/uploads/2014/07/GZ_BRT_Impacts_20110810_ITDP.pdf.

CHAPTER 9

An Environmental Crisis with Chinese Characteristics

LEARNING OBJECTIVES	KEY CONCEPTS AND TERMS
★ Develop a broad understanding of China's environmental problems with respect to air, water, land, and climate change. ★ Learn about the progress on high-environmental-cost issues, as well as the price of the national goal to sustain economic growth. ★ Recognize the effects of Mao's legacy, especially his "war against nature," on China's environmental woes. ★ Understand the notion of an environmental crisis with Chinese characteristics: top-down authoritarian control versus civilian initiatives.	"under the dome" (living with toxic smog); Green Olympics; water crisis (surface and underground); spatial disparity of water resources; "bad earth" (desertification); climate change; common but differentiated responsibilities (CBDR); environmental crisis with Chinese characteristics

CHINA'S ENVIRONMENTAL CRISIS: THE SETTING

We set the stage for a discussion of China's environmental crisis with a brief review of some facts about China presented in earlier chapters. China is the fourth largest country in the world in terms of area, after Russia, Canada, and the United States. Its territory of 9.56 million square kilometers (km^2; the area of the United States is about 9.82 million km^2) occupies about 6.5% of the world's total land area. But on this 6.5% of land surface, China has about one-fifth of the world's population. It is the most populous country in the world, with an estimated population of 1.373 billion in 2016. Table 9.1 shows the six largest countries in terms of area. China

TABLE 9.1. Largest Countries (by Area) of the World, with Their Populations and GDPs

Country	Area (km², thousands)	Population (millions)	Total GDP (purchasing power parity, in 2015 U.S. $)	GDP per capita (purchasing power parity, in 2015 U.S. $)
Russia	17,098	142.4	3,725	26,000
Canada	9,985	35.4	1,634	45,600
United States	9,827	323.9	18,040	56,100
China	9,597	1,373.5	19,700	14,300
Brazil	8,515	205.8	3,199	15,600
Australia	7,741	23.0	1,141	47,600

Note. Data from https://www.cia.gov/library/publications/resources/the-world-factbook (retrieved November 5, 2016).

has the highest total gross domestic product (GDP), which recently surpassed that of the United States. However, given its large population, China ranks sixth in per capita GDP. Geographically, China is endowed with great diversity in its physical resources, and these are critical to its long-term sustainable development.

China has achieved rapid economic growth since the inception of market-oriented economic reform in 1978. The country's economy, already large, is growing faster than any other nation's. The growth model adopted by China today is extensive and characterized by high energy consumption and heavy environmental pollution. As China's prosperity grows, so do its environmental problems: pollution in air, water, and land; biodiversity losses; cropland losses; depleted fisheries; desertification; disappearing wetlands; grassland degradation; and increasing numbers of human-induced natural disasters, among others. Many of these problems are the results of rises in invasive species (intentionally or unintentionally introduced), overgrazing, soil erosion, trash accumulation, industrial and other pollutants, and water shortages. The environmental crisis affects almost all aspects of people's lives.

In this chapter, we discuss the causes and effects of major environmental problems in China, addressing these problems in four major spheres: air, land, water, and climate change (as shown in Figure 9.1). Each of these sets of problems is significant in magnitude, and each is found in specific locations and geographical regions. The causes of these problems are associated with specific human activities. Specifically, air pollution is a serious problem in Chinese cities, particularly those in the northern region. China's water resources are dwindling in major river basins around the country, but many Chinese continue to use freshwater resources in an unsustainable manner. Moreover, land degradation is widespread throughout the country. In the dryland areas in the north and northwestern parts of China, improper use of land and incompatible human activities have led to an extensive desertification problem. Finally, since 2007, China has surpassed the United States as the world's number one producer of carbon emissions; meanwhile, it is also a major victim of extreme weather conditions. Therefore, China's role in tackling climate change issues cannot be underestimated. This chapter aims to examine the

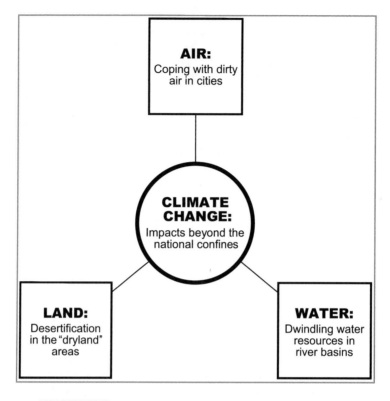

FIGURE 9.1 Major spheres of environmental concern in China.

environmental problems in these four areas by focusing on their unique Chinese characteristics.

COPING WITH DIRTY AIR

"Air pollution" is defined as the presence of chemicals in the atmosphere at concentration levels high enough to harm humans and the ecosystem. These pollutants, often found in industrialized and urban areas, are generated mostly by the burning of fossil fuels in power plants and industrial facilities, and from motor vehicles along major transportation routes. Air pollutants can cause respiratory problems, triggering asthma attacks, eye irritation, and much more.

Undoubtedly air pollution has become a major threat to public health worldwide, but the problem is particularly serious in Chinese cities. The severity of the air pollution problem in China was vividly shown in an investigative report entitled "Under the Dome" by a Chinese journalist, Chai Jing. The report, released in March 2015, has been the most high-profile investigation on the topic, and discussion of it soon flooded China's social media platforms.[1] Air pollution is currently the leading environmental problem in China. The World Health Organization (WHO) announced that air pollution, both indoors and outdoors, contributed to seven million deaths worldwide in 2012; more than one-third of those deaths occurred in the fast-developing nations of Asia, including China and India. Al Gore, a former vice president of the United States and now a leading advocate for environmental action, has claimed that air pollution has shortened the life of many Chinese—especially in northern China, where air pollution is the most severe.[2]

In order to gain better control of the country's air pollution problem, the Guideline on Strengthening Joint Prevention and Control of Atmospheric Pollution to Improve Air Quality was endorsed by China's State Council in May 2010. This comprehensive guideline was jointly developed by the Ministry of Environmental Protection (MEP) and other ministries, in part based on the lessons learned from the Beijing Olympics, the Shanghai Expo, and the Guangzhou Asian Games. The guideline explicitly acknowledges that air pollution in China is a national and regional problem that cannot be addressed by provinces acting individually. It was hoped that this new initiative would empower the MEP to better encourage and coordinate air quality management and strengthen policy implementation at the local level.

The MEP is responsible for monitoring air pollution levels in China, including the daily pollution levels in major Chinese cities. The air pollution index (API) computed from monitoring stations located throughout each city reports the levels of six atmospheric pollutants: sulfur dioxide (SO_2), nitrogen dioxide (NO_2), suspended particulate matter smaller than 10 microns (μm) in aerodynamic diameter (PM_{10}), suspended particulate matter smaller than 2.5 μm in aerodynamic diameter ($PM_{2.5}$), carbon monoxide (CO), and ozone (O_3). The major source of these pollutants is the combustion of fossil fuels, the dominant source of energy used in China. Table 9.2 summarizes the sources and impacts of major air pollutants in major cities in China.

Millions of Chinese citizens are living in and coping with an unhealthy atmosphere. For example, in 2013, the U.S. Embassy in Beijing issued an alert that the air quality in the city was at the "very unhealthy" or "hazardous" levels. The MEP published a statement on its website[3] noting that only 8 out of China's 74 biggest cities met the government's basic air quality standards in 2014. The MEP claimed that the result was already an improvement over the previous year, 2013, when only 3 cities had met the standard.[4] These cities included Haikou in the island province of Hainan, Lhasa in the Xizang (Tibet) autonomous region, and the coastal resort city of Zhoushan in Zhejiang province. They were joined in 2014 by Shenzhen, Huizhou, and Zhuhai in the southern province of Guangdong; Fuzhou in neighboring Fujian province; and Kunming in the southwestern province of Yunnan. Therefore, it is evident that the air quality in China showed a slight improvement—but only a slight one—when China "declared war on pollution" by starting to eliminate substandard industrial facilities and reduce coal consumption in the country beginning in 2013.

Table 9.3 shows the 10 cities with the best and worst air quality in China, according to the new air quality standards adopted in 2013. Figure 9.2 shows their locations. Geographically, the cities with the best air quality were located in the remote western part of China (such as Lhasa and Kunming), or were medium-size cities along the southeastern coast; an exception was Shenzhen, which is now one of the

TABLE 9.2. Sources and Impacts of Major Air Pollutants in Major Chinese Cities		
Air pollutants	**Sources/comments**	**Impacts**
Sulfur dioxide (SO_2)	Main source is coal combustion; more serious in northern cities than in southern China; slight decline due to changing fuel structure (from coal to natural gas).	Acid rain has negative impacts on the ecosystem; SO_2 is linked with a number of adverse effects on the respiratory system.
Nitrogen oxides (NO_x)	Worsening in major urban areas with increasing vehicle stocks and congested road networks; more serious in northern cities than in the south.	Can pose serious health risks in lowering lung function and raising the response to allergens.
Total suspended particulates (TSP) including PM_{10} and $PM_{2.5}$	Main source is combustion emissions, especially from thermal power stations using coal; particulates include "soot," "dust," and other smaller particles (including a variety of toxic heavy metals, acid oxides, and organic pollutants).	Adverse health effects, including increased mortality and morbidity, premature deaths; negative effects also on visibility and climate in general (radiation).
Carbon oxides	Carbon monoxide (CO) is a colorless, odorless, and highly toxic gas that forms during the incomplete combustion of carbon-containing materials; carbon dioxide (CO_2) is also a colorless and odorless gas, produced by the natural carbon cycle and human activities (especially burning of fossil fuel).	CO can kill people if inhaled in large quantities; CO_2 is a part of the natural carbon cycle, but is now regarded as a major greenhouse gas leading to climate change; China has become the world's largest producer of CO_2 since 2007.
Ozone (O_3)	Ground-level O_3 is not emitted directly into the air, but is created by chemical reactions between oxides of nitrogen (NO_x) and volatile organic compounds (VOC); O_3 is the main component of smog or haze.	O_3 is likely to reach unhealthy levels on hot, sunny days in urban environments; it contributes to what we typically experience as "smog" or "haze."

Note. Data summarized from various sources.

largest cities in China. Among the 10 cities with the worst air quality in 2014, 7 were located in the province of Hebei—a center of heavy industry that surrounds the capital, Beijing. The cities of Baoding, Xingtai, Shijiazhuang, Tangshan, Handan, and Hengshui, all in Hebei, filled the top six places. The other most polluted cities were found mainly in neighboring provinces such as Henan and Shandong; they also included the municipality of Tianjin. The MEP reported that the average reading for suspended particulate matter smaller than 2.5 μm ($PM_{2.5}$) in the Beijing–Hebei–Tianjin region stood at 93 micrograms per cubic meter (μg/m^3), significantly higher than the state standard of 35 μg/m^3 in 2014. The government has identified Hebei as a top priority when it comes to cutting smog, and the province has set targets to reduce coal consumption and close polluting industrial operations. However, Hebei is struggling to find alternative energy sources for growth in the years ahead. Nevertheless, the smog issue is often in the news in China, especially in the winter months. Citizens now have direct access to the haze/smog forecast for each city in real time,[5] as well as to real-time reports on the air quality of major cities in China and other cities all over the world.[6] These are attempts to

TABLE 9.3. The 10 Best and the 10 Worst Cities in China with Respect to Air Quality

Rank	Cities with the best air quality	Cities with the worst air quality
1	Haikou, Hainan	Baoding, Hebei
2	Zhoushan (Chusan), Zhejiang	Xingtai, Hebei
3	Lhasa, Tibet	Shijiazhuang, Hebei
4	Shenzhen, Guangdong	Tangshan, Hebei
5	Zhuhai, Guangdong	Handan, Hebei
6	Huizhou, Guangdong	Hengshui, Hebei
7	Fuzhou, Fujian	Jinan, Shandong
8	Xiamen, Guangdong	Langfang, Hebei
9	Kunming, Yunnan	Zhengzhou, Henan
10	Zhongshan, Guangdong	Tianjin, Tianjin

Note. Data from www.chinadaily.com.cn/china/2015-02/02/content_19466412.htm.

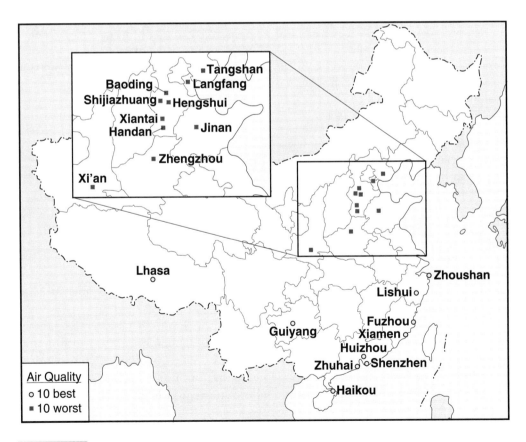

FIGURE 9.2 Spatial distribution of the 10 best and the 10 worst cities in China in terms of their air quality. Data from www.chinadaily.com.cn/china/2015-02/02/content_19466412.htm.

BOX 9.1. Air Quality and the Olympic Games

Beijing has long been ranked as one of the world's most polluted cities. When Beijing (along with six other Chinese cities) hosted the 29th Olympic Games in 2008, its air quality was the central focus for China and the world. To win its bid for the Games, China had to make a "Green Olympics" promise.[a]

To keep the "Green Olympics" promise, the city attempted to manipulate its air quality during the Games. Scientists treated the city as a laboratory by testing wind patterns and atmospheric structure, and pinpointing local and regional pollution sources. The Games were among the many driving forces for more stringent enforcement of air quality management (AQM) efforts in China. In order to comply with the pledge made by the Beijing Organizing Committee for the Games to the International Olympic Committee that "Beijing is determined to ensure the air conditions meet the necessary standards in August 2008," an Olympics contingency plan was approved for Beijing and the surrounding cities, but details were not made public. The plan included shutting down factories and restricting traffic during the Games. Records showed that in 2008, Beijing's air quality reached or exceeded the level of "good" on 274 days, which was an improvement of 28 days over the 2007 ratings. There were 61 days of "excellent" air quality in 2008, 29 days more than in 2007. This marked the best record for the city in the last 10 years.[b]

The Chinese AQM capacity was greatly strengthened when China successfully won the bid to host the 29th Olympic Games. However, the continued process of AQM in China remains a challenge, as the country continues its drive toward robust economic development with rapid urbanization and motorization. The toxic smog that covered Beijing and the surrounding areas 5 years after the Olympic Games demonstrated that the goal of a "blue sky" remained a major challenge for cities in China. As reported by Li Jingjing, a reporter for the *South China Morning Post* of Hong Kong, "The beautiful, sunny days of August 2008 came as a relief to Olympic organizers. But for Beijing residents, they are no more than a happy memory."[c] Undoubtedly, the rapid degradation of Beijing's air quality since 2008 has evolved into a public crisis, as more people now worry about the health impact of pollution.

---

[a]Chapter 2 of the *Bid Documents and Analysis: Passion behind the Bid* clearly spells out that the 2008 Olympic Games in Beijing would be a "Green Olympics" showcasing the ancient charm and modern vitality of the city. https://stillmed.olympic.org/Documents/Reports/Official%20Past%20Games%20Reports/Summer/ENG/2008-RO-S-Beijing-vol1.pdf.

[b]Jiao (2009).

[c]Jingjing (2013).

raise environmental awareness to win the general public's support for measures to combat the nation's air pollution problems.

The main force driving the rising air pollution levels in China is the rapid increase in energy consumption as a result of industrialization, urbanization, and motorization (due to growth in the number of vehicles). Unique meteorological conditions accentuate these anthropogenic factors. As noted earlier, air pollution is particularly acute in northern China, where the region is prone to intense anticyclone (high-pressure) systems in the winter season. Together, these factors explain why most of the smoggiest cities are found in northern China, where the winter monsoon (i.e., an anticyclone condition) creates descending air masses, keeping air pollutants near the ground (see Figure 9.3).

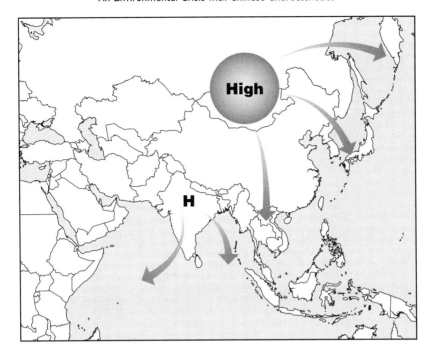

FIGURE 9.3 Winter monsoon system (a high-pressure belt or "anticyclone") dominating northern China. The arrows indicate the wind direction, but the descending air masses of high pressure in northern China keep the pollution in the lower atmosphere, hindering the quick dispersion of pollutants.

DWINDLING WATER RESOURCES

The Water Crisis in China

Apart from China's dirty air, its dwindling fresh water resources pose another major health risk to the public (Economy, 2004). According to Greenpeace East Asia, in fact, China is facing a water crisis: Its per capita water supply is significantly lower than the global average and is declining still further, but its overall demand for water is escalating. In addition to rising domestic water needs, both industrial and agricultural activities consume large quantities of fresh water, while simultaneously causing immense water pollution. Moreover, the geographical distribution of water resources is very uneven: Water resources are more abundant in the south, but scarce in the north.

China is clearly experiencing a severe water shortage; such a shortage can be defined as the lack of sufficient water resources to meet a country's or region's demands, especially not having safe, potable water for its people. The Chinese acute water shortage is caused by three general factors: physical shortage, overuse, and pollution. The physical shortage is made clear by the fact that China has 22% of the world's population, but only 7% of all freshwater runoff (Li & Liu, 2009). It is estimated that the national water shortage reaches 60 billion m³ on average. Among China's 600 or so cities, more than 400 are suffering from water shortages, and 110 cities are plagued by severe shortages (Jiang, 2009). Geographically, the shortage is particularly pronounced in northern China, including the watershed regions of the Yellow River (Huang He), Huai He, Hai He, and Liao He, where the per capita water supply is only one-third of the national average.

Water pollution is another reason for the water shortage. "Water pollution" is defined as the presence of harmful substances in watercourses. Key pollutants monitored by the Chinese government include organic matters (as measured by the "chemical oxygen demand" level), ammonia nitrogen, total nitrogen, total phosphorus, petroleum, volatile phenol, lead, mercury, cadmium, hexavalent chromium, total chromium, and arsenic. These pollutants can enter water bodies from discrete sources (or "point sources"), such as a factory or city sewer. Alternatively, they can also come from nonpoint sources, such as agricultural runoff or city street runoff.

According to China Water Risk, a nonprofit initiative dedicated to highlighting risk, the water pollution problem is worsening in China, and overall water quality is deteriorating. Water pollution has caused significant economic losses and constrained the socioeconomic and environmental development of the country. Even worse, it seriously threatens the safety of drinking water for many people in China. Among China's provinces, autonomous regions, and municipalities, China Water Risk defines 11 as "Dry" (including the "Deficit 6"), 9 as "At Risk," and only 11 as "Safe" (see Table 9.4).[7]

Water Quality of Major River Basins in China

There are seven major river systems in China: the Yangtze River, Yellow River (Huang He), Pearl River, Songhua Jiang, Huai He, Hai He, and Liao He. The flow directions of these rivers are controlled by topography. Most of these rivers drain from the high mountains in the west and enter the sea (East China Sea, Pacific Ocean) in the east. (See Figure 9.4; refer also to Chapter 2.) The water quality of these rivers differs. China attempts to categorize rivers into different grades according to their water quality status. Table 9.5 shows the major attributes and corresponding water quality status for each grade of water. Overall, the seven rivers in China have relatively low water quality levels.

TABLE 9.4. Water Risk Status in China: Who's Running Dry?

Water risk status	Provinces, autonomous regions, and municipalities	Remarks
"Safe" (11)	Xizang (Tibet), Qinghai, Hainan, Xinjiang, Yunnan, Guangxi, Sichuan, Jiangxi, Guizhou, Fujian, Hunan	Above national average (>2,023 m³)[a]
"At Risk" (9)	Heilongjiang, Zhejiang, Guangdong, Chongqing, Neimenggu (Inner Mongolia), Hubei, Anhui, Shaanxi, Jilin	Above World Bank Water Poverty Mark (≥ 1,000 m³)
"Dry" (11), including the "Deficit 6" (in boldface)	Gansu, Liaoning, Henan, Shandong, Shanxi, **Jiangsu**, **Hebei**, **Ningxia**, **Tianjin**, **Beijing**, **Shanghai**	Below World Bank Water Poverty Mark (<1,000 m³)

Note. Data from http://chinawaterrisk.org/big-picture/whos-running-dry.
[a]The national average is based on data from 2003 to 2011.

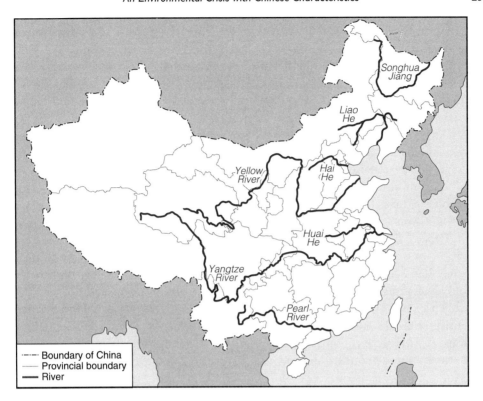

FIGURE 9.4 The seven main river systems in China.

TABLE 9.5. China's River Pollution Status: Grades and Attributes

Grade	Attributes	Status
I	Water source protection areas for centralized drinking water supplies; natural habitats for rare species of fish, and spawning grounds for fish and shrimp.	Drinking-water quality
II	Water source protection areas for centralized drinking water supplies; sanctuaries for common species of fish; swimming zones.	Drinking-water quality
III	Mainly applicable to bodies of water used for general industrial water supplies and for recreational purposes in which there is no direct human contact with the water.	Polluted
IV	Mainly applicable to bodies of water used for agricultural water supplies and for general landscape requirements.	Polluted
V	Essentially useless.	Highly polluted

Geographically, the water quality of the Pearl River basin, the rivers in south-western China (including the upper course of the Yangtze River), and the rivers in northwestern China (including the upper course of the Yellow River) are better, with water quality ranging from good to excellent. By contrast, the basins of the Songhua Jiang, Huai He, and Liao He are moderately polluted. The Hai He basin in northern China is the most heavily polluted river (Economy, 2004). The water quality levels of the upper courses of the main rivers are generally better, whereas many of their tributaries are often more polluted than their corresponding main rivers. As illustrated in Figure 9.5, four of the seven major rivers have more than half of their monitoring stations reporting water quality in the polluted to seriously polluted categories (i.e., Grade IV and higher).

In addition to the surface water pollution, groundwater is heavily contaminated. Despite the implementation of the National Groundwater Pollution Prevention and Control Plan at the end of 2011, about 60% of Chinese groundwater fell into the "bad" or "very bad" category of water quality in 2013 (Figure 9.6). This is troublesome, as 70% of China's more than 1.3 billion people and over 60% of China's cities rely on groundwater as their source of drinking water. For instance, in the entire Huai He basin, about 80% of the shallow groundwater has deteriorated to Grade V (highly polluted) status and has lost its biological functions. In some areas, the polluted groundwater extends down to 50 and even 300 m underground.

Water quality is as dire a challenge as water quantity in China. The pollution of water sources (both surface and underground) not only threatens the safety of the drinking water supply, but can result in "pollution-induced water scarcity" in many cities in China. About one-fifth of key cities' water supply is considered to have a Grade III pollution status, which means that water can only be used for general industrial water supply and recreational uses. To enhance the drinking water

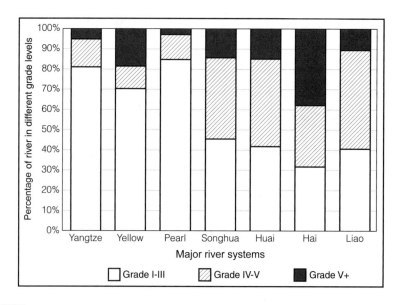

FIGURE 9.5 Water quality of China's seven major river basins in 2011. Data from China Water Risk (2012).

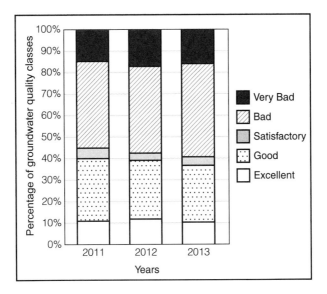

Quality of China's groundwater, 2011–2013. Data from China Water Risk (2012–2014).

quality for its citizens, the government announced a new Drinking Water Health Standard to be implemented in the summer of 2007.[8] However, monitoring data collected by the Urban Water Supply Water Quality Monitoring Center showed that out of more than 3,000 water plants and over 660 cities in China, no more than 10 plants can test all of the 106 items stipulated in the new standard. Fewer than 15% of water plants have the ability to test the 42 mandatory items in the standard, and approximately 51% of these plants have no testing capabilities at all (Jiang, 2009). Therefore, the currently available data are insufficient for deciding whether the drinking water is safe.

Overall, the water quality of China's freshwater resources is deteriorating. There are several reasons for this. First, vast quantities of industrial waste have been discharged into water bodies because of the lax laws and regulations. Second, agricultural pollutant runoff contaminates the surrounding water bodies. Finally, domestic sewage treatment facilities are inadequate, and sewage may even be discharged directly into rivers and lakes without treatment. Evidently, China's deteriorating water quality is intensified by ineffectual environmental law enforcement by the local governments. In a nation where pro-growth sentiment is so strong, environmental protection has rarely if ever been elevated to a high priority in the policy agendas of local government officials (Wong, 2010). The tradeoff between economic growth and protecting the environment is a dilemma that the country still has to resolve.

Health Checkup Report on the Yangtze River

The Yangtze River originates in the Qinghai–Tibetan Plateau. Figure 9.7 shows the extent of the Yangtze drainage basin, which transverses the three topographical regions of China: the Qinghai–Tibetan Plateau, the central mountains and plateaus,

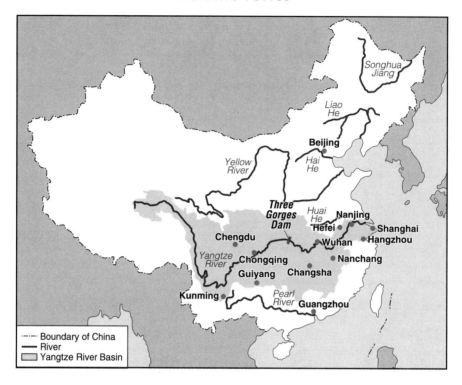

FIGURE 9.7 The drainage basin of the Yangtze River.

and the eastern plains. It flows for 6,300 km from glaciers in the Qinghai–Tibetan Plateau eastward and empties into the East China Sea near Shanghai. The Yangtze is the most important river in China. Its basin covers about one-fifth of China's land area and is the home of one-third of the country's population. Table 9.6 summarizes basic information on the Yangtze River (Wang, 2009).

The importance of the Yangtze River to China is indisputable, and conserving its hydrological environment is crucial to ensuring it as a long-term sustainable resource for the residents of the entire Yangtze basin. The Chinese government published a report on protection and development of the Yangtze River in 2007 (see Yang, 2008). This report concluded that the Yangtze River faces 10 important issues.[9] The report also highlighted several major ecological/environmental problems of the Yangtze River basin caused by recent development. First, overexploited hydroelectric power (HEP) in the basin has created immense ecological problems. For instance, many HEP stations and reservoirs were constructed along the upper reaches (tributaries) of the Yangtze River, such as the Jinsha Jiang, Yalong Jiang, Minjiang, Dadu He, and Wujiang. These stations and reservoirs have largely altered the hydrological regimes and damaged the aquatic ecosystem of the river. The upper course of the Yangtze River is a critical habitat for many migratory fish. These fish require three grounds for reproduction, breeding, and spawning, and one channel (i.e., the river channel) to complete their life cycle and perpetuate the species. Many migratory fish in the rivers have become endangered, due to the

TABLE 9.6. Yangtze River: Basic Information

Parameters	Units	Remarks
Total length	6,300 km	Longest river in China
Drainage area	1.8 million km²	18.7% of China's total land area
Total runoff volume	Five times the total runoff of the Yellow River, Huai He, and Hai He	Major source of exporting water for the South–North Water Diversion Project (SNWDP)
No. of provinces and municipalities drained	Eleven (nine provinces and two municipalities)	The basin has been incorporated into the country's Sustainable Development of Eastern China, Rising Central China, and Western Development projects
Population covered	480 million	36.4% of China's population
GDP of the basin	40.3% of the national total	

Note. Data from Wang (2009).

changing hydrological conditions created by the dams. Moreover, no fish ladders or channels have been built in existing dams to alleviate the problem, as they have in many Western countries. Instead, China has created breeding grounds to try to protect these endangered species. However, studies have found that many of these breeding grounds are ineffective to ensure the survival of these species.

Second, annual water storage and recession in the reservoir of the Three Gorges Dam area have imposed serious environmental risks on the river banks. The normal water storage level of the Three Gorges Dam is 175 m in winter. This level recedes to 145 m in summer as a flood prevention measure in the lower course of the river basin. The 30-m gap between the high- and low-water marks exposes part of the banks—the most fragile ecological zone in the area—to numerous environmental problems, such as landslides, pollutant accumulation, and loss of habitat. These have become recurring troubles for the area.

Third, records from the water quality monitoring stations show that the water pollution problems in the Yangtze River drainage area have been worsening. Water quality tests conducted in 58 provincial regions in 2003 and 2005 indicated that the volume of polluted water in the Yangtze River drainage area had increased (Wang, 2009). In 2003, the sections exceeding the Grade III standard constituted 41% of the entire region. In 2005, this percentage rose to 55%. The major pollutants found were amino nitrogen, total phosphorus, potassium permanganate, fecal bacteria, and petroleum. Studies also revealed that a riverside pollution zone extending over 600 km has been found along the Yangtze River. Sections of the Minjiang, Tuojiang, Xiangjiang, and Huangpujiang are very seriously polluted, especially those sections passing through major cities. Water quality monitoring data along these watercourses revealed that over 40% of the sections had water quality worse than the Grade III standard. Moreover, water flowed more slowly after the completion of the Three Gorges Dam, with a speed of only 1.2 cm/second in some areas. Slow-flowing water weakens diffusion ability and decreases the pollutant-carrying capacity of the surrounding waters, reservoirs, and bays.

BOX 9.2. Water Pollution Problems in Lakes and Reservoirs: The Blue-Green Algae Bloom in Taihu Lake

Water pollution is a serious problem in Chinese lakes and reservoirs. One of its most noticeable signs is the blue-green algae bloom[a] caused by the eutrophication problem in many lakes and rivers in China. Of the 28 major lakes in China, only 28% meet Grade II or III standards, with water quality ranging from fair to lightly polluted. Over 70% of the lakes have water quality poorer than Grade III. Among these 70% of lakes, 29% are polluted, and 43% are highly polluted.

On May 28, 2007, some residents of Wuxi on Taihu Lake found that their tapwater had a rotten odor, which gradually became so serious that the water was unfit for drinking (Zhang, 2009). Many residents swarmed stores in Wuxi to buy bottled water. The incident was caused by a serious blue-green algae bloom in Taihu Lake, polluting the water supply for most of the urban area in Wuxi, and affecting about 5 million people in the region. Taihu Lake administratively belongs to Jiangsu province and is a large freshwater lake in the Yangtze River Delta plain near Shanghai. The crisis was a wakeup call. The algae bloom incident drew people's attention to water safety issues in China. One immediate fix was to switch Wuxi's water intake pipe from Taihu Lake (from which the urban area was drawing about 70% of its water) to other sources. For instance, Wuxi is now pumping in about half of its drinking water from the Yangtze. The Jiangsu government also launched measures, such as relocating chemical plants, to reduce nutrient loading and reduce pollutants entering the lake.

According to an investigation in 2004 before the incident occurred, roughly 50% of the total nitrogen and phosphorus (sources of eutrophication) in Taihu, Chaohu, and Dianchi Lakes resulted from agricultural pollution. The amount of chemical fertilizer per hectare of cultivated land was 24.4 kg in the Taihu Lake watershed at the onset of economic reform in 1979. This level was slightly over the recommended amount adopted by other developed countries. In the 2000s, chemical fertilizer amounted to 66.7 kg/hectare, which was about three times higher than the recommended amount.

Moreover, the development of urban sewage treatment in China lags behind that of other developed countries by 30–40 years. The length and geographical coverage of sewage pipelines are grossly inadequate. The population density of the Taihu Lake area has reached 1,000 people/km^2 (one of the highest in the world); sewage discharge exceeded the treatment capacity. For instance, a plant with a disposal capacity of 20,000 tons per day received more than 40,000 tons of sewage a day, overwhelming sewage disposal facilities to the point that the treatment plants became sources of pollution themselves.

China generates a huge amount of urban wastewater. The amount is comparable to the total annual runoff of the Yellow River. The quantity of domestic wastewater is rising with urbanization, and industrial wastewater is underreported. In rural areas, agriculture pollution is still very serious; many industries opt to pay penalties for pollution rather than treat their wastes.

---

[a]Algal bloom often follows a massive discharge of phosphates and nitrates (from farming, untreated sewage and industrial plants) into the water. Most algae are harmless, but some algae can produce toxins that can be harmful to people and animals. Algal bloom can dramatically change the ecology of the environment beneath it. It blocks sunlight from entering the water and depletes oxygen from the water suffocating aquatic life.

Finally, algal blooms due to eutrophication[10] began to occur in the Three Gorges reservoirs, especially in areas where the water is stagnant. The 2007 report revealed that the absolute amounts of pollutants increased drastically because of rapid development in industrialization and urbanization in the drainage basin (Yang, 2008). Moreover, the non-point-source pollution has not been efficiently controlled, and irrigation projects have changed the water regimes and aggravated the deterioration of water quality. In addition, there has been a discernible decline in the amount of water feeding into the Yangtze River in recent years, due to abnormal precipitation caused by climate change. The *Second National Assessment Report on Climate Change,* released in 2011, pointed out that climate change would lead to severe imbalances in China's water resources in the future.

In a nutshell, fresh water is vital for humans and other life forms, and thus access to safe, clean freshwater is a global health issue. In China, the geographical distribution of water resources is uneven. The distribution is affected by both physical water shortages and severe scarcities caused by water pollution resulting from human activities. Moreover, China's water resources are considerably undervalued by its citizens; they do not treasure these resources. They are thus among the most poorly managed resources in the country, resulting in overuse, waste, and contamination. A growing population and unprecedented economic growth, as well as negligent environmental oversight, have augmented water demand and pollution in the nation.

China's South–North Water Transfer Project

Description

On December 12, 2014, China inaugurated one of its biggest engineering projects: the South-North Water Transfer (SNWT) project. When completed, it will have a 2,900-km network of canals and tunnels, designed to divert 44.8 billion m³ of water annually from China's humid south (mainly from the Yangtze River) to the Huang He and the thirsty, industrialized north.

The SNWT (南水北调工程)[11] is an infrastructure megaproject aimed at remedying the geographical imbalances of freshwater resource distribution. The project was first proposed in the early 1950s, in response to an offhand comment made by Mao Zedong that the north should "borrow" water from the south.[12] After much investigation, planning, design, and research, the project was finally approved 50 years later in 2002. The overall project has three main routes. The construction of the Eastern Route Project (ERP) started in December 2002, while the Central Route Project (CRP) commenced in 2003. The entire SNWT is projected to be completed by 2050. Table 9.7 summarizes basic information on the three routes of the SNWT, and Figure 9.8 shows the spatial distribution of the project's three routes.

The ERP follows the course of the Grand Canal, which connects the lower course of the Yangtze River to the eastern Huang–Huai–Hai Plain. The ERP will supply water for Jiangsu, Anhui, Shandong, Hebei, and Tianjin. However, the

TABLE 9.7. South-to-North Water Transfer (SNWT) Project: Basic Information

Parameters	Western Route Project (WRP)	Central Route Project (CRP)	Eastern Route Project (ERP)
Source of transferable water	Upper course of the Yangtze River (Jinshajiang)	Middle course of the Han River (a tributary of the Yangtze River)	Lower course of the Yangtze (Yangzhou)
Terminal point	Upper course of the Yellow River	Beijing–Tianjin	Tianjin Shandong
Length of canal/tunnel	450 km	1,273 km	1,156 km
Volume of transferable water	17.0 billion m³	13.0 billion m³	14.8 billion m³
Engineering works	Dams and tunnels	Dam extension (Danjiangkou), canals, and Huang He crossing	Diversion channel, pumping stations, and Huang He crossing
Status	Pending	Route completed in 2014	Route completed in 2013
Environmental impacts	Disruption of ecosystem/ seismic activity	Water pollution/ decreasing runoff/ resettlement	Water pollution/movement of water against gravity

Note. Data from www.nsbd.gov.cn/zx/english/mrp.htm.

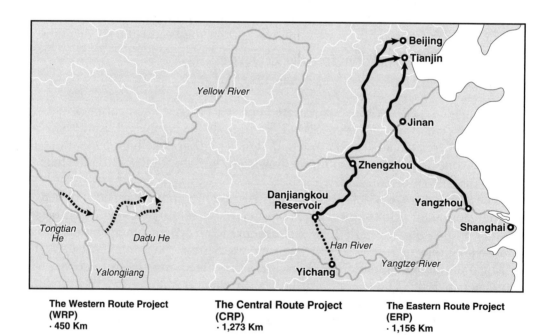

The Western Route Project (WRP)
· 450 Km

The Central Route Project (CRP)
· 1,273 Km

The Eastern Route Project (ERP)
· 1,156 Km

▪▪▪▪▪➤ Planned route

•••••••• Future plan to connect Yangtze River at Yichang with Danjiangkou Reservoir

➡ Completed route

FIGURE 9.8 The three routes of China's South-to-North Water Transfer (SNWT) project.

diversion plan has been delayed, due to severe water pollution problems in the source region. The total length of the trunk canal is about 1,156 km. It has 23 pumping stations to lift water from the source region to the importing region.[13] The entire ERP can divert about 14.8 billion m^3 of water annually.

The major source of the diverted water of the MRP is the Danjiangkou Reservoir, which is built in the middle course of the Han River, a tributary of the Yangtze River. The main MRP is composed of two parts. The reservoir's dam was raised from its existing crest elevation of 162 m up to 176.6 m (and the water level was raised from 157 to 170 m), to increase the reservoir's water storage capacity and to create sufficient hydraulic pressure to allow water to flow along the trunk canal by gravitational force from Danjiangkou to Beijing. New canals were built along the western edge of the Huang–Huai–Hai Plain to flow through Henan and Hebei to Beijing. The total length of the trunk canal is 1,273 km, and the mean annual transferable water quantity will be about 12.0–14.0 billion m^3. In December 2014, the MRP officially began carrying water from the Danjiangkou Reservoir to Beijing. This should mitigate the acute shortage of water resources in Beijing, Tianjin, and north China. However, there is now a concern about declining water reserves in the Danjiangkou Reservoir and Han River. The future plan is to build a canal to connect the Yangtze River near Yichang to the Danjiangkou Reservoir, as shown in Figure 9.8.

The WRP will divert water from the upper reaches of the Yangtze into the Yellow River (Huang He) to solve the water deficiency problem in northwest and north China. The feasibility of diverting water from the headwaters of the Yangtze River (i.e., the Tongtian, Yalong, and Dadu Rivers) into the headwaters of the Yellow River has been explored since the 1950s. Huge dams and long tunnels are needed to cross the Qinghai-Tibetan Plateau and the western Yunnan Plateau. The total length of the diversion tunnels is about 450 km, and they are designed to bring about 17 billion m^3 of water from the three tributaries of the Yangtze River to supply water for Qinghai, Gansu, Shaanxi, and Shanxi provinces, and for the Ningxia Hui and Neimenggu autonomous regions. However, the potential ecological destruction and the cost are major concerns. At this writing, therefore, the WRP remains largely conceptual.

Major Environmental Concerns

Many people doubt that the ambitious SNWT project can really help to resolve the geographical and temporal disparity of China's freshwater resources. The following are some of the prominent environmental problems related to this megaproject.

First, water pollution in the source regions is a foremost concern, especially for the MRP and ERP. Canals in the ERP receive large amounts of pollutants from agricultural and industrial runoff, untreated sewage, and vessels (barges) plying these waters. Indeed, the success or failure of the SNWT depends on improvement in the water quality along the channel route. People in Tianjin (a major port city of both the eastern and middle routes) are considering desalinization of seawater as a preferred alternative source of drinking water because they are so worried about the quality of the imported water from the Yangtze River.

Second, the Danjiangkou Reservoir dam extension project has changed the hydrological regime of the Han River. About one-third of the annual water flow of the river has been diverted to northern China, exacerbating the water supply and water pollution problems downstream.

Third, since much of the area in the WRP is considered ecologically fragile, the diversion could destroy the integrity of the headwaters' ecosystems for both the Yellow and Yangtze Rivers. Moreover, the WRP region is prone to seismic activity, and thus the potential exists there for landslides and slope failures.

Finally, the socioeconomic impact of the MRP is staggering. The construction of the Danjiangkou Reservoir dam extension project and the new trunk canal have displaced about 350,000 villagers. Most of them have been settled far away from their homes and given low-grade farmland.

Like other megaprojects in China, such as the Three-North Shelterbelt Program (see below) and the Three Gorges Dam, the SNWT project is an example of an ambitious Chinese leadership's determination to conquer nature. The reality is that the south may no longer have enough water to spare, due to its own growing demands and to rainfall fluctuations caused by climate change.

THE "BAD EARTH": DESERTIFICATION IN CHINA

In addition to major problems with the atmosphere (air) and hydrosphere (water), China suffers from serious land degradation problems. For instance, the fertile black soils (chernozems) in northern Heilongjiang province, which forms part of China's "breadbasket," are thinning. Much farmland in southern China is suffering from acidification, making the soil there generally unfavorable for agriculture.[14] In short, the quality of China's arable land is deteriorating, reducing its capacity to produce adequate food to feed its huge population. In this section, we examine the state of desertification in the dryland (or arid land) of the country.

The State of Desertification in China

China is one of the countries most severely affected by desertification. According to the United Nations Convention to Combat Desertification (UNCCD), "desertification" is defined as land degradation in arid, semiarid, and dry subhumid areas, resulting mainly from climatic variations and human activities. According to this definition, a huge area in China is subject to desertification, especially in the dryland areas. The natural vegetation of dryland, where annual precipitation is less than 380 mm (1.5 in), includes grassland, dry shrubs, and other desert vegetation (Hong, 2010). Geographically, these lands are situated primarily to the west of the Greater Khingan Range (see Chapters 2 and 11), which is north of the Great Wall, as well as in the western and northern parts of the Qinghai–Tibetan Plateau.

According to a report issued by the China National Committee for the Implementation of the UNCCD, of the 3.3 million km² of dryland in China, 2.64 million km² (or 79%) is affected by desertification; in other words, about 27.5% of China's total land area suffers from desertification, threatening the livelihood of nearly 400 million people (Chen, Dong, & Yan, 1996).

The immediate cause of desertification is the removal of vegetative cover. This is driven by a number of factors, acting on the land either alone or in combination with other factors, such as drought, climatic changes, tillage for agriculture, overgrazing, and deforestation for fuel or construction materials. Figure 9.9 shows the major causes of desertification in China in the 1980s, which included excessive collection of wood for fuel (31.8%), overgrazing (28.3%), cultivation of unsuitable land (25.4%), water misuse, wind erosion, and dune sand encroachment (Zhu & Liu, 1989). More recent studies have revealed that proportions of the contribution from different activities have changed. For instance, fuel wood collection has decreased as the economy has improved and other fuel sources are being used. Overgrazing and cultivation of marginal land are now the main drivers of desertification in China (Wang, 2003).

The human and economic consequences of desertification have been alarming. In 2006, the Vice Minister of the Forestry Ministry of China indicated that desertification led to direct economic loss of 54 billion yuan, or about 2.6% of China's GDP (Dong, 2007). Geographically, the most seriously desertified regions in China are found in Neimenggu (Inner Mongolia), Gansu, Xinjiang, Qinhai, Ningxia, and Shaanxi. Excessive human activities have been identified as the main factors leading to the development of desertification in these areas.

In China, the pace of land degradation and desertification has accelerated since the Communist party took control of the country in 1949. Figure 9.10 shows

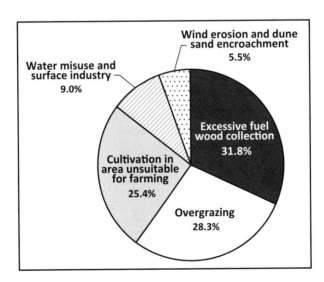

FIGURE 9.9 The major causes of desertification in China. Data from Zhu and Liu (1989).

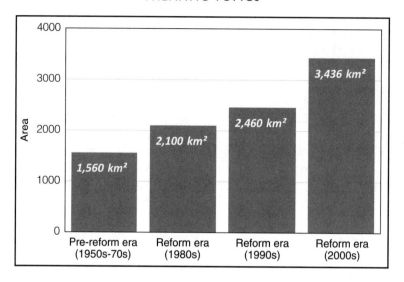

FIGURE 9.10 Increases in desertified area in China since the 1950s. Data from Meng, Wen, and Ma (2005).

the annual rate of desertification in China since the 1950s. During the pre-reform era, the rate was 1,560 km² annually. However, it increased to 2,100 km² in the 1980s, and then to 2,460 km² in the 1990s. It further increased to 3,436 km² at the turn of the 21st century. The desertified areas are generally deprived of vegetation cover, and the precipitation is low. The strong winds in winter and spring (also known as the "anticyclones") lead to the formation of severe dust storms. As Figure 9.11 shows, the number of severe dust storms in China has been rising steadily

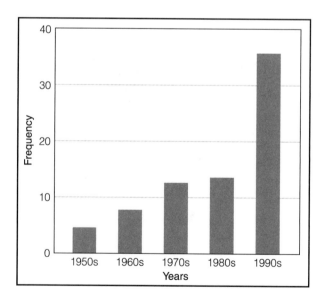

FIGURE 9.11 Frequency of dust storms in China over the past five decades. Data from Weng (2000).

over the years, particularly in the 1990s (Weng, 2000). This rise corresponds to the increase in desertified areas in China.

Apparently, the severity of desertification in China is closely related to the political–economic policies implemented by the Communist regime. Table 9.8 shows, chronologically, a selection of these policies. During Mao's era (1949–1976), the dominant environmental ideology was "battling with heaven and earth." Mao and his government deliberately ignored, abused, and destroyed the environment (Shapiro, 2001). The main policy objective in the 1960s was grain production, which was driven by the need to increase food production to feed China's people in the country's postfamine era.[15] The "grain-first campaign" encouraged people to exploit all available land resources to grow crops. Under this policy, many trees were felled, lakes were filled, and grassland was converted to cropland. The "grain-first campaign" has led to grave ecological destruction in China, especially in the dryland areas (Ho, 2003). Moreover, the traditional Mongolian economy of grassland, based on animal husbandry, was negated, and the cultivation of these dryland areas led to widespread land degradation and desertification.

Mao died in 1976, and China entered a phase of economic reform starting in 1978. The transition into the new economic reform era was led by Deng Xiaoping, who wanted to speed up economic growth. "Economic growth is the ultimate goal" was the principal ethos, and such growth has been used as the ultimate measure of people's achievement, both individually and collectively. In order to remedy some of the previous environmental flaws, the government launched the Three-North Shelterbelt Program, with the goal of stopping the spread of desertification in the dryland areas. However, an aggressive attitude toward the environment remained unchanged during the reform era. Despite a great deal of effort, too, the Shelterbelt Program has not achieved its goal. Furthermore, the drylands are home to several major ethnic groups, such as the Mongols, Uyghurs, Kazaks, and Hui; therefore, the development paths in this region should be sensitive to their ethnic and cultural

TABLE 9.8. Policies That Might Have Affected Desertification Development in China at Different Periods

Period	Policy
1950s (early Mao era)	Program of socialist construction (Mao's calls for "battling with heaven and earth")
Early 1960s (postfamine era)	Emphasis on grain production (conversion of grassland to cropland)
Cultural Revolution (1966–1976)	"Grain-first" rural policy (negating the traditional economy of grassland-based animal husbandry in several regions)
Immediate post-Mao era	Emphasis on economic growth (economic growth as the ultimate measure of achievement)
Economic reform era (from 1978 onward)	Relocation of people from degraded grassland, leading to further grassland degradation
Current problem	Unchecked economic growth

traditions. However, the contrary has been practiced in many places: The local cultures and practices have been ignored. Therefore, desertification in China is the result of many erroneous policies adopted by the government over the past several decades. We now present a detailed discussion of the Three-North Shelterbelt Program and its effects.

The Three-North Shelterbelt Program

The Three-North Shelterbelt Program (*San Bei Fang Hu Lin Gong Cheng*) is a major government initiative to control the spread of deserts and related environmental problems (such as dust storms) in China. According to the State Forest Administration, the program plans to plant 35.6 million hectares of protective forests in a belt 4,480 km long[16] and 560–1,460 km wide in north China. Geographically, the "Three-North" in the name of this program refers to northeast, north, and northwest China (see Plate 5). It is also known as the "Green Great Wall" program of China—the most ambitious tree-planting effort in the world, which began in 1978 and will last until 2050. However, it has been criticized as an unrealistic ecological plan, for multiple reasons.

Like the SNWT project discussed earlier, the Three-North Shelterbelt Program exemplifies a Chinese "state-planning mentality" and treats the environment as if it can be altered at will by human actions. The program has failed to improve the ecological environment or stop the spread of desertification in China. The failure can be attributed to the following factors. First, as mentioned above, rainfall in most of the areas covered by the program is too scarce to support large-scale afforestation. Second, the practice of monospecies planting makes the forest vulnerable to diseases and pests.[17] Third, government officials have been assessed by the number of trees they planted (a quantifiable parameter), rather than by the ecological benefits of their work. Finally, planting trees in drylands is usually costly, and without proper care, such as irrigation and pest control, the survival rates are extremely low.

China has planted many more trees than any country in the world since 1949. But the overall survival rate of the trees has been extremely low (only about 15%), and the overall ecological environment of the country has shown no significant improvement. Overall, the Three-North Shelterbelt Program has failed to achieve its intended goals because Chinese leaders and officials in the State Forestry Administration misread the essence of dryland ecology.

In China, desertification affects the livelihood of millions of people. Nevertheless, Mao's policy of aggression against nature is still the dominant view among many Chinese officials today. Some Chinese scientists have voiced criticisms of China's dryland policies favoring tree planting instead of promoting natural recovery by conservation. However, this natural recovery approach is unpopular among many local government officials who are rewarded for the number of trees planted. Environmental policies in China are often aimed at serving political ends, rather than achieving realistic environmental goals or promoting long-term sustainability.

COPING WITH CLIMATE CHANGE

"Climate change" refers to any long-term significant change in the weather pattern of an area. Climate is affected by many factors, including biotic processes, variations in solar radiation received by the earth, plate tectonic movements, and volcanic eruptions. Recently, human activities have also been identified as one of the significant driving forces of climate change. The buildup of greenhouse gases (GHGs), such as carbon dioxide, nitrogen oxide, and methane, in the atmosphere has altered the "energy budget" of the earth's surface,[18] causing global warming. This human-induced climate change is currently a major global concern. Since 2007, China has surpassed the United States in GHG emissions. Accordingly, any deal to attain substantial and sustained reduction of GHG emissions globally will not be successful without the active participation of China, as the largest anthropogenic producer of GHGs.

Initially, the Chinese leadership claimed that as a socialist nation, the country did not have environmental problems like those found in the capitalist states of the West. When the United Nations convened the first Human Environment Conference in Stockholm in 1972, the Communist party furiously debated whether to send a delegate. Eventually one was sent, and this led to cautious changes in the country's environmental protection attitudes and practices: The Chinese leaders began to admit that environmental problems did exist in China, and established the Environmental Protection Leadership Group in 1973. This group began developing environmental protection policies and legal systems. The first task of the group was to formulate a policy to recycle the "three industrial wastes" (or *sanfei*) of wastewater, waste gas, and solid waste residues. Many argued, however, that the central aim of the program was to increase economic efficiency rather than to improve environmental quality. Ten years later, in 1983, the government formally announced that environmental protection would become a state policy. In 1998, the government upgraded the Leadership Group into a ministry-level agency known as the State Environmental Protection Administration; in 2008, this agency became the MEP. The MEP is empowered and required by law to implement environmental policies and enforce environmental laws and regulations.

China's National Climate Change Assessment

China issued a preliminary national report on the state of climate change in 2006.[19] The report noted a rise in average surface temperature of approximately 0.5–0.8 degrees Celsius in China in the past 100 years, slightly higher than the global average surface temperature increase over the same period. Over the past 50 years, China's average surface temperature has increased by 1.1 degrees Celsius, with a warming rate of 0.22 degrees every 10 years; this rate is significantly higher than the average warming rate globally, or in other parts of the Northern Hemisphere. According to the report, China's average annual temperature will increase by 1.3–2.1 degrees Celsius by the year 2020. By the middle of the century (i.e., 2050), the temperature will increase by as much as 3.3 degrees Celsius, and by 2100 by as much as 6 degrees (Ding, Ren, & Shi, 2006; see Table 9.9).

In addition to the increase in average annual temperature, average annual precipitation may increase (see Table 9.9). However, rising temperatures will raise the evaporation rate of water in each river basin area. The evaporative capacity of the Yellow River, for instance, will rise by 15%, which will further aggravate the water shortage in the basin (Ding et al., 2006). Climate variability thus influences the stability of water systems. Water crises caused by the increasing frequencies of floods and droughts in China will become more and more severe. The annual flows of the seven major river basins in China are declining overall.

Undoubtedly, climate change affects China's agricultural prospects. Extreme weather events and the spread of plant diseases and pests have already increased the difficulty of producing enough food to feed China's huge population. Moreover, forests and other natural ecosystems, such as coastal zones and coastal ecological systems, are susceptible to the effects of global climate change. Socially, climate change has a more severe impact on disadvantaged groups in any society. This is the case for those living in China's poverty-stricken rural communities, particularly those in arid and disaster-prone areas in central and western China. China's economic growth over the past few decades has widened the gap between the rich and the poor. Socially disadvantaged groups may not have sufficient financial and technical capabilities to manage the risks associated with climate change, such as declines in safe drinking water and in food security.

China's Climate Change Policy

As noted above, the development of climate change policy in China has been slow. The most notable policy change occurred in 2007, subsequent to the official announcement of China's National Climate Change Program.[20] This was the country's first climate change policy initiative, in which the Chinese government adopted measures involving law, economics, administration, and technology to reduce GHG emissions. The 2007 program elevated climate change to the national policy agenda (Stensdal, 2012). For example, a "carbon intensity"[21] target for China was announced in 2009, marking a new phase in national climate change policies. Consequently, the climate change issue was incorporated into the nation's 12th Five-Year Plan in 2011.

TABLE 9.9. Projected Changes (Relative to 1961–1990) in China's Surface Temperature and Precipitation

Factor	2020	2023	2050	2100
Increase in temperature (degrees Celsius)	~1.3–2.1	~1.3–2.1	~2.3–3.3	~3.9–6.0
Increase in precipitation (%)	2–3	—	5–7	11–17

Note. Data from Ding, Ren, and Shi (2006).

As shown in Table 9.10, China rose from being the fourth largest emitter of GHGs in the world in 1988 to becoming the largest emitter in 2008. Therefore, China is a key actor in any global climate change negotiation. But Chinese delegates have encountered many difficulties during such negotiations. The major difficulty is that many of the proposed short-term carbon emission reduction plans are very costly for China to implement. Moreover, the long-term benefits suggested in the negotiations are not substantial. The lack of a strong global regime to enforce agreements is a major problem for many countries, including China. All along, China has taken a defensive position in the international climate change negotiation process, for fear that the proposed mitigation measures would be too politically and economically costly for the country to bear. Millions in China still live at various levels of poverty. China has therefore resisted international demands for the country to take on binding goals for climate change mitigation.

It is not surprising that China has taken a tough stance on climate change in the international arena. Similar to its views on other environmental issues, the Chinese government's position is that climate change will not be addressed by sacrificing economic development. This stance can be viewed as an assertion of sovereignty backed by its growing global influence. The Ministry of Foreign Affairs exercises great influence over which specific positions China should take in international negotiations. Moreover, China maintains its long-time viewpoint that as a developing country, it should not make any binding commitment to reduce absolute GHG emissions that could jeopardize economic development. China upholds the principle of "common but differentiated responsibilities" (CBDR), formulated by the United Nations Framework Convention on Climate Change, which was signed in Rio de Janeiro in 1992. The CBDR principle is that all countries have a shared interest in protecting the environment, but that nations have different responsibilities, depending on their capacities to act and their historic levels of emissions. Accordingly, developed countries should take the lead in combating climate change and its adverse effects. However, many developed nations argue that the CBDR principle is awkward and outdated, as the geopolitical reality now is very different from when it was first formulated more than two decades ago.

TABLE 9.10. China's Greenhouse Gas (GHG) Emissions and GDP

Year	CO_2 emissions (MtCO$_2$e)[a]	CO_2 emissions ranking	% of World's total emissions	US$ (trillion)
1988	2,191.0	4th	10.71	0.312
1998	3,423.4	3rd	14.87	1.029
2008	7,200.1	1st	24.1	4.598

Note. Emissions data from World Research Institute Climate Change Analysis Indicators Tool; GDP data based on World Bank database (https://data.worldbank.org/country/china).
[a]MtCO$_2$e, million tons CO_2 equivalents.

China's Climate Change Paradox

The primary difficulty in previous climate change meetings (such as the meeting in Copenhagen in 2009) has been a lack of compromise between economically "developed" and "developing" countries, particularly over historic emissions, climate justice, and current and future emissions. While China is now the world's largest emitter of GHGs, it still regards itself as a "developing country." In fact, China perceives itself as the leader of the "developing countries," claiming that developing countries have the "right" to develop, and that having higher emission levels than those of developed nations is inevitable. From this perspective, industrialization, urbanization, and modernization are critical to transforming China from a developing country into a modern state. China understands the intricate relationships between climate change on the one hand and economic development, resource management, poverty alleviation, and energy use on the other. Instead of a stringent cap on its total GHG emissions, China is more likely to consider adopting policies and methods to cut its relative emissions by improving energy efficiency, controlling pollution, and developing alternative energy sources. When compared with many developed countries, China's per capita carbon emissions (7 metric tons, or mt) are lower than that of the United States (17 mt), Australia (16 mt), and Germany (9 mt). However, during negotiations, total emissions are always more important than per capita emissions. China, as the largest producer of GHGs, has an undeniable responsibility to join forces with the international community to combat climate change.

Although coal still dominates China's energy mix, the country is rapidly developing its renewable energy capabilities, including solar, wind, and HEP. China's contribution to the development of renewable energy sources is crucial to combating climate change. Its efforts to make a rapid transition to greener energy will contribute to reducing carbon dioxide emissions globally, mitigating the impact of climate change. Cooperation between China and the West (especially the United States) is imperative for any successful deal in reducing carbon emissions to alleviate climate change impacts.

Overall, the Chinese government handles this paradox by prioritizing economic growth. The government considers economic growth as a critical means to prevent discontent among its citizens. However, the "Under the Dome" report mentioned earlier in this chapter suggests that concern for the environment and the pursuit of economic growth need not always be mutually exclusive. For instance, developing renewable energy capacity should allow China to maintain economic growth, while at the same time enabling the country gradually to use less coal and reduce GHG emissions.

Internationally, limiting warming to no more than 2 degrees Celsius[22] in the 21st century has become the de facto target for global climate policy. China's climate change paradox is threatening this warming limit. However, domestic air pollution is forcing China to embark on a new energy path away from coal. Therefore, it is important for the international community to work closely with China to tackle climate change by considering a range of options. It is almost certain that all sides will have to offer difficult concessions if there is to be a comprehensive climate deal. In 2016, China ratified the Paris climate agreement, which is a global effort to check temperature rise; this may have been the first sign of China's willingness to work with the international community to tackle climate change.[23]

• • • • • • • • • • • • • • • FINAL THOUGHTS • • • • • • • • • • • • • • • • •

China's environmental issues clearly demonstrate that people in China are critically affected by climate change. Blue skies, clean rivers, and green forests are becoming rarities. Cancer is now the leading cause of death in the country, partly as a result of the increasing levels of pollution. Toxic smog is choking its urban areas, including the capital city, Beijing.[24] Ambient air pollution alone is blamed for hundreds of thousands of premature deaths every year. Millions of people in China lack access to safe drinking water, and water resources are dwindling in major river basins. Moreover, land degradation is widespread, especially in the dryland areas in the north and northwestern parts of China, where human activities inappropriate for these arid regions have led to extensive desertification. China is now the country producing the highest levels of carbon emissions in the world, and is one among many nations that will be seriously affected by climate change.

China's environmental crises are unique. Many environmental problems are due to China's own economic success (the so-called "black" GDP). The Communist regime has also successfully done away with some traditional environmentally friendly Chinese philosophy. For instance, *tian ren heyi* (天人合一), or "the unity of humans and nature,"[25] was once a core concept in Chinese traditional philosophy. Under Mao Zedong, this traditional Chinese ideal was abrogated in favor of Mao's insistence that humans could conquer nature and bend it to their own will (*ren ding sheng tian*) (人定勝天) (Shapiro, 2001). But this thinking has resulted in enormous negative consequences for both the Chinese people and the country's natural environment (Wong, 2008). Although Mao's "war against nature" ended when he died in 1976, its effects have continued in the reform era that followed.

In China, environmental policies often contradict one another. For instance, Mao launched a large-scale, government-directed afforestation project soon after the founding of the People's Republic of China in 1949. However, during the Great Leap Forward (1958–1962), widespread deforestation was the norm; trees were cut to help fuel "backyard furnaces" that would push China ahead of the West in industrial production. Many similar examples could be cited.

It took more than four decades for China to establish a ministry-level government agency (i.e., the MEP) to administer the country's environmental issues. In reality, the MEP is still considered a "toothless tiger"—not only because it is a relatively "young" ministry, but also because the national ethos is still one of growth and development. Environmental protection has always been given a lower priority in government policy. Many environmental protection policies in China were formulated not to address environmental concerns alone, but to promote economic development or to fulfill other political aims. Many government officials believed that environmental protection should "slow down environmental deterioration but not stop it" (Tang & Zhan, 2008). For instance, the Three-North Shelterbelt Program has cleared away numerous wild and diverse vegetative covers in favor of planting single-species forests (Liu, 2009). Moreover, the Chinese government has always been criticized for regarding climate change "not as a cross-sectorial environmental issue, but largely an economic one" (Yang, 2009). In China, economic goals still underlie many "green" initiatives that have been implemented. "Sustainable development" seems to be an obvious solution for China, but the concept may be subject to different interpretations by different officials. Many are more interested in maintaining economic sustainability than social and environmental sustainability. Therefore, despite continued efforts to improve the environment, results in China are still limited. The overall environmental condition continues to be grim, and the country's environmental quality continues to deteriorate.

China has adopted a "top-down" approach in environmental policy formulation and implementation. Environmental awareness surveys in China often reveal that Chinese citizens hold an unusually strong attitude of reliance on the government when it comes to environmental protection (Wong, 2008, 2010). Public participation in the process is infrequent. Civil societies, including citizen-organized environmental nongovernmental organizations (ENGOs), are only recent phenomena in China. Friends of Nature, set up in 1994, was the first organization of this kind. By the end of the 1990s, there was an evident increase in the presence of international NGOs (INGOs) in China—such as Greenpeace China, based in Hong Kong, and World Wildlife Fund China, with nine offices around China. There is an unusual form of NGOs in China, known as government-organized NGOs (GONGOs). GONGOs are set up by the nondemocratic government so that the state can maintain some level of control of the organization's personnel, purposes, operations, or activities. Many GONGOs were set up in order to qualify for outside aid or to mitigate specific issues related to in-country projects or international relations. The China Red Cross Society, for instance, is a GONGO set up by the Chinese government. Because of the stringent registration standards for setting up these civil societies in China, many organizations remain unregistered (and are often mistaken for "underground" groups). In China, members of ENGOs are advocates for change who are trapped in an authoritarian state. As an important tactic to survive, ENGOs must avoid sensitive issues that might appear to threaten the structural status quo (Wong, 2010). The impact of civil societies in China cannot be measured in immediate policy outcomes. Instead, they must be seen as part of the wider sociopolitical spectrum and their potential to influence the society as a whole.

Myth lies at the root of Eastern (or Chinese) and Western (European and North American) cultural views on the relationship between humans and nature. Human domination over nature has been part of the Western tradition since ancient times, and this view is influenced by Judeo-Christian values. Chinese traditional thought, on the other hand, provides a unifying framework connecting humans with nature. However, modern experience has led to different trends in the West and the East. Environmental awareness and related movements have started to address the negative consequences of human domination in the West. China, under the Communist party, has sustained an extreme attack on the environment in ways even more severe than those seen in the West.

Therefore, China's environmental crisis is a result of policies and perceptions rather than of imperfect market mechanisms or poor technology. By limiting alternative discourses and environmental management options, China's top-down authoritarian control has been damaging its long-term environmental sustainability. New values of respect for nature have to be established—or old ones reestablished. Indeed, China should regain these values by drawing inspiration from traditional Chinese culture (with its roots in Confucianism, Taoism, and Buddhism), as well as by learning from modern ecological science. Environmental policies have to be formulated and assessed for their human and environmental effectiveness, rather than their political ideologies and convenience.

NOTES

1. There is a YouTube video on Chai Jing's report: "Under the Dome—Investigating China's Smog" (www.youtube.com/watch?v=T6X2uwlQGQM).

2. http://english.mep.gov.cn/News_service/media_news/201411/t20141127_292096. htm.

3. The MEP released the air quality status of key regions and 74 cities in 2014 (see http://english.mep.gov.cn/News_service/news_release/201502/t20150209_295638. htm).

4. www.chinadaily.com.cn/china/2015-02/02/content_19466412.htm.

5. The haze/smog forecasts for Chinese cities in real time are available on a website (http://tianqi.2345.com/zhuanti/haze/topic.html).

6. These reports are available on the Real-Time Air Quality Index Visual Map (http://aqicn.org/map/china).

7. The term "Deficit 6" refers to regions of China where annual renewable water use per capita is greater than annual renewable water resources per capita. These regions are part of the "Dry 11," in which the available water resource falls below the World Bank Water Poverty Mark (i.e., renewable water resources below 1,000 m³ per person per year). For all these Chinese ratings, see http://chinawaterrisk.org/big-picture/whos-running-dry.

8. In the government's 2006 report (GB 5749-2006; www.iwa-network.org/filemanager-uploads/WQ_Compendium/Database/Selected_guidelines/016.pdf), the number of indicators for water quality increased from 35 items to 106 items including organic substances, microbes and purification levels, and 42 of which are mandatory. This standard was to be applied nationwide no later than July 1, 2012.

9. The 10 important issues of the Yangtze River (Yang, 2008) are (1) water pollution; (2) soil erosion and sediments in the Yangtze basin; (3) decline in biodiversity; (4) the exploitation and use of the "Golden Watercourse"; (5) climate change and floods; (6) hydropower exploitation in the upper reaches; (7) flood prevention after the completion of the Three Gorges Dam; (8) ecological issues in the Three Gorges Reservoir area; (9) water quality protection in the water source regions of the middle route of

the South-to-North Water Diversion Project (to be discussed later); and (10) dammed lakes in the middle and lower reaches of the river.

10. "Eutrophication" is the enrichment of an ecosystem with chemical nutrients (typically compounds containing nitrogen, phosphorus, or both). An overgrowth can lead to an algal bloom, which may disturb life in the water.

11. The official English-language website of the Office of the SNWT Commission is www.nsbd.gov.cn/zx/english/mrp.htm.

12. Chairman Mao remarked on October 30, 1952, "The south has plenty of water, but the north is dry. If we could borrow some, that would be good."

13. www.water-technology.net/projects/south_north (retrieved March 9, 2017).

14. Southern China has become the third-largest producer of acid rain in the world (after the northeastern United States and central Europe), due to increased emission of sulfur dioxide and nitrogen oxides.

15. The Chinese Great Famine (1959–1961) killed more people than any other famine in history, with estimates ranging from 16.5 to 45 million individuals. The famine was caused mainly by social pressure, economic mismanagement, and radical changes in agriculture practice during the Great Leap Forward period.

16. By way of comparison, the driving distance between New York, New York, and Seattle, Washington, in the United States is about 4,500 km.

17. For instance, an insect known as *Anoplophora glabripennis,* or the Asian long-horned beetle, wiped out a large number of poplar trees in Ningxia in 2000. www.fao.org/forestry/9598-0ccc5d998559e4979e3695daf125e99aa.pdf (retrieved September 15, 2017).

18. The earth's "energy budget" refers to the accounting of energy entering and leaving the earth's system. A more detailed explanation of the concept can be found at http://scied.ucar.edu/longcontent/energy-budget.

19. China's Ministry of Science and Technology and six other ministries jointly issued the 2006 preliminary report. The full version of the country's first *National Assessment Report of Climate Change* was published in 2007.

20. www.china.org.cn/english/environment/213624.htm.

21. "Carbon intensity" is the average emission rate of carbon dioxide from a given source relative to the intensity of a specific activity—for example, grams of carbon dioxide released per megajoule of energy produced, or the ratio of carbon dioxide produced to GDP.

22. Two degrees Celsius above preindustrial temperatures has been agreed upon as an appropriate threshold, beyond which climate change risks become unacceptably high. See http://unfccc.int/paris_agreement/items/9485.php.

23. http://unfccc.int/paris_agreement/items/9485.php.

24. Wearing face masks because of toxic smog is a common scene in many Chinese cities. Some masks are stylish, and some are equipped with sophisticated filters. A CNN news story (http://edition.cnn.com/2014/01/20/health/pollution-china-pnas) discusses the Chinese toxic smog problem and links it to air pollution even in the western United States.

25. It is also referred to as "Harmony between Heaven and Humankind," according to Judith Shapiro (2001).

REFERENCES ●

Chen, G., Dong, Z., & Yan, P. (1996). [Desertification: International research topics and research strategies in China]. *Exploration of Nature, 15,* 1–5. (In Chinese)

China Water Risk. (2012–2014). Ministry of Environmental Protection 2011–2013 *State of Environment Report* reviews. Retrieved from http://chinawaterrisk.org/resources/analysis-reviews.

Ding, Y., Ren, G., & Shi, G. (2006). National Assessment Report of Climate Change (I): Climate change in China and its future trend. *Advances in Climate Change Research, 2*(1), 3–8.

Dong, J. (2007, June 15). Direct economic loss of land desertification surpasses 54 billion yuan. *Xinhua Net.* Retrieved from www.gov.cn/ztzl/fszs/content_649805.htm.

Economy, E. C. (2004). *The river runs black: The environmental challenge to China's future.* Ithaca, NY: Cornell University Press.

Ho, P. (2003). Mao's war against nature?: The environmental impact of the grain-first campaign in China. *China Journal, 50,* 37–59.

Hong, J. (2010). Desertification in China: Problems with policies and perceptions. In J. J. Kassiola & S. Guo (Eds.), *China's environmental crisis: Domestic and global political impacts and responses* (pp. 13–40). New York: Palgrave Macmillan.

Jiang, M. (2009). Water crisis in Chinese cities in 2007. In D. Yang (Ed.), *The China environment yearbook: Vol. 3. Crises and opportunities* (pp. 53–61). Leiden, The Netherlands/Beijing: Brill/Social Sciences Academic Press.

Jiao, L. (2009). Green Olympics and environmental improvements in Beijing. In Y. Dongping (Ed.), *The China environment yearbook: Vol. 3. Crises and opportunities* (pp. 135–151). Brill, NY/Beijing: Koninklijke/Social Sciences Academic Press.

Jingjing, L. (2013, August 10). Pollution-free days of Beijing Olympics now just a happy memory. *South China Morning Post.* Retrieved from www.scmp.com/news/china/article/1295644/pollution-free-days-beijing-olympics-now-just-happy-memory.

Li, J., & Liu, J. (2009, January). Quest for clean water: China's newly amended water pollution control law. *China Environmental Forum.* Retrieved from www.wilsoncenter.org/publication/quest-for-clean-water-chinas-newly-amended-water-pollution-control-law.

Liu, F. (2009). *[Resource utilization and environmental protection on the basis of environmental ethics].* Beijing: National Defense Industry Press. (In Chinese)

Meng, S., Wen, S., & Ma, D. (2005). [Consideration of law in China's desertification]. *Heibei Law Studies, 23*(10), 154–157. (In Chinese)

Second national assessment report on climate change. (2011). Beijing: Sciences Press. Retrieved from http://english.cas.cn/resources/archive/news_archive/nu2009/201502/t20150215_139339.shtml. (In Chinese)

Shapiro, J. (2001). *Mao's war against nature: Politics and the environment in revolutionary China.* Cambridge, UK: Cambridge University Press.

Stensdal, I. (2012). *China's climate-change policy 1988–2011: From zero to hero?* Lysaker, Norway: Fridtjof Nansen Institute,

Tang, S., & Zhan, X. (2008). Civic environmental NGOs, civil society and democratization in China. *Journal of Developmental Studies, 44*(5), 425–448.

Wang, T. (Ed.). (2003). *[Desert and desertification in China].* Shijiazhang, China: Heibei Science & Technology Press. (In Chinese)

Wang, Y. (2009). A health check on the ecology of the Yangtze River. In D. Yang (Ed.), *The China environment yearbook: Vol, 3. Crises and opportunities* (pp. 63–74). Leiden, The Netherlands/Beijing: Brill/Social Sciences Academic Press.

Weng, B. (2000). [The lonely wall: Reflections on the Three-North Shelterbelt Program after 20 years]. *Window of Southern Wind, 8,* 14–25. (In Chinese)

Wong, K. K. (2008). Greening of the Chinese mind: Environmentalism with Chinese characteristics. *Asian–Pacific Review, 12*(2), 39–57.

Wong, K. K. (2010). Environmental awareness, governance and public participation: Public perception perspectives. *International Journal of Environmental Studies, 67*(2), 169–181.

Yang, G. (2008). *Yangtze conservation and development report 2007.* Beijing: Science Press.

Yang, G. B. (2009). Civic environmentalism. In Y. Hsing & C. K. Lee (Eds.), *Reclaiming Chinese society: The new social activism.* London: Routledge.

Zhang, K. (2009). Blue-green algae bloom in Taihu Lake: Reflections on pollution and development. In D. Yang (Ed.), *The China environment yearbook: Vol. 3. Crises and opportunities* (pp. 39–52). Leiden, The Netherlands/Beijing: Brill/Social Sciences Academic Press.

Zhu, Z., & Liu, S. (1989). *[Desertification in China and its control].* Beijing: Science Press. (In Chinese)

FURTHER READING •••

Ding, D., Bao, H., & Ma, Y. (1998). Progress in the study of desertification in China. *Progress in Physical Geography, 22*(4), 521–527.

Liang, W. (2010). Changing climate?: China's new interest in global climate change negotiations. In J. J. Kassiola & S. Guo. (Eds.), *China's environmental crisis: Domestic and global political impacts and responses* (pp. 61–84). New York: Palgrave Macmillan.

PART III
SELECTED REGIONS

CHAPTER 10

Coastal China

LEARNING OBJECTIVES

- Recognize the variation in how China defines different geographical regions.

- Understand the geographical setting and historical development of the coastal region.

- Recognize the coastal region's shared characteristics and geographical variability.

- Learn the history of Shanghai's development.

- Develop an understanding of the economic geography of the Yangtze River Delta region.

- Recognize Hainan as a unique province in the region.

KEY CONCEPTS AND TERMS

regionalization scheme;
coastal development policies;
intraregional variability;
Yangtze River Delta region;
research and development (R&D);
growth pole development policy;
primary, secondary, and tertiary sectors;
unequal Treaty of Nanking;
concession districts;
transnational corporations (TNCs);
foreign direct investment (FDI);
spatial agglomeration; "Hawaii of China"

REGIONS IN CHINA

This is the first of three chapters in which we take a regional approach to study specific regions within the Chinese territory (see Chapter 1 for a brief discussion of the two major approaches in geography—"systematic" and "regional"). Unfortunately, there are no official regional definitions in China similar to the definitions of the nine census regions used in the United States.[1] How, then, are regions in China defined?

China has used region as a spatial planning concept to formulate numerous regionalization schemes. Since 1949, these schemes have reflected various political and economic concerns. For example, Mao's attempt to reduce unequal development between the coastal and inland regions led to the development of a scheme that included six economic regions. During the first Five-Year Plan, about two-thirds of government-initiated industrial projects were allocated to the interior region. In the mid-1960s, the intensification of the Cold War between China and western countries put national security at the top of Mao's agenda. As a result, a radical three-region scheme was adopted. The country's military and critical industries were shifted to the central and inland regions.

Since 1976, Mao's radical policies have been replaced with economic development polices, which seek to "let a small number of people get rich first." In this context, a new three-region division—east, central, and west—and a coastal development strategy was introduced. Despite the fact that this regionalization scheme received widespread acceptance among scholars and policy makers, government authorities developed their own schemes for specific purposes. For instance, when the National Bureau of Statistics of the People's Republic of China (PRC) reports census data for the nation, it organizes the data into six regional groups.[2] Beijing, Tianjin, Hebei, Shanxi, and Neimenggu form a group; Liaoning, Jilin, and Heilongjiang constitute another group; and Shanghai, Jiangsu, Zhejiang, Anhui, Fujian, Jiangxi, and Shandong form a third group. Three other groups include several southern provinces, provinces/autonomous regions in the southwest, and provinces/autonomous regions in the northwest. However, these regions are not commonly used for other governmental functions. The National Bureau of Statistics has also defined four economic regions[3]: east (Beijing, Tianjin, Hebei, Shanghai, Jiangsu, Zhejiang, Fujian, Shandong, Guangdong, and Hainan); central (Shanxi, Anhui, Jiangxi, Henan, Hubei, and Hunan); west (Neimenggu, Guangxi, Chongqing, Sichuan, Guizhou, Yunnan, Xizang, Shaanxi, Gansu, Qinghai, Ningxia, and Xinjiang); and northeast (Heilongjiang, Jilin, and Liaoning). These various regional schemes not only demonstrate inconsistency between government departments, but also confuse researchers and students studying China.

In this book, we use a relatively simple three-region scheme. This scheme is mainly geographical, but also takes into account the similarities among areas in terms of economic conditions, population, and cultural characteristics. Our three-region scheme consists of the coastal region, the interior, and the peripheral or border region (see Figure 10.1). We discuss the coastal region in this chapter. In the next chapter (Chapter 11), we focus on the peripheral region, covering areas near the Chinese border to the north, west, and south. Geographically between the coastal and peripheral regions is the central region, but we do not dedicate a chapter to this region, as many of its important and interesting aspects are already covered in other chapters. Instead, we focus in Chapter 12 on Chinese territories outside the mainland. These territories include the two special administrative regions (SARs) of Hong Kong and Macau, as well as Taiwan, which the PRC regards as part of China. Clearly, these territories are not spatially linked (contiguous), but they

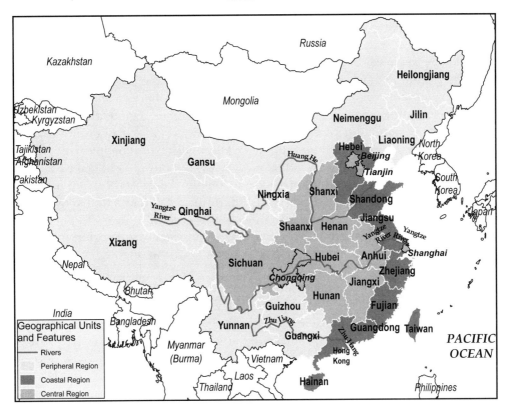

FIGURE 10.1 The three-region scheme we have adopted for this book: coastal, central, and peripheral.

exhibit many similarities in terms of history, current political situation, and future relationships with the Chinese central government (i.e., the PRC).

Located at the center of Asia, China borders 14 countries to the north, west, and southwest on land. However, given its huge territory, the remaining border is a coastline of 14,500 km to the east and southeast[4] (Figure 10.1). With more than 36,000 km of territorial boundary, slightly less than 40% is coastline, providing access to the Pacific Ocean through the Yellow Sea in the north, the East China Sea to the east, and the South China Sea to the south and southeast (Plate 6). Areas along the coastline not only have the locational advantage of ocean access, but they also include the estuaries and delta regions of three major rivers: the Huang He (Yellow River), the Yangtze River, and the Zhu Jiang (Pearl River). These delta regions are rich in alluvial soil, which is generally fertile. As a result, agricultural productivity in these delta regions has been relatively high, and therefore these regions have the capacity to support relatively large populations.

This coastal region includes any administrative unit near the coast or with a coastline. This regional definition is similar to the coastal region adopted by Wei (2004). The extent of this region, starting from the north, includes Hebei, the two municipalities of Beijing and Tianjin, Shandong, Jiangsu, the municipality of Shanghai, Zhejiang, Fujian, Guangdong, and Hainan. Although Liaoning is a province with a coast, it, Heilongjiang, and Jilin are often grouped together as the "north-three provinces" because they share many characteristics (see Chapter 11). Therefore, Liaoning is not included in our definition of the coastal region and is only mentioned once or twice in this chapter. Guangxi shares a small portion of the Chinese coastline to the south, but it is an autonomous region, and the coastal impact on the region is relatively insignificant. Therefore, we also do not include Guangxi in the coastal region, and it is not discussed in this chapter. Geographically, the two SARs of Hong Kong and Macau, as well as Taiwan, which have administrative status similar to that of a province, belong to the coastal region; however, Hong Kong, Macau, and Taiwan are discussed in Chapter 12, as noted above. Plate 6 highlights the relevant administrative units in this region.

In this chapter, we emphasize the importance of the coastal region to China. The physical setting of the region is reviewed first. Then we highlight some of the similarities and differences within the region. The importance of the coastal region is not accidental; it has been cultivated in recent Chinese history, particularly by economic development policy. We discuss relevant issues related to the region's growth and strengths. The coastal region is also characterized by the presence of two major economic engines: the delta regions of the Pearl and Yangtze Rivers. We focus here on the situation in the Yangtze River Delta, with Shanghai at its center. The chapter also provides a brief overview of Hainan—a province that is often ignored, partly because of its peripheral location, but that occupies a special niche in the increasingly important Chinese tourist industry.

PHYSICAL SETTINGS OF THE COASTAL REGION

The north–south geographical extent of the coastal region is defined by Hebei province in the north and Hainan province in the south. The latitudes range from slightly above 40 degrees North to 17 degrees North. This latitudinal range is equivalent to the spatial extent from Massachusetts and Connecticut in the north to the southern tip of Florida into Cuba and Jamaica. The southern tip of the Chinese coastal region is below the Tropic of Cancer (i.e., 23.5 degrees North); the island province of Hainan and a significant portion of Guangdong province are therefore in the tropical climate zone. This climate is characterized by hot summers with frequent thunderstorms and mild to cool winters with no clear dry season, although the summers are wetter than the winters.

The northern end of the region, Hebei province, is in the temperate climate zone. Winter can be cold at such a high latitude, especially when the region is under the influence of the cold air masses from Siberia in the far north. However, its proximity to the ocean allows the water to have a moderating effect, keeping the region from extreme climatic conditions. Ocean water off the coast is usually warmer than the temperature on land during winter, and therefore it raises the temperature of the coastal region. The summer situation is the opposite, with cooler water off the coast, reducing the summer temperatures from hot to warm.

Climate along the coastal region is very much affected by the powerful monsoon climate, a climatic system characterized by a reversal of wind direction between summer and winter (see Chapter 2 for a fuller description). During winter, wind blows from the frigid continental interior toward the coast, creating occasional cold fronts sweeping into the region. During summer, wind blows from the cooler oceans inland, creating sea breezes that moderate the hot summer temperature. Associated with the summer monsoon is the occasional formation of typhoons. Like hurricanes in the Atlantic Ocean, typhoons are tropical depressions (low-pressure cells) that form over the oceans. When they approach the continent or make landfall, they may bring disasters and significant amounts of rainfall. People living in the coastal region often have to endure this type of natural disaster. Evacuations along coastal and lowland areas are quite common during the typhoon season.

Overall, the coastal region in China does not have extreme or unbearable climatic conditions. Compared to the interior parts of China, where arid, desert climates (such as that in Xinjiang) or rugged terrains (such as that in Xizang) are found, the coastal region has physical conditions relatively favorable to human settlement. The coastal region also has moderate relief with relatively low elevations. North of Zhejiang province, the coastal lowland includes the delta regions of the two main rivers, the Huang He and Yangtze. The coastal area from Hebei to Zhejiang is relatively gentle, with no major mountain ranges (refer to the terrain map in Plate 1). Some of the areas near the river deltas are low-lying and thus have been historically subject to flooding. These areas also have the most fertile soil—partly because of the frequent flooding, which brings alluvium from the rivers to land to support the intensive agricultural system. The coastal areas of Zhejiang, Fujian, and part of Guangdong are more rugged, even though the region does not have major mountains. The delta region of Zhu Jiang (the Pearl River Delta) in Guangdong province is another major agricultural area with both desirable climate and landscape.

The coastal area has easy access to the oceans. East of Hebei and the two municipalities of Beijing and Tianjin is Bohai (*hai* [海] in Chinese means "sea"), which is the bay leading to the Yellow Sea and the East China Sea (Plate 6). The rest of China's coastline in the northeast is along Korea Bay in Liaoning province, which shares its international boundary with North Korea. The East China Sea and South China Sea surround the rest of the coastal region, with the Gulf of Tonkin adjacent to Vietnam at the western end of the ocean. The narrow Taiwan Strait between Taiwan and the mainland has been a political and military flashpoint for decades, with several islands heavily guarded by troops on both sides. Many major cities along the coastal area serve as seaports to facilitate trade and commerce. Although we do not include Liaoning province as part of the coastal region, its famous port, Dalian, at the southern tip of the Liaodong Peninsula,[5] has historically been an important naval base and provides convenient access to the Yellow Sea and then the East China Sea. Farther south is another famous seaport, Qingdao, which used to be spelled "Tsingtao" (this is now the name of a popular Chinese beer and brewery). Qingdao is in the eastern tip of the Shandong Peninsula next to the Yellow Sea. The city serves as a major seaport and also a naval base. Many other major cities are found near major bodies of water, such as rivers (e.g., Nanjing in Jiangsu and Hangzhou in Zhejiang) or lakes (Suzhou in Jiangsu), in this coastal region.

Despite the tremendous variation in the physical environment along the coastal region, this area has several consistent characteristics—including its relatively low-lying relief, strong agricultural potential, and (in recent decades) immense economic power. The rest of this chapter discusses some of these strengths in greater detail.

ECONOMIC DEVELOPMENT POLICY AND ITS IMPORTANCE TO THE COASTAL REGION

Out of the 31 major administrative units in China (excluding Hong Kong, Macau, and Taiwan), only 10 are found in the coastal region. However, this region contains an exceptionally large number of politically and economically important cities. Figure 10.2 shows the major cities found in the coastal region (and in nearby provinces). Three of the four municipalities directly under state control are in the coastal region: Beijing, Shanghai, and Tianjin. All of the cities designated earliest as special economic zones (SEZs) are coastal cities: Zhuhai, Shenzhen, Shantou, and Xiamen. Several of the 20 largest Chinese cities (see Chapter 6, Table 6.1) are found in this region, and four are seaports: Shanghai, Shenzhen, Dalian, and Qingdao. In terms of its number of administrative units and its area, the coastal region is relatively small. However, it has disproportional significance in the Chinese economy and history. Its significance in today's Chinese economy is partly attributable to the economic policies adopted in the past several decades.

Coastal Development Policies

The development of modern China's coastal region has been closely tied to the overall economic policy of the Chinese central government and various political movements in recent Chinese history. In the early Communist era, Mao Zedong was desperate to eliminate the development gap between the coastal and inland regions. He said:

> In the past our industries were concentrated in the coastal regions. . . . This irrational situation is a product of history. The coastal industrial base must be put to full use, but to even out the distribution of industry as it develops we must strive to promote industry in the interior. . . . Without doubt, the greater part of new industry should be located in the interior so that industry may gradually become evenly distributed. (1977, pp. 286–287)

Radical measures followed that emphasized local industrial production of all kinds, whether or not local conditions were favorable for such production. The Cultural Revolution not only created massive social protests, but sent many urban dwellers, including businessmen and intellectuals, to rural farming areas for

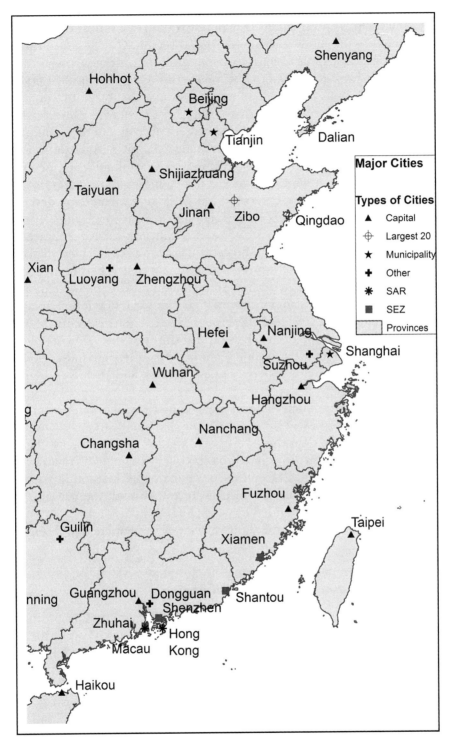

FIGURE 10.2 Major cities in the coastal region and in nearby provinces. The special administrative regions (SARs) of Hong Kong and Macau are also included in this figure, although they are discussed in detail in Chapter 12. SEZ, special economic zones.

"rehabilitation." This caused major disruption to the rebuilt postwar urban economy, particularly in the highly urbanized coastal region. Overall, the strategy was to shift emphasis away from the coast to the interior, in order to achieve more balanced development and to reduce the influence of the colonial and capitalist centers along the coast. Thus the development of coastal areas was not favored during the early Communist era.

Mao's death marked the beginning of a new era of "rational" economic reform, which to a large degree was initiated by Deng Xiaoping. Agricultural reform included the household responsibility system in which farmland was leased to farmers, giving them the incentive to produce more to increase income. On the business side, township and village enterprises (TVEs) were created, as described in Chapter 7. These production units were essentially private enterprises, owned and operated by the local jurisdictions. A market mechanism was also embraced in the new development era. Furthermore, the central government decided to accelerate the economic growth of the coastal region, realizing that it had many locational advantages over the interior. Accepting the economic principle of "comparative advantage,"[6] the Chinese government stimulated industrial development and trade in the coastal region, believing that these were effective means to lift the Chinese economy overall. Another major idea behind this shift was the "growth pole" development policy, or the idea that wealth accumulated in the coastal region would eventually trickle down to the less developed interior and therefore benefit the entire country.

One of the effective policies adopted early in the economic reform era was to establish the SEZs, mainly in southern China near the Pearl River Delta. Rules in these zones were relaxed so that local governments could attract foreign business to set up production facilities in China, taking advantage of cheap labor and other factors. Initially, four SEZs (Shenzhen, Zhuhai, and Shantou in Guangdong province, and Xiamen in Fujian province) were established; the great success of these four was envied and demanded by other jurisdictions. More SEZs were soon set up along the coastal region, and many port cities were opened to foreign investors.

The National Importance of the Coastal Region

Among the 20 largest cities in China (refer to the 20 largest cities according to the UN in Chapter 6), nine are in the coastal region. These nine cities together have a total population of almost 65 million, approximately 56% of the population in the 20 largest cities in 2008. The total population in the coastal region was almost 550 million, according to the 2010 census. That accounts for more than 38% of the total Chinese population, but the area of the coastal region is only about 9.7% of Chinese territory. Given the relatively small area and the large population size, this region has a population density of almost 554 people per square kilometer (km^2), versus 97 people/km^2 for the rest of the country in 2010. Table 10.1 includes some statistics comparing the coastal region with the rest of the country.

TABLE 10.1. Selected Statistics Comparing China as a Whole, Averages for the Coastal Region, and Averages for the Rest of the Country

	Countrywide	Coastal region (average by units)	Rest of country (average by units)
Population density (per km^2) (2000/2010)	131.46/141.01	484.53/554.48 (by region)	93.72/96.80 (by region)
% Nonagricultural population (2000/2010)	24.73/29.14	34.52/36.30	25.09/29.85
% Age 6 years and older with no education (2000/2010)	7.75/5.00	6.55/3.91	11.16/7.10
% Age 6 years and older with college education (2000/2010)	3.73/9.53	6.03/13.90	3.52/8.76
% of Population in Han ethnic group (2000/2010)	91.53/91.60	96.55/96.39	79.42/79.69
% of R&D expenditure of GDP (in 2009)	1.7	2.12	1.07
Average earnings, 2006 (in yuan)	20,856	25,338	18,263

Note. The statistics for the coastal region and the rest of the country are statistically different at the 90% confidence level (except for the nonagricultural population proportions in both years). Calculations are based on the fifth (2000) and sixth (2010) population censuses in China. Other calculations are based on special topic statistics provided by the National Bureau of Statistics of China (www.stats.gov.cn/tjsj/pcsj/rdzyqc/decrdzyqc).

Besides having nine of the 20 largest Chinese cities, the coastal region is also relatively highly developed, with significant manufacturing and commercial activities. The percentage of the population engaged in nonagricultural activities was more than 36% in 2010 in the region. Although this percentage is higher than the almost 30% for the rest of the country, the difference is not statistically significant (Table 10.1). Related to the level of development is education. Only 3.91% of the population 6 years old and older in the coastal region received no education in 2010, versus 7.10% for the rest of the country. More than 13.90% of the population 6 years old and older received at least a college-level education in this region, but only 8.76% of this group in the rest of country received that same level of education. Economic development is often stimulated by research and development (R&D) activities. In the coastal region, slightly more than 2% of total gross domestic product (GDP) was spent in R&D activities, almost twice the percentage for the rest of the country. Not surprisingly, the average earned income per person in this region was over 25,000 yuan, much higher than the average of 18,263 yuan for the rest of the country. Another interesting characteristic of the coastal region is the dominance of the Han ethnic group, with an average of 96.39% of the population. In the rest of the country, including all the autonomous regions, the average percentage of Han was only 79.69%.

To summarize, the coastal region is relatively well developed economically and has large numbers of major cities, including three of China's four independent municipalities. The population is relatively homogeneous and well educated, and its ethnic composition is dominated by the Han. Many of them are employed in nonagricultural sectors with relatively high income. But they are confined to a relatively small region, enduring high population density. Nevertheless, not all provinces in the region are equally prosperous. They vary tremendously in their historical and political legacies. A point to note is that the differences between the coastal region and the rest of the country narrowed between 2000 and 2010. This is evidence (supporting the growth pole development policy) that the benefits of development have been trickling from the coastal region to the interior.

HISTORICAL AND ECONOMIC VARIATIONS WITHIN THE COASTAL REGION

The coastal area is the most developed region in China, with major political and economic engines that have run exceptionally well in the past several decades. However, its current prosperity is not just the result of the Chinese government's development policy enacted during the past several decades. The region's success is also due to its deeply entrenched role in the political history of China.

Historical and Political Clout

The nine largest Chinese cities found in the coastal region are, in descending order of population size, Shanghai, Beijing, Guangzhou, Tianjin, Shenzhen, Dongguan, Nanjing, Jinan, and Qingdao. Quite a few of these cities (Shanghai, Guangzhou, Tianjin, Nanjing, Jinan, and Qingdao) and others in the coastal regions were once "treaty ports," some of which, like Shanghai, have "concession districts." That is, because of the terms of treaties signed in the 19th century, China had to make concessions to foreign powers and experienced occupation by these powers. The foreigners, however, brought industrial technologies with them. Therefore, these cities and the coastal region as a whole were more accustomed to industry and trade, and more ready to be engaged in the global economy, than the interior part of the country.

Three coastal cities are currently provincial capitals (Guangzhou, Nanjing, and Jinan). However, the three political powerhouses are Beijing, Tianjin, and Shanghai—municipalities that enjoy an administrative status equivalent to provinces and autonomous regions. Many of these cities were capitals of China in the past, and their historical importance has been carried into the present.

The rest of the large coastal cities are important from a different perspective. Qingdao in Shandong province, the smallest of these cities, was once a concession city occupied by Germany after foreign powers demanded the opening of Chinese seaports in the Qing dynasty. The two large southern cities of Shenzhen and Dongguan are economic powerhouses in the south, but have no important history and were not of any political significance. Geographically, there are three subregional clusters within the coastal region: Beijing–Tianjin is the political center; Shanghai–Jiangsu–Zhejiang is a combined political and economic center; and southern Guangdong province around the Pearl River Delta is an economic center. The last two clusters constitute the two major delta regions of China and are discussed in more detail later.

No large city of historical or political significance is found in the provinces of Fujian and Hainan. Although the provincial capital of Fujian is Fuzhou, the most well-known city in the province is probably Xiamen (known as Amoy in the past). Xiamen is one of the four original SEZs opened for foreign investment by the Chinese government in the early 1980s. However, it did not grow as fast as Shenzhen, another SEZ in Guangdong province, just north of the Hong Kong SAR.

Jinmen (or Kinmen)—an island or county officially controlled by the Taiwanese government (the Republic of China, or ROC)—is off the coast of Fujian province, just a few kilometers from Xiamen. It has been a political "hot button" on both sides of the Taiwan Strait, and there are ROC army outposts on the island, right on the doorstep of PRC territory. Occasional military drills conducted by the Taiwanese army on the island draw protests from the mainland government and stir up international concern. Hainan—an island in the South China Sea off the coast of Leizhou Peninsula, the southernmost tip of the Chinese mainland—was part of Guangdong province until 1988. It has a tropical environment like Hawaii's, which attracts tourists from all over Asia.

Economic and Social Variations

China's coastal region is the most developed and highly populated region in the country. But variations within the region should not be ignored. Figure 3.7 in Chapter 3 shows that the three municipalities and Jiangsu, immediately adjacent to Shanghai, have the highest population density levels. Fujian and Hainan have the lowest density levels in the coastal region.

To assess these variations at a finer geographical level, we calculated population density levels at the county level, and these are reported in Figure 10.3. There is relatively high population density in the stretch between Beijing–Tianjin and Shanghai that cuts through the southern part of Hebei, Shandong, and Jiangsu. The figure also shows clearly that in the provinces of Zhejiang, Fujian, and Guangdong, high population density is restricted to limited areas and is not widespread. Hainan's population is very small. Beyond the three municipalities, population distribution is clearly related to the locations of rivers, particularly the delta regions. Thus not all of the coastal region is densely populated.

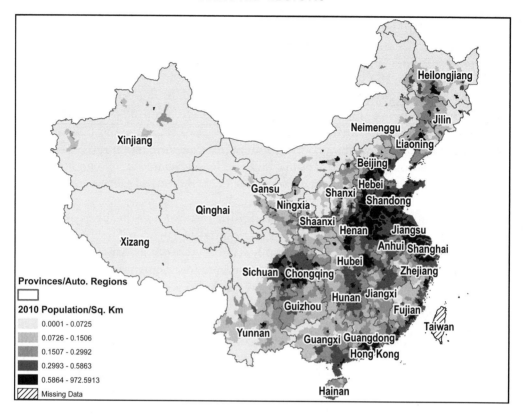

FIGURE 10.3 Population densities at the county level. Data from 2010 Chinese census.

To a large extent, the variation of population density within the coastal region reflects different levels of economic development. In Table 10.2, the region's political and administrative areas are arranged from north to south, together with selected population and economic statistics. The percentage of the nonagricultural population reflects the extent to which the area relies on industrial and commercial activities, an indicator of the strength of the modern economy. Not surprising are the high nonagricultural percentages in the three municipalities, ranging from 50 to 62%. Beijing is the national capital and the seat of the central government, which dominates employment in the municipality. There is a very low percentage of the nonagricultural population in the surrounding Hebei province (21%). In fact, Hebei has the lowest percentage of this population in the entire coastal region.

Extreme situations are found along the borders in the Beijing–Tianjin–Hebei region, and they constitute a very unusual geographical pattern. Typically, areas with similar characteristics are found close together, and dissimilar areas are usually far apart.[7] The two neighboring municipalities, Beijing and Tianjin, are surrounded by a very different environment in Hebei. Although Hebei did not have the highest percentage of people age 6 years and older without education (indicating low education level), its percentage of the population with at least a college education was the lowest among all areas in the coastal region. Its percentage of GDP spent on R&D was the second lowest, slightly more than twice the lowest in Hainan. Hebei's per capita earning was also the second lowest, slightly higher than that for Hainan. These extremely different economic conditions found in adjacent areas are mostly due to the artificial administrative boundaries that control resource allocation and policies across administrative borders. This is an example of the administrative zone economy, discussed in Chapter 5.

The lowest percentage of GDP spent on R&D was 0.35% in Hainan; this partly reflects Hainan's economic emphasis on tourism. This contrasts with the 5.5% GDP spending on R&D in Beijing. Hainan's percentage of the nonagricultural population was significantly higher than those in Hebei, Fujian, and Shandong, indicating that Hainan has significant nonagricultural sectors. But Fujian and Shandong have relatively low nonagricultural population levels, low averages in earning, and relatively low percentages of people with at least a college education. At the other end of the spectrum, the three municipalities have the most favorable statistics and conditions, followed by Guangdong, Zhejiang, and Jiangsu provinces. It is interesting to note that all the administrative units in the region, except for Hainan in the south, have populations that are more than 95% Han. In other words, the region is highly ethnically homogeneous. In Hainan, Li is the largest minority group.

Figures 10.4 and 10.5 provide a more detailed picture by comparing the economic structure of the coastal region with the rest of the nation. Using data from the 2008 China economic census, we classified employment numbers into primary, secondary, and tertiary sectors by provinces, municipalities, and autonomous regions. These areas were grouped into the coastal region and the rest of the country. The

TABLE 10.2. Selected Population and Economic Statistics for Provinces and Municipalities within the Coastal Region

Provinces/ municipalities	% of Nonagricultural population	% Age 6 years and older with no education	% Age 6 years and older with at least college education	% Population in Han ethnic group	R&D expenditure as % of GDP (in 2009)	Average earnings, 2006 (¥)
Hebei	21.26	3.26	7.93	95.83	0.78	16,456
Beijing	61.79	1.93	32.84	95.91	5.50	39,684
Tianjin	50.24	2.52	18.26	97.44	2.37	27,628
Shandong	23.43	5.96	9.32	99.24	1.53	19,135
Jiangsu	33.47	4.65	11.48	99.51	2.04	23,657
Shanghai	61.89	3.15	22.82	98.80	2.81	37,585
Zhejiang	25.02	6.55	9.86	97.77	1.73	27,570
Fujian	22.14	3.46	8.98	97.84	1.11	19,424
Guangdong	28.77	2.67	9.12	98.02	1.65	26,400
Hainan	34.96	4.91	8.43	83.56	0.35	15,843

Note. ¥, yuan. Data from the 2010 Chinese population census and other sources from the National Bureau of Statistics of China (www.stats.gov.cn/tjsj/pcsj/rdzyqc/decrdzyqc).

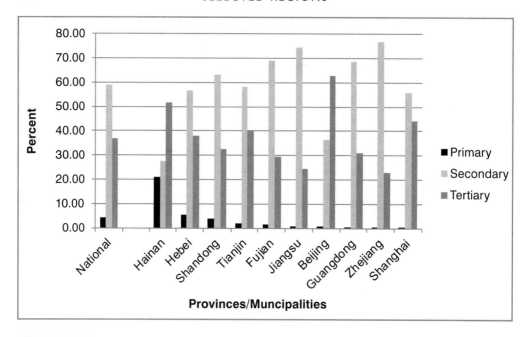

FIGURE 10.4 Employment compositions of legal establishments by economic sectors at the national level and in each province or municipality in the coastal region. Data from State Council Economic Census Leading Group (SC-ECLG) (2010).

percentages employed in the three sectors for these areas can be compared with the national percentages. At the national level, the percentage employed in the primary sector (agriculture, animal husbandry, fishery, foresting, and mining) was around 4%; those employed in the secondary sector (manufacturing, processing, construction, and energy) represented almost 60%; and those working in the tertiary sector (services) accounted for 36%. Figure 10.4 shows that the economic data for Hebei and Shandong were most similar to the national economic structure, meaning that they were dominated by the secondary sector. Hainan's data were most different from the national situation, with relatively large primary and tertiary sectors, but the smallest secondary sector in the coastal region. The three municipalities and other provinces had small or no percentages employed in the primary sector, but sizable secondary and tertiary sectors, indicating the dominance of industries and services in these provinces.[8]

Specifically, both Beijing and Hainan were dominated by the tertiary sector, although by different types of services. The government, which is part of the tertiary sector, is the largest employer in Beijing, while services in the hospitality industry are the largest sources of employment in Hainan. For all other provinces and municipalities in the coastal region, the secondary sector was the largest. The secondary sector was notably dominant in Fujian, Jiangsu, Guangdong, and Zhejiang provinces—the most industrialized areas in the nation. Hainan still has a significant primary sector.

As for the rest of the country (Figure 10.5), the economic data for the first four provinces and municipalities, Henan, Chongqing, Anhui, and Jiangxi, were most similar to the national situation: The secondary sector was the largest, followed by the tertiary sector and then the primary sector. Heilongjiang and Shanxi were similar in their economic structure, with a relatively large primary sector, and secondary and tertiary sectors of similar sizes. Xinjiang also had a relatively large primary sector, but its economy was dominated by the tertiary sector. For the other provinces and autonomous regions, the secondary sector was not as dominant as in the national situation. Xizang (Tibet) had a very large tertiary sector (around 70%). This outlier, similar to that of Beijing, was partly due to the large presence of government, but for a different reason: control and monitoring of the minority Zang (Tibetan) population. Another majority "contribution" to the tertiary sector consisted of religious organizations, which have a large presence in Xizang because of relatively large Buddhist institutions. Only three provinces and autonomous regions, Hubei, Guangxi, and Xizang (Tibet), had a relatively smaller primary sector than the national average. The relatively small primary sector in Xizang was mostly attributable to the lack of natural resources, including an undesirable climate for most crops.

The major difference between the coastal region and the interior, then, is in their differing emphases on the primary and secondary sectors. The strength of

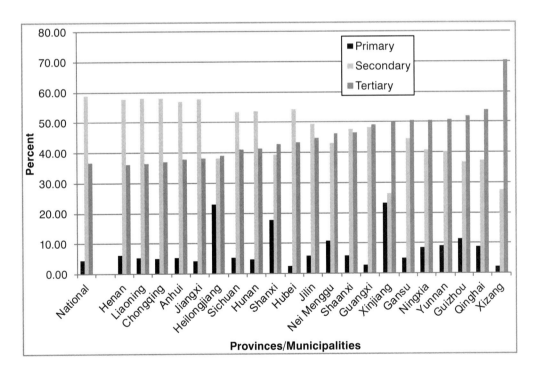

FIGURE 10.5 Employment composition of legal establishments by economic sectors at the national level and in each province or municipality outside the coastal region. Data from SC-ECLG (2010).

the secondary sector in the coastal region, and particularly in the two delta regions centered in Shanghai and Hong Kong–Guangzhou, separates the coast from the interior quite significantly.

THE YANGTZE RIVER DELTA REGION AS AN ECONOMIC ENGINE

The coastal region is no doubt the most economically vibrant region in China. But within it, the two delta subregions of the Yangtze and Pearl Rivers are the most powerful economic engines, lifting the economic prosperity of contemporary China to a new level. The composition, historical development, economic strengths, and the future development of the Pearl River Delta are discussed in Chapter 12. In this part of this chapter, we focus on the Yangtze River Delta, with the municipality of Shanghai at its center.

The city of Shanghai is located on the southern bank of the Yangtze River (Figure 10.6). Across the Huangpujiang (Huangpu River) to the east is the newer, more glamorous Pudong district. There, the 101-floor Shanghai World Financial Center—once the world's tallest building—rises among other tall skyscrapers, such as the 88-floor Jin Mao Tower and the iconic Oriental Pearl Tower with its communication

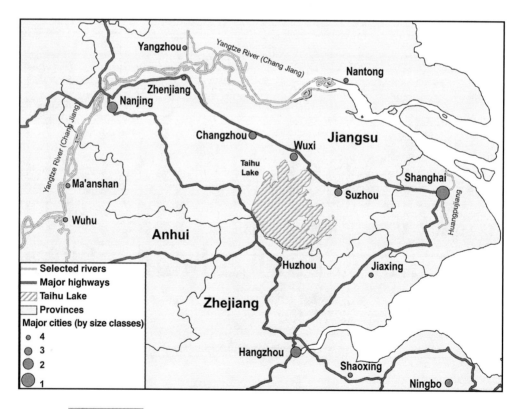

FIGURE 10.6 The municipality of Shanghai and the Yangtze River Delta region.

FIGURE 10.7 High-rises in the Pudong district along the Huangpujiang—a view from the "old" Shanghai city. (Photo: courtesy of Dr. Banggu Liao, Shanghai Normal University)

antenna ("needle") on top. Figure 10.7 shows the Pudong skyline across the Huang-pujiang from old Shanghai city. Although the city of Shanghai is no doubt the most prosperous and important economic center in the country, it is only one of the many well-connected and fast-growing economic nodes in the delta region (Figure 10.6). Less than 300 km (186 miles) to the west is Nanjing, and about 200 km (124 miles) to the southwest is Hangzhou; both are major second-tier cities. Within the territory bounded by these three cities is a region supported by an efficient transportation system, filled with pro-business local governments, and populated by a large pool of relatively inexpensive but skillful workers. These large cities—together with a large number of medium-size cities, such as Changzhou, Ningbo, Suzhou, and Wuxi, and smaller cities—form a very economically powerful network in the delta region. Because of the historical influence of Western powers, easy access to the global economy, and aggressive Chinese economic development policy, Shanghai and its surrounding area constitute one of the most prosperous and wealthiest regions in China.

The Historical Development of Shanghai

Within the coastal region, the economy of Shanghai was the earliest to take off. In the mid-19th century, the Qing dynasty's government was defeated by foreign powers in the Opium Wars (Chapter 12 describes these wars in greater detail).[9] As a result, China had to make many concessions to these foreign countries. These were formalized in treaties that opened up Chinese ports to these powers for business and trade. One of the major concessions was to let the foreigners occupy Chinese territories, particularly in cities. Shanghai was targeted by these foreign powers. Two "concession districts" were created within the city. The French Concession was located west of the walled city of Shanghai; a larger concession district, called the International Settlement and shared by other foreign powers (including the British and Americans), was located north of the old city along the Huangpujiang (Henriot, 2004). Figure 10.8 shows that the concession areas were quite dynamic, and that over time they expanded, reflecting the weakening and collapse of the Qing dynasty. Within these concession areas, foreigners controlled business and population settlements, even though most of the residents within the concession districts were Chinese.

The invasion of Shanghai by Westerners brought Western cultures and lifestyles to modernize the city. Knowing and learning foreign languages in Shanghai became highly desirable, as language proficiency could open doors to various job opportunities brought by the foreign occupants. Western fashions became popular, in contrast to traditional Chinese clothing. Tailors in Shanghai received exposure to Western sewing and tailoring techniques; the skills of Shanghainese tailors and the quality of their work were regarded as first-class. Remnants of these cultural influences are still visible in today's Shanghai.

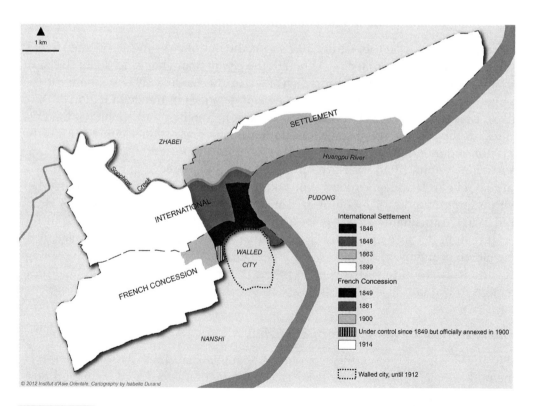

FIGURE 10.8 The French Concession and International Settlement districts in Shanghai before 1914. Based on Henriot and Durand (2012).

BOX 10.1. Shanghai: The Most Westernized Chinese City, Then and Now

Shanghai's earliest encounters with the Western world probably occurred after it became one of the treaty ports. China was forced to open these ports to foreign powers after the Qing dynasty was defeated during the Opium Wars (1839–1841). The Qing government signed the Treaty of Nanjing in 1841, granting foreigners the right to live and trade in "treaty ports." Shanghai was one of the five initial treaty ports. The other four were Canton, or Shamian Island near today's Guangzhou; Amoy, or Xiamen, and Fuzhou in Fujian province; and Ningbo in Zhejiang province. The major foreign occupants included the British, the Americans, the French, and later the Japanese. The treaty also allowed foreigners to establish their own jurisdictions as "concession districts" and to enjoy extraterritorial rights so that they were not subject to Chinese laws. In Shanghai, concession districts established by the four dominant foreign powers occupied most of the old city. Later the British and Americans merged their districts, and it became the International Settlement (see Figure 10.8).

The presence and influence of Western cultures in Shanghai were manifested in many ways. The historic district at the eastern end of Shanghai city along the Huangpujiang is a striking example. This area along the riverbank extends from north of the old walled city (Figure 10.7) toward the north in the Nanshi and Huangpu districts (Figure 10.9). The waterfront area, often called the "Bund," was the center of foreign powers in Shanghai, and this legacy is reflected in the 50 or so historical buildings in both classical and modern styles of architecture. The Bund is one of the most famous tourist sites in Shanghai (Figure 10.10). A favorite tourist activity is to take a sunset cruise along the Huangpujiang and see the Bund buildings lit up after dark (Plate 7).

Another dimension of Western cultural influence was entertainment. Although many Western or Westernized entertainment establishments in the former concession districts have ceased to exist, some structures remain and are historical landmarks in today's Shanghai. Figure 10.11 shows the historical building in downtown Shanghai, still called the "Great World" (大世界). It had been the center of the city's entertainment industry for decades before the Communist era. Located in the former French Concession, it today includes performance halls, theatres, roof gardens, and pavilions; in other words, it is a multimedia complex with all-day activities. During the occupation era, the building held a variety of shows, movies, and performances in its various sections, accommodating people of different tastes, including Western-style movies and dance. The complex also provided a gathering place for both foreign and domestic elites and dignitaries. Through entertainment, therefore, Western culture penetrated Chinese society in subtle ways. While glamorous and lavish entertainment may no longer exist in the building's current "amusement park" atmosphere, the Great World is a reminder of what Shanghai used to be—a confluence of traditional Chinese and Western cultures and values.

Figure 10.12 shows the Paramount, still another example of Western cultural influence in Shanghai before the Communist era. Completed in 1933, the Paramount is an Art Deco–style building (the Chrysler Building in New York City is another instance of Art Deco style). The building was financed by a group of Chinese bankers; it operated initially as a casino, and later as a nightclub and ballroom where wealthy people in Shanghai high society gathered. Famous taxi girls provided their services as dancing partners or escorts to wealthy men, Chinese and foreigners alike. Dancing became so popular and pervasive that even white-collar workers became frequent visitors to the Paramount and numerous other ballrooms in Shanghai. After years of decay, a Taiwanese businessman renovated the Paramount, restoring some of its old-time glory. Today, a modern disco coexists with the traditional ballroom. The ballrooms and buildings provide the Shanghainese with a place not just to enjoy the fox-trot, tango, or rumba, but also to indulge in the lavish atmosphere that once defined high society.

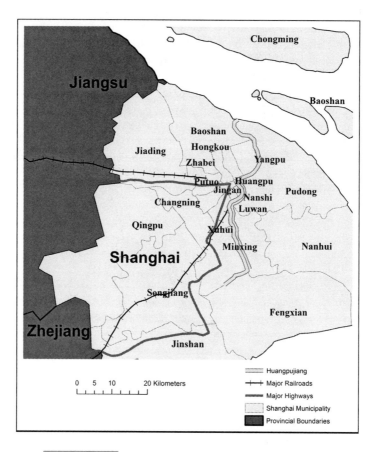

FIGURE 10.9 Regional layout of the Shanghai municipality.

FIGURE 10.10 Historic buildings along the Bund in Shanghai. Note the Chinese flags flying over the buildings. (Photo: courtesy of Dr. Banggu Liao, Shanghai Normal University)

FIGURE 10.11 The Great World entertainment complex, downtown Shanghai. (Photo: David W. S. Wong)

FIGURE 10.12 The Paramount in Shanghai—now including both traditional ballroom dance and modern dance clubs. (Photo: Dr. Banggu Liao, Shanghai Normal University)

The Western occupation also brought Western technology, which made Shanghai one of the most industrious light manufacturing centers in China at the time. A large number of industrial establishments owned by foreign powers were located in the concession districts of Shanghai. Among the foreign powers, the Japanese employed the largest workforce in the textile industry, followed by the British. British industrialists focused on textiles, paper processing, food, and public utilities, employing sizable workforces. The Americans shared interests with the British in public utilities and also in electrical equipment (Henriot & Durand, 2012). While the numbers of foreign-owned industrial establishments were significant, they were still not in the majority because the Chinese industrial base in Shanghai was quite massive. Businessmen and industrialists in Shanghai were extremely skillful.

The economic growth of Shanghai was interrupted by the invasion of Japan during World War II, and later by the Communist takeover of mainland China. Both disruptions triggered massive exits of entrepreneurs from Shanghai. Many Shanghainese businessmen and industrialists ended up relocating to Hong Kong, a British colony that provided some sense of security during the years of turmoil. These entrepreneurial migrants, part of the social and economic network of old Shanghai, became major economic forces in building the Hong Kong economy, which took off during the second half of the 20th century.

The exodus of industrialists and businessmen from Shanghai after the Communist takeover did not significantly cripple Shanghai's economic growth, however. Gradually, industries in Shanghai expanded and moved into the surrounding areas, creating positive economic spillover into these neighboring provinces and cities. Shanghai itself evolved to become a commercial business center, parallel to the political government center in Beijing. As a result, the municipality of Shanghai is China's largest city in terms of population, surpassing that of Beijing. However, the economic region centered in Shanghai is much bigger than the city itself. The entire region has become a major economic engine in China.

Shanghai: Market versus Policy; Local versus Global Forces

The economic status of Shanghai today is the result of the interplay among several factors: the central Chinese government's economic development policy, particularly the Four Modernizations in the early Communist era; the role of local government in creating favorable business environments; the emergence of a globalized economy; and the arrival of massive foreign capital. The early Communist economic policy that favored geographically balanced development definitely hurt Shanghai. Its importance and that of the surrounding Yangtze River Delta region were deemphasized. Its locational advantages—situated at the Yangtze River Delta, on the east coast between Beijing and Hong Kong, with access to the rest of the world—were ignored. Its pre–World War II legacy as a world trade, financial, and industrial center was not exploited under Communist rule. Before 1980, Shanghai and its surrounding region were told to be self-sufficient. Its manufacturing industries constituted its major economic engine.

But the economic reform that began in the late 1970s introduced market mechanisms and created a turning point for the entire country. For Shanghai, it meant an opportunity to regain its economic supremacy in the Chinese city system. The Shanghai municipal government realized that under the open-door economic policy, a strong tertiary sector was a must for Shanghai to be competitive—not just domestically, but internationally. A "spatial restructuring" of the economy in the region gradually took shape, with manufacturing industries moving away from the city proper to its suburbs and surrounding regions. The municipal government also adopted a land-leasing system (see Chapter 6): It actively collaborated with private capital in redevelopment projects, building megastructures and providing critical infrastructure. With the development of the Pudong district, east of old Shanghai city across the Huangpujiang, the municipal government showed that it was committed to putting Shanghai on the map of the global economy.

Besides managing land development and real estate projects, the government of Shanghai was also directly involved in business enterprises. A significant number of high-tech businesses in Shanghai are partly or wholly owned by the municipal government. Government resources serve as the foundation of economic development in the region. Local government has had a role in strengthening the competitiveness of Shanghai through the creation of a favorable economic environment. But the major forces propelling Shanghai into a world-class financial center were the arrival of transnational corporations (TNCs) and the accompanying overseas investment capital, often labeled "foreign direct investment" (FDI). Foreign countries regard Shanghai as an open window to accessing the gigantic Chinese economy. The strategic location of Shanghai and its business-friendly environment have made it the prime destination for FDI. Major Fortune 100 companies have chosen Shanghai to be their regional headquarters because of the abundant supply of relatively high-quality labor to support headquarters operations, as well as the availability of the stock exchange to raise capital.

Beyond Shanghai

The financial power and business glamor of Shanghai are not confined to the city proper. The headquarters of TNCs in Shanghai represent only the tip of the iceberg in terms of their economic impact. The foreign capital that flew into Shanghai did not stop there, but infiltrated the surrounding regions. To the west of the Shanghai municipality is Jiangsu province, where a large number of second- and third-tier cities are located within a 200-km (124-mile) radius of Shanghai. Several other smaller cities are within 200 km (124 miles) of Shanghai to the south, in the province of Zhejiang (Figure 10.6). These cities, together with two fourth-tier cities in the nearby province of Anhui (Ma'anshan and Wuhu) to the west, have a total population of more than 30 million (see Table 10.3). The total population of major cities in this region accounts for less than 2.4% of China's more than 1.3 billion people. Comparatively speaking, however, it is 50% larger than the approximately 20 million in the greater New York metropolitan area (2010).[10] Among this group of

TABLE 10.3. Population Size and Rank of Cities in the Greater Yangtze River Delta Region

City	Rank	Population	Province
Shanghai	1	14,348,535	Shanghai
Nanjing	12	3,624,234	Jiangsu
Hangzhou	24	2,451,319	Zhejiang
Ningbo	52	1,567,499	Zhejiang
Wuxi	67	1,425,766	Jiangsu
Suzhou	85	1,344,709	Jiangsu
Huzhou	129	1,145,414	Zhejiang
Changzhou	141	1,081,845	Jiangsu
Jiaxing	201	881,923	Zhejiang
Nantong	265	771,386	Jiangsu
Yangzhou	300	711,993	Jiangsu
Wuhu	304	697,197	Anhui
Zhenjiang	305	695,663	Jiangsu
Shaoxing	345	633,118	Zhejiang
Ma'anshan	392	567,576	Anhui
Total		31,948,177	

Note. Data from United Nations Statistics Division (2010).

Chinese cities are two provincial capitals, Nanjing (for Jiangsu province) and Hangzhou (for Zhejiang province). About half of these cities have a population size of more than 1 million, with the smallest city having a population exceeding 500,000.

The economic development in the Yangtze River Delta, with its group of medium-size and smaller cities, is closely tied to the rising financial status of Shanghai in the global economy. As TNCs and the associated FDI poured into Shanghai, the city had to find ways to physically accommodate these businesses. Land redevelopment was one mechanism for housing the new business and financial institutions establishing their presence in Shanghai. Manufacturing industries that used to occupy land in the city proper were relocated to the outskirts of the city or to neighboring provinces. The second- or third-tier cities became attractive candidates for such relocations because they provided an abundant supply of inexpensive but relatively skilled labor. Many TNCs establishing their headquarters in Shanghai intended to exploit the comparative advantage of Chinese manufacturing industries; setting up production in these second- and third-tier cities near Shanghai was an ideal logistical arrangement. As a result, these cities received massive amounts of FDI after 1990 as factories sprang up around the region.

As shown in Figure 10.6, the three cities of Suzhou, Wuxi, and Changzhou form a spatial agglomeration west of Shanghai. Each of these cities has a population of more than 1 million, and the total population of this tri-city region was more than 21 million in 2000 (not counting the 16 million in the Shanghai municipality).[11] These three cities and other cities in the region experienced a boom in manufacturing, fueled by the FDI brought in by TNCs, due in part to their proximity to Shanghai. Secondary production increased from 15% in 1980 to 55 or 60% after 2000, dominating the economy in the region (Chen, Xiang, Sun, & Chu, 2006).

Many international corporations established their presence in the tri-city region. Examples of these companies include Motorola, Philips, Sharp, Panasonic, and Siemens. Besides the locational advantage of being close to Shanghai, other location advantages made the region attractive to TNC investment. A very efficient transportation network, including several major highways and railroads, serves the region between Nanjing and Shanghai. Access to the international airports in Shanghai is relatively convenient. The region is heavily populated, and this population provides a pool of inexpensive but relatively well-educated workers. The physical environment is also desirable. Taihu Lake, one of the largest water bodies in China, provides an abundant supply of water. The climate in the region is relatively mild. Local governments have favorable and competitive business-friendly policies to attract FDI. These are all decisive factors for TNCs in deciding to invest.

Therefore, while Shanghai is the largest city and financial center in the region, it is highly integrated economically, organizationally, and spatially with the surrounding network of second- and third-tier cities focused on manufacturing. The Yangtze River Delta, together with the Pearl River Delta region in the south, is one of China's two major manufacturing belts, making China a global economic powerhouse. These manufacturing engines and their associated financial centers (Shanghai and Hong Kong) help integrate the coastal region of China into the global economic system.

HAINAN: ISOLATED BUT ATTRACTIVE

Unlike Shanghai, Hainan province is a remote and slowly developing region at the southern tip of Chinese territory. It is separated from the Leizhou Peninsula on the mainland (the southern tip of Guangdong province) by the Qiongzhou or Hainan Strait, which is about 30 km (19 miles) wide (see Figure 10.13). (There have been proposals to build a bridge or tunnel connecting Hainan to the Leizhou Peninsula.) West of the island is the Gulf of Tonkin, and then the Vietnamese coast. East of Hainan is the South China Sea. The northeastern part of the island has gentle relief, but the southwestern section is relatively rugged, with a coastal flatland surrounding the island.

After the island of Hainan had been part of Guangdong province for centuries, the island and approximately 200 other small islands in the Gulf of Tonkin and South China Sea became the separate Hainan province in 1988. The numerous

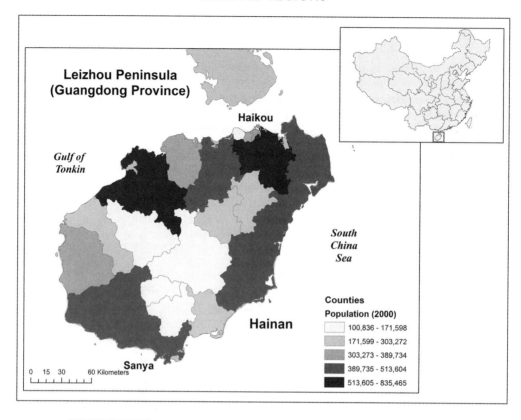

FIGURE 10.13 Hainan province: location, counties, and population distribution.

small islands are insignificant in terms of population, and their resource potential is unknown. Recently, however, the sovereignty of these islands has become a contentious political issue between China and neighboring countries, including the Philippines and Vietnam. The island of Hainan itself accounts for the majority of the population and land mass of the new province. The formation of the province was also accompanied by the island's designation as one of the SEZs, and so it shares that status with the four economically robust cities of Shenzhen, Zhuhai, Shantou, and Xiamen. However, this largest-in-area SEZ has not grown as fast as the other smaller zones economically. Hainan's industrial sector has grown slightly, but its overall growth has been relatively slow as compared to other parts of the mainland.

The island of Hainan has 20 counties and cities (see Figure 10.13). The total provincial population was slightly smaller than 8.7 million, according to the 2010 Chinese census. Compared to its 7.558 million people in 2000, the population had increased substantially by 2010. Its share of China's total population has increased slightly, from 5.33 to 5.36%, putting the province in the top third of all provinces in terms of population increase over the decade (Table 10.4). The provincial capital is Haikou, which is also the largest city in the province, located at the northern end of the island (Figure 10.13). Its location clearly provides the best shelter along

TABLE 10.4. Population Size of Provinces, Municipalities, and Autonomous Regions in 2010, and Changes in Their Shares of Total Population between 2000 and 2010					
Province, municipality, or autonomous region	Population (2010)	Share in 2000	Share in 2010	Difference	Coastal
Guangdong	104,303,132	6.83	7.79	0.96	Yes
Shanghai	23,0191,48	1.32	1.72	0.4	Yes
Beijing	19,612,368	1.09	1.46	0.37	Yes
Zhejiang	54,426,891	3.69	4.06	0.37	Yes
Tianjin	12,938,224	0.79	0.97	0.18	Yes
Xinjiang	21,813,334	1.52	1.63	0.11	No
Shanxi	35,712,111	2.6	2.67	0.07	No
Jiangxi	44,567,475	3.27	3.33	0.06	No
Yunnan	45,966,239	3.39	3.43	0.04	No
Hebei	71,854,202	5.33	5.36	0.03	Yes
Hainan	8,671,518	0.62	0.65	0.03	Yes
Ningxia	6,301,350	0.44	0.47	0.03	No
Tibet	3,002,166	0.21	0.22	0.01	No
Qinghai	5,626,722	0.41	0.42	0.01	No
Fujian	36,894,216	2.74	2.75	0.01	Yes
Jiangsu	78,659,903	5.88	5.87	−0.01	Yes
Shandong	95,793,065	7.17	7.15	−0.02	Yes
Inner Mongolia	24,706,321	1.88	1.84	−0.04	No
Heilongjiang	38,312,224	2.91	2.86	−0.05	No
Shaanxi	37,327,378	2.85	2.79	−0.06	No
Liaoning	43,746,323	3.35	3.27	−0.08	No
Guangxi	46,026,629	3.55	3.44	−0.11	No
Gansu	25,575,254	2.02	1.91	−0.11	No
Jilin	27,462,297	2.16	2.05	−0.11	No
Hunan	65,683,722	5.09	4.9	−0.19	No
Guizhou	34,746,468	2.78	2.59	−0.19	No
Anhui	59,500,510	4.73	4.44	−0.29	No
Henan	94,023,567	7.31	7.02	−0.29	No
Chongqing	28,846,170	2.44	2.15	−0.29	No
Hubei	57,237,740	4.76	4.27	−0.49	No
Sichuan	80,418,200	6.58	6.00	−0.58	No

Note. Data from Population Reference Bureau, www.prb.org/pdf11/china-2010-census-results-table.pdf (retrieved January 24, 2012).

the coast. The city was ranked 230th in population size among all Chinese cities, according to the United Nations *2008 Demographic Yearbook* (United Nations Statistics Division, 2010), with approximately 830,000 in population. The second largest city is Sanya, located at the southern end of the island, with a population of almost 500,000.

According to Figure 10.4, the economic structure and the industrial composition of Hainan are quite different from those of the other coastal provinces. Its secondary sector (manufacturing and fabricating) is the smallest of the three sectors, and the tertiary sector is the largest. The large primary sector is mainly attributable to its agricultural production: Its tropical climate makes the production of rice, tropical fruits, and natural rubber ideal. Besides agriculture, other activities in the primary sector exploit the natural resources available in the region. These resources include seafood (particularly in the South China Sea), minerals (including some precious metals), and oil extracted from oil shale and offshore drilling. All these activities contribute significantly to the primary sector. The secondary sector relies heavily on the foods produced and resources extracted from the primary sector; the processing of these foods and raw materials serves as the backbone of this sector. Crude oil has to be refined, another major secondary-sector activity on the island.

The tertiary sector is the largest sector in the Hainan economy, primarily due to its services industry targeting tourists. Because of its natural rainforest and picturesque beaches, Hainan Island was designated as a prime tourist destination by the Chinese central government in 2009. The intention is to establish Hainan as the "Hawaii of China"—an international destination attracting tourists from all over the world, but particularly from Asia. As a result of this designation, investment on the island has surged significantly. Real estate prices on Hainan have also risen.

Hainan has a long history within Guangdong province, and Han is the largest ethnic group in Hainan. The largest minority population is the Li people, who account for 10–15% of the total population. They are found mostly in the middle and southern parts of the island. The Miao people, originally from Guizhou province, are the second largest minority group; they are mostly located in the highland areas in the west (Figure 10.13).

• • • • • • • • • • • • • • FINAL THOUGHTS • • • • • • • • • • • • • • •

The coastal region is the most developed area in China, with a relatively high concentration of its population. Its prosperity is attributable to its relative location within China and globally, and to its physical environment, even though it does not have a strong natural resource base. Its largest resource is probably its relatively abundant supply of high-quality labor. However, levels of economic development within the region vary significantly, with the two delta regions leading manufacturing in the entire country. Areas outside the municipality clusters of Beijing–Tianjin, Shanghai, and Guangzhou are relatively less affluent and developed within the coastal region. Despite the intraregional variation, people in the region still enjoy the most affluent and modern lifestyles in China, with the best quality of life. The southern tip of the region in Hainan is at the lower end of the spectrum.

The coastal region's relationship with the rest of the country is an interesting and dynamic one. As its prosperity continues, more people from the interior will be attracted to the coastal region. It is not clear how many more migrants the coastal region can accommodate, however. It is also not clear when more of the coastal region's prosperity will trickle into less developed regions, so that more geographically balanced economic development can be achieved for the entire country. There are clear indications that the Chinese government has started paying more attention to the interior cities. In particular, the development of some provincial capitals—such as Xi'an (capital of Shaanxi), Zhengzhou (capital of Henan), Wuhan (capital of Hubei), and Chengdu (capital of Sichuan)—has recently outpaced the development of many cities in the coastal region. Whether a real development strategy of rebalancing is at work and sustainable has yet to be determined.

NOTES •

1. www.census.gov/geo/maps-data/maps/pdfs/reference/us_regdiv.pdf.

2. www.stats.gov.cn/tjsj/pcsj/rkpc/5rp/index.htm.

3. www.stats.gov.cn/tjzs/cjwtjd/201308/t20130829_74318.html (accessed on June 23, 2015).

4. https://www.cia.gov/library/publications/the-world-factbook/geos/ch.html.

5. Liaodong Peninsula (or, in Chinese, Liaodong Bandao) is the peninsula in Liaoning province that divides the coastal waters between Bohai Bay to the west and Korea Bay to the east.

6. According to the theory of "comparative advantage," when two parties or countries have different costs in producing two commodities, both parties will gain if each party produces the relatively cheaper one and trades with the other party.

7. The "First Law in Geography," coined by geographer Waldo Tobler (1970), is that "everything is related to everything else, but near things are more related than distant things." Such geographical regularity is often translated into the spatial statistical term of positive spatial autocorrelation.

8. This dataset consisted of the same 2008 Chinese economic census data used in Chapter 5 (State Council Economic Census Leading Group [SC-ECLG], 2010). The numbers of employees were for registered "legal entities." Therefore, these statistics probably represented undercounts, particularly in the agricultural sector.

9. Since the 18th century, the British had been illegally exporting opium from India to China. Chinese officials attempted to stop the import and ended up in conflict with the British troops. China was defeated and signed the "unequal" Treaty of Nanking (so called because it penalized China heavily) in 1842. The French joined the British in the subsequent conflict with China. China was defeated again, and the Treaty of Tianjin was signed in 1858, legalizing the importation of opium and opening several ports to foreign trade and residence.

10. www.census.gov/population/www/cen2010/cph-t/cph-t-5.html.

11. Tabulated by the authors based on census data for 2000.

REFERENCES •

Chen, W., Xiang, J., Sun, W., & Chu, S. (2006). Globalization and the growth of new economic sectors in second-tier extended cities in the Yangtze River Delta. In F. Wu (Ed.), *Globalization and the Chinese city* (pp. 252–270). New York: Routledge.

Henriot, C. (2004). Shanghai industries under Japanese occupation: Bombs, boom and bust (1937–1945). In C. Henriot & W. Yeh (Eds.), *In the shadow of the Rising Sun: Shanghai under Japanese occupation* (pp. 17–45). Cambridge, UK: Cambridge University Press.

Henriot, C., & Durand, I. (2012). Shanghai industrial surveys (1935–1940): A GIS-based analysis. *Annals of GIS, 18*(1), 45–55.

Mao, Z. (1977). On the ten major relationships. In *Selected works of Mao Tsetung* (Vol. 5, pp. 284–307). Beijing: Foreign Languages Press.

State Council Economic Census Leading Group (SC-ECLG). (Ed.). (2010). *Zhongguo jingjipucha nianjian 2008 [China economic census yearbook 2008]*. Beijing: Zhongguo Tongji Chubanshe.

Tobler, W. (1970). A computer movie simulating urban growth in the Detroit region. *Economic Geography, 46*(Suppl.), 234–240.

United Nations Statistics Division. (2010). *2008 demographic yearbook*. New York: Author.

Wei, Y. D. (2004). Trajectories of ownership transformation in China: Implications for uneven regional development. *Eurasian Geography and Economics, 45*(2), 90–113.

CHAPTER II

The Periphery of China

LEARNING OBJECTIVES	KEY CONCEPTS AND TERMS

LEARNING OBJECTIVES

* Recognize the peripheral areas as a distinct region, while acknowledging the large variability within these areas.

* Understand the diversities in the physical geography, population, and socioeconomic conditions across and within the peripheral region.

* Recognize the adverse physical environments encountered by the local populations and the low levels of economic development.

* Associate the dominance of different ethnic groups with different provinces and autonomous regions.

* Develop an understanding of the political volatility in some parts of the peripheral region.

KEY CONCEPTS AND TERMS

core periphery; ethnic diversity; human capital; terracing; karst landscape; "roof of the world"; intermittent streams; concentration of minority groups; cultural traits; tourism; the Silk Road (or Silk Route); "Siberian high"; dust storms; ethnic diversity; hydrocarbons

This is the second of three chapters devoted to geographical regions in China. This chapter focuses on a region we label the "periphery," the "peripheral region," or the "border region"—indicating that it consists of areas at the edge of Chinese territory, close to the borders between China and neighboring countries (see Figure 11.1). To some extent, we adopt a "core periphery" framework in defining the three main regions in China. In Chapter 1, we briefly mentioned the

FIGURE 11.1 Geographical extent of the peripheral region.

concept of "China proper," the area dominated by "Chinese culture" (i.e., the culture of the Han ethnic majority, for the most part). The peripheral region covered in this chapter includes territories outside China proper, but it also includes areas along the edge of China proper where Chinese culture and the cultures of minorities coexist. Geographically, these are also areas where Chinese political power has least penetrated historically. For instance, no Chinese dynasty has ever had its capital in the peripheral region.[1]

WHAT IS SPECIAL ABOUT THE PERIPHERAL REGION?

The peripheral region is quite diverse in environmental conditions, landscape characteristics, population, and cultural mix. All these topics are addressed in this chapter. Provinces and autonomous regions in the peripheral region also share some characteristics. Geographically, by definition, they are all close to the Chinese border. This proximity to neighboring countries suggests that some of the areas may be influenced by the cultures of these countries, or that their populations may share some characteristics with neighboring populations. Populations with characteristics similar to neighboring populations are likely to be minorities. All five autonomous regions—Guangxi, Neimenggu (Inner Mongolia), Ningxia, Xinjiang, and Xizang (Tibet)—are in the peripheral region, and they all have a strong minority presence. Some provinces in the periphery, such as Yunnan and Guizhou, are also famous for their high levels of racial/ethnic diversity. While some minority groups in Yunnan and Guizhou provinces are too small to be recognized officially, other groups are quite large, such as the Uyghur in Xinjiang and the Zang (Tibetans) in Xizang. But compared to the Han in the entire country, they are nevertheless minorities. Some of these issues were discussed in Chapter 3 on population.

Besides the dominance of minority populations, most areas within the peripheral region share relatively unfavorable environmental conditions. Areas in southern China have relatively rugged terrain and are highly inaccessible. In the west, Xizang has the world's highest plateau. Lhasa, the capital of this autonomous region, can be reached by train today, but visiting Xizang is always a challenge, particularly given the likelihood of altitude sickness due to the high elevation. The northwestern and northern parts of the region are dominated by a harsh, dry, hot environment. This is where the Gobi Desert is located. The northeast has to deal with extreme cold weather influenced by the Siberian climate of eastern Russia. The winter temperatures in northeast China can reach –40 degrees Celsius (–40 degrees Fahrenheit).

Most areas within the peripheral region also share low levels of economic development. With the exception of a few resource and industrial centers, such as Urumqi in Xinjing and Harbin in Heilongjiang, most areas within the region have a weak resource base, and therefore few industries have been or can be developed. Due to the adverse natural environment, intensive agricultural practices are also quite difficult. The local population has had to adapt to the local environments not just in agricultural production, but in other types of economic activities as well as their lifestyle. Thus the peripheral region is generally poor and is the least developed region of China.

All provinces and autonomous regions along the border and in the western part of the country share most of these characteristics to a large degree, and so we group them together as the peripheral or border region. Considerable variation across this region does exist, and in the rest of this chapter, we focus on these differences and special characteristics. This chapter takes the "regional approach" to studying this part of China. A regional approach usually studies different topics or themes within a region, but we are not studying a set of topics across the entire region. Instead, we divide the region further into subregions. In the discussion of these subregions, we highlight the uniqueness of each one and emphasize different topics across subregions.

We divide the peripheral region into three subregions according to their locations relative to the "core" region. The south–southwest includes Guangxi, Guizhou, and Yunnan. The west includes Gansu, Ningxia, Qinghai, Xinjiang, and Xizang. The north–northeast includes Heilongjiang, Jilin, Liaoning, and Neimenggu.

SOUTH–SOUTHWEST: LAND OF DIVERSITY

Physical Diversity and Complexity

The two provinces of Guizhou and Yunnan, and the autonomous region of Guangxi, constitute the south–southwestern subregion within the peripheral region. These three are at the southwestern tip of Chinese territory. Guizhou is buffered from the international border by Guangxi and Yunnan. The latter shares a border with Vietnam. Yunnan is bounded by Myanmar (formerly Burma) to the west and by Laos to the south (see Plate 8). Topographically, the southeast near the coastal area in Guangxi has relatively gentle relief, but the topography becomes more complex farther inland toward the north and west. Most parts of Guizhou, except the west, are not too rugged, but Yunnan definitely has very rugged terrain with high elevations. Elevations in this subregion range from 29 m (95 ft) below sea level to over 6,000 m (19,700 ft) above sea level. The highest point is still more than 2,000 m (6,560 ft) short of the highest point on earth (Plate 8).[2]

Although Plate 8 does not fully illustrate the physical and environmental complexity of this subregion, it still shows that the northern part of Yunnan has relatively high elevation, and that the elevations for the rest of the province vary tremendously. Such large variations are also found on the western side of Guizhou. Plate 8 clearly shows that the central part of Yunnan has a low-lying trench extending southeastward toward the Vietnamese border. This is part of the Red River (a fault), which extends all the way through Vietnam and into the Gulf of Tonkin. Also visible are several similar low-lying troughs running north and south at the western end of Yunnan. These are rivers and fault lines that extend into the Mekong River in Laos, and into the Salween and Irrawaddy Rivers in Myanmar. Two major rivers that flow across the subregion are also shown on Plate 8. They are the Yangtze River, cutting across the northern part of Yunnan, and the Xi Jiang (Xi River), extending from the eastern part of Yunnan to Guangxi and then Guangdong. The first sharp turn of the Yangtze River in northern Yunnan adds to the landscape complexity to the region. The Xi Jiang and its massive tributaries in Guangxi, together with the limestone landscape, have created a world-renowned scenic region that has become the backbone of a tourist industry. This is discussed in more detail later.

The subregion's complicated landscape with rivers and fault lines, particularly in Yunnan province, is the result of a larger geological process involving the collision of the Eurasian and Australian Plates (see Chapter 2, Figure 2.1, for an illustration of these tectonic plates).[3] This collision was partly responsible for the creation of the Tibetan Plateau and the Himalayas, the highest points on earth. As the two plates collided, part of the surface was uplifted, creating the highlands and mountains. As the Australian Plate in the south pushed against the Eurasian Plate in the north, it also squeezed the land mass eastward, "folding" the earth's crust in Yunnan and part of Guizhou province.

When the plates are set in motion (usually in association with earthquakes), the two sides may move in different directions (vertical, horizontal, and combined), resulting in natural disasters.[4] Besides the uplifting process that created the high mountains and highlands, the collision of the two plates also means that, geologically and seismically, this area is vulnerable to earthquakes. If one surveys the major earthquakes in China in recent years, Yunnan and Sichuan have been the "hot spots" so far, although these quakes were not necessarily the most historically deadly ones (see Chapter 2, Table 2.2).[5]

People: How Many "Nations" in This Part of the Country?

Chapter 3 already pointed out that besides the Han majority, the Chinese government officially recognizes 55 other ethnic groups or races. Two other groups are also reported in the Chinese census: "Foreign" refers to naturalized Chinese citizens, whereas "unofficial" refers to the aggregate of those groups that are not officially recognized. The Han majority accounts for more than 91% of the total Chinese population, while other groups are relatively small in size; their percentages of the total population are listed in Chapter 3, Table 3.1. Several points deserve attention here. Zhuang (1.27%) is the second largest ethnic group in China, and the full official name of Guangxi is the Guangxi Zhuang autonomous region, reflecting the concentration of Zhuang there. Of the 46 million total population of Guangxi, about 14.5 million are Zhuang (almost one-third). Han accounts for 63% of the total population in Guangxi. Besides Zhuang, Yao is the next largest minority group in Guangxi, with almost 1.5 million.

The ethnicities that make up the "unofficial" group constitute a relatively small percentage (0.048%) of the total Chinese population, but they total over 640,000 people. As mentioned before, these are ethnicities with relatively small population sizes, too small to be recognized officially. Table 11.1 shows where these people, and members of other ethnic groups, are found in the south–southwest. The majority (~94%) of the "unofficial group" are found in Guizhou. In other words, Guizhou houses a large number of population groups, but each group has a relatively small population. Guizhou also has high concentrations of Miao, Bouyei, Dong, and Tujia. The largest groups in Yunnan are Yi, Bai, Hani, Dai, and Lisu; note that these are not the same groups, and that the groups are not as large, as those found in neighboring Guizhou or Guangxi. In other words, while these two provinces and one autonomous region have significant numbers of minority groups, these groups are highly concentrated geographically instead of spread over a large area.

Such localized concentrations of minority groups could be the results in part of the physical landscape. As discussed above, most of this subregion has rugged terrain, and thus little space that is desirable for settlement. People do not have many choices of where to settle, and so they tend to concentrate in the relatively few desirable locations. Many groups are found in these few locations. The rugged terrain also discourages movement of populations, and thus population groups are less likely to travel and interact. Their settlements are inaccessible, even by today's standards. As a result, they do not have much interaction with the outside world or even with groups that are not too far away. This lack of interaction with other cultural systems means that they are able to preserve their own customs and cultural practices, including languages (both written and spoken), clothing, traditional customs, and lifestyles. Today, many tourists visit this part of China because they want

TABLE 11.1. Distributions of Major Ethnic Groups in Guangxi, Guizhou, and Yunnan			
	Guangxi	**Guizhou**	**Yunnan**
Total	46,023,761	34,748,556	45,966,766
Han	28,916,096	22,344,156	30,617,580
Non-Han	17,107,665	12,404,400	15,349,186
Hui	32,319	184,788	*698,265*
Miao	475,492	*3,968,400*	*1,202,705*
Yi	9,700	834,461	*5,041,210*
Zhuang	*14,448,422*	52,577	1,215,260
Bouyei	20,072	*2,510,565*	58,790
Dong	305,565	*1,431,928*	4,389
Yao	*1,493,530*	40,879	219,914
Bai	2,489	179,510	*1,564,901*
Tujia	9,155	*1,436,977*	5,963
Hani	474	1,092	*1,629,508*
Dai	796	1,217	*1,222,836*
Lisu	154	337	*668,336*
Unofficial	205	*612,780*	3,415
% non-Han	37.17	35.70	33.39

Note. Data for ethnic groups with significant proportions of their populations in one of these three areas are given in bold italics. Data from 2010 Chinese census from www.stats.gov.cn/tjsj/pcsj/rkpc/6rp/indexch.htm (retrieved September 15, 2017).

to see these minority populations, including their clothing, handicrafts, food, and other cultural practices. (See our discussion of tourism in Chapter 13.)

To summarize, minority groups constitute at least one-third of the population in each of these two provinces and one autonomous region (Table 11.1). Yunnan has 34 ethnic groups with more than 1,000 people each, while Guangxi has 22 groups. In other words, Yunnan has more but smaller groups, and Guangxi has fewer but larger groups. Guizhou includes almost all of the "unofficial" group; the number of these ethnic groups is large, but the size of each tends to be relatively small.

What Do the People Do?

A characteristic shared by most provinces and autonomous regions in the periphery is relatively low socioeconomic status. Part of the reason is that the industrial base in the peripheral region is quite weak. Among all subregions in the peripheral region, the south–southwest is probably among the weakest in industrial development, according to several measures. According to the 2010 Chinese census, the average percentage of nonagricultural population across all provinces and autonomous regions was 29.14%, with the lowest level at 14.77% in Xizang and the highest level at 61.89% in Shanghai. However, next to Xizang, the lowest percentages were in Yunnan (16.45%), Guizhou (18.81%), and Guangxi (19.03%). In other words, the south–southwest, together with Xizang, had the largest proportions of population relying on the agricultural sector.

The heavy reliance on agricultural production is expected in this subregion, partly because people's education level in this region is relatively low; it can be said that in this respect, the south–southwest is weak in human capital. According to the 2010 census, only about 5% of the entire Chinese population 6 years or older had never attended school. Xizang had the highest percentage at 34%, but Guizhou had more than 10% and Yunnan had almost 8%, whereas Guangxi had less than 4% (below the national average). Nationwide, 9.5% of the population had at least a college-level education. Guizhou had the lowest percentage of the college-educated at 5.8%, followed by Xizang, but Yunnan and Guangxi followed Xizang with 6.2% and 6.6%, respectively. Commercial and high-tech industries thus cannot be the economic backbone in this subregion, due to the lack of educated human capital. This subregion also has few valuable natural resources, except beautiful scenery.

Another reason why this subregion has to rely on agricultural production is its desirable climate. The latitudinal positions of these provinces and region ensure that most areas do not experience extremely cold weather, except in high elevations. In addition, the region is well drained by large rivers (the Xi Jiang and the Yangtze River) and streams, and so an adequate water supply is usually not a concern. However, two physical factors limit agricultural practice in this subregion: the quality of the soil, and the availability of land with gentle topography. While plenty of land in the subregion is reasonably fertile and appropriate for growing crops, a significant portion of the region has limestone as the bedrock. A limestone landscape is not suitable for agriculture, for two main reasons: Limestone is not suitable for many crops, and it is often exposed with no topsoil.

Rugged terrain, particularly in the western part of the region, poses another serious challenge to agricultural production. However, the native people have adapted to the local environment in order to feed themselves and have invented techniques to grow crops even on steep slopes. The cash crops include sugar cane, tobacco, and tea, while paddy rice is the major staple crop. For paddy rice, the fields need to be flooded with water over extensive periods; this is a challenge, given the rugged terrain. Terracing, or cutting steps along steep slopes to hold water in the rice fields, is the major farming technique for creating land to grow sufficient crops to feed the massive population (Figure 11.2).

While the occupations of most people in the subregion are classified as agricultural (80–85%), a significant proportion of the nonagricultural population works in the service sector supporting the tourist industry. The scenic views created by the karst (limestone) landscape have made Guilin, in Guangxi, a prime tourist attraction for decades. Due to the varying levels of resistance to erosion, different kinds of interesting limestone shapes have formed, such as the Elephant Trunk Hill

FIGURE 11.2 Terraced field in Longsheng (Longji), north of Guilin, Guangxi. The terraces are about 1,900 m long, with 70 km² of terraced rice fields and several Zhuang villages.

(Xiangbi Mountain in Chinese) in Guilin (upper left, Plate 9). Using your imagination, you may see other creatures or objects in the stone shapes, such as a saddle (upper right, Plate 9). Sometimes steep rocks cut through by water are breathtaking enough (lower left, Plate 9). Water going underground dissolves limestone to create caves. Dissolved limestone dripping from the roof of a cave forms stalactites, and stalagmites grow up from the floor of the cave. When stalactites and stalagmites join together, they form pillars (lower right, Plate 9). According to an old Chinese saying, the scenery in Guilin is "the best under heaven." The boat ride from Guilin to Yangshuo to the south along the Li Jiang is a must for both domestic and international tourists (lower left, Plate 9), and the Stone Forest (石林; *Shilin* in Chinese) near the provincial capital of Kunming is the must-see tourist spot in Yunnan.[6]

WEST: LAND OF EXTREMES

The western subregion of the periphery is not as diverse as the south–southwestern subregion, but it is distinct from the rest of Chinese territory in many ways. These include extreme landscape characteristics; the dominance of two major religions and ethnic minorities; and disparities in resources that in turn create dramatically different types of economies within this subregion.

The two largest administrative units in the western subregion are the Xinjiang and Xizang (Tibet) autonomous regions. Xizang has several international neighbors; these include Myanmar (Burma), India, Bhutan, and Nepal. The boundary with India has been the subject of dispute for an extended period. Xinjiang has a long international boundary, and the number of bordering countries in central Asia is quite large: From south to north, these include Pakistan, Afghanistan, Tajikistan, Uzbekistan, Kyrgyzstan, Kazakhstan, Russia, and Mongolia. Some of these neighboring countries affect the political stability of this border region.

Among all administrative regions in China, Gansu probably has one of the most irregular shapes. Its elongated territory marks the northeastern end of the western subregion, with the tiny autonomous region of Ningxia tucked into part of northeastern Gansu (Plate 10). The relatively large province of Qinghai is bounded by Gansu to the north and east, Xinjiang to the northwest, and Xizang to the west and south. Its only neighbor not in the peripheral region is Sichuan to the southeast.

Landscape: From the Highest Mountains to the Lowest Land

We pointed out in our discussion of the south–southwest that the complex and rugged terrain in Yunnan and Guizhou can be partly attributed to the "folding" of the earth's crust when the Eurasian and Australian Plates collided. Their collision also affected all of southwestern China. When the plates collided, the uplifting of the surface created the highest ground on earth: the Qinghai–Tibetan Plateau in Xinjiang and Qinghai, and the Himalayas, which are on the border between Xizang and Nepal. Plate 10 shows that the southern Chinese border has an extremely high elevation at over 8,000 m (26,000 ft), higher than the cruising altitude of propeller airplanes. Most of Xizang is a plateau with high elevation (over 5,000 m or 16,400 ft); it is clear why Xizang is sometimes called the "roof of the world."

The plateau is geographically extensive, covering most parts of the Xizang autonomous region. The northern edge of the plateau is the Kunlun Shan (*shan* means "mountains" in Chinese), which is along an escarpment with a sharp drop in altitude from 4,000 m (6,562 ft) to about 1,000 m (3,280 ft) over a distance of several hundred kilometers. Plate 10 shows a fairly sharp line where the color changes indicating the drastic change in elevation. After the quick descent from the mountains to the north is the Tarim Basin, a desert. The dryness of the basin is partly due to its low-lying land surrounded by mountains and highlands. To its north is another mountain range, the Tian Shan (or Tien Shan), which serves as the natural border between Xinjiang and several central Asian countries to the west. Farther north of the Tian Shan is another low-lying basin, the Junggar Basin or Dzungaria, with elevation in some areas below 100 m (328 ft). In fact, a small region east of the Tian Shan, Tulufan or the Turfan Depression, is below sea level.

Clearly, this western peripheral subregion includes dramatically different landscapes and contrasting elevations, from the highest mountain and plateau in the world to a depression below sea level. Thus there is also a wide range in temperature. The Turfan Depression in Xinjiang is famous for its hot temperatures, which in the summer can reach the high 40s in degrees Celsius (over 110 degrees Fahrenheit). In Tibet, the high elevation in general keeps the temperature cool, but extreme temperatures may occur.[7] In this western subregion, the extreme land-scape characteristics are found at an extensive geographical scale, unlike in Yunnan and Guizhou, where landscape varies more locally. In other words, landscape variations are manifested at different geographical scales in the western and the south–southwestern subregions within the peripheral region.

Dryness is a major characteristic in Xinjiang, but water sources are not completely absent. Several major rivers flow through the region, although they are not shown on the map in Plate 10. The Tarim River cuts through part of the Tarim Basin, the longest inland river in China. It is fed by intermittent streams (streams that have water only part of the year, not year-round) from the two surrounding mountain ranges, the Tian Shan in the north and the Kunlun Shan to the south. In general, the Tarim River flows eastward, but its lower streams become intermittent streams. Other rivers in Xinjiang mostly dissipate in the deserts and dry land. The arid condition of Xinjiang is also shared by Gansu and Qinghai, to a certain degree. Note that both the Yangtze River and Huang He have their sources in the high Qinghai–Tibetan Plateau. The rivers' water comes partly from melting snowcaps (in fact, this area is sometimes called the "third pole").

Population and Cultures: Minorities Are the Majority

The five provinces and autonomous regions in the western subregion are as culturally diverse as those in the southwest subregion, but this diversity has a different pattern. Table 11.2 lists the major ethnic groups found in each province and region. "Major" is loosely defined here as a population of at least 10,000 people.

From this table, we can observe several distinctive population characteristics in the five areas of the western subregion. The bottom row of this table shows the percentages of minority (i.e., non-Han) populations in each area. Gansu has the lowest proportion of non-Han residents (~9%), while Xizang has more than 90%. About 50% of the populations of Qinghai and Xinjiang are non-Han, and Ningxia has about 35%. Clearly, the minorities equal the Han or constitute the numerical majority in three of the five areas in this subregion. However, Gansu has the largest population (approximately 25 million), and over 90% are Han. The second largest population is that of Xinjiang, with approximately 22 million. In these five provinces and autonomous regions as a whole, almost 37% of the population is non-Han. If we exclude Gansu, about 56% of the population in the remaining four areas is non-Han.

Three of the areas in this subregion are autonomous regions, accounting for the large presence (if not the dominance) of minority groups. The full name of Ningxia is the Ningxia Hui autonomous region, reflecting the large presence of Hui in Ningxia. In fact, the Hui constitute more than 2.1 million of Ningxia's 6.3 million total population. They also have large numbers in the entire western subregion, except in Xizang. Another major minority group in Ningxia is the Manchu, but they are much smaller in number. The name Xizang (Tibet) combines *xi*, which means "west" in Chinese, with the name of the Zang minority group. The Zang are clearly the dominant group in Xizang (see Table 11.2). The full name of the

Xinjiang Uyghur autonomous region indicates the large presence of Uyghur—over 10 million out of a total of almost 22 million. Besides the Uyghur, Xinjiang also has large numbers of Mongols, Kazakhs, Kyrgyz, Tajiks, Uzbeks, and Russians, all of which are also ethnic populations in neighboring countries (as indicated by the boldface for the names of these groups in Table 11.2). In other words, while the Uyghur have relatively distinctive cultural traits, significant proportions of the Xinjiang population have cultural characteristics of language and religion similar, if not identical, to populations in neighboring countries. While it is difficult to assess whether Xinjiang populations and their neighboring nations have kinship ties, it is undeniable that they share cultural traits.

TABLE 11.2. Distribution of Major Ethnic Groups in the Two Provinces and Three Autonomous Regions in the Western Peripheral Subregion

	Gansu	Ningxia	Qinghai	Xinjiang	Xizang
Total	25,575,263	6,301,350	5,626,723	21,815,815	3,002,165
Han	23,164,817	4,086,367	2,983,521	8,829,994	245,263
Non-Han	2,410,446	2,214,983	2,643,202	12,985,821	2,756,902
Mongol	10,935	6,661	99,815	*156,280*	307
Hui	1,258,641	*2,173,820*	834,298	983,015	12,630
Zang	488,359	656	*1,375,059*	8,316	*2,716,388*
Uyghur	1,937	613	209	*10,001,302*	205
Manchu	14,206	*24,902*	8,029	18,707	718
Tujia	2,092	1,441	1,537	*17,850*	451
Kazakh	4,444	190	680	*1,418,278*	2,143
Dongxiang	*546,255*	1,261	6,331	61,613	757
Kyrgyz	48	12	4	*180,472*	2,678
Tu	30,781	326	*204,412*	3,455	1,068
Salar	13,517	72	*107,089*	3,728	255
Xibe	299	184	128	34,399	6
Tajik	13	1	3	*47,261*	0
Uzbek	15	3	2	*10,114*	4
Russian	48	18	38	*8,489*	3
Bonan	*18,170*	21	904	568	15
Yugur	*13,001*	48	163	391	4
% non-Han	9.42	35.15	46.98	59.52	91.83

Note. Data for ethnic groups with significant proportions of their populations in one of these provinces/autonomous regions are given in bold italics. Names of minority groups of the same ethnicity as in a neighboring country are given in bold. Data from 2010 Chinese census. www.stats.gov.cn/tjsj/pcsj/rkpc/6rp/indexch.htm (retrieved September 15, 2017).

Another way to consider these minority groups is to analyze their concentration levels. Among the largest groups, the Uyghur, with a population of more than 10 million, are largely restricted to Xinjiang; their populations are relatively small in other provinces and autonomous regions. The Zang are highly concentrated in Xizang and to some degree in Qinghai, and the Kazakh group is mostly in Xinjiang. Among the largest groups, the Hui are spread widely across the subregion, although the group has its largest population in Ningxia.

Note that the current population mixes in this subregion are the result of many years of a China population policy that has involved "moving" (both voluntarily and involuntarily) Han populations into the peripheral region, in order to dilute the dominance of the minority groups. In other words, without the intervention of the Chinese central government, this western subregion would have had more minority-dominant populations. This has been an uncomfortable situation for the Chinese state for a long time. The Chinese government is extremely sensitive to potential influence from foreign powers (see the brief discussion of the Chinese constitution in Chapter 1). Having large populations of groups highly similar or related to those of neighboring countries increases the chance of undue influence, in the government's view. Therefore, most areas within this peripheral region are closely monitored by the government.

When a group of people is labeled as a minority, the group is likely to have cultural traits different from those of the Han majority. Usually the main differences are in language and religion. Many of the ethnic groups identified above have their own languages. In terms of religion, most, if not all, of the Zang practice Buddhism. Buddhism is one of five religions officially recognized by the Chinese government (see Chapter 1). Buddhism in Xizang is a specific sect, sometimes labeled as Tibetan Buddhism. Buddhism came to Xizang from India and Nepal, but over time it evolved into the specific sect in Xizang.

While the Chinese government imposes tight controls over all religious groups, its restrictions on Tibetan Buddhism have been extremely tight because religion and politics mix in Xizang. The most influential leader of Tibetan Buddhism is the Dalai Lama, whose title can be translated into English as "Great Teacher." The current (14th) Dalai Lama is in exile.[8] In the past, some Dalai Lamas not only were the spiritual leaders of Tibet, but also had power over the Tibetan government. Thus the Zang in Xizang strongly support the return of the Dalai Lama, but the Chinese consider the Dalai Lama a "separatist" or "rebel," and thus he has been denigrated by the Chinese government and forbidden to enter China.

Compared to that in Xizang, the population mix in Xinjiang is more diverse: It includes many large minority groups, with Uyghur being the largest. Uyghur is one of the Turkic ethnic groups (others include the Kazakh, Kyrgyz, and Uzbek groups), all of which are found in central Asian countries as far west as Turkey. All of these Turkic groups are also found within Xinjiang. Although they share the same Turkic language family, this family includes several dozen languages, and so the groups are far from homogeneous in language. The religion of most of the Turkic ethnic groups, including the Uyghur, is Sunni Muslim.

After the Republican revolution in 1912 that successfully overthrew the Qing dynasty, Turkic-speaking Muslims in present-day Xinjiang, partly backed by Russia, tried unsuccessfully to break away from Chinese authority and form the republic of East Turkestan. Since 1949, the Chinese Communist government has been successfully controlling the region, despite Uyghur separatists' constant claims that the region is not part of China. Adding to this history of political conflict is the Chinese suppression of the Uyghur culture. Overall, this is a politically volatile area within China's peripheral region.

Economies: Agriculture, Industries, and Tourism

The western subregion of the periphery is physically diverse, with many different types of landscape (highlands, mountains, basins, deserts, and grassland). Different landscape features may provide different types of natural resources or offer environments to support different types of economic activities. For instance, many deserts, such as those in the Middle East, have significant deposits of hydrocarbons (petroleum and natural gas). Mountains often have significant deposit of minerals and precious metals; the Ural Mountain range in Russia is an example. The diverse landscapes in the western peripheral subregion also offer great potential for various economic activities.

Table 11.3 reports the percentages of the labor force in selected categories in the western subregion's economy. Other categories are not included here because they have relatively low percentages. The averages of all provinces and autonomous regions in the nation for the selected labor categories are also provided, for comparison. Percentages higher than the national provincial averages are highlighted by shading in the table. A region probably has a diverse economy if the labor force is not highly concentrated in one or only a few sectors. In other words, a diverse economy should have a labor force distribution similar to the provincial average.

TABLE 11.3. Percentages of the Labor Force in Selected Categories for Provinces and Autonomous Regions in the Western Peripheral Subregion

Labor category	Average for all provinces/aut. regions in China	% of Provincial/aut. region labor force in selected categories				
		Xizang	Gansu	Qinghai	Ningxia	Xinjiang
Primary (except for mining)	1.89	0.08	0.49	1.09	1.56	16.48
Mining	4.82	1.95	4.52	7.58	6.96	6.84
Manufacturing	30.00	5.62	22.59	19.15	24.55	13.44
Energy	1.88	1.77	2.47	2.26	3.45	1.91
Construction	13.49	15.68	15.34	11.08	8.07	6.59
Resource and public management	0.98	0.52	1.12	1.07	1.64	1.55
Education	7.85	11.10	10.52	8.49	9.46	10.70
Public admin. and organizations	11.35	40.69	17.84	21.41	14.44	15.87

Note. Percentages higher than the national averages are shaded. Data from State Council Economic Census Leading Group (SC-ECLG) (2010).

Among the five provinces and autonomous regions in the western subregion, Xizang seems to have the most unusual economic structure. In the 2008 Chinese economic census, more than 40% of the labor force was in the "public administration and organizations" category—the highest percentage among all provinces and regions. Qinghai had the second highest percentage. In fact, all these provinces and regions had percentages in this category higher than the national average for all provinces/regions (11.35%). In comparison, the national capital, Beijing, had only 4.61% of its labor force in this category. All provinces and regions outside this subregion (except Guizhou) had percentages below 15%. Such high percentages of the public administration and organizations sector indicate a strong presence of government officials. Given the relatively high proportions of minority populations in this subregion, the officials are likely to be there for extensive monitoring and control.

The education sector in this subregion was also relatively large: All areas in the subregion had percentages larger than the national provincial average of 7.85%. Such high percentages may reflect national and local policies emphasizing the investment in human capital in these peripheral regions.

The percentages of the labor force in the manufacturing sector for all five provinces and regions were significantly below the national provincial average of 30%. In other words, this subregion has little manufacturing activity. Except for Xinjiang, this subregion is also quite weak in primary-sector agricultural activities. This should not be a surprise, given the extreme physiographic characteristics discussed earlier. However, some areas north and south of the Tian Shan (Plate 10) in Xinjiang have an adequate supply of water, including rivers, groundwater, and snowmelt from the mountains. Some areas are even oases. Together with reliable sunshine and relatively high daytime temperatures, these areas turn out to be agriculturally productive. Primary-sector activities also include herding, and cattle and sheep herding are significant businesses in this subregion. In fact, agricultural activities in Xinjiang are becoming high-tech: They are being transformed from traditional, small-scale, family-based operations to corporate-style businesses. The percentage of the labor force in the agricultural sector in Xinjiang was second highest in the nation in 2008. It was highest in Hainan province at 20%.

Overall, Xizang seems to have the least economic power in this subregion, as most of its economic sectors are small, and the labor force is dominated by the government and construction sectors. By contrast, Xinjiang also has relatively little manufacturing, but is strong in agriculture and has reasonable mining, energy, and resource management activities. Ningxia and Qinghai have more balanced economies.

Certain aspects of the economy are missing from Table 11.3. Some areas in the western subregion, like some parts of the south–southwest, are tourist "hot spots." Tibet is a land of mystery to many people, Chinese and foreigners alike. Travel between Tibet and the rest of China has been greatly improved, as trains now run between Beijing and Tibet. The trip takes approximately 48 hours (2 days) and rises more than 5,000 m (16,400 ft) in altitude. Another popular tourist venue is the traditional "Silk Road," including cities like Xi'an in Shaanxi; Lanzhou and Dunhuang in Gansu; and Turpan or Turfan and Urumqi in Xinjiang. Tourism is one of the major industries in this peripheral region of China.

BOX 11.1. Where Is the "Silk Road" Today?

Major cultural and historical attractions in western China include the "Silk Road" (also sometimes called the "Silk Route"). Geographically, the Silk Road is not a particular road, but a general route that ancient traders took, carrying not only silk but also other merchandise. About one-third of the route is inside today's Chinese territory. Marco Polo, the Italian explorer, documented what he saw on this road to China in the Yuan dynasty. His writings fascinated Europeans of the time who were unfamiliar with China and the Far East. The term "Silk Road" was coined by German historian-geographer-traveler Ferdinand von Richthofen. The extensive route usually originated from today's Xi'an (or Chang'an, one of the capitals of the Tang dynasty). It then went west.

Major cities on the Silk Road included Lanzhou and Dunhuang in Gansu province. This is the so-called Hexi ("west of the river," in Chinese) corridor. The Mogao Cave in Dunhuang is a major tourist attraction today. The ancient traders could then take three different routes, partly depending on which areas they wanted to pass and their final destinations.

Two routes went along the northern and southern slopes of the Tian Shan; the northern one continued to Central Asia, the eastern Mediterranean, and Europe. The third major route ran along the northern slope of the Kunlun Shan, toward Pakistan and India.

These routes existed before the Yuan dynasty and carried trading activities between ancient China and central Asia, Persia, the Arab territories, and Asia Minor. Along this lengthy trade route, many settlements were established. What is amazing is how well preserved many artifacts are. As a result, many sites along the route inside China (i.e., the route from Xi'an/Chang'an to the Tian Shan) have been designated as UNESCO cultural heritage sites.[a] Because all three routes went through vast territories, crossing multiple countries, nations, and cultures, the term "Silk Road" has come to represent diversity and multiculturalism—as manifested, for example, in cellist Yo-Yo Ma's musical Silk Road Ensemble and Silkroad Project.[b]

[a]http://whc.unesco.org/en/list/1442.

[b]www.silkroadproject.org/#home-carousel.

NORTH–NORTHEAST: LAND OF ADVERSITY

The north–northeastern subregion of the periphery includes three provinces and an autonomous region: Heilongjiang, Jilin, Liaoning, and Neimenggu (also known as Nei Mongol or the Inner Mongolia autonomous region). We present these areas in alphabetical order, which also corresponds to a spatial order going from north to south and west. The three provinces of Heilongjiang, Jilin, and Liaoning are traditionally known as "northeast China," and sometimes as historical "Manchuria"—the home of the Manchu people who conquered all of Chinese territory and established the Qing dynasty, the last dynasty in China. This peripheral subregion also includes the Neimenggu autonomous region—part of the home of the Mongols, another nation that conquered all of Chinese territory, along with a large part of Asia and part of Europe. Was it coincidental that these two minority nations that once ruled over China came from the same subregion?

Compared to the western and south–southwestern peripheral subregions, the north–northeast is less topographically dramatic: It has only one moderate-height mountain range and no large, low basins. Only a small portion of the Huang He flows through a small part of southern Neimenggu (see Plate 11). Other rivers in the subregion are not significant in size or economic value, although politically Heilongjiang (which literally means "Black Dragon River" in Chinese) serves as part of the border between China and Russia. It is also called the Amur River (Amur is its Russian name). No part of the subregion is dominated by a minority group as Xizang is, and no province has a minority population that constitutes more than 21% of its total population. Some provinces in this subregion are quite well developed economically (relative to other peripheral subregions), with significant concentrations of heavy industries. Nevertheless, this subregion faces many challenges, mainly due to its physical landscape characteristics, its climatic conditions, and (more recently) the restructuring of the economy. Perhaps the physically adverse conditions in this subregion forced the Mongol and Manchu nations to invade China, seeking a better environment.

Physical Environment

Plate 11 shows that with the exception of a small portion of southwestern Neimenggu, the rest of the subregion is north of the 40th parallel, Beijing, and most of the two Koreas. The three northeastern provinces are not too far from the ocean, which provides moderating effects, warming up the cold winters and cooling down the hot summers. These moderating effects dissipate farther inland. Liaoning, which shares part of the Chinese coastline, tends to have milder weather than Heilongjiang, which is completely landlocked.[9]

In winter, proximity to the ocean is only a secondary factor affecting the climate in this part of China. North and northwest of Heilongjiang is the vast eastern section of Russia known as Siberia. The continental "anticyclones" (high-pressure centers) usually originate there during winter. This so-called "Siberian high" draws the cold air mass from the pole toward lower-latitude areas. Thus the dominant factors affecting the climate in the three northeastern provinces, and to some extent in Neimenggu, are the strength and the temperature of the Siberian jet stream that brings frigid Arctic air to eastern China and Asia. For instance, Harbin, the provincial capital of Heilongjiang, has an average minimum temperature of –24.5 degrees Celsius (–12 degrees Fahrenheit) in January, but it can be as cold as –37 degrees Celsius (–35 Fahrenheit).[10]

To turn to landform characteristics, Plate 11 shows that Neimenggu has higher elevation (the highest point is at 3,400 m or 11,155 ft) in the west than in the rest of the subregion. In general, elevation declines toward the eastern coastal area. The high elevation in western Neimenggu may be regarded as an extension of the Tibetan Plateau from the southwest toward the northeast. The Greater Khingan Range is the only major mountain system in this subregion, although some areas along the coast have relatively higher elevation than inland.

Another major landscape feature in this subregion is the Gobi Desert. In fact, most of the Gobi Desert is inside Mongolia, but its southern and eastern sections are within Neimenggu's territory. This is one of the largest deserts in Asia.

BOX 11.2. Ice and Snow for Fun, but How Much Longer?

Humans know how to have fun, regardless of the weather. Having fun in tropical paradises, such as Hawaii or the Caribbean, is a "no-brainer." Having fun in frigid weather, by contrast, requires some snow or ice and some creativity. In North America, the Canadians created a winter carnival, Le Carnaval de Québec, as early as 1894.[a] In Asia, the Sapporo Snow Festival in Sapporo, the capital of the island of Hokkaido in Japan, has a long history of ice sculpting and attracts millions of visitors worldwide annually. Places suitable to hold this type of winter event need to have daytime high temperatures too low for the ice to start melting. Winter in Heilongjiang meets this condition. The Snow and Ice Festival in Harbin takes advantage of the frigid winter climate.

In Harbin's Snow and Ice Festival, domestic and international teams compete by creating sculptures and structures made of packed snow or ice. The festival includes exhibits of various sizes, from life-size sculptures of animals to replicas of gigantic structures such as castles or towers (see Plate 12). Some ice or snow structures allow people to walk through them. There are also fun participatory exhibits, such as slides for children and adults. The ice exhibition is especially amazing at night because many of the ice structures are lit in color from within.

Given Harbin's cold climate, supplies of ice and snow to build the structures for the festival are usually plentiful. The ice supply usually comes from the river. Flowing through the city of Harbin is the Songhua River, one of the main tributaries of the Amur River (Heilongjiang). In deep winter, ice on the river is so thick that trucks can drive down the river's channels to transport the big blocks of ice to shore. These ice blocks are cut up with chainsaws and pulled from the river to the festival site; they then become the material for crafting the ice sculptures and gigantic structures.

Although the weather in Heilongjiang is usually cold enough to keep the ice and snow from melting, some recent winters in Harbin have been unusually warm. The ice and snow melted quickly, and the exhibits did not last for the entire festival. Global warming makes the future of Harbin's Snow and Ice Festival uncertain.

---

[a]http://carnaval.qc.ca/en.

The boundary of the desert is expanding toward the grassland or steppe (this is an instance of the process of desertification, discussed in Chapter 9). Dust from the desert, and the loess (yellow earth) from the Loess Plateau, are the two main sources of the dust storms experienced by major northeast China cities, including Beijing and Tianjin.

People

Like the other two peripheral subregions, the north–northeast has a significant number of minority groups, but proportionally these groups are not as dominant as in the other subregions. For instance, Neimenggu has the largest proportion of minorities in this subregion, and they make up slightly more than 20% of its total population. By contrast, all provinces and autonomous regions in other subregions of the periphery, with the exception of Gansu (9.42%), have larger non-Han populations than Heilongjiang and Jilin do.

The largest minority groups in the north–northeast include the Mongol, Hui, Korean, Manchu, Daur, and Ewenki groups. Their numbers in the areas where significant proportions of these populations are present are given in italics in Table 11.4. The Hui and Manchu are the third and fourth largest groups in the country. The Mongols rank 10th, and the Koreans rank 15th. Still, the size of the Hui group in this subregion is relatively small. Although these minority groups are not sizable by China's standards, two of them are historically significant, as mentioned earlier: The Mongols governed China during the Yuan dynasty, and the Manchus during the Qing dynasty.

Table 11.4 clearly shows that the largest minority group in Neimenggu is the Mongol group, and in Liaoning the Manchu. It may come as a surprise that the largest minority in Jilin is Korean, but geographically it should be expected, as Jilin borders North Korea. Heilongjiang has the smallest proportion of minorities among all the subregion's units, with the Manchu as the largest group. Although Heilongjiang borders Russia, a much larger Russian group is found in Neimenggu. Table 11.4 also indicates that some minority groups are the same ethnicities as those found in neighboring countries (the names of these groups are given in boldface in the table).

The largest minority groups in the north–northeast have a significant presence over large areas, although they do cluster around one or two areas. (This is somewhat different from the western subregion, where the largest minorities tend to be concentrated in one or a few provinces and autonomous regions.) For instance, the Mongols have a significant presence in all four areas, but they are mostly found in Neimenggu (Table 11.4). Koreans are mostly found in Jilin, but their presence is also sizable in Heilongjiang, Liaoning, and to a lesser extent Neimenggu. The Manchus are mostly found in Liaoning, but their size is quite large in other three areas. In other words, these minority groups are not restricted to just one or two provinces, but widely spread out.

The population mix in this subregion is not as diverse as in the other subregions in the periphery. A common measure of racial/ethnic diversity is the entropy-based "diversity index."[11] This index is scaled so that it ranges from 0 to 1, with 0 indicating that an area is dominated by one group, and 1 meaning that all groups have equal shares in the area. Since Han is the largest population group in most provinces and autonomous regions, including Han in the calculation of the index will skew it toward a low diversity level. For instance, including Han in the index for Heilongjiang results in the low diversity index of 0.1455 because the minority groups constitute the smallest proportion of the population in that province. The highest diversity index is found in Neimenggu at 0.4621 because its Han and non-Han proportions are the most even. If we remove the Han group to determine to what degree all minority groups have equal shares, Heilongjiang is the most diverse, and Neimenggu is the least diverse.

We have calculated the diversity indices for all 12 provinces and autonomous regions in the peripheral region for all population groups except the Han. The results are reported in Table 11.5 in descending order. Yunnan is the most diverse, as it has a large number of officially recognized minority groups of similar sizes, although Guizhou has the largest number of "unofficial" (i.e., officially unrecognized) groups. When all official minority groups are counted, Heilongjiang is the third most diverse area in the peripheral region. Jilin is around the middle of the pack, and Liaoning and Neimenggu are below the median, as the Manchu and Mongol groups, respectively, are dominant there. The lowest-diversity area is Xizang, as the Zang group dominates the region and is much larger than other groups in this autonomous region.

TABLE 11.4. Distributions of Major Ethnic Groups in Heilongjiang, Jilin, Liaoning, and Neimenggu

	Heilongjiang	Jilin	Liaoning	Neimenggu
Total	38,313,991	27,452,815	43,746,323	24,706,291
Han	36,939,181	25,267,110	37,103,174	19,650,665
Non-Han	1,374,810	2,185,705	6,643,149	5,055,626
Mongol	*125,483*	*145,039*	*657,869*	*4,226,090*
Hui	*101,749*	*118,799*	*245,798*	*221,483*
Zang	589	652	1,881	3,259
Uyghur	884	1,127	1,917	658
Miao	2,575	1,446	3,952	3,349
Yi	730	558	1,693	2,854
Zhuang	2,070	1,547	4,285	2,319
Korean	*327,806*	*1,040,167*	*239,537*	*18,464*
Manchu	*748,020*	*866,365*	*5,336,895*	*452,765*
Tujia	2,175	1,523	5,190	3,096
Li	477	545	1,765	981
Kyrgyz	1,431	36	125	141
Daur	*40,277*	*587*	*1,858*	*76,255*
Xibe	7,608	3,113	132,431	3,000
Russian	312	48	185	4,673
Ewenki	2,648	104	448	*26,139*
Oroqen	3,943	111	196	3,632
Hezhen	3,613	212	154	50
% non-Han	3.59	7.96	15.19	20.46

Note. Data for ethnic groups with significant proportions of their populations in one of these provinces/autonomous regions are given in bold italics. Names of minority groups of the same ethnicity as in a neighboring country are given in bold. Data from 2010 Chinese census. www.stats.gov.cn/tjsj/pcsj/rkpc/6rp/indexch.htm (retrieved September 15, 2017).

TABLE 11.5. Diversity Index Values for the 12 Provinces and Autonomous Regions of the Periphery, Including All Racial/Ethnic Groups except the Han	
Provinces or autonomous regions	Diversity index
Yunnan	0.5708
Guizhou	0.5068
Heilongjiang	0.3296
Gansu	0.3106
Qinghai	0.3002
Jilin	0.2755
Xinjiang	0.2156
Liaoning	0.1886
Neimenggu	0.1651
Guangxi	0.1624
Ningxia	0.0302
Xizang	0.0271

Economic Characteristics: Most Diverse

Northeast China has a unique contemporary history, having been under both Russian and Japanese occupation. Today there are still signs of those historical legacies. As mentioned earlier, this area is the home of the Manchu, who governed during the Qing dynasty. After being defeated in international disputes, however, the weakened Qing dynasty had to cede land to foreign powers, including Russia. As a result, the three northeastern provinces were under the strong influence of Russia for much of the late 19th and early 20th centuries. This homeland of the Manchu was also one of the earliest regions lost to the Japanese invasion through Korea in 1931. Today, Russian-style buildings, including Eastern Orthodox Church buildings, Czarist villas, and other buildings, are common in some northeastern cities like Harbin (Plate 13). Some Japanese-style structures are also still standing.

Before their invasion, Japan had invested heavily in various mineral and natural resource-based industries in the region. Japan had no significant natural resources, whereas northeast China was quite rich in significant deposits of coal and metallic ores (iron, copper, etc.). The Japanese set up the puppet state of Manchukuo and installed Puyi, the last emperor of the Qing dynasty, as its head. Manchukuo included the three northeastern provinces and part of Neimenggu. After the Japanese took over the region, they turned it into a zone for heavy manufacturing, to produce supplies they needed for their army to expand their invasion. The industrial strength of the region was later used to support the Communist party during the civil war when it fought with the Kuomintang party.

After the Communist party took over the mainland, the northeastern provinces, together with a few regions in central China, formed the backbone of heavy industry in the early Communist era. This region has been and is still rich in natural resources, particularly hydrocarbons (including, coal, petroleum, and natural gas). For example, the three major oil fields of Daqing, Jilin, and Liaohe are located in the northeastern provinces of Heilongjiang, Jilin, and Liaoning, respectively.[12] While many provinces, including all those in the northeast, have significant coal deposits, Neimenggu is among the four provinces and autonomous regions with the country's most coal resources. (The other three are Shanxi, Shaanxi, and Xinjiang.)[12] The north–northeast is also quite rich in metallic ores, including iron and copper. Although the future supply of high-quality timber from the northeast is now a concern, it has played an important role in the economic development throughout China.[13] Thus this subregion has been endowed with abundant resources that provide a solid foundation for manufacturing industries.

Table 11.6 shows the percentages of the labor force in selected sectors in this subregion in 2008. Again, the averages for these sectors of all provinces and autonomous regions in the nation are included here. Area percentages higher than the national provincial average are highlighted. In the primary sector, Neimenggu was slightly below the average. Again, the primary sector does not just consist of farming, which is relatively weak in Neimenggu because of the harsh environment; it also includes herding (cattle, sheep, and horses), which is quite a significant activity, and the timber industry. Heilongjiang had the highest labor percentage in the primary sector in 2008. The high percentages of the labor force in mining should not be a surprise, given the rich energy and metallic resources in Neimenggu. Strongly associated with the mining sector is the energy sector, which had higher

TABLE 11.6. Percentages of the Labor Force in Selected Categories for Provinces and Autonomous Regions in the North–Northeastern Peripheral Subregion

| Labor category | % of provincial/aut. region labor force in selected categories | | | | |
	Average for all provinces/aut. regions in China	Neimenggu	Liaoning	Jilin	Heilongjiang
Primary (except for mining)	1.89	1.82	0.12	0.66	13.02
Mining	4.82	9.00	5.32	5.19	9.73
Manufacturing	30.00	21.73	38.79	29.52	21.97
Energy	1.88	2.94	2.05	2.89	3.07
Resource and public management	0.98	1.57	1.09	1.23	0.99

Note. Percentages higher than the national averages are shaded. Data from SC-ECLG (2010).

percentages than the national provincial average in all areas in this subregion. The "resource and public management" sector was also relatively large, compared to the national average.

A small surprise is that the percentages for the manufacturing sector were below the national average in all areas except in Liaoning, despite this subregion's rich energy and metallic resources. These somewhat unexpected statistics could be due to an accounting issue. Another possible reason is that the industries in this subregion are likely to be heavy manufacturing, which involves heavy machinery and may not require many workers. Provinces with the highest percentages of the labor force in manufacturing were Guangdong (57%), Zhejiang (50.50%), and Jiangsu (50.43%). The Greater Pearl River Delta region in southern Guangdong has been regarded as the "world's factory"; light manufacturing industries producing consumer products have sprung up there in big and small towns (see the discussion in Chapter 10). Zhejiang and Jiangsu provinces are also light manufacturing centers. Heavy industries in the north–northeast are still very important, but they hire proportionally fewer people than do light industries.

• • • • • • • • • • • • • • FINAL THOUGHTS • • • • • • • • • • • • • • • •

The peripheral region is far from being a homogeneous region. Each subregion has its own physiographic, population, cultural, and economic uniqueness. Many provinces and autonomous regions in the periphery also have unique histories, particularly in their relationships with the rest of China. This chapter illustrates that many aspects of China differ from the stereotypes of big cities such as Beijing or Shanghai. It is a country with many ethnicities; it is also a country dominated by big, modern, but polluted metropolises that also has small, traditional, and pristine communities in the mountains, plateaus, and deserts. It is a country more diverse than the face it usually presents to the world, perhaps because that diversity is often suppressed or ignored by the Han majority and the central government.

Most parts of the peripheral region of China have adverse and challenging natural environments. These provinces and autonomous regions are economically less developed and have populations with racial/ethnic and cultural characteristics different from those of the majority Han. Some of these population groups share more characteristics with neighboring countries than with the Han and may not identify with the rest of China. At the same time, some parts of the peripheral region are resource-rich and thus are of economic significance to China. As the people of coastal and southern China experience unprecedented economic prosperity, it is unclear how economic benefits will spread to the people of the peripheral regions. Currently, the disparities between the periphery and core are at alarming levels. The economic engine in China cannot sustain high growth rates endlessly. The government is in a race with time—a race to spread wealth to the peripheral areas before the economy runs out of steam.

Recently, the Chinese central government launched a new "one belt, one road" economic development scheme, as discussed in Chapter 5 (see Box 5.1). Contrary to the open-door policy and the marketization movement of the late 1970s and early 1980s, which focused on the coastal region, this new scheme seems to focus more on the interior and the west. China intends to improve its infrastructure to connect with other countries in Central Asia, South Asia, and then with Europe, and so the scheme will have especially important impacts on the peripheral region. Many infrastructure-building activities have been and will be launched in the provinces and autonomous regions in the periphery. This scheme will pour more capital and resources into the peripheral region, and thus it should help shrink the economic disparities with the rest of the country.

NOTES

1. http://afe.easia.columbia.edu/timelines/china_timeline.htm (retrieved March 21, 2017).

2. To provide some reference points for comparison, Mount Everest, which lies at the southern edge of the Tibetan Plateau, is about 8,800 m (almost 29,000 ft). The cruising altitude of most airplanes (jets) is between 30,000 and 33,000 ft.

3. http://pubs.usgs.gov/gip/dynamic/himalaya.html.

4. www.iris.edu/gifs/animations/faults.htm.

5. http://earthquake-report.com/2014/05/12/important-historic-earthquakes-in-china.

6. www.globalgeopark.org/aboutGGN/list/China/6414.htm.

7. Lhasa, the capital of Tibet, has a record daily maximum of 85 degrees Fahrenheit and minimum of –2 degrees Fahrenheit (www.britannica.com/EBchecked/topic/594898/Tibet).

8. See the Dalai Lama's website (www.dalailama.com).

9. The southeast tip of Heilongjiang province does not quite touch the coast. Russia claims a narrow strip along the coast, sealing off the Chinese province from reaching the ocean.

10. www.hko.gov.hk/wxinfo/climat/world/eng/asia/china/harbin_e.htm and http://weatherspark.com/history/34136/2013/Harbin-Heilongjiang-China. Note that the Celsius and Fahrenheit temperature scales converge at –40 degrees.

11. Please refer to Chapter 3, note 18, for the calculation of the diversity index.

12. www.eia.gov/countries/cab.cfm?fips=CH.

13. http://news.xinhuanet.com/english2010/china/2010-06/29/c_13375864_2.htm.

REFERENCE

State Council Economic Census Leading Group (SC-ECLG). (Ed.). (2010). *Zhongguo jingji-pucha nianjian 2008 [China economic census yearbook 2008]*. Beijing: Zhongguo Tongji Chubanshe.

FURTHER READING •

Chow, C.-S. (2005). Cultural diversity and tourist development in Yunnan province, China. *Geography, 90*(3), 294–303.

Owen, R. B. (2005). Physical geography and geology: Imprints on a landscape, Yunnan, China. *Geography, 90*(3), 279–287.

Wong, K. K. (2005). Diverse botanical communities in Yunnan and the Yangtze River shelter forest system. *Geography, 90*(3), 288–293.

CHAPTER 12

Beyond the Mainland
Hong Kong, Macau, and Taiwan

LEARNING OBJECTIVES

- Comprehend the historical contexts that led to the formation of the three special regions.

- Recognize these three regions' unique economic development histories, trajectories of development, and physical and economic characteristics, as well as their differences from other regions of China.

- Develop an understanding of the political and economic uncertainties facing these three regions.

KEY CONCEPTS AND TERMS

"one country, two systems"; special administrative regions (SARs); Greater Pearl River Delta region; entrepôt; land reclamation; public transportation; "Monte Carlo of the Orient/ Vegas of the East"; domestic workers; "four little dragons of Asia"; integration; identity crisis

Any comprehensive discussion of contemporary China has to include Hong Kong, Macau, and Taiwan. These three political entities have been strongly influenced by colonial powers and their historical legacies. While each of the three is unique in certain ways, they are similar in their geographical and political situations, as well as in their recent relationships with China. Hong Kong, located at the southern tip of Guangdong province on the east side of the Pearl River (Zhu Jiang) Delta, is a global metropolis famous for its fast-paced lifestyle, its nightlife, and its numerous shopping opportunities. This vibrant economy is a focal point of international trade, supported by its extreme pro-business legal, economic, and cultural systems. A former British colony, Hong Kong earned the nickname "Pearl of the Orient" because of its harbor skyline dominated by high-rises and its captivating night scene. The recent addition of laser light shows on the buildings along the harbor during holidays has increased the city's attractiveness still further. Beginning in the mid-19th century, Hong Kong was a colony of the United Kingdom; it was returned to China in 1997.

The city of Macau, a western neighbor of Hong Kong on the other side of the Pearl River Delta, has always been in the shadow of Hong Kong in terms of economic prosperity. It was the first seaport in China controlled by a foreign power (Portugal), and was the last territory returned to Chinese sovereignty in 1999. The dominance of its tourist industry, particularly gambling, earned the city the nicknames "Monte Carlo of the Orient" and (more recently) "Vegas of the East."

Taiwan, off the coast of mainland China, is a political entity with an identity crisis. Over the centuries, it has played a unique role in the history of East Asia, as a refuge, a mythical land, or a land of opportunity. Its geographical isolation has not stopped it from reaching a high level of economic development. Although Taiwan is a prosperous and fully functional capitalist democratic entity in East Asia, it is not recognized diplomatically by many nations.

Geographically, all three entities are located in the southeastern periphery of the Chinese mainland. Hong Kong and Macau are seaports, and Taiwan is an island separated from the mainland by the Taiwan Strait (see Figure 12.1). Both Hong Kong and Taiwan were once regarded as two of the "four little dragons of Asia" (or "four tigers of Asia") because of their vibrant economic power and prosperity in the postwar years. (The other two "little dragons" were South Korea and Singapore.) Hong Kong and Macau were designated as special administrative regions (SARs) in

FIGURE 12.1 The geographical settings of Hong Kong, Macau, and Taiwan in southern China.

1997 and 1999, respectively. Each has its own administrators, but both are overseen by the Hong Kong and Macau Affairs Office of the State Council, an administrative branch of the central government of the People's Republic of China (PRC). On the other hand, Taiwan has been governed independently as the Republic of China (ROC) since 1949.

The majority of people in Taiwan have close historical and cultural relationships with the mainland. The presence of foreigners—including the Portuguese, Spanish, Dutch, French, and Japanese—on the island has been intermittent. After World War II and the Chinese civil war, the island of Taiwan, which has also been called Formosa, became the ROC, while the PRC was established on the mainland. Taiwan's political relationship with the mainland has always been sensitive and volatile. Mainland China still regards Taiwan as part of China,[1] and the Taiwan Affairs Office of the State Council of the PRC handles China's relationship with Taiwan.[2] Ironically, most older Taiwanese always regard Taiwan as part of "China," and reclaiming mainland China had always been the ROC's ultimate official goal. However, Taiwan's economic ties to the mainland have been strengthened in recent years, and its economic development has been rapid. There is also once-unimaginable, but now intense, movement of people and goods between these two places.

This chapter focuses mainly on the geographical and historical backgrounds of these three places. Because Hong Kong and Macau are similar in many respects, we discuss their geographical settings, population characteristics, and levels of economic development together, while also pointing out their uniqueness. We discuss Taiwan separately in terms of its geographical setting, historical development, and population characteristics. Finally, we discuss the opportunities and challenges of economic and political integrations with mainland China that these three entities are facing.

HONG KONG AND MACAU

The Greater Pearl River Delta Region

The Pearl River (Zhu Jiang) in the south is the third longest river in China. Its three main tributaries—the Xi Jiang ("West River"), the Bei Jiang ("North River"), and the Dong Jiang ("East River")—converge in Guangdong province. In the Pearl River Delta region, Guangzhou (Canton), the capital of Guangdong province, is the focus and is the largest city in southern China (Figure 12.2). The Pearl River empties into the South China Sea through its extensive delta region, which includes many counties and two of the initial special economic zones (SEZs), Shenzhen and Zhuhai. These cities account for a large proportion of the population in the region. The Pearl River Delta thus forms the economic powerhouse of southern China (Li, 2009b).

Geographically and administratively, neither Hong Kong nor Macau is part of the Pearl River Delta. However, the delta region, together with Hong Kong and Macau, functions as the Greater Pearl River Delta region, which is working toward social, political, economic, and bureaucratic integration. The entire region, called

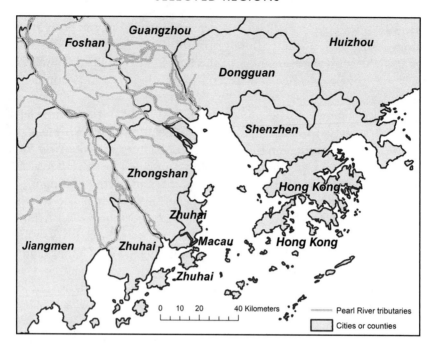

FIGURE 12.2 The Greater Pearl River Delta region, including Hong Kong and Macau.

the "world's factory," has immense economic power supported by a massive and diverse manufacturing system (Wong, 2009).

The delta region provides convenient water access to most parts of the Greater Pearl River Delta. All the cities mentioned above have access to either waterways (Guangzhou) or seaports (Hong Kong, Macau, Shenzhen, and Zhuhai). The historical occupation of Macau by the Portuguese came about partly because of its port. Hong Kong was able to transform itself from a small fishing village into an "entrepôt" (a transshipment point for import and export of goods into and from China), and then into an international financial center.

Macau, on the river's estuary, has had to deal with siltation—the accumulation of alluvial deposits. The presence of silt is clearly seen in the yellowish water in the Outer Harbour of Macau, and is a major drawback for Macau to function effectively as an important trading port. On the other hand, Hong Kong is farther away from the Pearl River Delta, and it has the advantage of a deep harbor free from siltation. As a result, Hong Kong has one of the largest container terminals in the world. As the Chinese economy continues to open up to foreign trade and investment, seaports serving the Shenzhan area, adjacent to Hong Kong, have been growing significantly during the past several decades.

Geographical Settings, People, and Land Shortages

Hong Kong and Macau share many characteristics besides their former colonial status. Both are cities of limited size. The area of Hong Kong is approximately 1,100 square kilometers (km²) or 420 square miles, about six times the size of Washington, D.C. (Central Intelligence Agency [CIA], n.d.). Macau is even smaller, with an area of approximately 28 km² (10 square miles). Since both are cities, very little land is devoted to farming nowadays.

The Hong Kong SAR (HKSAR) consists of several districts: Hong Kong Island (ceded to the British in 1842), Kowloon Peninsula (ceded in 1860), and the New Territories and numerous islands (leased for 99 years in 1898) (see Figure 12.3). North of the HKSAR boundary in the New Territories is the Shenzhen SEZ. Between Hong Kong Island and Kowloon Peninsula is Victoria Harbour, forming the famous skyline captured by numerous photographers (Figure 12.4). The area of this harbor has been decreasing, due to land reclamation for urban developments on both sides of the harbor.

The Macau SAR (MSAR) consists of three parts: Macau Peninsula and the islands of Taipa and Coloane to the south (see Figure 12.5). The northern part of the peninsula is connected to Zhuhai, another Chinese SEZ, through the Barrier Gate. About 85% of the population resides on the peninsula (MSAR, 2009). Zhuhai is also to the west of Taipa and Coloane, which used to be two separate islands in Macau's territory. Over the years, as the demand for land increased, new land resulting from reclamation was used to form the area known as Cotai. It connects the two islands to form a bigger island. Three bridges connect the peninsula and the islands.

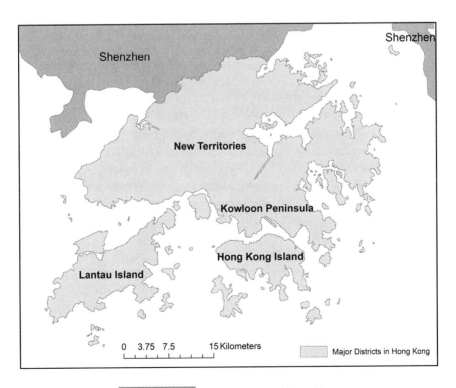

FIGURE 12.3 The territories of Hong Kong.

FIGURE 12.4 Victoria Harbour and the commercial high-rises along the northern edge of Hong Kong Island. (Photo: David W. S. Wong)

Although both Hong Kong and Macau are relatively small in size, they both have relatively large populations: slightly over 7 million for Hong Kong (according to the 2011 Hong Kong census[3]) and 552,503 for Macau (according to the 2011 Macau census[4]). These population numbers and areas translate into population density levels of almost 6,500 people/km² for Hong Kong in the middle of 2009 (HKSAR, 2010) and over 20,000 people/km² for Macau (MSAR, 2009). However, Kwun Tong, the most densely populated district in Hong Kong, has a population density of 53,110 persons/km². This compares to the following average population densities in 2010[5] for various nations: Monaco, 35,835 persons/km²; Singapore, 7,526/km²; Japan, 337/km²; Canada, 3/km²; and the United States, 32/km².

These population statistics for Hong Kong and Macau may be slightly misleading. The topography of Hong Kong is very hilly, with mountains on the main island and around the city. More than 90% of the population lives and works on 20% of the land near the center of the city. Although it is one of the world's great metropolises, about three-quarters of its land is countryside, and about 40% of the land is designated as country parks protected by laws. To some extent, Hong Kong has adopted a "smart growth" policy, restricting development to limited areas. Thus the effective population density (i.e., the density people actually experience) is much higher than the overall density level. High-rises with 40 or more stories are common in urban areas on both sides of Victoria Harbour and in the remote new towns in the New Territories. On the other hand, most of Macau Peninsula is open to development. Its population is more spread out in the region, but it still has relatively high population density.

Moreover, the populations of Hong Kong and Macau have been increasing. For instance, Macau's population increased from 355,693 in 1991 to 435,235 in 2001 and then to 552,503 in 2011. According to the 2011 Macau census, among the 325,892 non-Macau-born residents, 78.3% had mainland China as their previous residence. Thus migrants from the mainland accounted for the significant increase in population. Similarly, Hong Kong also received a large number of mainland immigrants. The percentage of Chinese with Hong Kong as their place of domicile (i.e., those born in Hong Kong) decreased from 93.3% in 2001 to 91.8% in 2011, while the percentage of Chinese with places other than Hong Kong as their place

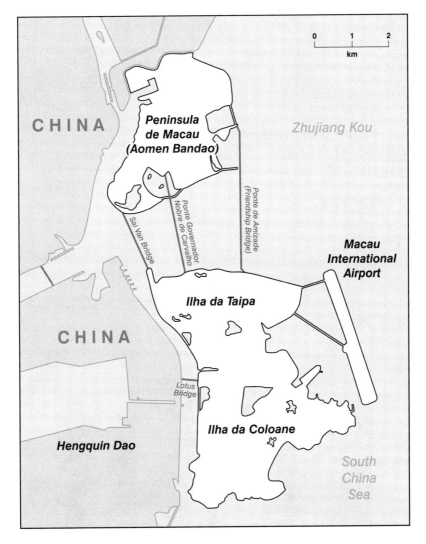

FIGURE 12.5 Territory of Macau. From https://www.cia.gov/library/publications/the-world-factbook/geos/mc.html (retrieved June 22, 2016).

of domicile (i.e., migrants) increased from 1.1% in 2001 to 1.4% in 2011, although the absolute sizes of these changes were relatively small (76,898 and 97,084, respectively). Concomitant with these changes were the increasing numbers of Indonesians (mostly as domestic workers), Indians, Pakistanis, and Australians. In order to accommodate their increasing populations, both cities have created more land by reclamation. In the early 1990s, about 5% of land in Hong Kong and 33% of land in Macau were reclaimed from the sea (Glaser, Haberzettl, & Walsh, 1991), and these percentages have since been increasing.

The massive land reclamation efforts in Hong Kong and Macau have had only a minimal to moderate impact on the land shortage problem. Most people in Hong Kong live in apartments, not houses. Many ordinary citizens cannot afford to buy or even rent a flat at market rates. The Hong Kong government has played an important role by providing public housing ownership. In 2010, about 30% of the population in Hong Kong lived in public rental apartments, and about 16% of the population resided in subsidized ownership units. About 50% of the population lived in privately owned apartments. Most units are quite small. Almost half the units have an internal area between 30 and 39.9 square meters (m^2), or 322–429 square feet (ft^2), and the average living space per person was 12.6 m^2 (135.6 ft^2) in 2010.

Given such a high-density environment, commuting between home and work locations may not be a simple task. The transportation system has to move large volumes of people between places within reasonable time frames. Hong Kong's residents have to rely heavily on public transportation. Over the year, Hong Kong has developed an extensive and efficient public transportation network that combines subways, trains, and bus routes served by double-deckers (see Figure 12.6). These public transportation modes are assisted by privately owned mini-buses and taxis. Although the city has adopted numerous policies to discourage car ownership,

FIGURE 12.6 Double-decker buses at a bus terminal in Hong Kong. (Photo: David W. S. Wong)

FIGURE 12.7 Skywalks allow people to cross busy streets in Hong Kong. Crossing at street level is prohibited. (Photo: David W. S. Wong)

traffic jams are still part of everyday life in Hong Kong. In order to keep the traffic moving through critical intersections, some of these intersections are blocked to prevent pedestrians from crossing the streets, but skywalks and tunnels have been built for pedestrians to cross (Figure 12.7). Still, crossing the street may not be simple.

Historical Development

The Qing dynasty, the last dynasty to rule China, was overthrown in 1912, and the country was then led by the Kuomintang party, entering the rather short Republic era on the mainland. In the 1920s, Mao Zedong led the Communist party's uprising against the Kuomintang. However, the two parties cooperated in fighting the invading Japanese until the end of World War II. After that, a civil war broke out, and the two parties continued to fight each other to gain control of the country. The Communists won and took over the mainland, forming the PRC in 1949; the Kuomintang fled to Taiwan to continue the ROC regime.

Hong Kong: The Birth of a Business Powerhouse

Before the 19th century, Hong Kong was a small fishing village. Like many European countries, Britain established many colonies in different continents, including India in South Asia around the early 1800s. These colonies provided valuable merchandise for trade, such as spices and tea. India, especially the city of Bombay (now Mumbai), served as a major trading post in Asia for the British. Another British colony of significant strategic and trading value in Asia was Singapore. British and other European merchants, including the Portuguese, were eager to do business with China, as many Chinese goods (including silk and tea) were in high demand in Europe. However, the Qing government restricted European trading operations to the city of Canton (today Guangzhou; see Figure 12.1). In order to sustain and expand its trading activities further, the British wanted to occupy another port in southern China to align with its strategic occupations of Bombay and Singapore. British officials identified the island of Hong Kong as a promising candidate.

While Asian merchandise was shipped to Europe from China, China also imported goods from European merchants, including opium. Opium was produced in South Asia, particularly in British-controlled India, and had been legally imported to China for some time. But the Qing government officially denounced it and banned its import in 1800, alleging that smoking opium was damaging to people's health. Nevertheless, European merchants and corrupt Chinese officials still smuggled opium into China. In 1839, a special Imperial Commissioner, Lin Ze-xu, was sent to Canton to seize all the opium. The same year, the British launched a war against the Qing government. The island of Hong Kong was occupied by British naval forces in 1841. China was defeated in this first "Opium War," and the Qing government signed a treaty in 1842 with the British government in Nanking (present-day Nanjing). The Treaty of Nanking was the first of a series of unequal treaties that the Qing government was forced to sign with foreign imperialist powers. In the Treaty of Nanking, China paid the British an indemnity and ceded the island of Hong Kong. In addition, British merchants were allowed to trade in five "treaty ports": Canton (Guangzhou), Amoy (Xiamen), Foochow (Fuzhou), Shanghai, and Ningbo.

Western powers including Britain, France, and the United States demanded still more trading privileges and more ports to be opened for trading activities.[6] British and French troops entered the Forbidden City in Beijing in 1860, concluding the second Opium War. The Qing dynasty, in the first Convention of Peking, ceded Kowloon Peninsula south of Boundary Street, together with other concessions. In 1898, the Qing dynasty signed the second Convention of Peking, leasing the New Territories (the area from north of the Kowloon Peninsula to the south of the Shenzhen River) to the United Kingdom for a 99-year term, expiring on June 30, 1997.

In 1984, through the Sino-British Joint Declaration, China declared that it would resume its exercise of sovereignty over Hong Kong (Hong Kong Island, Kowloon Peninsula, the New Territories, and all surrounding islands). However, it would implement a so-called "one country, two systems" plan, so that the capitalistic system and lifestyle in Hong Kong would remain unchanged for another 50 years until 2047, and so that the Communist system would not be implemented in Hong Kong. The Hong Kong Basic Law[7] lays out the fundamental laws and policies that govern the HKSAR.

Hong Kong was acquired by the British as an entrepôt at the very beginning. Over the years, the economic role of Hong Kong has changed quite a few times: from an entrepôt between the Western world and China, to a light manufacturing industrial center after World War II, then to a center of tertiary and financial services before the handover back to China, and then today back to its role as an entrepôt, but in a version different from the old one.

Although there was no significant economic progress before World War II, the British had set up the foundation for future economic growth. They established modern municipal infrastructure and services, such as an efficient public transportation system and utilities. Some western and British trading companies, such as Jardine Matheson, had already set up their regional offices in the Colony. Some modern banking systems, including the Hong Kong and Shanghai Banking Corporation (now known simply as HSBC), started operating in the mid-19th century.

After World War II, the global political economy changed significantly in many ways. A new international division of labor moved some industrial production from developed nations to some less developed nations, taking advantage of the cheap labor supply. Hong Kong was able to benefit from this new global economic restructuring, and it became a leading manufacturing center for textiles, clothing, plastics, and electronics. The dominance of light manufacturing continued into the 1980s, providing jobs for more than 40% of the labor force at one point (Li, 2009a). Production was mainly carried out by subcontractors of multinational firms in small to medium-size factories with little capital investment. Small-scale production relying heavily on cheap labor was the main advantage of the industry. The production system was highly resilient and flexible, adapting to new requirements and environments easily and quickly.

The manufacturing industries in Hong Kong gradually shifted emphasis from low-skill, small-scale production to more capital-intensive and larger-scale production. The manufacturing sector overall was declining, due to the accelerated open-door policy in mainland China. A cheaper labor supply was available in the Pearl River Delta region, and thus relocation of manufacturing facilities from Hong Kong to the mainland began in the mid-1980s, creating the "world's factory" of light manufacturing along the corridor between Hong Kong and Guangzhou. However, many corporations still had their headquarters in Hong Kong. Hong Kong regained its entrepôt status as external trade increased tremendously, due to the industrial relocation process and the spatial restructuring of the regional production system. Import of raw material to China and export of finished products to the rest of the world benefited Hong Kong's trading position. Associated with the increasing importance of trading activity was the growing service sector, supporting the global production system. The percentage of gross domestic product (GDP) derived from the service sector increased from more than 60% in 1980 to over 90% in 2006 (Li, 2009a). The finance, insurance, accounting, legal services, advertising, and product design subsectors were all fueled by the growth of manufacturing in the Pearl River Delta region, and Hong Kong consolidated its role as an entrepôt. Today Hong Kong operates one of the world's largest container terminals, competing with several other Chinese seaports and international hubs such as Singapore.[8]

Hong Kong's role as a bridge between China and the rest of the world continued after Britain handed Hong Kong back to China in 1997. Despite the rising competition from mainland cities and ports such as Beijing and Shanghai, where multinational corporations began choosing to establish their Chinese headquarters, Hong Kong is still attractive to many international firms. Among its advantages are its location, including an efficient international airport well connected to different parts of China; a government committed to promoting business by not intervening in market mechanisms (the so-called "positive noninterventionism" or laissez-faire policy implemented by former Financial Secretaries under British rule); a well-educated and relatively inexpensive labor force; and well-established infrastructure for various types of businesses. Thus the number of regional headquarters settling in Hong Kong has been on the rise, pushing the service sector to providing more than 90% of jobs in the city.

The opening up of the mainland Chinese economy forced many Chinese companies to expand and become internationalized. One channel for such growth has been attracting foreign investment through the stock market. A *Time* magazine article, "A Tale of Three Cities" (Elliott, 2008), described the international financial connections among New York, London, and Hong Kong—or, collectively, "NyLonKong"—and highlighted the critical status of Hong Kong due to its stock market. Many Chinese companies were able to raise massive amounts of capital through their initial public offerings and listings on the Hong Kong Stock Exchange. As a result, financiers, brokerage firms, accounting firms, and legal consultants all congregated in Hong Kong to serve their Chinese corporate clients. Thus Hong Kong became an international financial center and metropolis, serving as a hub of air transportation and telecommunication as well (Breitung & Günter, 2006; Meyer, 2000).

Macau: From a Portuguese-Run Entrepôt to "Vegas of the East"

Unlike the British presence in Hong Kong, the Portuguese presence in Macau dates back to the middle of the 1500s. In fact, Macau was the first and the last place occupied by Europeans in Chinese territory.[9] The Chinese name for Macau is Aomen. The A-Ma Temple, a major landmark then and now, was there when the Portuguese first arrived. The locals called this temple A-Ma Gao, and the Portuguese thought that this was the name of the place. Subsequently, Aomen was named Amacuao, Amacao, and then Macau in Portuguese or Macao in English. The city served as a transshipment point in China for the Portuguese traders who developed the new market in Japan. Thus Macau developed into an entrepôt, serving three main trade routes: Macau–Melaka–Goa–Lisbon; Guangzhou (Canton)–Macau–Nagasaki; and Macau–Manila–Mexico. The trading business of the Portuguese in Southeast Asia broke down after 1600 because they were unwelcome in Japan, and because of the entrance of other Europeans (such as the Dutch and British) into the trading business. Nevertheless, trading activities in Macau still flourished, as it was the only port opened to Europeans for trade in China until Guangzhou (Canton) was officially designated a trading port in the early 19th century. The cession of Hong Kong to Britain in 1842 created another port to compete with Macau on trade with China. This prompted Portugal to seek formal recognition of Macau as a colony from the Qing dynasty's government. Eventually, the colonial status of Macau (the peninsula) was established through the Protocol of Lisbon and the Sino-Portuguese Treaty of Peking in 1887. The two islands of Taipa and Coloane were also ceded to Portugal. Portugal agreed not to cede Macau to a third party without China's permission.

After Portugal gained control of Macau, the country went through several stages of decolonization. During the 19th and 20th centuries, Portugal was not enthusiastic about occupying Macau. It expressed the desire to hand Macau back to China on two occasions. One was after a pro-Communist riot broke out in 1966 in Macau; the second was in 1974, after the the fall of the Salazar dictatorship that had ruled Portugal for many years. But on both occasions, China refused to settle the issue. One year after the Sino-British Joint Declaration that determined the future of Hong Kong, Portugal and China started official discussions for handling the Macau situation. The Joint Declaration on the Question of Macau was signed in 1987, declaring that Macau would return to China with full sovereignty as an SAR in December 1999, approximately 2 years after the British handover of Hong Kong. Similar to the Basic Law of the HKSAR, the Basic Laws of the MSAR were adopted—another case of the "one country, two systems" plan.[10]

A considerable difference from Hong Kong's role as a financial center, however, is that the economy of Macau has been concentrated in the gambling industry. In the early 20th century, labor-intensive, low-skill manufacturing occupied only a small part of Macau's economic landscape. Four other economic activities predominated in Macau at this point: import of rice, export of fish, manufacturing of fireworks, and gambling. Although gambling was a part of life in Macau for a long time, the activity began to be licensed by the middle of the 19th century. The starting of the casino franchise in 1934 marked a new era for the city and steered the direction of its development irreversibly toward gambling.

Macau earned the nickname "Monte Carlo of the Orient" to share in the fame of the well-known Monte Carlo Casino in the city-state of Monaco along the northern Mediterranean coast. The patrons of Macau's casinos were Chinese from the mainland before 1949. After 1949, they were mostly Hong Kong residents; more recently, they are predominantly mainland Chinese again. Before 2002, Macau's casino-gaming industry was dominated by a few local businessmen and families; Stanley Ho Hung Sun (also known simply as Stanley Ho) has been associated with this industry for decades. After 2002, the casino-gaming industry in Macau started to change. Casino moguls from Las Vegas, including Stephen (Steve) Wynn and Sheldon Adelson, started launching their operations in Macau. In 2007, of the 26 casinos in Macau, most were owned by Stanley Ho's company; six were owned by Galaxy (a joint venture between Adelson's Venetian and businessmen from Hong Kong); and one was owned by Wynn (Lo, 2008, p. 101). The entry of Steve Wynn, father of the "new" Vegas, into Macau's casino landscape created a significant change in the business. Wynn is famous for using casinos as means to promote "sustainable" tourism and cultural development. In the past, casinos and the gaming industry in Macau were associated with bribery and organized crime; it shared a "sin city" image with the old Las Vegas. Just as Wynn transformed the crime-plagued old Vegas into a more family-friendly, entertainment-oriented, upscale gaming and vacation center, Macau has undergone a similar transformation.

BOX 12.1. Let's Take a Day Trip to "Vegas"

The glamor of Las Vegas used to be out of reach for most people in Asia. But with Macau's recent reinvigorating development, it has definitely come within their reach. Part of the Vegas landscape has been replicated in Macau. Big-name casinos such as the MGM Grand, the Sands, the Venetian, and Wynn Resorts are all present in Macau. The gambling-oriented, sin-plagued city has been transformed into a more family-friendly, upscale gaming and shopping center that attracts visitors from southern China and other Asian countries (Figure 12.8). Macau used to be served only by slow ferries and a few hydrofoils from Hong Kong, but visiting Macau is now as easy as visiting Hong Kong, if not easier. Macau is already very well connected to different parts of the Pearl River (Zhu Jiang) Delta region, and the level of connection will increase in the future.

Macau has its own international airport, bringing flights from all of China and from Taiwan, as well as from Japan and many other Asian countries. Several ferry terminals in Hong Kong have frequent service to Macau with high-speed catamarans and jetfoils (Figure 12.9). The trip between Hong Kong and Macau now takes about an hour; this is even shorter than some local trips within Hong Kong, given all the traffic jams. The highways between Macau and several cities in Guangdong province, including Guangzhou, Zhuhai, and Shenzhen, allow more mainland Chinese to visit Macau. The plan to connect Zhuhai, Macau, and Hong Kong with a set of bridges will surely increase the accessibility of Macau even further, although the bridge project remains incomplete at this writing.[a]

Not all visitors to Macau like gambling. Macau provides a rich cultural environment, both Chinese and Portuguese, with many historical sites and some local specialties. The Ruins of St. Paul's are the facade and stairs of St. Paul's Church, also known as Mater Dei, a Catholic church that was originally completed in 1640. The ruins were left after the church burned down for the third time. The facade resembles a Chinese gate. Another historical site is the A-Ma Temple, which is older than the city itself. The Dr. Sun Yat-sen Memorial House and Lin Ze-xu Museum are other notable historical sites in the city.

Despite the internationalization of the gaming industry in recent decades, the number of "high rollers" and other visitors from the mainland has dropped significantly.[b] The speculated reason is the anti-bribery, anti-corruption campaign within the PRC government. The campaign has sent many high-level government officials to jail, and therefore "high rollers" in Macau may consider themselves too noticeable to anti-bribery officials.

[a]www.scmp.com/news/hong-kong/economy/article/2087509/hong-kong-zhuhai-macau-bridge-open-end-year.

[b]www.forbes.com/sites/muhammadcohen/2016/06/03/not-everyone-ready-to-bury-macau-after-two-years-of-declines/#5ac53e471ad7.

The casinos in Macau have been regarded as some of the most profitable in the world. The gaming industry, together with the tourist sector, provides most of the employment opportunities and the major portion of government revenue. Some scholars have labeled Macau a "casino state," given that the government is built around the gaming industry. According to the CIA (n.d.), the breakdown of Macau's GDP is 0% from agriculture, 7% from industry, and 93% from services, based on estimates in 2012. The traditional manufacturing sector has almost completely disappeared. By 2006, Macau's gaming revenue surpassed that of the Las Vegas strip; gaming-related taxes accounted for more than 70% of total government revenue, and gambling accounted for slightly more than 35% of the city's GDP

FIGURE 12.8 The Venetian–Macau, one of several Vegas-style casinos/resorts in Macau. (Photo: David W. S. Wong)

(Lo, 2008). This city has a population slightly more than 500,000, but it received more than 28 million visitors in 2012, and about 60% of these visitors came from mainland China (CIA, n.d.).

As China relaxes travel restrictions on Chinese citizens visiting Macau from the mainland, the tourist industry in Macau has had to accommodate an influx of Chinese tourists. While most tourists visiting Macau are attracted by the gambling industry and related entertainment, the city has another side, including museums, monuments, and restored historic architecture. A Grand Prix race has also been a regular annual event in Macau for decades.

FIGURE 12.9 A hydrofoil, a major means of commuting between Macau and Hong Kong. (Photo: David W. S. Wong)

Population Characteristics

The original importance of Hong Kong was not related to natural resources, as it had none of significance. Its location was its most valuable asset. In the late 20th century, the growing importance of Hong Kong was partly due to opportunistic economic and political developments in the macroregion, and partly due to its most valuable resource—its people. The overall population characteristics are of less importance in the development of Macau, but several individuals and groups have played major roles in the past several decades.

As noted earlier, the population of Hong Kong was slightly over 7 million in 2011, while Macau had about 552,000. The Chinese are in the majority in both places (over 90% in Hong Kong and 85% in Macau). In Hong Kong, the largest groups of foreign residents are Filipinos and Indonesians, most of whom came to Hong Kong as domestic workers. In both cities, most Chinese speak Cantonese, although the number of residents speaking Mandarin has been increasing. Macau has about 10,000 "Macanese" or "Macaense," who are of mixed Portuguese–Chinese or Portuguese–Chinese–Malayan ancestry (CIA, n.d.). These terms may also refer to any non-Chinese person born in Macau (e.g., someone of any type of mixed ancestry who speaks Portuguese with a Macau accent). However, their actual numbers are unknown. Counting them has not been easy because Macau statistics use only three population categories: Portuguese, Chinese, and "foreigner." The Macaense are mainly lumped into the Portuguese category. Most of the Portuguese have been administrators from Portugal on assignment and their dependents.

Immigration from China has been a major factor in the population growth of Hong Kong. The population of Hong Kong around the middle of the 19th century was about 20,000, but it was over 1 million by 1940, rose to over 3 million by 1960, and reached 7 million recently (Shen, 2010). Because the overall rate of natural increase (birth rate minus death rate) has not been high, population growth in Hong Kong has been attributable to in-migration, mainly from the mainland. After 1961, 30–40% of population growth has been attributable to immigration from China (Shen, 2010). While Hong Kong has been receiving a steady stream of immigrants from China, several influxes were triggered by major political and economic events on the mainland, and these influxes boosted the population base of this tiny place.

During World War II, Japan's invasion of China chased many mainland Chinese into the British and Portuguese colonies. The Japanese occupied many territories in Asia, including Hong Kong (for 3 years and 8 months). But, interestingly, the Japanese never took control of Macau, although Japanese troops "visited." Soon after the end of World War II, the civil war between the Kuomintang and Communist parties, and the eventual takeover of the mainland by the Communists, created large numbers of refugees; many of these went to Hong Kong, although a much smaller number went to Macau. By 1951, the population of Hong Kong was over 2 million (Li, 2009a, p. 219). While most of the refugees were not well educated or highly skilled, they formed a pool of cheap labor and allowed the infant manufacturing industry in Hong Kong to develop rapidly. Some economic and industrial elites from Shanghai were among these refugees. Although they did not have much capital to launch new businesses in Hong Kong, they did have entrepreneurial skill and the social networks to establish new factory operations in Hong Kong. This group formed the earliest generation of industrialists, setting up small to medium-size textile and clothing factories in the 1950s and 1960s in Hong Kong. They include some who are now billionaires and are well known internationally. The so-called "cottage industry"[11] also emerged in this economic environment. During the early 1980s, and after the Asian financial crisis that began around 1997, several new waves of immigration occurred. The arrivals from the mainland occasionally created high levels of unemployment.

While immigration from the mainland has been a consistent phenomenon, out-migration was intense for an extended period before Hong Kong reverted to China in 1997. Impending Communist rule and fear of restricted liberty and freedom led many Hong Kong citizens to emigrate overseas. Besides the United Kingdom (because of the colonial connection), other popular destinations included Canada, particularly the cities of Vancouver and Toronto, and Australia. These emigrants took substantial financial and human capital away from Hong Kong, as some visa programs required investment capital or viable business plans.

The populations of Hong Kong and Macau share some demographic character-istics. The fertility levels in both places have been low to moderate, resembling the fertility levels of developed nations. The populations in both cities have relatively high life expectancies at birth. In 2012, the estimated life expectancy of babies born in Hong Kong was 81 years for males and 87 for females; for Macau, life expec-tancy was 79 and 86 years, respectively.[12] These were not only among the highest in Asia, but some of the highest in the world, including all North American countries. Both Hong Kong and Macau also experienced a "baby boom" after World War II (see Chapter 3). As they do in many developed nations, the baby boomers form the largest cohorts in the populations of the two cities. As these cohorts approach retirement age, the overall populations are also aging. Thus the populations in both cities are relatively old, and the demand for social services for the elderly has been increasing tremendously.

About 93% of Hong Kong's 7 million Hong Kong residents are ethnic Chi-nese.[13] The Filipinos and Indonesians (together, more than 260,000 in 2011) are almost all domestic workers and account for about 60% of the non-Chinese popula-tion. Many Filipino domestic workers are well educated. The live-in workers take care of household chores, including (but not limited to) grocery shopping, cooking, laundry, and house cleaning. Recently, taking care of the elderly has become the main responsibility of some workers, partly due to the aging Hong Kong popula-tion. Employers give the workers food and living space (although the space is usu-ally tiny). Thus almost their entire salary can be pocketed, or sent back home to support families in their home countries. Importing household workers to Hong Kong from the Philippines started in 1970s and 1980s. After 1990, the source of these workers began shifting from the Philippines to Indonesia. On average, over 10% of households in Hong Kong have either a Filipino or an Indonesian domestic worker; in fact, some households have multiple workers.

BOX 12.2. Occupy Central/the Umbrella Movement

"Occupy Wall Street" was a demonstration that began on September 17, 2011, in the financial district of New York City, near Wall Street. It was a protest against social and economic inequality; as such, it became a movement that was picked up by people all over the world.[a] In 2014, some Hong Kongers launched "Occupy Central"—a civil disobedience protest that demanded the right for people in Hong Kong to elect their administrative leaders.[b] (The Central district is the financial center of Hong Kong, the equivalent of Wall Street.)

The protest began on September 22, 2014, with a sit-in of high school and college students expressing anger at the Chinese government's announced process for electing the Hong Kong Chief Executive and other officials in 2017. The plan was that the Chinese government would hand-pick a 1,200-member committee to nominate two to three candidates for the Chief Executive position. More than 5 million voters would then cast their votes for one of the preapproved nominees. The nomination committee would thus essentially control the election's outcome, regardless of how the general public voted. After a week of the student sit-in, a separate group that had been planning Occupy Central joined the students. In the evening of September 28, 2014, a Sunday, police fired tear gas and pepper spray into the crowd, raising the tensions between the occupiers and the government. The protest became known after this as the "Umbrella Movement" because during one confrontation on the 28th, the occupiers opened their yellow umbrellas to protect and defend themselves against the pepper spray the police were using. The yellow umbrellas became the symbols of the movement. The venues in the Central district regularly used by Filipino and Indonesian domestic helpers on Sundays as gathering spots were taken over by the demonstrators during the movement period. Eventually, the protest occupied the Admiralty (the district east of Central, thick with government and legislative offices), and the commercial and shopping districts of Causeway Bay and Mongkok, for more than 2 months.

During the occupation period, students and political activists set up tents and shelters on the streets in the three sites, blocking off major streets in the three typically very busy districts, and hoping that the Chinese government would revise the announced election plan (see Plate 14a). Despite some interactions between Hong Kong government officials and the students and activists, no concrete agreement was reached. In the middle of December, the police cleared the tents and shelters from the three sites, ending the occupation (see Plate 14b). The failure of both the Hong Kong and Chinese central governments to make any concessions deepened the pro-democracy supporters' distrust of the governments.

It is indisputable that the 2014 mass protests in Hong Kong were the largest anti-establishment movement the city had ever experienced, and that the movement was a referendum on the city's relationship with the PRC government. The yellow umbrellas used by the protesters became symbols of courage and defiance in the struggle to full democracy for the city. In his book *Umbrellas in Bloom*, Jason Ng (2016) stated: "The Umbrella Movement has shown me possibilities in our future that I did not know existed. It has brought out qualities in our citizens that I did not think they possessed. It has reminded me that no matter how hopeless and helpless we feel, Hong Kong is still a place worth fighting for." The Umbrella Movement put Hong Kong on the world map and elevated this docile, money-minded Asian city to a model for pro-democracy campaigns across the globe.

---

[a]There have been many "Occupy . . ." protests after Occupy Wall Street (see http://en.wikipedia.org/wiki/List_of_Occupy_movement_protest_locations).

[b]www.scmp.com/topics/occupy-central (retrieved June 25, 2016).

TAIWAN

Historical Background and Current Political Status

The Han Chinese first settled in Taiwan about 1200 C.E., joining the indigenous Taiwanese, who were Austronesian. The island had not been of strategic importance to China, and so the Portuguese, Dutch, Spanish, and French subsequently landed on the island. The Japanese had attempted to control the island since the 16th century because of its location along Japan's expansion route in Asia, but it was not successful until it defeated the Qing government during the first Sino-Japanese War in 1895. Taiwan was then occupied by the Japanese from 1895 to 1945, until the end of World War II. After World War II, the Chinese civil war broke out between the Communists, led by Mao Zedong, and the Kuomintang party, led by Chiang Kai-shek. When the Communists took over the mainland and established the PRC in 1949, about 2 million Nationalists, mostly members of Kuomintang, retreated and sought refuge on Taiwan. The island of Taiwan (which has also been called Formosa) became the ROC. The fleeing Kuomintang members brought millions in gold and foreign currency from the mainland's treasury to Taipei. The influx of capital, entrepreneurs, and skilled laborers from the mainland were crucial for the subsequent economic development of the island, which became one of Asia's economic "four little dragons," along with Hong Kong, South Korea, and Singapore.

The PRC has always maintained that Taiwan is part of China, despite the fact that Taiwan has not been under the control of the mainland since 1949. The PRC views the island as a province, while the Taiwanese have different views on the island's status and relations with the mainland. Formal and informal discussions between the PRC and ROC about the island's political status and future have been intermittent. The status of Taiwan as the legitimate government of China has been challenged numerous times. Partly due to the Cold War between Western capitalist nations and the Communist Soviet Union, the United Nations regarded the ROC as the legitimate Chinese government until 1971. In 1971, the ROC lost its seat representing China at the United Nations to the PRC. Since then, the PRC has been internationally considered the rightful government of China. Through back-channel diplomacy in the 1970s, the United States eventually reversed its support of the ROC's claim to represent China; it extended formal recognition to the PRC in 1979, and it terminated diplomatic relations with the ROC government in Taiwan. But soon after, the U.S. Congress passed the Taiwan Relations Act, retaining important unofficial ties with the island. The new legislation replaced the previous bilateral defense treaty, but asserted U.S. commitments to maintaining the island's security. Strategically, the long-standing security relationship between Taiwan and the United States has always been a critical political issue that the three political entities involved have needed to deal with carefully. Today, except for about 20 countries that maintain official diplomatic relations with Taiwan, all other countries only maintain some form of unofficial relations with Taiwan to deal with all the issues relating to political, economic, and cultural matters.

The Geography, People, and Economy

The size of Taiwan is almost 36,000 km²; it is thus slightly smaller than the states of Maryland and Delaware combined. Besides the main island, it also includes a few nearby islands in the Taiwan Strait, and several surrounding the main island. Taiwan lies in the subtropical region, with the Tropic of Cancer cutting across the island, and its climate is influenced by the East Asian monsoon (see Chapter 2). The island also lies on the tracks of typhoons (or hurricanes) in the Pacific, which are major factors affecting the island's summer. The terrain of Taiwan is mostly mountainous (the highest peak, Yu Shan, is 3,952 m or 12,966 ft) in the east, with gently sloping plains in the west (see Figure 12.10). Geologically, Taiwan sits along the Pacific Rim or "Ring of Fire," and it is seismically active. For instance, on September 21, 1999, an earthquake with a magnitude of 7.3 on the Richter scale hit the island, and smaller tremors are quite common. About 24% of the land is arable in Taiwan, but the agricultural sector provides only about 5% of total employment. The largest employment sector is the service sector (58.8%), followed by industry (36.2%), according to 2012 estimates (CIA, n.d.). Though Taiwan is small in size, it is a land of abundance and great diversity, in terms of both its natural environment and its culture. Besides its largest city, Taipei, which is the ROC capital, the island also has several seaports on the west and south (Chilung or Keelung, Kaohsiung, and Taichung) that keep the economy prospering.

Taiwan's population is about 23 million, with a relatively low population growth rate of 0.27% (2013 estimate; CIA, n.d.). This rate is lower than those of many

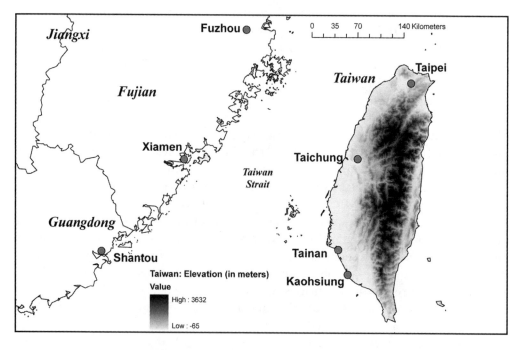

FIGURE 12.10 Taiwan: Major cities and topography.

European countries, such as the United Kingdom, Norway, and Switzerland, and the population is also aging. To a large degree, the demographic characteristics of Taiwan closely resemble those in the developed nations.

The Taiwanese are also diverse in ethnicities and cultures. They include the Hakka, a subgroup of Han speaking the Hakka dialect, and the long-term residents who originally came from China's southeastern provinces of Guangdong and Fujian. The latter prefer to speak Minnanese (or Taiwanese or Holo), although the official language of Taiwan is Mandarin (see Chapter 1 about Guoyu). Another significant group includes the descendants of the mainland Chinese who fled to Taiwan in 1949 after the civil war. A further 2% of the population in Taiwan belongs to the indigenous group; as mentioned earlier, the island's original residents were part of the Austronesian population found in Oceania and Southeast Asia. (Plate 15 depicts a food store run by someone from an indigenous tribal group.) Finally, about 400,000 "foreigners" resided in Taiwan in 2000. These included Japanese, partly due to the Japanese occupation prior to World War II, and people from Southeast Asia, who came to Taiwan as domestic workers.[14]

Morphing into a "Little Dragon"

Taiwan and Hong Kong were considered two of the "four little dragons" of Asia, due to their economic success in the postwar years. The economic development trajectories of these two places are somewhat similar. Like Hong Kong, Taiwan has no significant natural resources and has had to rely on its most valuable asset—relatively cheap and skillful labor—as well as the huge influx of capital from the mainland after the Communists took over the country in 1949. Earlier industries in Taiwan also took advantage of the international division of labor, focusing on labor-intensive light manufacturing industries. Electronics, textiles, processed foods, and consumer products were the major exports. A difference from Hong Kong was that Taiwan deliberately moved away from relying on light manufacturing as its major economic base because the cost of labor in Taiwan could no longer compete with that in other Asian countries, including mainland China. The economy then developed the more capital-intensive and technology-oriented industries, with the help of the ROC government, which established industrial and science parks to promote research and development. The discovery of oil and natural gas reserves also helped boost the economy, as did related industries such as machinery, refining, chemicals, and transportation.

Yet another situation also helped Taiwan flourish economically. During the early era when the Kuomintang controlled Taiwan, martial law was imposed to restrict people's activities in many aspects. The lifting of martial law in Taiwan during the 1980s coincided with the open-door economic policy in the mainland. As a result, many Taiwanese businessmen started investing in mainland China. The direct flow of capital (including human capital) between China and Taiwan was prohibited, and so it all went through Hong Kong and Macau. This indirect trade has increased tremendously over the decades. Still, Taiwan has been able to maintain a surplus of trade with the mainland, which became Taiwan's largest export destination, replacing the United States in 2000 (Lei & Yao, 2009). As many manufacturing activities have relocated from Taiwan to the mainland, Taiwan has gradually transformed itself from an industrial economy into a service economy, playing an important role in import–export activities between China and the rest of the world.

ECONOMIC INTEGRATION OF THE GREATER CHINA REGION

At the turn of the 21st century, Hong Kong and Macau became China's SARs, under the "one country, two systems" principle. However, the political status of Taiwan is still unsettled. In 1992, the representatives of the Communist and the Nationalist parties (the latter was still the ruling party of Taiwan at that time) reached an understanding referred to as the 1992 Consensus. The Consensus states that there is only "one China," but this term has been interpreted differently on both sides, especially the ROC's. The Nationalist party still accepts the Consensus as the starting point for future negotiations with the Communists. However, the island's new president (as of 2016), Tsai Ing-wen, leader of the Democratic Progressive Party, has refused to reference the 1992 Consensus when speaking about cross-strait relations. No concrete vision for how to handle the situation has been set forth. The issue often creates anxiety on both sides of the strait, and disturbs the mutually beneficial economic cooperation.

As noted above, Taiwan began investing in China after China launched its economic reform policies in the late 1970s. Despite intermittent frictions, the cross-strait economic relationship has blossomed. Bilateral trade between China and Taiwan in 2014 reached $198.31 billion, up from $8 billion in 1991. China (the mainland, Macau, and Hong Kong combined) is Taiwan's largest trading partner, accounting for 30% of the island's total trade, according to Taiwan's bureau of foreign trade (see Albert, 2016).

Nevertheless, Hong Kong, Macau, and Taiwan have all established much closer economic ties to mainland China over the last several decades, despite some tensions and uneasiness in the political arena. These three places now enjoy varying degrees of political autonomy. Still, despite the apparent success of this economic integration, the best way to achieve further political or social integration (under the "one China" principle) is still unclear.

Hong Kong has deepened its economic dependence on the mainland since the 1997 handover. Many clients of Hong Kong firms providing financial and business services are Chinese companies. A significant proportion of Hong Kong's residents also work on the mainland. Before 1999, Macau's gambling industry was highly dependent on Hong Kong. However, the reversion to China, along with the Chinese government's increasing relaxation of travel, has meant that Macau's gambling and tourism industries rely more on visitors from southern China than on those from Hong Kong. Among the 22 million people visiting Macau in 2006, more than 21 million were from Asia (Lo, 2008). The mainland was the major source of tourists visiting Macau, followed by Hong Kong and then Taiwan. The tourists' average length of stay was slightly more than a day, but their spending was impressive. Finally, during the second half of 2003, China officially launched the Closer Economic Partnership Agreement, giving the two SARs preferential terms and conditions for trade and investment in China. These terms allow capital to flow more freely from the SARs into China, and marked a new era in the process of economic integration between China and the SARs.

Although the economies of both Hong Kong and Macau continue to flourish under the closer economic ties with the mainland, they also have fierce competition from neighboring SEZs—Zhuhai on the west; Shenzhen on the north; to some extent, Guangzhou, and even the financial center of Shanghai. Many international or multinational corporations have bypassed Hong Kong and Macau to set up their operations in China, especially in the SEZs. These SEZs have attracted massive amounts of foreign direct investment (FDI) from international conglomerates such as Mitsubishi, Toshiba, Canon, Panasonic, and Siemens, just to name a few. Major industries settled in these SEZs include electronics, instruments, textiles/garments, plastics, metals, pharmaceuticals, food/beverages, chemicals, and paper. Governments in these cities give priority to developing industries in electronics and communications, electrical machinery, petrochemicals, biomedicine, and software. As a result, major manufacturing clusters surround Hong Kong and Macau, while these cities themselves are dominated by service activities.

The comparative advantages of SEZs over SARs in manufacturing will continue as long as the SEZs have a cheaper labor supply and lower production costs. But forces have emerged for integrating the SARs with the SEZs, and to some extent creating an integrated Greater Pearl River Delta region. For example, a set of new bridges and tunnels, collectively known as the "Hong Kong–Zhuhai–Macau Bridge," is being constructed across the estuary of the Pearl River Delta to link Hong Kong, Zhuhai, and Macau. The project, which was begun in 2009, will connect the two SARs with Zhuhai by highways and rail. The main bridge was expected to be completed by 2016, but there have been many delays, and at this writing the bridge is not expected to be open before the end of 2017.[15] The project involves many engineering feats, including the creation of two artificial islands in the middle of the Pearl River estuary so that traffic can switch between bridges and underwater tunnels. When the project is completed, the trip from Hong Kong to Macau will be shortened to 30 minutes. Imagine how convenient it will be for Hong Kong residents or tourists to visit "Vegas"! Moreover, the bridge will improve the flow of labor and goods between China and the rest of the world through Hong Kong. Apart from economic benefits, the bridge will have significant implications for the sociopolitical development of the region; in particular, it may reinforce the "one country, two systems" political ideology and the operational relationships among the SARs, the SEZs, and the rest of the mainland. However, the potential economic benefits achieved could easily be upset by the increasing sociocultural and political conflicts among citizens from these different entities.

As another example, there are plans to promote economic and social integration between Hong Kong and Shenzhen by allowing more mainland residents (up to 2 million) to visit Hong Kong. Such integration will create Greater Hong

Kong–Shenzhen, a megalopolis with over 16 million people, comparable in size and economic status to the New York metropolitan area or the Tokyo–Yokohama conurbation. If both SARs are integrated with the SEZs to this extent, then this question arises: Will the "one country, two systems" concept still be applicable, or should it be "one country, one system"? This concern has surfaced in an alarming increase in confrontational incidents between mainlanders and Hong Kong residents in recent years.

Regarding Taiwan, China (i.e., the PRC) has launched numerous campaigns to promote the "one China" principle. Back in 1979, China called for the establishment of three types of links across the Taiwan Strait to connect the mainland with the island: direct transportation, business/trade, and postal services. The Taiwanese government was initially ambivalent about this call for a closer relationship. However, Taiwanese capital has poured into the Chinese economy indirectly through Hong Kong and Macau since 1987. Over time, direct postal services and trade across the strait were gradually established. The year 2000 marked an important breakthrough, as the Taiwanese government officially embraced the "three links" policy and allowed direct transportation services by ship between the two regions. When the Kuomintang leader won the presidential election in 2008, the government became even more aggressive about promoting cross-strait relationships and established direct flights to the mainland. Taiwan's current president, elected in 2016, is less enthusiastic about promoting further integration, although she resolves to open more communication channels to ensure stability in cross-strait relations.

These developments align with the Taiwanese government's desire to promote Taiwan, particularly Taipei and the surrounding region, as an international logistical center. For example, they have made a series of efforts to elevate Taipei's economic status as an international metropolis. These efforts include promoting Taipei as a logistics center in east Asia; building "Taipei 101" (see Figure 12.11), one of the tallest buildings in Asia; and developing the clusters of industrial and science parks around the Taipei region. Taiwan's economic connections across the strait, especially to the Yangtze River Delta and Shanghai, have become very robust and are still expanding. To take further advantage of the cross-strait division of labor, Taiwan has emphasized its role in research and development.

Relationships between Taiwan and Macau have also been strengthening over the years. Because Macau's economy is dominated by a narrow set of service industries, finding other types of jobs in Macau is quite challenging. Some people from Macau have found other types of job opportunities in Taiwan, and Macau students have found promising educational opportunities in Taiwan. Although Chinese from the mainland have constituted the largest group of visitors to Macau, the Taiwanese also visit as tourists. Connections between Macau and Taiwan have been further strengthened by the establishment of direct flights between the two places. Thus a "Greater China" seems to be emerging, with strong linkages and frequent movement of residents among all these places. While the Basic Laws of both Hong Kong and Macau state that there will be no significant changes for 50 years after the handover, it is not difficult to see the economic relationships among these places growing tighter as the 50-year mark comes closer.

BOX 12.3. Evolving National Identities of Residents in Hong Kong and Taiwan

A recent report revealed that the national "Chinese" identity has been losing ground in both Hong Kong and Taiwan (Tran, 2015). The unprecedented protests in Taiwan (the Sunflower Movement)[a] and Hong Kong (Occupy Central/the Umbrella Movement; see Box 12.2) in 2014 pointed to an increasingly localized sense of identity among residents in both entities, combined with a decreasing sense of a national "Chinese" identity. The *New York Times* also reported that according to a survey conducted before the beginning of the Umbrella Movement in 2014, the number of people self-identified as "Hong Kongers" increased significantly, while the number of people self-identified as either "Chinese" or "citizens of the PRC" fell to their lowest levels since Hong Kong reverted to China in 1997 (Wong & Wong, 2014).

Similarly, a survey conducted in Taiwan in 2014 after the Sunflower Movement (in October) showed that most people in Taiwan no longer identified themselves as "Chinese." Instead, most people only identified themselves as "Taiwanese" (Zhong, 2016). In fact, a long-term survey conducted since 1992 shows that more people have been self-identified as "Taiwanese" over the years and fewer as "Chinese," and that the gap is widening.[b] The percentage of Taiwan residents considering themselves to be only "Taiwanese" also reached a record high in another report (Tseng & Chen, 2015). Undoubtedly, the trends toward localized "Hong Konger" and "Taiwanese" identities are unwelcome and annoying developments for the mainland Chinese government.

The fading "Chinese" identity among residents in Hong Kong and Taiwan, to a certain extent, is a natural by-product of well over a century of historical separation from the mainland. The colonization of Hong Kong by the British in 1842 and of Taiwan by the Japanese in 1895 created powerful collective historical memories and experiences for people in these two locales. Obviously, these memories and experiences are divergent from those of people living in mainland China. While many people in these two locales do not deny their ethnic and cultural Chinese identity, some of them object to being called "Chinese nationals," an identity subsumed under the PRC. The identity is alien to many residents in Hong Kong and Taiwan today, as neither place has ever been ruled by the Chinese Communist party, nor has either had much exposure to the party's ideologies or directives, something that many residents in Hong Kong and Taiwan reject.

The perception of "national identity" is not static, and it does trend only in one direction. The Beijing government maintains an optimistic outlook that economic integration will eventually lead to political accommodation and social integration. Therefore, Beijing has made many efforts to maintain close ties with Hong Kong and Taiwan on economic matters.

---

[a]The Sunflower Movement was a protest movement driven by a coalition of students and civic groups in the spring of 2014 in Taiwan. The activists protested the passing of the Cross-Strait Service Trade Agreement by the ruling Nationalist party in the legislature without clause-by-clause review. The protesters perceived that the trade pact with the PRC would hurt Taiwan's economy and leave it vulnerable to political pressure from Beijing. www.scmp.com/news/china/article/1740013/one-year-impact-sunflower-movement-protests-taiwan-continue-blossom.

[b]www.cfr.org/china/china-taiwan-relations/p9223 (retrieved March 28, 2017).

FIGURE 12.11 "Taipei 101," one of the tallest buildings in Asia. (Photo: David W. S. Wong)

• • • • • • • • • • • • • • • • • **FINAL THOUGHTS** • • • • • • • • • • • • • • • • •

Can economic integration lead to a politically and socially integrated "Greater China"? Economic collaborations and logistical networks among Taiwan, Hong Kong, Macau, and mainland China improved tremendously before 2010, partly because of the economic prosperity that they all enjoyed. However, with its huge economy and massive population, the mainland has been in the dominant position. When the Chinese government cracked down on corruption in recent years, fewer high-stakes gamblers visited Macau, and the gambling industry suffered. The number of mainland tourists visiting Hong Kong has also been declining, partly due to the slowing down of the Chinese economy and partly to the increasingly negative attitude of some Hong Kong residents toward mainlanders. The Hong Kong economy has also suffered mildly. Taiwan's economy has stagnated, as the mainland can no longer provide cheap labor to facilitate Taiwan's industrial expansion on the mainland. Taiwan has thus begun struggling to become less economically dependent on the mainland.

Unquestionably, Hong Kong, Macau, and Taiwan are more integrated economically with the mainland than they were two or three decades ago. Moving capital between Hong Kong and China is now enabled by the Shanghai–Hong Kong Stock Connect, a system that links the Hong Kong and Shanghai stock markets so that investors in one market can invest in the other market. Through this link and the future one between the Hong Kong and Shenzhen stock markets, China is establishing channels to access and attract global capital.[16] The Hong Kong financial market may benefit from these links between stock exchanges, and the financial systems of the two entities are getting closer to integration as well.

Despite the fact that China, Taiwan, Hong Kong, and Macau are four political entities sharing cultural and historical links to a civilization that has flourished on earth for more than 5,000 years, residents of these four places live in societies with different (and often contrasting) political ideologies, lifestyle orientations, and economic conditions. The political and cultural gaps among fractions of people in these places have been widening rather than narrowing in recent years. Economic integration alone may not be sufficient to restore a sense of "Chinese" identity to residents in Hong Kong, Macau, and Taiwan. A political system that governs a locale, and the corresponding social values its people hold, are crucial in identity formation. In these respects, many "Hong Kongers" and "Taiwanese" feel that they are different from their "Chinese" counterparts on the mainland.

It requires tremendous effort to maintain both Hong Kong and Macau within the "one country, two systems" economic and political framework. Numerous contradictions need to be resolved, or at least managed. Antagonisms between pro-democracy residents of Hong Kong and the Chinese government have emerged in recent years. These antagonisms were manifested in the somewhat unpleasant ending of the "Umbrella Movement," an extended occupation of several Hong Kong districts by demonstrators demanding "true" universal suffrage (see Box 12.2). Some extremists in Hong Kong have even promoted the idea of an independent Hong Kong—an idea strongly condemned, and labeled as a violation of the Basic Law, by the Chinese government. The political road toward the "50-year" mark may be treacherous. Macau, located on the other side of the Pearl River Delta, seems to be more submissive toward Chinese rule (or, at least, tolerates it more passively).

The "one country, two systems" concept is a constitutional principle formulated by Deng Xiaoping, Mao Zedong's successor as the Chinese Communist leader, for the reunification of Hong Kong and Macau with China during the early 1980s. It was also showcased as a model for Taiwan's reunification with China in the future. However, Taiwan continues on its road to democratization. New political parties have formed to challenge the political hegemony of the Nationalist party, and candidates from other parties have won elections. The Taiwanese enjoy political freedoms in line with those of Western democracies, and there is no incentive for their government to become politically closer to the mainland. Some Taiwanese feel uneasy about the closer economic relationship between the mainland and their island; economic dependence on the mainland has been viewed as undesirable. Thus maintaining the status quo, or even achieving greater distance from the political and economic influence of the mainland, seems to be Taiwan's general desire for the near future.

Therefore, the chances of these four political entities' becoming a unified "Greater China" without friction seem low for now. Macau, Hong Kong, and Taiwan are at different points along the path to integration with mainland China, and the road leading to unification will not be smooth. Increasing Chinese economic strength, and improving China's overall standing in the world, would be advantages of creating "one China." Achieving such a goal, however, will require the people of the PRC, Taiwan, and Hong Kong (and, to a lesser extent, Macau) to exercise wisdom, ingenuity, and thoughtfulness in coming up with consensual ways to resolve their differences and to close the gaps among them perceptively and intelligently.

NOTES

1. See the Chinese government website on the listing of local governments (http://english.gov.cn/archive/china_abc/2014/08/27/content_281474983873401.htm, retrieved May 21, 2016).

2. www.gwytb.gov.cn, retrieved May 21, 2016.

3. www.census2011.gov.hk/pdf/summary-results.pdf.

4. www.dsec.gov.mo/getAttachment/7a3b17c2-22cc-4197-9bd5-ccc6eec388a2/E_CEN_PUB_2011_Y.aspx?disposition=attachment.

5. www.prb.org/pdf10/10wpds_eng.pdf (retrieved May 21, 2016).

6. One of many historical reports about the U.S. involvement in the opium trade is provided in a *New York Times* article (www.nytimes.com/1997/06/28/opinion/the-opium-war-s-secret-history.html).

7. www.basiclaw.gov.hk/en/index/index.html.

8. www.joc.com/port-news/joc-top-50-world-container-ports_20130815.html.

9. According to Puga (2013), Macau was not officially a Portuguese colony at first. Puga asserts that early Chinese officials simply allowed Portugal to station itself in Macau without a political concession because the Portuguese were so effective at controlling pirates' activities off the southern China coast.

10. One of the English translations of the Macau Basic Law can be found in the University of Macau website, www.umac.mo/basiclaw/english/main.html (retrieved September 16, 2017).

11. Cottage industry in Hong Kong includes home-based and small-scale factories and workshops, producing products that require little machinery or other equipment. Workers are unskilled and may include family members.

12. www.prb.org/pdf12/2012-population-data-sheet_eng.pdf (retrieved June 25, 2016).

13. www.census2011.gov.hk/en/index.html.

14. http://ebas1.ebas.gov.tw/phc2010/english/rehome.htm (retrieved June 26, 2016).

15. www.hzmb.hk/eng/about.html.

16. http://fortune.com/2016/11/27/china-hong-kong-shenzhen-trade.

REFERENCES ●

Albert, E. (2016, December 7). China–Taiwan relations. Council on Foreign Relations. Retrieved from www.cfr.org/china/china-taiwan-relations/p9223.

Breitung, W., & Günter, M. (2006). Local and social change in a globalized city: The case of Hong Kong. In F. Wu (Ed.), *Globalization and the Chinese city* (pp. 85–107). New York: Routledge.

Central Intelligence Agency (CIA). (n.d.). *The world factbook.* Retrieved January 22, 2015, from https://www.cia.gov/library/publications/the-world-factbook.

Elliott, M. (2008, January 17). A tale of three cities. *Time,* pp. 30–33.

Glaser, R., Haberzettl, P., & Walsh, R. P. D. (1991). Land reclamation in Singapore, Hong Kong and Macau. *GeoJournal, 24*(4), 365–373.

Hong Kong Special Administrative Region Government (HKSAR), Information Services Department. (2010). Hong Kong: The facts. Retrieved January 22, 2015, from www.gov.hk.

Lei, C. K., & Yao. S. (2009). *Economic convergence in Greater China.* New York: Routledge.

Li, S. M. (2009a). Hong Kong's changing economy in national and global contexts. In K. K. Wong (Ed.), *Hong Kong, Macau and the Pearl River Delta: A geographical survey* (pp. 210–223). Hong Kong: Hong Kong Educational.

Li, S. M. (2009b). The Pearl River Delta: The fifth Asian little dragon? In K. K. Wong (Ed.), *Hong Kong, Macau and the Pearl River Delta: A geographical survey* (pp. 178–209). Hong Kong: Hong Kong Educational.

Lo, S. S. H. (2008). *Political change in Macau.* New York: Routledge.

Macau Special Administrative Region (MSAR) Government, Statistics and Census Service. (2009). *Population estimate of Macau.* Macau: Author.

Meyer, D. R. (2000). *Hong Kong as a global metropolis.* New York: Cambridge University Press.

Ng, J. (2016). *Umbrellas in bloom: Hong Kong's Occupy movement uncovered.* Hong Kong: Blacksmith Books.

Puga, R. M. (2013). *The British presence in Macau, 1635–1793.* Hong Kong: Hong Kong University Press.

Shen, J. F. (2010). Population. In C. Y. Jim, S. M. Li, & F. Tung (Eds.), *A new geography of Hong Kong* (Vol. 2, pp. 7–36). Hong Kong: Friends of the Country Parks.

Tran, E. (2015, March 4). Hong Kong and Taiwan: Evolving identities. *The Diplomat.* Retrieved March 28, 2017, from http://thediplomat.com/2015/03/hong-kong-and-taiwan-evolving-identities.

Tseng, W., & Chen, W. (2015, January 26). "Taiwanese" identity hits record level. *Taipei Times.* Retrieved March 28, 2017, from www.taipeitimes.com/News/front/archives/2015/01/26/2003610092.

Wong, E., & Wong, A. (2014, October 7). Seeking identity, "Hong Kong people" look to city, not state. *New York Times.* Retrieved March 28, 2017, from www.nytimes.com/2014/10/08/world/asia/hong-kong-people-looking-in-mirror-see-fading-chinese-identity.html?_r=1.

Wong, K. K. (2009). A geographical survey of the region. In K. K. Wong (Ed.), *Hong Kong, Macau and the Pearl River Delta: A geographical survey* (pp. 2–23). Hong Kong: Hong Kong Educational.

Zhong, Y. (2016). Explaining national identity shift in Taiwan. *Journal of Contemporary China, 25,* 336–352.

FURTHER READING ●●●●●●●●●●●●●●●●●●●●●●●●●●●●●●●●●●●●

Chen, H. N. (2006). New configuration of Taipei under globalization. In F. Wu (Ed.), *Globalization and the Chinese city* (pp. 147–164). New York: Routledge.

Edmonds, R. (1989). *World bibliographical series: Vol. 105. Macau.* Oxford, UK: Clio Press.

Forêt, P. (2006). Globalizing Macau: The emotional costs of modernity. In F. Wu (Ed.), *Globalization and the Chinese city* (pp. 108–124). New York: Routledge.

Lin, C. P. (2001). Goodwill and proactive exchange policy: How Taipei manages the cross-strait relations. *Journal of Contemporary China, 10*(29), 711–716.

Lo, C. P. (1992). *Hong Kong.* London: Belhaven Press.

U.S. Department of State. (n.d.). U.S. bilateral relations fact sheets. Retrieved January 22, 2015, from www.state.gov/r/pa/ei/bgn.

Vogel, E. F. (1991) *The four little dragons: The spread of industrialization in east Asia.* Cambridge, MA: Harvard University Press.

Wong, D. W., Strang, G., Tang, W.-Y., & Wu, W. (2015). How diverse can a "Chinese city" be?: A case of Hong Kong. *Eurasian Geography and Economics, 56*(3), 331–355.

Yang, C. (2006). Cross-boundary integration of the Pearl River Delta and Hong Kong. In F. Wu (Ed.), *Globalization and the Chinese city* (pp. 125–146). New York: Routledge.

CONCLUSION

CHAPTER 13

China at the Crossroads

INTRODUCTION

Rostow's (1960) model of economic growth suggests that a country moves through five stages of economic development: traditional (most likely agricultural) society; preconditions for economic take-off; take-off; drive to maturity; and an age of high mass consumption.[1] China after World War II may be roughly characterized as experiencing an initial period of political turmoil and then several decades of rapid economic growth, in which it progressed through the stages of take-off and drive to maturity. There have been indications during the last two decades that China has been moving toward the stage of high mass consumption (e.g., Tse, Belk, & Zhou, 1989). The undeniable facts include economic prosperity and the associated benefit of lifting millions of Chinese out of poverty. Internationally, China has moved up from being a poor, developing Third World country laden with a huge and fast-growing population to becoming the largest economy in the world in terms of total gross domestic product (GDP).[2] The country that used to be quiet in the international arena is now highly visible. China is not just a recipient of, but a major player in, foreign direct investment (FDI); its large-scale acquisitions range from mines and land to factories and firms. Its construction projects, mostly related to infrastructure building, are found on many continents. The Chinese president frequently makes international deals to bring more economic opportunities from overseas to China, while the Chinese premier likes to comment publicly on the rise of international trade protectionism, as free trade is advantageous to the Chinese export-oriented economy. The progress of this country over the last 50 years is historical and unique.

This book has covered major aspects of China from a geographical perspective, and one of its objectives has been to provide readers with the background knowledge to understand how this country has transformed itself so rapidly. However, all the glamor of China's economic success cannot overshadow existing concerns and potential problems. The book not only discusses developments in those areas but, to a certain extent, assesses the rates and levels of accomplishment in overcoming these various problems. Clearly, China is facing some substantial issues that may disrupt its trajectory of further prosperity. This concluding chapter highlights several of these significant issues, as well as areas with promise for the future.

THE STATE OF THE NATION

International and Regional Arenas

An international issue that has not been discussed in detail to this point is this: China is deeply entrenched in territorial disputes with many Pacific Rim nations. All these territorial disputes can be labeled "island disputes," as the claims all involve islands. In the South China Sea, several groups of islands have been claimed by China, while Vietnam, the Philippines, Malaysia, and Brunei dispute Chinese authority over these islands from a historical perspective.[3] Although there is historical evidence indicating that Chinese territory in the South China Sea had traditionally been limited to the northern part of this body of water, China has been unilaterally building infrastructure and occupying those islands with military presence.[4] In the East China Sea, Japan has been struggling with China and Taiwan over the sovereignty of several small uninhabited islands (the islands are called the Senkaku Islands, according to Japan, and the Diaoyudao or Diaoyutai Islands, according to China/Taiwan). The Chinese occupation of these islands and the large presence of the Chinese navy in the South China Sea have gradually pulled the United States into the arena of this territorial dispute.

Many Asian countries have had to accept China as a global power, if not yet a superpower, and have been willing to cooperate with China in international development. When China launched its initiative to create the Asian Infrastructure Investment Bank (AIIB)[5]—its version of the World Bank, intended to counterbalance the roles of the World Bank (with its U.S. dominance) in global economic development projects—most Asian countries joined the AIIB. These included most of the countries with territorial disputes with China, Australasian countries, Russia, and some countries in central Asia and the Middle East. China is also a very prominent member of the Association of Southeast Asian Nations[6] and the Asia–Pacific Economic Corporation[7], both of which are very influential regionally and globally in trade negotiation and economic development. After China joined the World Trade Organization, its international economic status was elevated still further.

On the one hand, most of China's neighbors want to befriend China and are willing to be on its side in economic issues; on the other hand, the territorial disputes have created a great deal of tension between China and its neighbors. The neighboring countries, with a few exceptions, are traditionally allies of (or at least friendly to) the United States, and they are accustomed to U.S. naval dominance in the Pacific region. However, the recent island disputes and the expanding Chinese military establishments on those islands have resulted in an increased presence of U.S. naval forces (particularly the famous Seventh Fleet of the U.S. Navy) in the region. As China has grown stronger economically, politically, and militarily, its relationships with other countries have also become more contentious, sensitive, and even volatile.

Another source of international uneasiness consists of the great many unknown factors in the relationship between China and North Korea, a country famous for its missile testing, nuclear power development, and other threats to stability and peace in the region. China is the only country that has had a long-term diplomatic relationship with North Korea since the founding of the Communist regime after World War II. While Western nations want to punish North Korea for violating agreements and initiating provocative actions,[8] China has been regarded as the only political and influential channel for convincing North Korea to "behave better." However, China's exact political positions on North Korean issues are unclear.

Within the "Greater China" region, the plan to create stronger connections among Hong Kong, Macau, and southern Guangdong province seems to be proceeding well, to a certain degree. The bridges connecting these places are scheduled to be completed by the end of 2017. People's ability to travel from one of these places to another will reach a new level, despite the relatively efficient transportation networks currently linking these locations. There is little doubt that Hong Kong and Macau will continue to be economically integrated with the larger Chinese economy. However, the distrust of a fraction of Hong Kong residents is a political reality that the Chinese government has to face, regardless of how the spatial separations among different population groups have been reduced by technologies. Similarly, the new (as of 2016) president of Taiwan seems to feel no urgency about improving the island's relationship with the mainland, and the general desire of the Taiwanese seems to be to maintain the current level of cooperation and interaction. The attitude of mistrust toward the Beijing government is also shared by the minority populations in the western periphery; thus far, China's only approach to handling this mistrust has been to emphasize the "one China" principle and to reiterate China's sovereignty over these peripheral regions.

Multifaceted Disparities in the Domestic Realm

Several chapters of this book have clearly highlighted a side effect of China's economic growth—a large degree of economic and spatial disparity. (In particular, see Chapter 5 on economic geography, Chapter 6 on urbanization, Chapter 7 on rural China, Chapter 10 on the coastal region, and Chapter 11 on the periphery.) Physical geography has arguably played a significant role in the disparities between eastern/coastal and western/interior China, and human efforts to reduce the disparities in natural environments have had and are likely to have limited results. (Indeed, many Chinese environmental policies have only inflicted further damages; see Chapter 9 on the environment.) However, other significant disparities in China are those between rural areas and cities, and these divisions are partly the results of government policies.

Whatever the root causes of the various disparities may be, the Chinese government has to deal with these inequalities across the country at various geographical scales and in multiple sectors of society. Migrations at various scales are reactions to different types of disparities. Athough the Chinese household registration (*hukou*) system is now acknowledged to be inadequate and out of date, it mildly deterred migrants from flooding into cities in the past (see Chapter 6). The problems with the *hukou* system are well recognized, and reform of the system has been called for.[9] The central government launched a reform in 2014, in which the differences between rural and urban *hukous* are being removed, and relocating *hukous* to cities will be evaluated according to each applicant's job, place of residence, and number of years in a city.[10] Thus the relocation process is under the control of the government. Although the implementation and execution of the new policies have been slow, this slowness is actually ensuring an orderly process, such that cities will not experience large influxes of rural immigrants and the local entities' social welfare resources will not be depleted (Tiezzi, 2016).

On the surface, these new policies put the government back in control to evaluate and determine who can legally relocate to cities, and provide a mechanism for those illegal immigrants in the cities to legalize their city residencies. However, these policies fail to address the fundamental and powerful force driving the migration: regional disparities. In today's China, the "pull forces" attracting migrants to cities and coastal areas are significantly larger than the "pull forces" in the rural and western regions that might keep these residents from moving. Meanwhile, the rural and western regions have many "push factors" encouraging residents to migrate elsewhere (Newbold, 2013). In other words, the mild reform of the *hukou* system is unlikely to slow down the migration trends significantly, unless the gradients of disparities can somehow be reduced in the near future. As migration continues, the disparities across the regions may even be exacerbated; that is, migration may continue weakening the origins (the less developed regions) and strengthening the destinations (the more developed areas).

One of the factors causing the large degree of regional disparity is the high concentration of minority populations in the peripheral regions (see Chapters 3 and 11). These people are not only culturally and ethnically different from the majority Han, but they are also the disadvantaged groups, both economically and politically. Economically, many of them are not engaged in the "mainstream" economic sectors; even if they are, they are often working only at the lower levels of the hierarchy. Politically, they have always been under the watchful eye of the central government because of their cultural and ethnic similarities to citizens of neighboring countries, as well as their occasional calls for greater autonomy. Policies dealing with the minority regions have not been successful in creating a more integrated society. Despite massive migrations in parallel with economic reform, only a few ethnic groups, such as the Koreans and Hui, have shown relatively high propensities to migrate; the majority of minority populations stay in their remote peripheral regions, mix little with the Han, and experience little improvement (Gustafsson & Yang, 2015). It is not clear whether China will achieve any breakthrough in its policies toward minorities in the near future.

The Environment and Economic Growth

The economic success of China clearly comes with a cost: environmental degradation. Chapter 9 provides a detailed assessment of the state of the environment. Most environmental problems are either directly or indirectly the results of industrial development and economic growth. Aside from concerns about the economic and environmental sustainability, which are both very important, the most immediate and troubling effects of environmental degradation are its negative impacts on human health. Having a clear blue sky is the news of the day for some Chinese cities, and the sales of air purifiers and face masks have skyrocketed.[11] The most heavy-duty industrial-grade masks have found a big market in China. The sale of bottled water has also increased, as people do not trust the safety of the public water supply anymore. Although it is not closely related to the general trend toward environmental degradation, the increasing frequency of avian flu outbreaks and the emergence of new flu strains constitute another significant public health concern.[12] While all these urgent concerns about health are justifiable, the various types of concerns, particularly environmental, about the sustainability of China's present course of development are equally important.

Although the Chinese government recognizes many of the problems mentioned above and has been formulating and implementing more stringent environmental policies at the national level, the effectiveness of these policies (assuming that the policies are sound in the first place) is dependent on the local authorities' power and capacity to enforce them. Unfortunately, short-term economic gains often conflict with environmental preservation, and financial advancement is the winner in many situations. Therefore, despite some success in protecting the environment, China is still on the verge of a collapsing environmental system. Something drastic has to take place before it is too late to reverse the current trajectory of environmental degradation.

China's economic success during the past several decades is undeniable. China transformed itself from an agricultural economy into one that was developing the preconditions for take-off in the postwar era. The economic reform enabled China to become an industrial economy, and more recently a service and information economy. Although China has experienced high growth rates in the past, sustaining that high level of growth is quite impossible, and a slowdown is expected.[13] While the slowdown may be viewed as unavoidable, the trend may reflect the presence of some structural issues in the economy. The Chinese education system has been structured around the needs of the current economy, producing a labor force to reinforce the existing economic structure (Kwong, 2016). Instead, the system should aim at producing an innovative workforce to stimulate further economic growth.

FURTHER DEVELOPMENT AND TOURISM

As the preceding discussion has suggested, China's current economic policies are outdated. Export-led, investment-led, and GDP-centered models that focus on productivity are no longer applicable to the current situation, which requires more comprehensive economic, social, political, and environmental changes (Ryan & Huang, 2013). Nevertheless, China needs to keep the economy afloat without a "hard landing." As briefly discussed in Chapter 5, maintaining the circulation of capital will facilitate capital accumulation and economic growth. Therefore, China has been exploring different means to keep capital flowing in all directions, including overseas infrastructure projects and investments (Pitlo, 2015).[14] The launching of the "one belt, one road" initiative (see Chapter 5) is clearly reinforcing the "going-abroad" direction, channeling potential growth on multiple fronts.

Today's Chinese society is very different from the one during the pre-reform era. A significant proportion of Chinese, especially many members of minority groups in western China, are still living in poverty, and lifting them above the poverty line remains a goal. On the other hand, the more affluent portions of the population are not satisfied merely with material well-being; they are seeking a higher-quality living environment and more individual rights. One economic sector that can play a number of significant roles in this new societal reality is tourism (Ryan & Huang, 2013). In fact, tourism was recognized by the Chinese government as a "strategic pillar industry" in 2009; that is, China began treating "tourism as an approved form of development" (Sofield & Li, 2011, pp. 513–516). Globally, tourism has been regarded as a major means of promoting socioeconomic development, partly through the creation of jobs and the improvement of infrastructure. International tourism is also treated as a category of international trade, since it involves importing and exporting services and goods (United Nations World Tourism Organization [UNWTO], 2016).

Tourism is regarded as a service industry. It has to be supported by other sectors of the economy, including transportation, hospitality, and tourist agencies. Tourism activities may be generally classified into "domestic" and "international" categories, and international tourism has two components: "inbound" and "outbound." From an international trade perspective, outbound tourists spend money in foreign lands, and inbound tourists bring in foreign currencies. Having the largest population in the world, the Chinese economy generates a huge demand for various types and levels of tourism activities. The demand for domestic and outbound international tourism has been rising quickly during the past two decades, as many Chinese have become more affluent. On the other hand, China's huge territory, fascinating landscapes, and rich historical and cultural heritage offer tremendous resources (which may be treated as supply) for domestic and inbound international tourism. Due to their physical or cultural characteristics, numerous sites are highly attractive to tourists, domestic and international alike. Objective circumstances therefore make tourism a key impetus of economic development in today's China.

Domestic tourism is still the dominant component of the tourism industry in China. The almost 3 billion domestic tourists dwarfed the 132 million international arrivals in 2012.[15] Although the inbound international sector has exhibited a long-term growth trend with fluctuations over the years, the domestic sector has been expanding tremendously, with a 12.0% increase in tourists and a 17.6% increase in revenue in 2012. Clearly, the international sector is a less significant component of the industry, but it presents a rather complicated picture. Table 13.1 reports the foreign arrivals in China in 2013.

Although Hong Kong and Macau are officially special administrative regions (SARs) of China, the Chinese tourism accounting system still treats arrivals from

TABLE 13.1. Foreign Visitor Arrivals in China, January–December 2013

	Person-times (10,000s)	% of total
Total	12,907.77	100.00
Hong Kong	7,688.46	59.56
Macau	2,074.03	16.07
Taiwan	516.25	4.00
Actual foreigners	2,629.03	20.37
Total actual foreigners	2,629.04	100.00
Asia	1,608.83	61.19
America	312.38	11.88
Europe	566.00	21.53
Oceania	86.34	3.28
Africa	55.27	2.10
Others	0.22	0.01

Note. "Person-times" are numbers of visits, not unique visitors. The top portion of the table gives data for all visitors reported by the Chinese tourism accounting system as "foreigners"; the bottom portion gives data for tourists coming from places other than mainland China, China's SARs, and Taiwan. Data from http://en.cnta.gov.cn/Statistics/TourismStatistics/201507/t20150707_721713.shtml (retrieved February 22, 2017).

Hong Kong and Macau as "foreigners," lumping them together with visitors from Taiwan. Among the almost 130 million total visitors, only about 26 million (approximately 20%) were from non-Chinese-dominant countries (i.e., actual "foreigners"). Just visitors from Hong Kong and Macau accounted for more than 75% of what the tourism accounting system called "foreign visitors." It is necessary to point out that all of these figures represent visits (or "person-times"), not unique visitors. Many residents in Hong Kong and Macau (and, to a lesser extent, Taiwan) visit China multiple times a year. In fact, many visitors from the two SARs take day trips to the mainland frequently. Therefore, these figures need to be interpreted within this unique geographical context. Nevertheless, residents of these SARs generate tremendous demand for tourism in the mainland.

On the other hand, most actual "foreign" tourists came from Asia (61%), followed by Europe (22%). These figures seem to indicate that the proximity and population size factors play an important role in the Chinese tourism industry. Asian countries are closer to China than to countries on other continents, and they have some of the largest populations (and thus demand for tourism) globally. Countries farther away—even those with large populations, such as the United States and some Latin American countries—generate fewer visits to China. In other words, China's current inbound tourism has a regional emphasis, and it should be quite possible in the future to expand the "catchment area" to other regions. However, studies show that international inbound tourism has not contributed significantly to the Chinese enormous economy, as it is still relatively small compared to the domestic tourism sector (Oosterhaven & Fan, 2006).

The UNWTO provides a different picture when China's tourism is put into an international perspective. (As usual, the dollar values that follow are U.S. dollars.) Despite the relatively small proportion of inbound foreign visitors in respect to the total number of tourists (domestic and international), China was the second largest earner, with $114 billion (behind the top earner, the United States, with $205 billion) in 2015 (UNWTO, 2016). In terms of arrivals, China was in 4th place with 57 million (behind France with 84 million, the United States with 78 million, and Spain with 68 million; Hong Kong and Macau were considered separately and were ranked 9th and 10th, respectively).

As the number of foreign arrivals in China has been slowly growing, the number of outbound tourists has been increasing by double digits every year since 2004 (UNWTO, 2016, p. 13). This growth in outbound tourism is partly related to the prosperity of the Chinese economy over the past two decades, and partly to the government's changing policies over time (Dai, Jiang, Yang, & Ma, 2017). Chinese citizens can visit only foreign countries approved by the government (currently, there are about 115 of these). As Hong Kong and Macau were opened to mainland Chinese visitors in the early years of relaxations on tourism, the SARs have been the most popular destinations. In 2008, Chinese tourists were allowed to visit Taiwan. Still, only about 5% of Chinese took overseas trips in 2011, including those visiting Hong Kong and Macau. If we put aside the tourists visiting the two SARs, only about 1.65% of the population made outbound trips—a much smaller percentage than that of many other countries (e.g., Taiwan's outbound tourists represented 41% of the population in 2011) (Dai et al., 2017). Data regarding the regions of China from which travelers came were unsurprising: The more affluent coastal region generated the most outbound tourists, followed by the central region. The west produced the smallest number of outbound tourists. Despite the small proportion of Chinese engaged in international travel, the impact of the 1–2% of over 1.3 billion Chinese going overseas is not inconsequential (*The Economist*, 2014). The world should be expecting to see more Chinese tourists in major tourist sites.

On the domestic front, rural collectives and township and village enterprises (TVEs) tried to lift themselves out of poverty by taking advantage of rurally based tourism (see Chapter 7) before the economic reform. Their efforts were not very successful. Since then, however, domestic tourism has been expanding rapidly (Ryan & Gu, 2009; Wen, 1997). This rapid growth has been supported by several factors: the stable, high level of economic growth since the economic reform; the changing policies to accommodate the development of both international inbound and domestic tourism; and the abundant, high-quality resources to support tourism development (Wen, 1997). As the Chinese population becomes more affluent, government policies in promoting domestic tourists help channel the wealth to the poorer rural and minority areas. Therefore, tourism may become a major economic engine with the potential to cure persistent ills in China—the strong economic disparities between rural and urban areas, and between the minority regions in the west and the highly developed east.

Tourism is a service industry. It is also a "smokeless" industry, unlike the traditional manufacturing industries. Therefore, it is in general more environmentally friendly. Its ability to generate income for the economy is well recognized, and therefore it seems to be a promising tool for enabling wealth to "trickle down" to the poorer rural and western regions. While the demand for tourism is not highly constrained by geography, as people do travel to distant places (although we have acknowledged the effect of the proximity factor on the numbers of inbound tourists), the supply of resources for tourism is. In other words, only places with physical, historical, and/or cultural attractions can support the business of tourism. Moreover, the presence of attractive sites is only one prerequisite for developing tourism; the supporting infrastructure (e.g., transportation and accommodation) is another. Thus, only locales with both these sets of advantages can really benefit from tourism development.

LOOKING FORWARD

Developments in Chinese history over the past 150 years or so have been not only unique, but monumental. Following a series of attacks from imperial powers and the signing of unequal treaties was the downfall of the Qing dynasty. China then stepped into further political chaos: World War II and the civil war between the Communist and Kuomintang parties. The first two decades under Communist rule were chaotic, if not disastrous. Despite such a shaky start, China was able (though not without controversies) to reduce its high population growth to a level lower than those for some of the most affluent nations. It successfully lifted hundreds of millions of people out of poverty, and recently took over the position of the world's largest economy (in terms of total GDP). China accomplished all these in its own style; that is, China developed its unique approaches to reaching these goals through social experimentation.

China is likely to continue pursuing its goals in this style for the foreseeable future. For instance, Western policies and technologies to control environmental pollution will not be entirely transplanted to or adopted by China even to slow down, let alone reverse, environmental degradation. Similarly, the types of policies toward minority populations implemented by other countries will not be considered by the Chinese government as ways of handling issues involving the massive minority populations in the west. China is facing the extremely challenging task of sustaining its economic growth in the midst of a slowing economy on the one hand, and improving the economic well-being of the massive poor population in the less developed regions on the other. Therefore, China cannot count on a single means to tackle this extensive set of challenges. A multipronged approach is needed to coordinate different initiatives and to integrate them into the larger economic system (Ryan & Gu, 2009). The "one belt, one road" initiative has a clear westward orientation, focusing on the less developed parts of the country. If this initiative is combined with the tourism industry, economic development may trickle down to the less developed regions, including some of the minority-dominant areas traversed by the roads and belts. Such a government-initiated coordinated effort, which is a Chinese-style approach toward development, may further reduce regional disparities.

On the other hand, China is likely to continue along its current trajectories in several strategic areas. Information and communications technology (ICT) in general, and e-commerce in particular, are likely to maintain their dominance in the world economy in the near future. Whereas the Silicon Valley in northern California has been one of the centers of this wave of industrial revolution, China's Silicon Valley may be emerging in Hangzhou, the capital of Zhejiang province and the headquarters of the Alibaba Group.[16] Whether e-commerce can shoulder the growth of the entire Chinese economy is difficult to determine, but the wide adoption and expansion of ICT have surely boosted the economy to a large extent.

Specific aspects of China's future development are difficult to predict. However, we can all rest assured that China is aspiring to become a world superpower, on par with the United States. China has tremendous influence on multiple fronts—economic, military, and political. No other country except China has the attributes and qualifications to compete with the United States and attain superpower status. In addition, China and the United States have many areas of competing interests.[17] Therefore, the international arena is likely to be dominated by these two nations in the near future. Statements from U.S. government officials, to a certain extent, acknowledge that China needs to be treated with respect and care.[18]

NOTES

1. "Traditional society" in this context refers to subsistence economies relying heavily on primary production, such as farming and mining, with little technology or low levels of it. During the precondition stage, saving increases, and investment in infrastructure also expands; both of these increases prepare a society for economic take-off. Take-off is often characterized by industrialization. The economy enters the drive to maturity stage when the economy diversifies and when economic growth spreads from centers to the peripheries. The final stage is characterized by high mass consumption, reflecting the affluent level of the society.

2. www.cia.gov/library/publications/the-world-factbook/rankorder/2001rank.html#ch (retrieved February 24, 2017).

3. www.bbc.com/news/world-asia-pacific-13748349.

4. www.forbes.com/sites/timdaiss/2016/06/01/ newly-found-maps-dispute-beijings-south-china-sea-claims/#5ae7292d6492.

5. www.aiib.org/en/index.html.

6. http://asean.org.

7. www.apec.org.

8. www.foxnews.com/world/2016/09/15/ un-chief-demands-urgent-response-to-stop-north-koreas-provocative-actions.html.

9. Geographer K. W. Chan has been advocating a comprehensive reform of the *hukou*

system. See www.paulsoninstitute.org/wp-content/uploads/2015/04/PPM_Hukou_Chan_English.pdf (retrieved February 16, 2017).

10. http://china.org.cn/china/2016-04/29/content_38354489.htm (retrieved February 16, 2017).

11. www.theguardian.com/environment/2014/mar/07/china-pollution-smog-air-purifiers-masks.

12. www.nytimes.com/2017/02/18/world/asia/china-bird-flu.html.

13. www.economist.com/blogs/economist-explains/2015/03/economist-explains-8.

14. These two links provide examples of such projects: www.scmp.com/business/china-business/article/1211846/china-railway-groups-project-venezuela-hits-snag; and www.scmp.com/business/companies/article/2068199/chinese-overseas-investment-electricity-projects-surges-2016.

15. These are the latest (at this writing) annual figures reported by the China National Tourism Administration (http://en.cnta.gov.cn/Statistics/TourismStatistics/index.shtml, retrieved February 23, 2017).

16. www.bloomberg.com/news/articles/2014-12-21/alibaba-s-millionaires-fuel-startup-boom-to-rival-silicon-valley.

17. www.washingtonpost.com/opinions/five-myths-about-us-china-relations/2016/12/09/beedb888-bccc-11e6-91ee-1adddfe36cbe_story.html?utm_term=.5db6be8e8363.

18. www.telegraph.co.uk/news/2017/03/18/us-secretary-state-questions-us-china-will-live-coming-half.

REFERENCES ●

Dai, B., Jiang, Y., Yang, L., & Ma, Y. (2017). China's outbound tourism: Stages, policies and choices. *Tourism Management 58*, 253–258.

The Economist. (2014, April 19). Coming to a beach near you: How the growing Chinese middle class is changing the global tourism industry. Retrieved February 21, 2017, from www.economist.com/news/international/21601028-how-growing-chinese-middle-class-changing-global-tourism-industry-coming.

Gustafsson, B., & Yang, X. (2015). Are China's ethnic minorities less likely to move? *Eurasian Geography and Economics, 56*(1), 44–69.

Kwong, J. (2016). Embedded models of development: Educational changes in the People's Republic of China. In C. P. Chou & J. Spangler (Eds.), *Chinese education models in a global age* (pp. 3–14). Singapore: Springer.

Newbold, K. B. (2013). *Population geography: Tools and issues.* Lanham, MD: Rowman & Littlefield.

Oosterhaven, J., & Fan, J. (2006). Impact of international tourism on the Chinese economy. *International Journal of Tourism Research, 8,* 347–354.

Pitlo, L. B., III. (2015). Chinese infrastructure investment goes abroad. *The Diplomat.* Retrieved February 21, 2017, from http://thediplomat.com/2015/08/chinese-infrastructure-investment-goes-abroad.

Rostow, W. W. (1960). *The stages of economic growth: A non-Communist manifesto.* Cambridge, UK: Cambridge University Press.

Ryan, C., & Gu, H. (2009). Introduction: The growth and context of tourism in China. In C.

Ryan & H. Gu (Eds.), *Tourism in China: Destination, cultures and communities* (pp. 1–8). New York: Routledge.

Ryan, C., & Huang, S. (2013). The role of tourism in China's transition: An introduction. In C. Ryan & S. Huang (Eds.), *Tourism in China: Destinations, planning and experiences* (pp. 1–8). Bristol, UK: Channel View.

Sofield, T., & Li, S. (2011). Tourism governance and sustainable national development in China: A macro-level synthesis. *Journal of Sustainable Tourism, 19*(4–5), 501–534.

Tiezzi, S. (2016). China's plan for 'orderly' *hukou* reform. *The Diplomat.* Retrieved February 16, 2017, from http://thediplomat.com/2016/02/chinas-plan-for-orderly-hukou-reform.

Tse, D. K., Belk, R. W., & Zhou, N. (1989). Becoming a consumer society: A longitudinal and cross-cultural content analysis of print ads from Hong Kong, the People's Republic of China, and Taiwan. *Journal of Consumer Research, 15,* 457–472.

United Nations World Tourism Organization (UNWTO). (2016). UNWTO tourism highlights: 2016 edition. Retrieved February 23, 2017, from www.e-unwto.org/doi/pdf/10.18111/9789284418145.

Wen, Z. (1997). China's domestic tourism: Impetus, development and trends. *Tourism Management, 18*(8), 565–571.

FURTHER READING ●

Lew, A., Hall, C. M., & Timothy, D. (2008). *World geography of travel and tourism.* Oxford, UK: Elsevier.

APPENDIX

Websites

WEBSITES FOR DATA

Central Intelligence Agency, *The World Factbook,* China:
    https://www.cia.gov/library/publications/the-world-factbook/geos/ch.html

China's Ministry of Environmental Protection: http://english.mep.gov.cn

China's National Tourism Administration: http://en.cnta.gov.cn

National Bureau of Statistics of China: www.stats.gov.cn/english

Population Reference Bureau: www.prb.org

United Nations Statistics Division: https://unstats.un.org/unsd/demographic

U.S. Census Bureau: www.census.gov

World Bank: http://data.worldbank.org

WEBSITES ABOUT CULTURE

Chinatownology: www.chinatownology.com

Heilbrunn Timeline of Art History, Metropolitan Museum of Art, New York:
    www.metmuseum.org/toah/hd/chem/hd_chem.htm

Timeline of Chinese History and Dynasties:
    http://afe.easia.columbia.edu/timelines/china_timeline.htm

UNESCO World Heritage Sites in China: http://whc.unesco.org/en/statesparties/cn

WEBSITES FOR ORGANIZATIONS

Asian Infrastructure Investment Bank: www.aiib.org/en/index.html

Asia-Pacific Economic Corporation: www.apec.org

Association of Southeast Asian Nations: http://asean.org

Food and Agricultural Organization of the United Nations: www.fao.org/home/en
United Nations World Tourism Organization: www2.unwto.org/en

WEBSITES FOR NEWS MEDIA

Bloomberg News: www.bloomberg.com
British Broadcasting Company (BBC): www.bbc.com
The China Daily: http://usa.chinadaily.com.cn
The Diplomat: http://thediplomat.com
The Economist: www.economist.com
Fortune: http://fortune.com
The Guardian: www.theguardian.com
People's Daily Online: http://en.people.cn
South China Morning Post: www.scmp.com/frontpage/international
U.S. News & World Report: www.usnews.com

Author Index

Subject Index

Note. *f*, *n*, or *t* following a page number indicates a figure, a note, or a table.

About the Authors

David W. S. Wong, PhD, is Professor in the Department of Geography and Geo-information Science at George Mason University. Formerly, he was Professor in the Department of Geography at the University of Hong Kong. His primary thematic research interests are in population and health geographies. His primary technical interests include spatial analysis statistical methods and geovisualization. He has published extensively in measuring spatial segregation, with recent research focusing on uncertainty in spatial data. Dr. Wong has served on the editorial boards of journals including *Computers, Environment, and Urban Systems*; *Demography*; and *Geographical Analysis*.

Kenneth K. K. Wong, PhD, was Professor in the Department of Geography at Hong Kong Baptist University until retiring in 2015. He served as Visiting Research Scientist in the Department of Geography at National Taiwan University and as Visiting Professor in the Asian and Asian American Studies Program at Binghamton University, The State University of New York. His research focuses on people's attitudes toward environmental problems, environmental policy implementation, and, more recently, the sustainable use of urban green spaces and green urbanism issues. Dr. Wong has published widely in journals including *Environment and Planning B, Sustainable Development, Area, Managing Leisure, International Journal of Environmental Studies*, and *Public Administration Review*.

Him Chung, PhD, is Associate Professor in the Department of Geography at Hong Kong Baptist University. His research interests span the rural, urban, and regional geography of China, with foci including rural transformation, urban redevelopment, rural-to-urban migration, and town and regional planning. He has published in journals including *Environment and Planning A, International Journal of Urban and Regional Research, Eurasian Geography and Economics, Planning Practice and Research,* and *China Perspective*. Dr. Chung is also involved in the promotion and curriculum development of high school geography in Hong Kong.

James J. Wang, PhD, is Associate Professor (retired, honorary) in the Department of Geography at the University of Hong Kong. His research focuses on transportation geography, with special interests in port development, port–city relations, and public transportation in China. He is a member of the Steering Committee of the Transport and Geography Commission of the International Geographical Union, a council member of the Hong Kong Society for Transport Studies, and a Fellow of the Chartered Institute of Logistics and Transport. Widely published, Dr. Wang serves on the editorial boards of the *Journal of Transport Geography, Transportmetrica A, Transportmetrica B, Travel Behaviour and Society,* and *Asian Geographer.* He has participated in port–city planning projects and strategic studies for more than 30 Asian port cities and regions.